MW01030584

Between Philosophy and Social Science

Between Philosophy and Social Science

Selected Early Writings

Max Horkheimer

translated by G. Frederick Hunter, Matthew S. Kramer, and John Torpey

introduction by G. Frederick Hunter

The MIT Press
Cambridge, Massachusetts
London, England

First MIT Press paperback edition, 1995
©1993 Massachusetts Institute of Technology

For original publication information, see the Note on the Translation and Sources.
The translations are based on versions of the writings published in Horkheimer's *Ge-sammelte Schriften*, edited by Alfred Schmidt, © S. Fischer Verlag, Frankfurt am Main.
This edition prepared by arrangement with S. Fischer Verlag.

This book was set in Baskerville by Maple-Vail Book Manufacturing Group and printed and bound in the United States of America.

Library of Congress Cataloging-in-Publication Data

Horkheimer, Max, 1895–1973.
    Between philosophy and social science : selected early writings/
Max Horkheimer ; translated by G. Frederick Hunter, Matthew S.
Kramer, and John Torpey ; introduction by G. Frederick Hunter.
        p.   cm.—(Studies in contemporary German social thought)
    Includes bibliographical references and index.
    ISBN 0-262-08221-7 (HB), 0-262-58142-6 (PB)
    1. Philosophy and social sciences.   2. Frankfurt school of
sociology.   3. Critical theory.   I. Title.   II. Series.
B3279.H8473E5   1993
193—dc20   93-18720
                                                          CIP

Contents

Introduction

G. Frederick Hunter

Until recently Max Horkheimer's image was twofold: on the one hand, imperious director of the Frankfurt Institute for Social Research after 1931; on the other, theoretical junior partner to his colleague Theodor Adorno. In the last decade, however, there has been a notable shift in image, in Germany especially, as attention has focused on the remarkable early work collected in this volume. (A companion volume in this series, *On Max Horkheimer: New Perspectives,* will offer appraisals of Horkheimer's contributions to the development of critical theory.)

The 1984 Ludwigsburg Symposium on the early work of the Frankfurt School, sponsored by the Humboldt Stiftung and resulting in a book published by de Gruyter under the title *Die Frankfurter Schule und die Folgen,* was a watershed in the scholarly attention paid to this work. Scholars at that symposium argued that Horkheimer played a central role in defining the integration of philosophy and social science that was to become a hallmark of the Frankfurt School; other studies on the initial phases of critical theory, such as Helmut Dubiel's *Theory and Politics,* supported this contention.

The overall project of critical theory of this period was to develop an empirically and historically grounded research program that was fundamentally interdisciplinary, with the aim of overcoming the inadequacies of received Marxist theories of historical and social development. Although the Institute's work in this period retained in large part the Hegelian/Marxist philosophy of history that today has come under attack in "post-Marxist" circles (with Jürgen Habermas at the forefront), this is also the period in which it started to incorporate elements previously rejected as "bourgeois" by Marxists of every stripe, such as the work of Nietzsche, Schopenhauer, Weber, Freud, and, of course, Hegel—elements whose interweaving came to define critical theory for decades.

Some critics have charged that Horkheimer's early works were exercises in plain, orthodox Marxism; less bluntly, Habermas has suggested that they were caught up in a nineteenth-century "philosophy of history" paradigm that is no longer tenable. Horkheimer's essays are in fact peppered with Marxist notions that today are seldom expressed so unambiguously. Hence it is all the more remarkable how strikingly contemporary Horkheimer's words are on balance. The following excerpt from "Materialism and Morality," for example, might well have issued from the ranks of present-day defenders of the Enlightenment:

Today it is claimed that the bourgeois ideals of Freedom, Equality, and Justice have proven themselves to be poor ones; however, it is not the ideals of the bourgeoisie, but conditions which do not correspond to them, which have shown their untenability. The battle cries of the Enlightenment and of the French Revolution are valid now more than ever. The dialectical critique of the world, which is borne along by them, consists precisely in the demonstration that they have retained their actuality rather than lost it on the basis of reality. These ideas and values are nothing but the isolated traits of the rational society, as they are anticipated in morality as a necessary goal. . . . Materialist theory certainly does not afford to the political actor the solace that he will necessarily achieve his objective; it is not a metaphysics of history but rather a changing image of the world, evolving in relation to the practical efforts toward its improvement.

Horkheimer's goal for the Institute for Social Research, whose directorship he assumed in 1931, was to pursue a program of empirical research into social-theoretical issues that had previously been restricted to abstract philosophical discourse on the one hand or to formulaic economic analyses on the other. The "task of putting a large empirical research apparatus in the service of social-philosophical problems" announced in his 1931 inaugural address, "The Present Situation of Social Philosophy and the Tasks of an Institute for Social Research," was an attempt to bring the various conceptual tools and social-scientific methodologies of historical materialism under one roof.

Until recently, the reception of this earlier work of the Frankfurt School has been overshadowed by the momentous theoretical turn later made by Horkheimer, and more conspicuously by Adorno, toward the *aestheticization* of critical social theory. *Dialectic of Enlightenment,* the major work of this "second phase" of critical theory, has come to be regarded, with some justification, as the major work of Frankfurt critical theory as a whole. The experience of European fascism and the Second World War disillusioned Horkheimer and Adorno as to the possibility of a positive program of social inquiry based ultimately on an emancipatory and emphatically normative concept of Reason derived from the tradition of the Enlightenment. In abandoning orthodox Marxist theory and methodology and turning more and more to Weberian and Nietzschean themes, Horkheimer and Adorno considered themselves only to be soberly facing the new, dark reality of the age. This skepticism regarding the emancipatory potential of science as a whole during this period led them to abandon the former goal of an empirical, scientific interdisciplinary research program and to focus their theoretical attention increasingly on cultural and aesthetic criticism.

Jürgen Habermas, the following generation's most significant practitioner of Frankfurt School social theory (or any other German social theory, for that matter), has been primarily responsible for critical theory's reengagement with empirical, interdisciplinary social research. The now-famous "linguistic turn" into which he has almost single-handedly steered critical theory since 1970 is neither a regression to Marxist scientism nor an abstracting away from concrete social inquiry in the manner of the Anglo-American tradition of analytic philosophy. Moreover, his theoretical project marks a radical departure from the aestheticized critical theory of his mentor Adorno. The prodigious scholarly output of the latest generation of critical theorists is rooted in Habermas's redemption of the Enlightenment ideal of the emancipatory potential of normative social science.

While Habermas's research program is partly responsible for the current resurgence of interest in Horkheimer's earlier work—Habermas himself has stressed the continuity between his program and that of the "first phase" of the Frankfurt Institute—a further factor in this renewal is a reaction against what some commentators view as a neo-Kantian, formalistic aspect of Habermas's own work. This charge has been raised in particular against his "communicative ethics." Horkheimer's 1933 essay "Materialism and Morality," arguably the most decisive materialist critique of Kantian ethics ever written, will be of particular interest in this context.

This volume also includes essays pertaining to the current "foundations" debate within critical theory, and within Continental philosophy in general. Both "On the Problem of Truth," with its special focus on pragmatism, and "The Rationalism Debate in Contemporary Philosophy," a sustained critique of the post-Cartesian "philosophy of consciousness," rank as contemporary contributions to the "post-philosophy" debate. The rationality question is sustained throughout the essays in this volume, including the two major historical studies with which it concludes. Nowhere is Horkheimer's engagement with this most contemporary of themes in greater evidence than in the following passage from *Beginnings of the Bourgeois Philosophy of History*, his first published work, with which it seems appropriate to close these introductory comments:

The fact that reason can never be certain of its perpetuity; or that knowledge is secure within a given time frame, yet is never so for all time; or even the fact that the stipulation of temporal contingency applies to the very body of knowledge from which it is derived—this paradox does not annul the truth of the claim itself. Rather, it is of the very essence of authentic knowledge never to be settled once and for all. This is perhaps the most profound insight of all dialectical philosophy.

A Note on the Translation and Sources

The original translations presented in this volume were the result of a cooperative effort on the part of the three translators. Each of the translators, nevertheless, assumed primary responsibility for particular works, as follows: G. Frederick Hunter, for *Beginnings of the Bourgeois Philosophy of History*, the retranslations of "Egoism and Freedom Movements" and "Materialism and Morality," and the editing of "On the Problem of Truth"; Matthew S. Kramer, for "Remarks on Philosophical Anthropology"; and John Torpey for "The Present Situation of Social Philosophy and the Tasks of an Institute for Social Research," "History and Psychology," "A New Concept of Ideology?," "The Rationalism Debate in Contemporary Philosophy," and "Montaigne and the Function of Skepticism."

The original titles and sources of the writings are as follows:

"Die gegenwärtige Lage der Sozialphilosophie und die Aufgaben eines Instituts für Sozialforschung," *Frankfurter Universitätsreden* 27 (1931).

"Materialismus und Moral," *Zeitschrift für Sozialforschung* 2, no. 2 (1933). A previous English translation by G. Frederick Hunter and John Torpey appeared in *Telos* 69; retranslated for this volume.

"Egoismus und Freiheitsbewegung: Zur Anthropologie des bürgerlichen Zeitalters," *Zeitschrift für Sozialforschung* 5, no. 2 (1936). A previous English translation by David J. Parent was published in *Telos* 54; retranslated for this volume.

"Geschichte und Psychologie," *Zeitschrift für Sozialforschung* 1, nos. 1/2 (1932).

"Ein neuer Ideologiebegriff?," *Grünbergs Archiv* 15, no. 1 (1930).

"Bemerkungen zur philosophischen Anthropologie," *Zeitschrift für Sozialforschung* 4, no. 1 (1935).

"Zum Problem der Wahrheit," *Zeitschrift für Sozialforschung* 4, no. 3 (1935). An English translation was done by Maurice Goldbloom for inclusion in Andrew Arato and Eike Gebhardt, eds., *The Essential Frankfurt School Reader* (New York: Urizen Books, 1978), and is used here, in modified form, by permission of Continuum Publishing Company.

"Zum Rationalismusstreit in der gegenwärtigen Philosophie," *Zeitschrift für Sozialforschung* 3, no. 1 (1934).

"Montaigne und die Funktion der Skepsis," *Zeitschrift für Sozialforschung* 7, no. 1 (1938).

Anfänge der bürgerlichen Geschichtsphilosophie (Stuttgart: Kohlhammer, 1930).

Between Philosophy and Social Science

The Present Situation of Social Philosophy and the Tasks of an Institute for Social Research

Although social philosophy may be at the center of the broader interest in philosophy, its status is no better than that of most contemporary philosophical or fundamental intellectual efforts. No substantive conceptual configuration of social philosophy could assert a claim to general validity. In light of the current intellectual situation, in which traditional disciplinary boundaries have been called into question and will remain unclear for the foreseeable future, it does not appear timely to attempt to delineate conclusively the various areas of research. Nonetheless, the general conceptions that one connects with social philosophy can be put concisely. Its ultimate aim is the philosophical interpretation of the vicissitudes of human fate—the fate of humans not as mere individuals, however, but as members of a community. It is thus above all concerned with phenomena that can only be understood in the context of human social life: with the state, law, economy, religion—in short, with the entire material and intellectual culture of humanity.

Understood in this way, social philosophy grew into a decisive philosophical task in the course of the development of classical German idealism. The most compelling aspects of the Hegelian system are the supreme achievements of that type of social philosophy. This is not to say that philosophy before Hegel had not been concerned with matters of social philosophy; to the contrary, Kant's major works contain philosophical theories concerning the knowledge of law, of art, and of religion. But this social philosophy was rooted in the philosophy of the isolated subject [*Einzelpersönlichkeit*]; those spheres of being were understood as projections [*Entwürfe*] of the autonomous person. Kant made the closed unity of the rational subject into the exclusive source of the constitutive principles of each cultural sphere; the essence and the organization of culture were to be made comprehensible solely on the basis of the dynamics of the individual, the fundamental modes of activity of the spontaneous ego. Even if the autonomous subject could hardly be equated with the empirical individual in Kant's philosophy, one was nonetheless supposed to be able to investigate all possible culturally creative factors in the mind of each individual rational being. Overarching structures of being which could only belong to a supraindividual whole, which could only be discovered in the social totality, and to which we must subordinate ourselves, do not exist in this conception. To assert their existence would be considered dogmatic, and action oriented to them would be considered heteronomous. In the *Metaphysical Principles of Virtue*, Kant writes of the moral subject that a person "is subject to no laws other than those that it gives to itself (either alone or at least together with others)."[1]

The idealist tradition linked with Kant elaborated the meshing of autonomous reason and empirical individuals. The tension between the finite human being and the self as infinite demand also emerges, of course, in Fichte's first philosophy of the ego that posits itself in self-reflection. The eternal Ought, the insistence that we should be adequate to our human vocation [*Bestimmung*], originates in the depths of subjectivity. The medium of philosophy remains that of self-consciousness. But Hegel liberated this self-consciousness from the fetters of introspection and shifted the question of our essence—the question of the autonomous culture-creating subject—to the work of history, in which the subject gives itself objective form.

For Hegel, the structure of objective Spirit, which realizes in history the cultural substance of absolute Spirit—that is, art, religion, philosophy—no longer derives from the critical analysis of the subject, but rather from universal dialectical logic. Its course and its works originate not from the free decisions of the subject, but from the spirit of the dominant nations as they succeed each other in the struggles of history. The destiny of the particular is fulfilled in the fate of the universal; the essence or substantive form of the individual manifests itself not in its personal acts, but in the life of the whole to which it belongs. In its essential aspects, idealism thus became social philosophy with Hegel: the philosophical understanding of the collective whole in which we live—and which constitutes the foundation for the creations of absolute culture—is now also the insight into the meaning of our own existence according to its true value and content.

Let me consider this Hegelian perspective for a moment longer. The current situation of social philosophy can be understood in principle in terms of its dissolution, and of the impossibility of reconstructing it in thought without falling behind the current level of knowledge. Hegel left the realization of the purposes of reason to objective Spirit, and ultimately to World Spirit. The development of this Spirit represents itself in the conflict of "concrete ideas," of "the minds of the nations"; from them, the world-historical realms emerge in necessary succession "as signs and ornaments of its grandeur."[2] This development takes place independently of whether the individuals in their historical activity know it or desire it; it follows its own law. Like the French Enlightenment and English liberalism, however, Hegel certainly considers the individual interests, drives, and passions of human beings to be real driving forces. Even the actions of great men are determined by their individual aims. "Initially these individuals satisfy their own needs; the aim of their actions is not that of satisfying others in any case."[3] Indeed, "they are the most far-sighted among their contemporaries; they know best what issues are involved, and whatever they do is right."[4] But nothing in history "has been accomplished without the active interest of those concerned in it."[5] To be sure, this rational law of development makes "cunning" use of the interests of great men as well as of the mass in order to realize itself. And just as Hegel explains previous history only indirectly on the basis of this law, and directly on the basis of the conflict of interests, so it is with the life process of contemporary society. He refers to the liberal economists Smith, Say, and Ricardo in his attempt to elaborate how the whole is maintained out of the "medley of arbitrariness"[6] that emerges from individuals' efforts to satisfy their needs. "In civil society," according to the *Philosophy of Right*, "each member is his or her own end; everything else is nothing to them. But except in contact with others, they cannot attain the whole compass of their ends, and therefore these others are means to the end of the particular member. A particular end, however, assumes the form of universality through this relation to other people, and it is attained in the simultaneous attainment of the welfare of others."[7] According to Hegel, the State can exist in this and no other way; it is directly conditioned by the conflict of social interests.

But although history and the State appear from without as evolving from the "medley of arbitrariness"; though the empirical historical researcher must descend into a chain of suffering and death, stupidity and baseness; though determinate being [*Dasein*] meets its demise under indescribable torments; and though history can be viewed, as Hegel put it, as the "altar on which the happiness of nations, the wisdom of states, and the virtue of individuals are slaughtered,"[8] philosophy raises us above the standpoint of the empirical observer. For "what is usually called reality," as he tells us in the *Lectures on the Philosophy of World History,*

is seen by philosophy as no more than an idle semblance which has no reality in and for itself. If we have the impression that the events of the past are totally calamitous and devoid of sense, we can find consolation, so to speak, in this awareness. But consolation is merely something received in compensation for a misfortune which ought never to have happened in the first place, and it belongs to the world of finite things. Philosophy, therefore, is not really a means of consolation. It is more than that, for it transfigures reality with all its apparent injustices and reconciles it with the rational; it shows that it is based upon the Idea itself, and that reason is fulfilled in it.[9]

This "transfiguration" [*Verklärung*] of which Hegel speaks thus occurs precisely by way of that doctrine according to which the true human essence does not exist in the mere interiority and in the actual fate of finite individuals, but is instead carried out in the life of nations and realized in the State. In the face of the notion that this substantive essence, the Idea, maintains itself in world history, the demise of the individual appears to be without philosophical significance. The philosopher can thus declare: "The particular is as a rule inadequate in relation to the universal, and individuals are sacrificed and abandoned as a result. The Idea pays the tribute which existence and the transient world exact, but it pays it through the passions of individuals rather than out of its own resources."[10] Only to the extent that the individual participates in the whole in which he lives—or rather, only insofar as the whole lives in the individual—does the individual acquire reality, for the life of the whole is the life of Spirit. The whole in this sense is the State. The State "does not exist for the sake of the citizens; it might rather be said that the state is the end, and the citizens are its instruments."[11]

According to Hegel, the finite individual can attain a conceptual consciousness of its freedom in the State only through idealistic speculation. He saw the achievement of his philosophy—and thus of philosophy as a whole—in this mediating function. To him, that function is identical with the transfiguration of reality "with all its apparent injustices." As the prestige of his system withered around the middle of the last century in Germany, the metaphysics of objective Spirit was replaced in an optimistic, individualistic society by the direct belief in the prestabilized harmony of individual interests. It appeared as though mediation between empirical existence and the consciousness of one's freedom in the social whole no longer required a philosophy, but simply linear progress in positive science, technology, and industry. But as this belief was increasingly proven empty, a scorned metaphysics exacted its revenge. Abandoned by the philosophical conviction of having its true reality in the divine Idea intrinsic to the whole, the individual experienced the world as a "medley of arbitrariness" and itself as "the tribute which existence and the transient world exact." A sober look at the individual and the other [Nächste] no longer revealed—beneath the surface of conflicting individual wills, in a constantly renewed scarcity, behind the everday humiliation and the horror of history—the cunning of which Reason was said to avail itself. Hegel's greatest adversary, Schopenhauer, lived to see the beginnings of the development indicated in his antihistorical, pessimistic, and well-meaning philosophy.

The conviction that individuals took part in the eternal life of Spirit by virtue of their membership in one of the self-regulating historical unities, the dialectic of which constitutes world history—this notion, which was supposed to save the individual from the infamous chain of becoming and fading away, disappeared along with objective idealism. The suffering and death of individuals threatened to appear in their naked senselessness—ultimate facts in an age that believed naively in facts. With the deepening of this contradiction in the principle of individualism—that is, between the unbroken progress of individual happiness within the given social framework, on the one hand, and the prospects of their real situation on the other—philosophy, and social philosophy in particular, was ever more urgently called to carry out anew the exalted role ascribed to it by Hegel. And social philosophy heeded this call.

From the cautious theory of Marburg neo-Kantianism that human beings are not mere individuals, but stand "in various pluralities . . . in rank and file" and "first complete the circle of their being in the larger totality [*Allheit*]," [12] to the contemporary philosophies according to which (as with Hegel) the meaning of human existence fulfills itself only in the supraindividual unities of history, whether these be class, state, or nation—from Hermann Cohen to Othmar Spann, philosophy in recent decades has brought forth the most variegated social-philosophical systems. The newer philosophical attempts to ground moral and legal philosophy anew, against positivism, are almost entirely at one in the effort to demonstrate—above the level of actual empirical events—the existence of a higher, autonomous realm of being, or at least a realm of value or normativity in which transitory human beings have a share, but which is itself not reducible to mundane events. Thus these, too, lead to a new philosophy of objective Spirit. If it can be said that Kelsen's individualistic and relativistic theory of justice contains such elements, this is even more true of the formalistic value philosophy of the Southwest German school, and indeed of Adolf Reinach's phenomenological theory that the essence of "legal forms" [*Rechtsgebilde*], such as property, promises, legal claims, etc., may be viewed as "objects" unto themselves. Scheler's nonformal ethics of values, his theory of the givenness [*An-sich-sein*] of values, has recently found a conscious connection to the philosophy of objective Spirit in its most significant exponent, Nicolai Hartmann. Scheler himself had already adumbrated afresh the theory of "group minds" [*Volksgeister*] before the appearance of Hartmann's ethics.[13]

All of these contemporary versions of social philosophy seem to share the effort to provide insight into a supraindividual sphere which is more essential, more meaningful, and more substantial than their own existence. They measure up well to the task of transfiguration laid out by Hegel. Thus in the only modern philosophical work that radically rejects any aspiration to being a social philosophy, and which discovers true Being exclusively within the individual's inner self—namely, in Heidegger's *Being and Time*—"care" [*Sorge*] stands at the center of attention. This philosophy of individual human existence is not, according to its simple content, transfigurative in Hegel's sense. For this philosophy, on the contrary, human Being is only being unto death, mere finitude; it is a melancholy philosophy. If I may speak here in catchphrases, it could be maintained that social philosophy is confronted with the yearning for a new interpretation of a life trapped in its individual striving for happiness. It appears as part of those philosophical and religious efforts to submerge hopeless individual existence into the bosom or—to speak with Sombart—the "gilded background" [*Goldgrund*] of meaningful totalities.

In the face of this situation of social philosophy, however, ladies and gentlemen, we must be permitted to characterize its shortcomings. Contemporary social philosophy, as we have seen, is in the main polemically disposed toward positivism. If the latter sees only the particular, in the realm of society it sees only the individual and the relations between individuals; for positivism, everything is exhausted in mere facts [*Tatsächlichkeiten*]. These facts, demonstrable with the means of analytic science, are not questioned by philosophy. But philosophy sets them more or less constructively, more or less "philosophically" over against ideas, essences, totalities, independent spheres of objective Spirit, unities of meaning, "national characters," etc., which it considers equally foundational—indeed, "more authentic"—elements of being. It takes the discovery of certain unprovable metaphysical preconditions in positivism as grounds for outdoing positivism in this regard. The Pareto school, for instance, must deny the existence of class, nation, and humanity due to its positivistic concept of reality. In contrast, the various viewpoints which maintain the existence of such entities appear simply as "another" world view, "another" metaphysics, or "another" consciousness, without any possibility of a valid resolution of the matter. One might say that several concepts of reality are involved. It would be possible to investigate the genesis of these different concepts, or to which kind of innate sensibility or social group they correspond; but one cannot be preferred to another on substantive grounds.

Now it is precisely in this dilemma of social philosophy—this inability to speak of its object, namely the cultural life of humanity, other than in ideological [*weltanschaulich*], sectarian, and confessional terms, the inclination to see in the social theories of Auguste Comte, Karl Marx, Max Weber, and Max Scheler differences in articles of faith rather than differences in true, false, or at least problematic theories—it is in this dilemma that we find the difficulty that must be overcome. Of course, the simultaneous existence and validity of various concepts of reality is an indication of the contemporary intellectual situation as a whole. But this variety is rooted in different areas of knowledge and spheres of life, not in one and the same object domain. Thus, for instance, the constitutive categories of philology and of physics may diverge today so greatly that it appears difficult to bring them under one hat. But within physics itself, indeed within the sciences of inorganic nature as a whole, no such tendency exists to develop irreconcilable concepts of reality; the opposite is the case. Here, the corrective is supplied by concrete research on the object.

One might be tempted to object that social philosophy is not an individual discipline, and that it is material sociology which must investigate the specific forms of sociation. This sort of sociology investigates the various concrete ways in which human beings live together, surveying all kinds of associations: from the family to economic groups and political associations to the state and humanity. Like political economy [Nationalökonomie], such a sociology is capable of objective judgment, but it has nothing to say about the degree of reality or about the value of these phenomena. Such issues are rather matters for social philosophy, and in those fundamental questions with which it deals, there can be ultimate positions but no generally valid truths that are woven into broad and variegated investigations.

This view is rooted in a no longer tenable concept of philosophy. However one may draw the boundary between social philosophy and the specialized discipline of sociology—and I believe a great deal of arbitrariness would be unavoidable in any such attempt—one thing is certain. If social-philosophical thought concerning the relationship of individual and society, the meaning of culture, the foundation of the development of community, the overall structure of social life—in short, concerning the great and fundamental questions—is left behind as (so to speak) the dregs that remain in the reservoir of social-scientific problems after taking out those questions that can be advanced in concrete investigations, social philosophy may well perform social functions (such as that of transfiguring and mystifying reality), but its intellectual fruitfulness would have been forfeited. The relation between philosophical and corresponding specialized scientific disciplines cannot be conceived as though philosophy deals with the really decisive problems—in the process constructing theories beyond the reach of the empirical sciences, its own concepts of reality, and systems comprehending the totality—while on the other side empirical research carries out its long, boring, individual studies that split up into a thousand partial questions, culminating in a chaos of countless enclaves of specialists. This conception—according to which the individual researcher must view philosophy as a perhaps pleasant but scientifically fruitless enterprise (because not subject to experimental control), while philosophers, by contrast, are emancipated from the individual researcher because they think they cannot wait for the latter before announcing their wide-ranging conclusions—is currently being supplanted by the idea of a continuous, dialectical penetration and development of philosophical theory and specialized scientific praxis. The relations between natural philosophy and natural science, as a whole and within the individual natural sciences, offer good examples of this approach. Chaotic specialization will not be overcome by way of bad syntheses of specialized research results, just as unbiased empirical research will not come about by attempting to reduce its theoretical element to nothing. Rather, this situation can be overcome to the extent that philosophy—as a theoretical undertaking oriented to the general, the "essential"—is capable of giving particular studies animating impulses, and at the same time remains open enough to let itself be influenced and changed by these concrete studies.

The eradication of this difficulty in the situation of social philosophy thus appears to us to lie neither in a commitment to one of the more or less constructive interpretations of cultural life, nor in the arbitrary ordainment of a new meaning for society, the state, law, etc. Rather—and in this opinion I am certainly not alone—the question today is to organize investigations stimulated by contemporary philosophical problems in which philosophers, sociologists, economists, historians, and psychologists are brought together in permanent collaboration to undertake in common that which can be carried out individually in the laboratory in other fields. In short, the task is to do what all true researchers have always done: namely, to pursue their larger philosophical questions on the basis of the most precise scientific methods, to revise and refine their questions in the course of their substantive work, and to develop new methods without losing sight of the larger context. With this approach, no yes-or-no answers arise to the philosophical questions. Instead, these questions themselves become integrated into the empirical research process; their answers lie in the advance of objective knowledge, which itself affects the form of the questions. In the study of society, no one individual is capable of adopting such an approach, both because of the volume of material and because of the variety of indispensable auxiliary sciences. Even Max Scheler, despite his gigantic efforts, came up short in this respect.

In this situation, it is appropriate that the chair in our university which is connected with the directorship of the Institute for Social Research is to be transformed into a chair in Social Philosophy, and reassigned to the Department of Philosophy. Carl Grünberg held the chair in conjunction with teaching responsibilities in a specific discipline, namely political economy [*wirtschaftliche Staatswissenschaft*]. Given the novel, difficult, and weighty task of putting a large empirical research apparatus in the service of social-philosophical problems, I have been only too aware since being called to this chair of the immeasurable distance between this great scholar, whose name is accorded the highest respect and gratitude wherever research in his field is in progress, and the young, unknown man who is to succeed him. His long illness belongs among those senseless facts of individual life in the face of which philosophical transfiguration comes to naught. In accordance with his precisely determined interests, rooted in the tradition of the historical school of political economy, he himself worked primarily in the area of the history of the labor movement. Due to his comprehensive knowledge of the relevant literature throughout the entire world, it has been possible to collect, in addition to rich archival material, a unique specialized library of approximately 50,000 volumes—a library of which the students of our university and many scholars from both here and abroad make copious use. The series of Institute writings which he edited contains works which expert researchers of the most varied perspectives have recognized as uniformly outstanding scientific contributions.

If I now undertake to orient the work of the Institute toward new tasks after the lengthy illness of its director, I have the benefit not merely of the experience of his colleagues and of the collected literature, but also of the Institute charter which he inspired. According to

The Present Situation of Social Philosophy

that charter, the director named by the Minister is fully independent "in all respects, . . . vis-à-vis the university administration as well as the sponsors," and rather than a collegial administration there exists, as Grünberg liked to put it, a "dictatorship of the director." It will thus be possible for me to make use of that which he created and, at least in narrow terms, together with his colleagues, to erect a dictatorship of planned work in place of the mere juxtaposition of philosophical construction and empirical research in social inquiry. As a philosopher in the sense of my teacher Hans Cornelius, I have heeded the call to lead this research institute mindful of this opportunity, which is equally important for philosophy and empirical research, and not in order to make the investigation of facts into an *ancilla philosophiae*.

But now many among you would like to know how these ideas can really be applied, how one is to conceive of their practical execution. Of course, I cannot go into that issue with the time available to me here in the necessary detail to give you an adequate idea of the work plans that the Institute has set for itself. In conclusion, however, I would like to give an example of the possible application of the above-outlined approach—and by no means an arbitrary example made up for this occasion, but rather one that brings the aforementioned methodological conviction to a head in a particular problem that will constitute a leading theme of the Institute's collective work in the immediate future.

Not just within social philosophy in the narrower sense, but in sociology as well as in general philosophy, discussions concerning society have slowly but ever more clearly crystallized around one question which is not just of current relevance, but which is indeed the contemporary version of the oldest and most important set of philosophical problems: namely, the question of the connection between the economic life of society, the psychical development of individuals, and the changes in the realm of culture in the narrower sense (to which belong not only the so-called intellectual elements, such as science, art, and religion, but also law, customs, fashion, public opinion, sports, leisure activities, lifestyle, etc.). The project of investigating the relations between these three processes is nothing but a reformulation—on the basis of the new problem constellation, consistent with the methods at our disposal and with the level of our knowledge—of the old question concerning the connection of particular existence and universal Reason, of reality and Idea, of life and Spirit.

To be sure, the tendency has been to reflect metaphysically on this theme (I would point to Scheler's *Sociology of Knowledge*), or to proceed more or less dogmatically from some general thesis—that is, one usually takes up in a simplifying manner one of the theories that have arisen historically and then uses it to argue against all others, remaining dogmatically in the realm of the general. It can thus be asserted that economy and Spirit are different expressions of one and the same essence; this would be bad Spinozism. Or, alternatively, one maintains that ideas or "spiritual" contents break into history and determine the action of human beings. The ideas are primary, while material life, in contrast, is secondary or derivative; world and history are rooted in Spirit. This would be an abstractly and thus badly understood Hegel. Or one believes, contrariwise, that the economy as material being is the only true reality; the psyche of human beings, personality as well as law, art, and philosophy, are to be completely derived from the economy, or mere reflections of the economy. This would be an abstractly and thus badly understood Marx. Such notions naively presuppose an uncritical, obsolete, and highly problematic divorce between Spirit and reality which fails to synthesize them dialectically. Moreover, such assertions—to the extent that they are taken seriously in their abstractness—are fundamentally immune from all experimental control: everyone is equally likely always to be right. Such dogmatic convictions are generally spared the particular scientific difficulties of the problem because, consciously or unconsciously, they presuppose a complete correspondence between ideal and material processes, and neglect or even ignore the complicating role of the psychical links connecting them.

The matter is different if one puts the question more precisely: which connections can be demonstrated between the economic role of a specific social group in a specific era in specific countries, the transformation of the psychic structure of its individual members, and the ideas and institutions as a whole that influence them and that they created? Then the possibility of the introduction of real research work comes into view, and these are to be taken up in the Institute. Initially, we want to apply them to a particularly significant and salient social group, namely to the skilled craftspeople and white collar workers in Germany, and then subsequently to the same strata in the other highly developed European countries.

There remains just enough time to give you a brief, inadequate summary of the most important paths which the Institute's permanent colleagues must pursue in order to acquire the empirical material with which to study the relationships involved. First, of course, is the evaluation of the published statistics, reports from organizations and political associations, the material of public agencies, etc. This process can only be carried out in tandem with the continuous analysis of the overall economic situation. Furthermore, we must undertake the sociological and psychological investigation of the press and of fiction, both because of the value of its findings concerning the situation of the examined groups itself, and because of the categorial structure of that literature, on the basis of which it has its effects on the group's members. Of special importance then will be the development of the most varied methods of investigation. Among other things, survey research could be integrated into our investigations in various ways and could serve valuable purposes, so long as one bears in mind that inductive conclusions based exclusively on such research are premature. Survey research has two advantages for our objectives. First, it should provide an initial stimulus to research and keep it in constant connection to real life. Second, surveys can be used to verify insights gleaned from other studies, and thus to prevent errors. American social research has made great preliminary contributions to the design of survey questionnaires, which we hope to adopt and develop further for our own purposes. In addition, we will have to consult extensively with expert specialists. Where it is possible to pursue certain questions by way of hitherto unanalyzed findings of competent researchers, the latter must be approached wherever they may be found. For the most part, this will involve appropriating for scientific purposes the insights of men of affairs. It will be important, furthermore, to compile and evaluate documents not available in book form. A branch office of our Institute will be opened in Geneva in order to facilitate the scholarly evaluation of the sociologically important material contained in the rich archives of the International Labor Office. Mr. Thomas, the director of the ILO, greeted our plan with approval, and has most cordially promised his cooperation. In addition to all these means, of course, is the methodical study of already existing and new scholarly writings in the area of research.

Each of these methods alone is completely inadequate. But all of them together, in years of patient and extensive investigations, may be fruitful for the general problem if the permanent colleagues, in constant connection with the material, understand that their views must be developed not according to their own wishes, but rather according to the matters at hand, if they decisively reject all forms of transfiguration, and if we are successful in protecting the unified intention both from dogmatic rigidity and from sinking into empirical-technical minutiae.

To conclude, it has only been possible for me to describe the tasks of the Institute concerning collective research, upon which the main emphasis will be placed in the coming years. In addition to this, we envision the continuation of the independent research activities of individual colleagues in the areas of theoretical economics, economic history, and the history of the labor movement. The Institute will fulfill its concurrent teaching responsibility to the university by regularly offering lecture series, seminars, and individual lectures. These activities should supplement the educational mission of the university by introducing the university community to the work of the Institute, reporting on its current progress, and offering a curriculum consistent with the notion of philosophically oriented social research described above.

I have only been able to suggest these particular tasks. Yet it seems to me that even my brief report concerning the details may have undermined recollection of the essentials. This lecture has thus become symbolic of the peculiar difficulty of social philosophy—the difficulty concerning the interpenetration of general and particular, of theoretical design and individual experience. My exposition was undoubtedly inadequate in this respect. If I may nonetheless hope that you indulged me with your attention, I also ask of you your goodwill and your trust regarding the work itself. At the inauguration of the Institute, Carl Grünberg spoke of the fact that everyone is guided in their scholarly work by impulses deriving from their own world views. May the guiding impulse in this Institute be the indomitable will unswervingly to serve the truth!

Materialism and Morality

Autonomously attempting to decide whether one's actions are good or evil is plainly a late historical phenomenon. A highly developed European individual is not only able to bring important decisions into the light of clear consciousness and morally evaluate them—such individuals also have this capacity in regard to most of the primarily instinctual and habitual reactions that make up the bulk of their lives. But human actions appear more compulsive the earlier the historical formation to which their subjects belong. The capacity to subject instinctual reactions to moral criticism and to change them on the basis of individual considerations could only develop with the growing differentiation of society. Even the authority principle of the Middle Ages, whose convulsions mark the starting point of modern moral inquiry, is an expression of a later phase of this process. Given that the unbroken religious faith which preceded the dominance of this principle was an already tremendously complicated mediation between naive experience and instinctual reaction, the medieval criterion of the tradition sanctioned by the church (whose exclusive validity surely still carried a strongly compulsive character) already indicates a moral conflict. When Augustine declares: "Ego vero evangelio non crederum nisi me catholicae ecclesiae commoveret auctoritas,"[1] this affirmation already presupposes—as Dilthey[2] recognized—a doubting of faith. The social life process of the modern period has presently so advanced human powers that in the most developed countries, at least the members of certain strata are capable, in a relatively wide range of their existence, not merely of following instinct or habit but of choosing autonomously among several possible aims. The exercise of this capacity admittedly takes place on a much smaller scale than is commonly believed. Even if deliberations about the technique and the means applied to a given end have become extremely refined in many areas of social and individual life, the aims of human beings nonetheless continue to be rigidly fixed. Precisely in those actions which in their totality are socially and historically significant, human beings in general behave in a quite typical manner—which is to say, in conformity with a definite scheme of motives which are characteristic of their social group. Only in nonessential, private affairs are people occasionally given to examine their motives conscientiously and to apply their intellectual powers to the determination of aims. Nonetheless, the question regarding the proper goals has been put energetically within contemporary society, especially among younger people. As the principle of authority was undermined and a significant number of individuals acquired substantial decision-making power over the conduct of their lives, the need emerged for a spiritual guideline that could substitute for this principle's eroding bases in orienting the individual in this world. The acquisition of moral principles was important for members of the higher social strata, since their position constantly demanded that they make intervening decisions which they had earlier been absolved of by authority. At the same time, a rationally grounded morality became all the more necessary to dominate the masses in the state when a mode of action diverging from the their life interests was demanded of them.

The idealist philosophers of the modern period did what they could to meet this need through the construction of axioms. In accordance with the conditions which, since the Renaissance, forced individuals back upon themselves, they sought to authenticate these maxims with reason—that is, with reasons that are in principle generally accessible. As distinctive as the systems of Leibniz, Spinoza, and the Enlightenment may be, they all bear the marks of an effort to use the eternal constitution of the world and of the individual as the basis for establishing some determinate manner of conduct as being appropriate for all time. They therefore make a claim to unconditional validity. Those standards characterized as correct are admittedly quite general for the most part and, with the exception of several materialist and militant theories of the French Enlightenment, offer little in the way of specific instruction. For the past few centuries, life has demanded of both religion and morality such capacity for conforming that substantively elaborated precepts cannot possibly retain even the mere semblance of permanence. Even modern moral philosophers who decisively attack the formalism of earlier moral teachings hardly diverge from them in this respect. "Ethics does not teach directly what ought here and now to happen in any given case," writes Nicolai Hartmann, "but in general how that is constituted which ought to happen universally. . . . Ethics furnishes the bird's-eye view from which the actual can be seen objectively."[3] Idealist moral philosophy purchases the belief in its own unconditionality by making no reference whatsoever to any historical moment. It does not take sides. As much as its views may be in harmony with or even benefit a group of individuals in collective historical struggle, it nonetheless prescribes no position. Hartmann declares: "What a man ought to do, when he is confronted with a serious conflict that is fraught with responsibility, is this: to decide according to his best conscience; that is, according to his own living sense of the relative height of the respective values."[4] Ethics "does not mix itself up with the conflicts of life, gives no precepts coined *ad hoc;* it is no code, as law is, of commandments and prohibitions. It turns its attention directly to the creative in man, challenges it afresh in every new case to observe, to divine, as it were, what ought here and now to happen."[5] Morality is understood in this connection as an eternal category. Just as the judgment of propositions according to their truth or falsity, or of fashioned objects according to their beauty or ugliness, both belong to the essence of being human, so too, the argument goes, should it be possible to judge whether any given character or action is good or evil. Despite the most vigorous discussions concerning the possibility or impossibility of an eternal morality, modern philosophers are in accord as to its concept. Both the mutability of content and the connateness of certain propositions are variously asserted and contested, but the capacity for moral value judgments is generally taken as an essential characteristic of human nature of at least equal rank with that of theoretical knowledge. A new category of virtue has entered philosophy since the Renaissance: moral virtue. It has little in common with either the ethical conceptions of the Greeks, which concerned the best path to happiness, or the religious ethics of the Middle Ages. Although connections exist between moral virtue and these phenomena, the modern problem of morality in its essentials has its roots in the bourgeois order. To be sure, just as certain economic elements of the bourgeois order are to be found in earlier forms of society, aspects of this problem of morality appear in these earlier forms as well; it can itself, however, only be understood from the standpoint of the general life situation of the epoch now about to end.

The moral conception of the bourgeoisie found its purest expression in Kant's formulation of the categorical imperative. "Act only according to that maxim by which you can at the same time will that it should become a universal law."[6] According to Kant, actions which conform to this principle and which are done solely for its sake are distinguished from all others through the quality of morality. Kant further proposed that "the specific mark"[7] distinguishing this imperative from all other rules of action lay in the "renunciation of all interest." Even if reason itself takes a pure and unmediated interest in moral actions,[8] this still does not mean that they are done out of any interest in the object or out of need. Acting out of duty is contrasted with acting out of interest. But virtue does not amount to acting contrary to one's individual purposes; rather, it consists in acting independently of them. Individuals are supposed to liberate themselves from their interests.

As is well known, Kant's view here was contested from the most various directions; his critics included, among others, Schiller and Schleiermacher. Interest-free action was even declared to be impossible. "What is an interest other than the working of a motive upon the Will? Therefore where a motive moves the Will, there the latter has an interest; but where the Will is affected by no motive, there in truth it can be as little active, as a stone is able to leave its place without being pushed or pulled," says Schopenhauer.[9] Certainly Kant did not want to have moral action understood as action without a motive, even if he viewed acting out of interest as the natural law of human beings. On the contrary, the moral impulsion[10] lies in respect for the moral law. But Schopenhauer's critique, which he transformed positively through the construction of his own ethics, hits one thing on the mark: to the moral agent in the Kantian sense, the actual reasons for action remain obscure. The agent knows neither why the universal should stand above the particular, nor how to correctly reconcile the two in any given instance. The imperative, which "of itself finds entrance into the mind and yet gains reluctant reverence (though not always obedience),"[11] leaves the individual with a certain uneasiness and unclarity. Within the soul, a struggle is played out between personal interest and a vague conception of the general interest, between individual and universal objectives. Yet it remains obscure how a rational decision based upon criteria is possible between the two. There arise an endless reflection and constant turmoil which are fundamentally impossible to overcome. Since this problematic tension playing itself out in the inner lives of human beings necessarily derives from their role in the social life process, Kant's philosophy, being a faithful reflection of this tension, is a consummate expression of its age.

The basis of the spiritual situation in question is easily recognized upon consideration of the structure of the bourgeois order. The social whole lives through unleashing the possessive instincts of all individuals. The whole is maintained insofar as individuals concern themselves with profit and with the conservation and multiplication of their own property. Each is left to care for himself as best as he can. But because each individual must produce things that others need in the process, the needs of the community as a whole end up being addressed through activities that are apparently independent of one another and seem only to serve the individual's own welfare. The circumstance that production and maintenance in this order coincide with the subjects' striving after possessions is a fact that has left its impression upon the psychic apparatus of its members. Throughout history, people have accommodated themselves in their entire being to the life conditions of society; a consequence of this accommodation in the modern period is that human powers orient themselves to the promotion of individual advantage. This life-dominating principle inescapably leaves its mark on the individual's feelings, consciousness, form of happiness, and conception of God. Even in the most refined and seemingly remote impulses of the individual, the function he performs in society still makes itself felt. In this era, economic advantage is the natural law under which individual life proceeds. The categorical imperative holds up "universal natural law," the law [Lebensgesetz] of human society, as a standard of comparison to this natural law of individuals. This would be meaningless if particular interests and the needs of the general public intersected not just haphazardly but of necessity. That this does not occur, however, is the inadequacy of the bourgeois economic form: there exists no rational connection between the free competition of individuals as what mediates and the existence of the entire society as what is mediated. The process takes place not under the control of a conscious will but as a natural occurrence. The life of the general public arises blindly, accidentally, and defectively out of the chaotic activity of individuals, industries, and states. This irrationality expresses itself in the suffering of the majority of human beings. The individual, completely absorbed in the concern for himself and "his own," does not only promote the life of the whole without clear consciousness; rather, he effects through his labor both the welfare and the misery of others—and it can never become entirely evident to what extent and for which individuals his labor means the one or the other. No unambiguous connection can be drawn between one's own labor and larger social considerations. This problem, which only society itself could rationally solve through the systematic incorporation of each member into a consciously directed labor process, manifests itself in the bourgeois epoch as a conflict in the inner life of its subjects.

To be sure, with the liberation of the individual from the overarching unities of the Middle Ages, the individual acquired consciousness of itself as an independent being. This self-consciousness, however, is abstract: the manner in which each individual contributes to the workings of the entire society through his labor, and in which he is in turn influenced by it, remains completely obscure. Everyone cooperates in the good or bad development of the entire society, yet it appears as a natural occurrence. One's role in this whole, without which the essence of the individual cannot be determined, remains unseen. Hence each necessarily has a false consciousness about his existence, which he is able to comprehend only in psychological categories as the sum of supposedly free decisions. Due to the lack of rational organization of the social whole which his labor benefits, he cannot recognize himself in his true connection to it and knows himself only as an individual whom the whole affects somewhat, without it ever becoming clear how much and in what manner his egoistic activity actually affects it. The whole thus appears as an admonition and demand which troubles precisely the progressive individuals at their labor, both in the call of conscience and in moral deliberation.[12]

Materialism attempts to delineate—and not simply with the broad strokes just suggested, but with a specific focus on the distinct periods and social classes involved—the actual relationships from which the moral problem derives and which are reflected, if only in distorted fashion, in the doctrines of moral philosophy. The idea of morality, as it was formulated by Kant, contains the truth that the mode of action informed by the natural law of economic advantage is not necessarily the rational mode. It does not, as might be supposed, set up an opposition between the interest of the individual and feelings or, worse, set such interest over against the return to blind obedience. Neither interest nor reason is maligned. Instead, reason recognizes that it need not exclusively serve the natural law and the advantage of the individual once it has absorbed the natural law of the whole into its will. To be sure, the individual cannot fulfill the demand to rationally shape the whole. Mastery of the overall process of society by human beings can only be achieved when society has overcome its anarchic form and constituted itself as a real subject—that is, through historical action. Such action issues not from the individual but rather from a constellation of social groups, in the dynamics of which conscience certainly plays an important role. Moral anxiety by no means burdens the labor of individuals in the production process alone; their entire being is affected by it. Whenever people follow the law which is natural to them in this society, they attend immediately only to the interests of the subject [*Angelegenheiten des Interessensubjekts*] that bears their own name. Insofar as the reason of the bourgeois individual extends beyond his particular purposes, insofar as he is not just this determinate X with his private worries and wishes, but rather at the same time can ask himself what concern these worries of X actually are to him even as they immediately affect his personal existence— insofar, that is, as he is not this mere X but rather a member of human society—the "autonomous" will that Kant's commandment formulates stirs within him. As Kant consistently detailed,[13] the interest of another is to be understood in this connection as equally contingent as one's own, for the relation of the strivings of Y to the life of the general public is for X, as a rule, no more transparent than his own. Whoever is in the economic situation of the bourgeois and is incapable of experiencing this whole conflict has not kept pace developmentally, and lacks a type of reaction belonging to individuals of this period.

Morality, therefore, is by no means simply dismissed by materialism as mere ideology in the sense of false consciousness. Rather, it must be understood as a human phenomenon that cannot possibly be overcome for the duration of the bourgeois epoch. Its philosophical expression, however, is distorted in many respects. Above all, the solution of the problem does not lie in the observance of rigidly formulated commandments. In the attempt to actually apply the Kantian imperative, it immediately becomes clear that the general interest the moral will is concerned about would not be helped in the least. Even if everyone were to comply with the imperative, even if everyone were to lead a virtuous life in its sense, the same confusion would continue to reign. Nothing essential would be changed.

The four examples of moral action which Kant himself adduces place this helplessness and powerlessness of the good will in bold relief. In the first, a desperate man turns away from suicide in consideration of the moral law. The dubiousness of his decision is so obvious, however, that the reader is astonished that Kant does not seriously pursue it. Why should a person "who, through a series of misfortunes which has grown into hopelessness, tires of this life,"[14] not at the same time be able to will that the maxim of this action become a universal law? Is not this world rather in such a condition that the rational actor must take solace in the possibility of that way out? Hume's essay on suicide, in which this philosopher proves himself a true Enlightenment figure, admittedly was published before the *Foundations of the Metaphysics of Morals* and was written long before it; nonetheless, it makes the impression of being a response to Kant's peculiar opinion. "A man, who retires from life," he says, "does no harm to society: He only ceases to do good; which, if it is an injury, is of the lowest kind. . . . But suppose that it is no longer in my power to promote the interest of society; suppose that I am a burthen to it; suppose that my life hinders some person from being much more useful to society. In such cases my resignation of life must not only be innocent but laudable. And most people who lie under any temptation to abandon existence, are in some such situation; those, who have health, or power, or authority, have commonly better reason to be in humor with the world."[15] Kant's deliberations, which take no notice of the contradictions in society, seem quite lame by comparison.

In the second example, a person decides against procuring money by the false promise of later repayment. Kant has him morally reflect that if everyone were to do this, in the end no promise would be taken seriously. In order to evaluate this example, it would be necessary to have knowledge of the purpose to which the money was to be put and the nature of the relationship between the two contracting parties. There are cases in which Kant is incapable of defending the solution he takes to be the moral one without resorting to the same kind of artificiality that characterizes his entire discussion of the reasons for lying.[16] In the third example, the disregard for reality proves more ominous than in the first. A rich man discovers that he has a certain talent, but is too indolent to develop it. Kant says that the man could not possibly want all others to remain idle in his situation, and that he therefore must undergo the effort. But, contrary to Kant's view, the idea of the will of the gifted man stirring all his competitors (if there were any to begin with) into action would undoubtedly dissuade him from devoting any effort whatsoever to this enterprise. In the context of this competitive society, should he decide to plunge into the rat race, he must wish precisely that his will does *not* become a universal rule.

The fourth example deals with charity. Kant's attempt to make an argument for charity is based less on respect for the moral law than on the not very persuasive observation that the rich person may himself someday require charity. If this example is supposed to concern not just the paltry take of a beggar but a really tempting amount, the rich person will quite justifiably prefer the secure present to the questionable future. But should this problem be considered morally in the Kantian sense—that is, with a view to universality—rather than ego-istically, then the rich person's theory regarding what is good for society at large will be quite different from that of the beggar: the former will declare with the utmost sincerity that large contributions are detrimental. Once the focus shifts to weightier matters, such as social burdens or wages, there will be as many beliefs about what befits universal law as there are social groups.

Were everyone to act on the basis of conscience, this would prevent neither the chaos nor the misery engendered thereby. The formal directive to be true to oneself and to have a will without contradiction fails to provide a guiding rule that could remove the basis of moral uneasiness. Is there no misdeed that has been committed at some time or other in all good conscience? What is decisive for the happiness of humanity is not whether the individuals consider their action to be reconcilable with the natural law of the general welfare [*Naturgesetz der Allgemeinheit*], but rather the extent to which it is actually reconcilable with it. Both the belief that a good will—as important an impulse as this may be—is the sole Good, and the evaluation of an action merely according to its intent and not also according to its real significance at a particular historical moment, amount to idealist delusions. From this ideological side of the Kantian conception of morality, a direct path leads to the modern mysticism of sacrifice and obedience, a mysticism which can only unjustly lay any further claim to the authority of Kant. If the development and happy employment of the powers present in society at large is to be the highest aim, it in no way suffices to set great store by a virtuous inner life or mere spirit—suppressing the instinct for acquisition through discipline. Rather, it is necessary to ensure that the external arrangements which can effect that happiness actually come to pass. What people do is at least as important as how they do it: it is precisely when the chips are down that the motives of those who pursue a goal matter less than the achievement of the goal. To be sure, the inner life of the acting individual is necessary for the very determination of both object and situation, for the internal and the external are every bit as much moments of manifold dialectical processes in all of history as they are in the life of the individual. But the prevalent tendency in bourgeois morality to lay exclusive value upon conviction proves to be a position that inhibits progress, especially in the present. It is not consciousness of duty, enthusiasm, and sacrifice *as such,* but consciousness of duty, enthusiasm, and sacrifice *for what* which will decide the fate of humanity in the face of the prevailing peril. A will that is prepared to make sacrifices may well be a useful resource in the service of any power, including the most reactionary; insight into the relation in which the will's content stands to the development of the entire society, however, is given not by conscience but by the correct theory.

This idealist trait, according to which all would be right in the world so long as all were right in Spirit, this lack of distinction between fantasy and reality through which idealist philosophy proves itself to be a refined form of the primitive belief in the omnipotence of thought—in other words, magic—comprises only one side of Kant's doctrine. It also has a very active relation to reality. In this society of isolated individuals, the categorical imperative, as was suggested above, runs up against the impossibility of its own meaningful realization. Consequently, it necessarily implies the transformation of this society. By extension, the very individual to whom the imperative make its appeal, and whose shaping seems to be its sole aim, would also have to disappear. Bourgeois morality presses toward the superseding of the order that first made it possible and necessary. If people want to act in such a way that their maxims are fit to become universal law, they must bring about an order in which this intention—so dubious in the cases enumerated by Kant—can really be carried out according to criteria. Society must then be constructed in a manner that establishes its own interests and those of all its members in a rational fashion: only under this condition is it meaningful for the individuals finding themselves involved in such a project, subjectively and objectively, to organize their lives around it. If modern ethics has borne witness to the elaboration of the negative side of Kant's position—namely subjectivism, which holds back change—at the expense of the development of this dynamic trait which points beyond the given set of relations, then the reason for this lies less with Kant than in subsequent history.

To be sure, the Kantian doctrine contains the impossible concept of an eternal commandment addressed to the free subject, but at the same time it includes tendencies anticipating the end of morality. This doctrine manifests the contradiction which had saddled the bourgeoisie throughout its entire epoch: it created and clung to an order which is in tension with its own concept of reason. Kant asserts the absoluteness of morality yet must necessarily view it as transitory and proclaim its supercession. Morality rests upon the distinction between interest and duty. The task of reconciling both was put to bourgeois society by its protagonists, but the philosophical exponents of "enlightened self-interest" (Bentham) hardly dared to declare it fulfilled. This is impossible in the prevailing form of society, in which humanity has neither voice nor consciousness except perhaps as theory, which criticizes (as contrasted with public opinion) the various particular interests and powers that falsely pretend to universality. The idea that the precondition of morality in the bourgeois sense—the distinction between particular and general interests—could be dissolved by a historical act is a doctrine which had achieved currency early on in the materialist anthropology of the bourgeoisie. Helvétius says one can "only make men happy if one reconciles their personal interest with the general. Under the condition of this principle it is apparent that morality is only a vain science if it is not fused with politics and legislation, from which I conclude that the philosophers must consider matters from the same standpoint as the legislator if they want to prove useful. Without, of course, being animated by the same spirit. The concern of the moralist is to fashion the laws; the legislator secures their execution by impressing upon them the seal of his power."[17] Kant also considered the reconciliation of happiness and duty to be possible in a better society. There is for him "no conflict of practice with theory,"[18] "the pure principles of right have objective reality, i.e., they may be applied."[19] It is his conviction that the true task of politics is to "accord with the public's universal end, happiness."[20] To be sure, political maxims may by no means "be derived from the welfare or happiness which a single state expects from obedience to them, and thus not from the end which one of them proposes for itself."[21] Accordingly, neither a single state nor any power group may make itself out to be the universal. In the last analysis, according to Kant, genuine politics is concerned not with the reconciliation of individual interests with those of such particularities, but rather with the achievement of the end whose principle is given through pure reason. If he preferred to define this end not as the condition of the greatest possible happiness but as the constitution of the greatest human freedom according to laws,[22] he nonetheless rejected any contradiction between this freedom and that happiness, declaring instead that the one follows of itself from the other. Kant did not emphasize the fundamental distinction between interest and duty with respect to the perfected order itself, but instead always with respect to the human beings who aspire to it. In the society to be aimed at, the purposes of any given individual could exist together with those of all others, and although the private purposes of the individuals would be different with respect to their content, the necessity of mutual obstruction would be absent. Moral action would coincide with the natural law or would not lead to conflict with it in any case. Despite unambiguous references to the possibility of this future society, Kant may have wavered in regard to the extent of its actualization. In the formulation in the *Critique of Pure Reason,* it was his conviction that the realization of the ideal can "pass beyond any and every specified limit."[23] He had harsh words for so-called "politic" men who pride themselves on their praxis but who in reality only fawn on the powers that be, because they claim that human nature precludes the possibility of any meaningful improvement. To them, "the legal constitution in force at any time is . . . the best, but when it is amended from above, this amendment always seems best, too."[24] The philosopher does not skeptically refer to how he "knows men"; rather, he knows "Man" and knows "what can be made of him."[25] There are no valid anthropological arguments against the overcoming of bad social relations. Kant's arguments against the psychological defense of absolutism are valid for every epoch in which the human sciences (among other sciences) are exploited in the struggle against progress. What Schopenhauer called the "setting up [of] a moral utopia"[26]—the fulfillment of morality and simultaneously its overcoming—is for Kant no illusion but the goal of politics.

Kant's philosophy certainly exhibits utopian elements: they lie not in the idea of a perfect constitution, but rather in the undialectical conception of a continuous approach to it. Kant holds that all determinations of bourgeois society return to themselves as identical in that final state, only they are better reconciled with each other than in the present. Even Kant eternalizes the categories[27] of the prevailing system. The order he postulates as a goal would be composed of autonomously acting individuals whose individual decisions smoothly yield the welfare of the whole. This ideal is indeed a utopia; as in every utopia, the yearning thought forms a beautiful vision out of the unchanged elements of the present. The harmony of the interests of all in Kant's utopia can only be understood as a prestabilized harmony, as a charitable miracle. In contrast, science takes account of the fact that historical transformation also changes the elements of the earlier condition at the same time.

The materialist theory of society is needed in order to supersede the utopian character of the Kantian conception of a perfect constitution. After all, the disparate interests of the individual are not ultimate facts; they do not have their basis in an independent psychological constitution, rather they are based on both the material relations and the real total situation of the social group to which the individual belongs. The absolutely incommensurable disparity of interests derives from the disparity of the relations of ownership; human beings today stand against one another as functions of various economic powers, of which each reveals to the others contradictory developmental tendencies. Only after this antagonistic economic form, whose introduction once meant tremendous progress (including among other things the developmental possibility of self-reliant human beings), has come to be superseded [*abgelöst*] by a social life form in which productive property is administered in the general interest not just out of "good intentions" but with rational necessity, only then will the concordance of individual ends cease appearing to be a miracle. Moreover, individuals at that point cease to be merely the exponents of private ends. Each is no longer simply a monad, but rather, in Kant's language, a "limb" of society at large [*ein "Glied" der Allgemeinheit*].

This expression, with which he characterizes a dynamic element in the moral phenomenon that points beyond itself to a more rational society, has assumed an unhappy function in modern sociology: it is supposed to prompt people, despairing of this mechanism run amok that is contemporary society, to give themselves over blindly to the particular "whole" into whose realm they have fallen by birth or by fate, regardless of the role it happens to play in human history. But this is an interpretation of the organic phraseology that runs precisely counter to Kant. Instead of pointing toward an era in which human relations will be really governed by reason, it betokens outmoded stages of society in which all processes were mediated simply by instinct, tradition, and obedience. Kant employs the image of the organism in order to indicate the frictionless functioning of the future society; nothing in this suggests the faintest denial of the role of rational thought. Today, by contrast, the image of the organism characterizes a system of dependency and economic inequality, one which can no longer justify itself before the world's expanded critical understanding and which therefore requires metaphysical phrases in order to reconcile people to it. The organism is drawn into the matter in order to rationalize—as an eternal relationship based on blind nature—the fact that certain people make decisions and certain others carry them out, a state of affairs which the growth of all forces has made questionable. Today, as in the time of Menenius Agrippa, suffering human beings are supposed to rest content with the thought that their role in the whole is as innate to them as are the members in the animal body. The obdurate dependency in nature is held up as an example to the members [*Gliedern*] of society. In contradistinction to this idealist sociology, which believes that it puts an end to injustice insofar as it strives to remove from people's heads the mounting consciousness of that injustice, the Kantian moral theory tends toward a society in which the material arrangements are indeed precisely linked [*gegliedert*], but in which the possibilities of development and the happiness of the individuals are neither subordinated to a sequence of stages nor surrendered to fate. "That there should be no discord in the body; but that the members may have the same care one for another," as it says in the New Testament.[28] With Kant, the organism is defined precisely by the concept of ends. Organic events, according to him, always refer to the "causality of a concept,"[29] that is, to purpose and planning.

In the future society toward which the moral consciousness aspires, the life of the whole and of the individuals alike is produced not merely as a natural effect but as the consequence of rational designs that take account of the happiness of individuals in equal measure. In place of the blind mechanism of economic struggles, which presently condition happiness and—for the greater part of humanity—unhappiness, the purposive application of the immeasurable wealth of human and material powers of production emerges. According to Kant, each individual "gives universal laws while also [being] subject to these laws."[30] The individual is a "lawgiver" not merely in the juridical sense of formal democracy, but in the sense of receiving as much consideration as everyone else, given the individual's possibilities in the total social reality. In Kant's sense, no specific totality can claim the status of an absolute end, but only individuals: only they have reason. Kant developed the idea of a society worthy of human beings, one in which morality loses its basis, by his analysis of moral consciousness; it appears as the demand and consequence of the latter. Hegel made this idea the foundation of his philosophy. According to Hegel, rationality consists concretely in the unity of objective and subjective freedom; that is, in the unity of the general will and the individuals who carry out its ends.[31] To be sure, like his liberal teachers of political economy, he considered this condition already to have been realized in his time.

Morality as a human power distinct from interest played no major role in his system; with this definitive metaphysics of history, it is no longer necessary as driving force. Hegel's concept of Spirit, however, contains the same ideal that the bourgeois world as well as the Kantian philosophy impressed upon every able thinker. The theory of its realization leads from philosophy to the critique of political economy.

With the recognition that the will and the appeal to it have their roots in the contemporary mode of production and, like other forms of life, will change with it, morality is simultaneously comprehended and made mortal. In an epoch in which the domination of the possessive instincts is the natural law of humanity, and in which by Kant's definition each individual sees the other above all as a means to his own ends, morality represents the concern for the development and happiness of life as a whole. Even the opponents of traditional morality presuppose in their critique an indeterminate moral sentiment with such strivings. When Nietzsche maps out his own problem in the Foreword to *The Genealogy of Morals,* the materialist question, "Under what conditions did man deem those value judgments good and evil?," is followed immediately by the moral one: "And what value have they themselves? Have they so far inhibited or advanced human development? Are they a sign of need, impoverishment, of deformation of life? Or, on the other hand, do they betray the fullness, the power, the will of life, its courage, its optimism, its future?" As a standard, the universal conception of humanity is as operative here as it is in Kant. To be sure, Nietzsche commended very perverse means for its liberation in a period in which the conditions for a more prosperous form of organization were already clearly visible; his challenge to humanity in his time, that it must "set its goal above itself—not in a false world, however, but in one which would be a continuation of humanity,"[32] applies to him too, for his practical suggestions all rest upon a false extrapolation. From his psychological investigation of the individuals that act under the natural law of their personal interest he concluded that the universal fulfillment of that for which they strove—namely security and happiness—would have to produce a society of philistines, the world of the "last" men. He failed to recognize that the characteristics of the present which he so detested derive precisely from the dearth of propitious conditions for society at large. With the spread of reason that he feared, with its application to all of the relations of society, those characteristics—which in truth rest upon the concentration of all the instincts on private advantage—must be transformed, as must ideas and indeed the drives themselves. Nietzsche's ignorance of dialectics allows him to foresee the same "dearth of justice" that Kant had seen. "If it were as we would like, all morality would transform itself into self-interest."[33] But in reality, self-interest would transform itself into morality, or rather the two would merge in a new form of human interest that would accord with the more rational condition. Nietzsche's theory of history misses the mark; he places the goal in an inverted world, if not quite in another one, because he misunderstands the movement of the contemporary world due to his ignorance of economic laws. His own moral philosophy, however, contains the same elements as that which he struggles against. He fumes against himself.

Bergson claims as well that moral philosophy contains the notion of the progress of humanity. "De la société réelle dont nous sommes nous nous transportons par la pensée à la société idéale, vers elle montre notre hommage quand nous nous inclinons devant la dignité humaine en nous, quand nous déclarons agir par respect de nous-mêmes."[34] He claims that morality has two aspects: a "natural" one which arises from society's accommodation to its life conditions—consisting in socially functional reactions consolidated in customs, similarly characteristic of members of both primitive tribes and civilized nations as well as of cases of brutish associations—and a truly human aspect, the "élan d'amour." This second aspect contains within itself "le sentiment d'un progrès"[35] and is no longer oriented to the preservation and security of the particular association to which the individual happens to belong, but is oriented rather to humanity. The difference between the two aspects, one of which appears as the "pression sociale" and the other as the "marche en avant," is none other than Kant's distinction between natural law and respect for humanity. Even today Bergson's vision extends deep enough to hit upon the distinction between publicly esteemed sentiment and forward-pointing morality. The "tendances innées et fondamentales de l'homme actuel"[36] are aimed at family, interest formations, and nation, and necessarily include possible enmity between groups. Hate, but not in the least the solidarity of forward-pointing moral sentiment, belongs to this purposeful love. "C'est qu'entre la nation, si grande soit-elle, et

l'humanité, il y a toute la distance du fini à l'indéfini, du clos à l'ou-
vert."[37] As with Nietzsche, Bergson indeed loses his sharpness of vision in the face of the question of how the ideal society prescribed by
genuine morality is to be realized, which of the present forces work
against it, who promulgates it, and who sides with it. Here he repeats
the theory of the heroes, "dont chacun répresente, comme eût fait
l'apparition d'une nouvelle espèce, un effort d'évolution créatrice."[38]
According to old superstition they are to arise only in isolation and at
the beginning of long periods of time. Indeed, Bergson is so certain
of their rarity that he forgets to ask whether today these heroes of the
"société idéale" in the end might not exist in abundance and be found
in a relation of struggle, without philosophers regarding them in a
manner other than that which is peculiar to the "closed soul." In this
forgetting, in the indifference to the mortal struggles for the society
anticipated in morality, in the deficient connection with the forces
that are driving forward, is that bit of immorality which can presently
be discovered even in genuine philosophy.

Materialism sees in morality an expression of life of determinate
individuals and seeks to understand it in terms of the conditions of its
emergence and passing, not for the sake of truth in itself but rather
in connection with determinate historical forces. It understands itself
as the theoretical aspect of efforts to abolish existing misery. The features it discerns in the historical phenomenon of morality figure into
its consideration only on the condition of a determinate practical interest. Materialism presumes no transhistorical authority behind morality. The fear which moral precepts—be they ever so spiritualized—
still carry from their origin in religious authority is foreign to materialism. The consequences of all human actions work themselves out
exclusively in the spatiotemporal world. As long as they have no effect
on their author in this world, he has nothing to fear from them. Even
the splendor in which philosophers—as well as public opinion in general—cloak "ethical" conduct, all arguments by which they recom-
mend it, cannot withstand the test of reason. With the notion that one
could investigate the "field of distinctive values"[39] in a manner similar
to any other field of inquiry, the modern "value research" of Scheler
and Hartmann has only hit upon another method for the solution of
an impossible task: the grounding of practices in mere philosophy.
The proposition of a science of "the structure and order of the realm

of values" necessarily entails such a promulgation of commandments. For even if this knowledge is characterized as being "in a rudimentary stage,"[40] an "Ought,"[41] which in certain cases is transformed "into the Ought-to-Do of the subject,"[42] still clings to all values which the ethicist strives to come up with. Despite the explanation that decision is constantly in the conscience of the subject, despite the universality that indeed belongs to the essence of the philosophical doctrine of morality, it is claimed that there exist differences of degree to which behavior supposedly conforms: "Thus, for example, brotherly love is evidently higher in value than justice, love for the remotest higher than brotherly love, and personal love (as it appears) higher than either. Likewise bravery stands higher than self-control, faith and fidelity higher than bravery, radiant virtue and personality again higher than these."[43] Such assertions, whose content moreover is connected only very diffusely with moral sentiment due to the intensely reactionary function of philosophy since Kant, have the same kind of command-ment-like character as the categorical imperative. They are the mys-tified expression of psychic states of affairs in which "pression sociale" and "élan d'amour" indeed enter into a connection which is difficult to analyze. There is no eternal realm of values. The needs and de-sires, the interests and passions of human beings change in relation to the historical process. Psychology and other auxiliary sciences of history must join together to explain the accepted values and their change at any given time.

Binding moral laws do not exist. Materialism finds no transcendent authority over human beings which would distinguish between good-will and the lust for profit, kindness and cruelty, avarice and self-sacrifice. Logic likewise remains silent and grants no preeminence to moral conviction. All attempts to ground morality in terms of tem-poral prudence rather than in terms of a view to a hereafter—as the cited examples show, even Kant did not always resist this inclination—are based on harmonistic illusions. First of all, in most cases morality and prudence diverge. Morality does not admit of any grounding—neither by means of intuition nor of argument. On the contrary, it represents a psychic constitution. To describe the latter, to make its personal conditions and its mechanisms of transmission intelligible, is the business of psychology. Characteristic of moral sentiment is an interest which diverges from "natural law" and which has nothing to do with private acquisition and possession. At present, all human impulses are determined, whether through this law or through mere convention. It follows from the definitions of the bourgeois thinkers that in this period even love falls under the category of property. "Videmus . . . quod ille, qui amat necessario conatur rem, quam amat, praesentum habere et conservare," says Spinoza.[44] Kant describes marriage as the "joining together of two people of the opposite sex for the lifelong mutual ownership of their sexual attributes"[45] and speaks of the "equality of possessions" of the married couple not merely in terms of material goods, but also in terms of "two people who mutually own each other."[46] Even insofar as modern accounts have not become completely ideological, they still contain similar definitions. According to Freud, the sexual aim of the infantile instinct, in which according to his teachings the essential features of the instinctual life of the adult are also to be discovered, consists in "obtaining satisfaction by means of an appropriate stimulation of the [selected] erotogenic zone."[47] Accordingly, the loved person appears mainly as the means to fulfill said stimulation. On this point, one is struck by the way in which Freud's theory is an elaboration of Kant's definition of marriage.

Moral sentiment is to be distinguished from this kind of love, and Kant is right to distinguish the former not only from egoism but from any such "inclination." He indicates the psychic state of affairs by his doctrine that in morality (as opposed to that which is the rule in the bourgeois world), a person is to be not simply a means but always at the same time an end. Moral sentiment has something to do with love, for "love, reverence, yearning for perfection, longing, all these things are inherent in an end."[48] However, this love has nothing to do with the person as economic subject or as an item in the property of the one who loves, but rather as a potential member of a happy humanity. It is not directed at the role and standing of a particular individual in civil life, but at its neediness and powers, which point toward the future. Unless the aim of a future happy life for all, which admittedly arises not on the basis of a revelation but out of the privation of the present, is included in the description of this love, it proves impossible to define. To all, inasmuch as they are, after all, human beings, it wishes the free development of their creative powers. To love it appears as if all living beings have a claim to happiness, for which it would not in the least ask any justification or grounds. It stands in primordial contradiction to stringency, even though there may be psychic processes which sustain both moments in themselves. In bourgeois society, training in strict morality more often stood in service to natural law than under the sign of liberation from it. Not the rod of the corporal but the climax of the Ninth Symphony is the expression of moral sentiment.

This sentiment is active today in a twofold manner. First, as compassion. While in Kant's period social production mediated by private acquisition was progressive, today it signifies the senseless crippling of powers and their misuse for purposes of destruction. The struggle of great economic power groups, which is played out on a world scale, is conducted amid the atrophy of kind human inclinations, the proclamation of overt and covert lies, and the development of an immeasurable hatred. Humanity has become so rich in the bourgeois period, and has at its disposal such great natural and human auxiliary powers, that it could exist united by worthy objectives. The need to veil this state of affairs, which is transparent in every respect, gives rise to a sphere of hypocrisy which not only extends to international relations but penetrates into even the most private of relations; it results in a diminution of cultural endeavors (including science) and a brutalization of personal and public life, such that spiritual misery is compounded with material. At no time has the poverty of humanity stood in such crying contradiction to its potential wealth as in the present, at no time have all powers been so horribly fettered as in this generation, where children go hungry as the hands of the fathers are busy churning out bombs. It appears as if the world is being driven into a catastrophe—or rather, as if it already finds itself in one—which can only be compared, within known history, to the fall of antiquity. The futility of the fate of the individual, which was caused earlier on by dearth of reason and by the bare naturalness of the production process, has risen in this present phase to become the most striking characteristic of existence. Whoever is fortunate could, as regards their inner worth, just as easily take the place of the most unfortunate, and vice versa. Everyone is given up to blind chance. The course of one's existence has no relation to one's inner possibilities, one's role in the present society has for the most part no relation to that which could be achieved in a rational society. Accordingly, the behavior of the moral agent is not capable of being oriented to one's dignity; the extent to which dispositions and deeds are really meritorious does not come to light in the chaotic present, "the real morality of actions, their merit or guilt, even that of our own conduct, . . . remains entirely hidden from us."[49] We view human beings not as subjects of their fate, but rather as objects of a blind occurrence of nature, to which the response of the moral sentiment is compassion.

That Kant did not see compassion on the basis of the moral sentiment can be explained in terms of the historical situation. He could expect from the uninterrupted progress of free competition an increase in general happiness, for he beheld the coming of a world dominated by this principle. All the same, even in his time compassion could not be separated from morality. As long as the individual and the whole have not really become one, as long as it is not the case that the easy death of the individual freed from fear is looked upon by the individual himself as something external, because he rightly knows his essential purposes to be looked after by society at large—as long, therefore, as morality still has a reason for existence, compassion will have its place in it. Indeed, compassion may outlast it; for morality belongs to that determinate form of human relations which was assumed on the basis of the mode of production of the bourgeois epoch. With the transformation of these relations through their rational arrangement, morality will, at the very least, step into the background. Human beings may then struggle in concert against their own pains and maladies—what medicine will achieve, once it is freed from its present social fetters, is not to be foreseen—although suffering and death will continue to hold sway in nature. The solidarity of human beings, however, is a part of the solidarity of life in general. Progress in the realization of the former will also strengthen our sense of the latter. Animals need human beings. It is the accomplishment of Schopenhauer's philosophy to have wholly illuminated the unity between us and them. The greater gifts of human beings, above all reason, by no means annul the communion which they feel with animals. To be sure, the traits of human beings have a certain imprint, but the relationship of their happiness and misery with the life of animals is manifest.

The other form in which morality today finds appropriate expression is politics. The happiness of the general public is consistently characterized as its proper aim by the great moral philosophers. To be sure, Kant had to deceive himself about the structure of future society, since he considered the form of the contemporary one to be eternal. The materialist critique of political economy first showed that the realization of the ideal in terms of which the present society was established—namely the union of general and particular interest—can take place only by the sublation of its own conditions. Today it is claimed that the bourgeois ideals of Freedom, Equality, and Justice have proven themselves to be poor ones; however, it is not the ideals of the bourgeoisie, but conditions which do not correspond to them, which have shown their untenability. The battle cries of the Enlightenment and of the French Revolution are valid now more than ever. The dialectical critique of the world, which is borne along by them, consists precisely in the demonstration that they have retained their actuality rather than lost it on the basis of reality. These ideas and values are nothing but the isolated traits of the rational society, as they are anticipated in morality as a necessary goal. Politics in accord with this goal therefore must not abandon these demands, but realize them—not, however, by clinging in a utopian manner to definitions which are historically conditioned, but in accordance with their meaning. The content of the ideas is not eternal, but is subject to historical change—surely not because "Spirit" of itself capriciously infringes upon the principle of identity, but because the human impulses which demand something better take different forms according to the historical material with which they have to work. The unity of such concepts results less from the invariability of their elements than from the historical development of the circumstances under which their realization is necessary.

In materialist theory, the main point is not to maintain concepts unchanged but to improve the lot of humanity. In the struggle for this, ideas have altered their content. Today, the freedom of individuals means the sublation of their economic independence in a plan. The presupposition of the ideas of Equality and Justice hitherto was the prevailing inequality of economic and human subjects; it must disappear in a unified society, whereupon these ideas will lose their meaning. "Equality exists only in contrast to inequality, justice to injustice; they are therefore still burdened with the contrast to the old, previous history, hence with the old society itself."[50] Hitherto, all these concepts took their determinate content from the relations of the free market, which with time were supposed to function to the benefit of all. Today they have transformed themselves into the concrete image of a better society, which will be born out of the present one, if humanity does not first sink into barbarism.

The concept of Justice, which played a decisive role as a battle cry in the struggle for a rational organization of society, is older than morality. It is as old as class society, i.e., as old as known European history itself. As a universal principle to be realized in this world, Justice in connection with Freedom and Equality first found recognition in bourgeois philosophy; though only today have the resources of humanity become great enough that their adequate realization is set as an immediate historical task. The intense struggle for their fulfillment marks our epoch of transition.

In previous history, every task of culture was possible only on the basis of a division between ruling and ruled groups. The suffering that is connected with the continual reproduction of the life of the masses at a particular level and especially with every advance, and which, so to speak, represents the costs expended by society, has never been distributed equitably among its members. The reason for this is not to be found, as the high-minded philosophers of the eighteenth century thought, in the avarice and depravity of the rulers, but in the disproportion between the powers and needs of human beings. Right up till the present, the general level of development of the whole of society (including the upper class) conditioned, in view of the available tools, the subordination of the masses at work and thus in life generally. Their coarseness corresponded to the inability of the rulers to raise them to a higher stage of development, and both moments were constantly reproduced along with the harshness of social life, which changes only slowly. Historical humanity, in danger of sinking into chaos, did not have the option of abandoning relations of domination. The emergence and dissemination of cultural values cannot be separated from this division. Leaving aside the material goods which result from a production process based on the division of labor, the products of art and science, the refined forms of social intercourse, their sense of an intellectual life, all point to their origin in a society which distributes burdens and pleasures unequally.

It has often been asserted that class division, which has left its imprint on all previous history, is a continuation of the inequality in nature. The genera of animals may be divided up into predators and prey, such that some genera are both at the same time, whereas others are principally only one of the two. Even within genera there are spatially separated groups, some of which appear to be blessed by fortune, some pursued by a series of inconceivable blows of fate. In turn, the pain and death of the individuals within the groups and genera are unequally distributed, and depend on circumstances which lack any meaningful connection to the life of the those so affected. The inequality which is constantly determined by the life process of society is related to that inequality which pertains to the whole of nature. Both of these permeate the life of humanity, in that the natural diversity of external form and abilities, not to mention diseases and further circumstances of death, further complicate social inequality. Of course, the degree to which these natural differences are operative in society depends on historical development; they have different consequences at the various levels of different social structures: the appearance of the same disease can mean quite different things for members of different social circles. Attention, pedagogical artifice, and a range of gratifications afford the poorly gifted wealthy child the opportunity to develop the aptitudes which still remain, whereas the slow child of poor people struggling for existence will go to ruin mentally as well as physically: his shortcomings will be intensified throughout his life, his hopeful first steps will come to nothing.

In this history of humanity, in which inequality constitutes such a fundamental trait, a certain human reaction has repeatedly become apparent, whether as inequality's other side or as its effect. The abolition of inequality has been demanded at different times and in different places. Not only the dominated classes but also renegades from the ruling classes have denounced inequality. The equality which was to be brought about (and which, in the materialist view, developed with the exchange relationship) has been understood in the most various ways. From the basic demand that everyone should receive an equal share of the consumer goods produced by society (e.g., in early Christendom) to the proposition that to each should be allotted that share which corresponds to his labor (e.g., Proudhon), to the thought that the most sensitive should be the least burdened (Nietzsche), there is an exceedingly wide range of ideas about the correct state of affairs. All of them make reference to the point that happiness, insofar as it is possible for each person in comparison with others on the basis of their lot in society, is not to be determined by fortuitous, capricious factors which are external to the individual—in other words, that the degree of inequality of the life conditions of individuals at least be no greater than that dictated by the maintenance of the total social supply of goods at the given level. That is the universal content of the concept of Justice; according to this concept, the social inequality prevailing at any given time requires a rational foundation. It ceases to be considered as a good, and becomes something that should be overcome.

To have made this principle a universal one is an achievement of recent times, during which there has certainly been no lack of defenders of inequality and of eulogists of the blindness in nature and society. Although representative philosophers of past epochs, such as Aristotle and Thomas Aquinas, had extolled the differences in people's fate as an eternal value, the Enlightenment (in connection with old humanistic doctrines, to be sure) described inequality as an evil to be abolished; in the French Revolution, Equality was raised to a principle of the constitution. Recognition of this principle was not mere inspiration or, in Bergson's terms, an incursion of open morality into the sphere of closed morality. Rather, such recognition belonged in that epoch to the process of society's adaptation to changing life conditions. Like all living entities, society makes such adaptation both continuously and spasmodically in consequence of its own intrinsic dynamics. The idea of Equality "résulte logiquement des transformations réelles de nos sociétés."[51] The idea of Equality necessarily brings that of Freedom to the fore. If indeed no individual is initially less worthy than any other of developing and of finding satisfaction in reality, it follows that the utilization of coercion by one group against the other must be acknowledged as evil. The concept of Justice is as inseparable from that of Freedom as it is from that of Equality.

From the beginning, the proclamation of Equality as a constitutional principle was not only an advance for thought, but a danger as well. As a sublation of determinate inequalities (which were no longer necessary, which were indeed hindrances in the context of the expanded powers of human beings) in fact came to pass in the new constellation of the relations of Justice, this step was additionally proclaimed as the realization of Equality in general. It had become unclear whether the social equality of human beings was still a demand to be met or a description of reality. The French Revolution had not only helped the universal concept of Justice to gain theoretical recognition, but had to a great extent realized it at that time as well. This concept came to dominate the ideas of the nineteenth century and turned into a decisive feature of all thought, indeed even the feeling of the European and American world. But the institutions which at the time aptly embodied the principle have grown old, as has the overall constitution of bourgeois society. At the time, equality before the law had signified a step forward in the direction of Justice, inequality of property notwithstanding; today it has become inadequate because of this inequality. Freedom of public expression was a weapon in the struggle for better conditions; today it acts primarily to the advantage of conditions that have become obsolete. Sanctity of property was a protection of bourgeois labor against the clutches of the authorities; today it brings in its wake monopolization, the expropriation of further bourgeois strata, and the tying up of social resources.

The alliance struck between the ruling power and the ideas of the bourgeoisie since the victory of the French Revolution confounds thought for this reason: these propelling ideas are alienated from and set against their logical proponents, the progressive forces of society. But it is precisely in the present, as humanity confronts the danger of ruin, that humanity is charged with their realization. The abolition of economic inequality, which would soon have to lead to a far-reaching sublation of the distinction between the ruling and the ruled groups, signifies for the first time today not an abandonment of cultural values, but on the contrary their redemption. While the unequal distribution of power was among the prerequisites of culture in earlier epochs, today it has turned into a threat to the same. But those forces which benefit from wretched social relations presently make use of those ideas to avert the possible change of which humanity stands in need. They snatch these ideas from those who have a genuine interest in their realization. The peculiar present perplexity in the ideological [*weltanschaulichem*] domain is a consequence of this. The provisions of justice, which today find expression in the institutions of a merely

formal democracy and in the ideas of those raised in its spirit, have
lost any clear connection to their origin. Otherwise they would now
be leveled at the ruling powers which fetter the development of
humanity, just as they were during the time when the latter understood the bourgeoisie itself in a productive sense—except that today
the change would signify a much more decisive step. However, although the powerful themselves have for centuries proclaimed the
principles of a good order to be holy, they are willing to twist them
around or betray them the instant that their meaningful application
no longer serves their interest but runs against it. Indeed, they are
ready to throw overboard and pull from the curriculum all the ideals
which the fathers of the bourgeois revolution championed, worked
for, and fought for, as soon as people are developed and desperate
enough to no longer apply them mechanically to the preservation
of institutions, but to apply them dialectically to the realization of a
better order. The requirements of internal and external control entail that all progressive elements of bourgeois morality be stifled or
deliberately eliminated in many places. There is a steady reduction in
the number of countries in which those values which aspire to the
increase of the happiness of individuals have not yet fallen into disrepute; it appears that the period in which the bourgeois world produced morality was too short for it to be converted into universality
in flesh and blood. It is not only secular morality which rests on such
shaky ground; the same can be said of whatever elements of kindness
and charity made their way into the soul as a result of Christianity
(the civilizing influence which preceded secular morality), such that
in a few decades even these forces could atrophy. The moral sentiment in governments, peoples, and spokesmen of the civilized [*gebildeten*] world is so weak that, although it is indeed expressed in relief
efforts after earthquakes and mine disasters, it is nevertheless easily
silenced and forgotten in the face of the monstrous injustice which
takes place for the sake of pure property interests, i.e., in the enforce-
ment of the "natural law" and amidst the mockery of all bourgeois
values.

The appeal to morality is more powerless than ever, but it is not
even needed. In contrast to the idealistic belief in the cry of conscience as a decisive force in history, this hope is foreign to materialist
thinking. Yet because materialism itself belongs to the efforts to attain

a better society, it well knows where the elements of morality that are pushing forward are active today. They are produced time and again, under the immense pressure which weighs heavily upon a large segment of society, as the will to rational relations which correspond to the present state of development. This part of humanity, which necessarily counts on this change due to its situation, already contains (and attracts ever more) forces to whom the realization of a better society is a matter of great importance. It is also psychologically prepared for it, since its role in the production process forces it to rely less on the unlikely increase of property than on the employment of its labor power. These conditions facilitate the generation of personalities in which the acquisitive instincts are not of prime importance. If the inheritance of morality thus passes on to new classes, there are nevertheless many proletarians who exhibit bourgeois traits under the domination of the natural law, as delineated in an earlier edition of this journal.[52] The works of later bourgeois writers such as Zola, Maupassant, Ibsen, and Tolstoy constitute testimonials to moral goodness. But in any case, the common efforts of that part of humanity which is guided by knowledge contain so much genuine solidarity with respect to their liberation and that of humanity, so much lack of concern about their private existence, so few thoughts of possessions and property, that the sensibility of future humanity already seems to manifest itself in them. While the putative consciousness of equality in existing society generally bears the flaw of overlooking the actual inequality in the existence of human beings, and thus embraces untruth, the forces pressing for change place actual inequality in the forefront. To the authentic concept of Equality belongs the knowledge of its negativity: contemporary human beings differ not only in terms of economic fortunes, but also in terms of their intellectual and moral qualities. A Bavarian farmer differs radically from a factory worker in Berlin. But the certainty that the differences are based on transient conditions—and above all that inequalities of power and happiness, as they have become entrenched today through the structure of society, no longer correspond to the developed forces of production—engenders a respect for the inner possibilities of the individual and for that "which can be made out of him" (Kant), a feeling of independence and goodwill, which politics must positively connect with if it is concerned to build a free society.

There is no obligation to this politics, any more than there is an obligation to compassion. Obligations refer back to commands and contracts, which do not exist in this case. Nonetheless, materialism recognizes in compassion as well as in forward-directed politics productive forces that are historically related to bourgeois morality. According to materialism, however, not only the explicit forms of command but the ideas of duty and metaphysical guilt, and above all the maligning of desire and pleasure, exercise constraining effects in the present social dynamic. Materialist theory certainly does not afford to the political actor the solace that he will necessarily achieve his objective; it is not a metaphysics of history but rather a changing image of the world, evolving in relation to the practical efforts toward its improvement. The knowledge of tendencies that is contained in this image offers no clear prognosis of historical development. Even if those who maintain that the theory could be misleading "only" in regard to the pace of development, and not its direction, were correct (a frightful "only," since it concerns the agonies of generations), merely formally understood time could, after all, turn around and affect the quality of the content, i.e., humanity could be thrown back to earlier stages of development simply because the struggle had lasted too long. But even the sheer certainty that such an order would come to pass would not alone provide even the slightest of grounds on which to affirm or precipitate this order. That something in the world gains power is no reason to revere it. The ancient myth of the rulers, that that which has power must also be good, passed into occidental philosophy by way of Aristotle's doctrine of the unity of reality and perfection. Protestantism reaffirmed this myth in its belief in God as the lord of history and the regulator of the world. It dominates the whole of life in present-day Europe and America. The blind worship of success determines people even in the most private expressions of life. For the materialist, the presence of a historical magnitude alone, or the prospects which it has, by no means constitutes a recommendation. The materialist asks how this dimension at a given point in time relates to the values he affirms, and acts according to the concrete situation. In the prevailing social conditions, this action is burdened by the unhappy situation that compassion and politics, the two forms in which moral sentiment finds expression today, can only rarely be brought into a rational relationship with each other. Regard for those close at hand and those far away, support for the individual and for humanity are contradictory in most cases. Even the best harden some place in their hearts.

The insight that morality cannot be proven, that not a single value admits of a purely theoretical grounding, is one that materialism shares with idealist currents of philosophy. But both the derivation and the concrete application of the principle within the sphere of knowledge are completely different. In idealist philosophy it is necessarily connected with the doctrine of the absolutely free subject. Just as the subject (at least according to later exponents) supposedly produces knowledge of itself, so too is the positing of value thought to be subjective. Without any foundation at all, it issues from autonomous Spirit, from "the *intellectus*." Nicholas of Cusa already teaches: "Without the power of judgment and of comparison there ceases to be any evaluation, and with it value must fall as well. Herefrom springs the wonder of the mind, since without it everything created would have been without value."[53] Even though, according to Cusanus, the autonomous subject does not of itself produce the *essence* of value, it nonetheless freely decides how much of that essence is accorded to each object. In this creative activity it is supposed to be similar to God, even another God itself, as it were. Since Cusanus, this doctrine has been definitive in science and philosophy. According to it, the differences in value of things are by no means material; the object in itself is indifferent to value. Science can indeed describe the human acts which posit value, but cannot itself decide among them. In modern methodology this principle is formulated as the demand for value neutrality. Max Weber's view is characteristic of the main tendencies of idealistic philosophy (with the exception of theories of objective value), which for the most part display romantic, at any rate antidemocratic tendencies. It is his view "that we are *cultural beings*, endowed with the capacity and the will to take a deliberate attitude toward the world and to lend it significance. . . . Undoubtedly, all evaluative ideas are 'subjective.' "[54] As a result of this doctrine, in idealist philosophy and science any value judgment is accordingly ruled out. Indeed, in recent decades it has increasingly been made a duty of the human or cultural sciences not to take up and develop its material in connection with larger social objectives, but rather to establish and to classify "theory-free" facts. The application of the earlier objectives of the bourgeoisie—above all that of the greatest happiness of all—to the problems of those areas of inquiry would necessarily lead to conflicts in increasing measure. In the original works of the bourgeoisie these motives are absolutely decisive. Even the originators of positivism defended themselves against the neutralistic degeneration of knowledge, in contrast to many of their later disciples. "The 'dispersive specialty' of the present race of scientific men," writes John Stuart Mill in his work on Auguste Comte, "who, unlike their predecessors, have a positive aversion to enlarged views, and seldom either know or care for any of the interests of mankind beyond the narrow limits of their pursuit, is dwelt on by M. Comte as one of the great and growing evils of the time, and the one which most retards moral and intellectual regeneration. To contend against it is one of the main purposes towards which he thinks the forces of society should be directed."[55] Such voices have become very rare precisely among the progressive scholars of our day. They must be satisfied with defending their work against the increasing predominance of those who, without respect for rigor or integrity, would like to lead knowledge back behind the position it has attained by way of its subjugation to goals that have become questionable, and who would like to reduce it to the handmaiden of whatever power happens to hold sway. In seeking to protect knowledge and the interest in truth from the presently invading barbarism, those scholars are rendering a service to civilization similar to those places where today genuine bourgeois values are still held up for respect in the public mind through education.[56]

Materialism recognizes the unconditional respect for truth as a necessary if not sufficient condition of science. It knows that interests stemming from social and personal circumstances also condition research, whether the creator of knowledge at any given time knows it or not. On both a small and a large scale, historical factors are operative not only in the choice of objects, but in the direction of attention and abstraction as well. In each case, the result has its origin in a determinate interrelation between investigators and objects. But in contrast to idealist philosophy, materialism in no way traces interests and objectives that are operative on the part of the subject back to the independent creative activity of this subject and to his free will. On the contrary, they are themselves seen as a result of a development in which both subjective and objective moments have a part. Even exchange value in the economy is not based on free valuation but rather ensues from the life process of society, in which use values are determining factors. The undialectical concept of the free subject is foreign to materialism. It is also well aware of its own conditionality. Apart from personal nuances, this latter is to be sought in connection with those forces which are devoted to the realization of the aims stated above. Because materialist science never takes its eyes away from these aims, it does not assume the character of false impartiality, but is consciously biased. It is concerned not so much with originality as with the extension of the theoretical knowledge which it has already attained on this course.

In its acknowledgment of the decisive significance of theory, materialism is to be distinguished from present-day positivism, though not from concrete research, which often comes to the same findings as materialism itself. Some of its exponents have grasped well the relation of morality and praxis to theory on account of intimate acquaintance with social problems. "Loin que la pratique se déduise de la théorie, c'est la théorie qui, jusqu'à présent, est une sorte de projection abstraite de la morale pratiquée dans une société donnée, à une époque donnée."[57] Theory is a cohesive body of insights that stems from a determinate praxis and from determinate ends. The world reveals a consistent image to whomever looks at it from a consistent point of view—an image which changes, to be sure, with the period to which acting and knowing individuals are subject. Praxis already organizes the material of which each individual takes cognizance; the demand to establish theory-free facts is false, if this is to mean that subjective factors are not already operative in the given objective facts. Understood productively, it can only mean that the description is veracious [wahrhaftig]. The whole cognitive structure from which every description gets its meaning, and which this description should serve in return—as well as theory itself—these are all part of the efforts and aspirations of the human beings that create them. These may arise from private whims, from the interests of retrograde powers, or from the needs of developing humanity.

Egoism and Freedom Movements: On the Anthropology of the Bourgeois Era

I

A contradiction in the conception of human nature that has great significance for the political literature of the bourgeois era came to light in two brilliant works at the beginning of the sixteenth century. Although Machiavelli's instructions for statesmen are not based on as pessimistic an anthropology as implied by the familiar statement in chapter 18 of *The Prince* that all men "are bad and would not observe their faith,"[1] subsequent centuries understood him essentially in that manner. In fact, Machiavelli found so many followers in this direction that Treitschke could state that "all truly great political thinkers reveal a trace of cynical contempt for man, and even if it is not too strong it always has a strong basis."[2] Thomas More's *Utopia* expresses a different view. This vision of a rational society proclaims the conviction of an originally happier constitution of human nature by the mere fact that its realization, according to the fable, is not separated temporally from the present but only spatially. More does not cite bestial instincts as constraints to the association of free people who regulate their lives according to plans that respect the claims of each member equally. Unlike Machiavelli, More does not describe a cycle of state forms in which every tolerable condition is necessarily followed by the same confusion and misery out of which society emerged after a long and arduous process.[3] Nor was More the only one to hold this view. Rousseau did not need to invoke More in his attacks on the Hobbesian doctrine of the dangerous aggressiveness of human nature, because he could cite a whole series of bourgeois theoreticians who held the same view.[4]

These representative writers of the Renaissance and the Enlightenment were sparing in applying the attributes "good" and "bad" to human nature. Aspects of their work not only evince points of view that reject such characterizations—Machiavelli's concept of *virtù* comes to mind here—but as modern thinkers they strive to exclude value judgments as much as possible. In contrast to the medieval view, which understood human beings mainly in reference to a norm, and in which nature, as opposed to the unnatural, connoted the divinely ordained constitution of human beings within all creation, early modern thought began to regard as human those traits which proved to be so in terms of historical, political, and psychological analysis. Human nature was no longer to be derived from biblical exegesis or other authorities, but ultimately from directly accessible facts. Knowledge of human beings becomes a specialized problem of natural science. To the extent that the basic natural-scientific categories contain any pervasive value judgment, it is based on the view that for everything in nature, and thus for the body and its indwelling soul, to perish represents the greatest evil, while self-preservation and all actions toward that end constitute the highest good. This simple naturalism, which drew upon the doctrines of antiquity, found expression in the Renaissance doctrine of emotions, especially as formulated by Cardano and Telesio, and was systematically elaborated in the philosophies of Hobbes and Spinoza.[5] This seemingly unprejudiced concept of nature was in reality individualistic in that it maintained each being's self-preservation to be its law and standard, corresponding to the social existence of the bourgeois individual. What starts as a conception of nonhuman nature, one lacking any conscious relation to this social origin, is eventually projected back onto human beings.

Yet, although philosophy and science were convinced of their own value neutrality, the spirit of the times imbued not only the effect but the very composition and implementation of their models: not just in the sense of the unquestioned individualistic principle that regulated the relationships of owners to one another, but also by the mental and instinctive barriers caused by the combination of this principle with the fact of the increasing differentiation of social classes. The nature of the isolated individual is itself a dubious topic for anthropology. This isolated individual is not the same as human beings in general, which is supposed to be anthropology's frame of reference. But due to the contradictions of the bourgeois order, especially the constant need for the physical and psychic repression of the masses, the analysis of this abstract subject is further obscured and constricted by unconscious considerations. With or without the author's intention, anthropological ideas take on moral significance; confidence or disgust, indifference or sympathy contaminate the descriptions of psychic structures as well as ideas about the nature and course of the emotions and all other impulses. The individual, which under the simplified rubric of Man constitutes the major theme of the anthropological ideas of this epoch, has in turn been considered by this epoch's philosophers in a manner that is fragmentary in many respects.

The explanation for this state of affairs seems obvious. The sociological attribution of thoughts and feelings to social groups and historical movements has an especially easy task in this instance. The anthropological contradiction corresponds to a political one. Historians have tried to explain the contradiction between Machiavelli and More psychologically by pointing to "differences in their mental attitude and ethical disposition," or politically by contrasting a divided Italy, always threatened by invasions, with England, an administratively united island, practically safe from all enemies.[6] Yet sociological analysis teaches us that in the subsequent development of anthropology, the emphasis placed on the aggressive "bestial" drives of human beings indicated an interest in oppression, whereas the emphasis placed on educability, or simply the moral indifference in the judgment of instinctual life, was an expression of emancipatory tendencies. Those philosophers of history differ not so much in anthropology as in politics. Had politics not separated them, they could have concurred on anthropology. Only the circumstance that anthropology was used to support political goals widened the gap between the two ways of thinking. The task of applying this theory to the anthropological ideas of modern history and of tracing the changes, reversals, and complications of this model is not just a historical problem. It is of systematic and scientific interest: the instructional content of the great bourgeois anthropological doctrines will be uncovered and appropriated by psychological knowledge.

But this obvious connection with politics will not be treated in the following pages when we speak of how anthropological thoughts are permeated with ideas about value. Rather, a closer look at the optimistic and pessimistic trends reveals a trait common to the two ways of thinking as they developed in history, one which drastically diverted and weakened the intention shared by Machiavelli and the Enlightenment to establish knowledge about human beings: the condemnation of egoism, indeed of pleasure itself. Not only in the cynical proclamation of the dangerous wickedness of human nature which must be kept in check by a strong governmental apparatus, and in the corresponding Puritanical doctrine of the sinfulness of the individual, who had to suppress his own desires with iron discipline and in absolute subjection to the law of duty, but also in the contrary assertion of man's originally pure and harmonious nature which is disturbed only by the restrictive and corrupt present conditions—in all of these, the absolute renunciation of every egoistic urge is the self-evident premise. This appears as a contradiction to practice. As the dominance of bourgeois society grows more undiluted and its influence less restricted, people come to view one another with increasing hostility and indifference as individuals, families, economic groups, and classes. In the context of sharpened economic and social contradictions, the originally progressive principle of free competition takes on the character of a permanent state of war, internally and externally. All who are drawn into this world develop the egoistic, exclusionary, hostile sides of their being in order to survive in this harsh reality. In the historically effective grand anthropological notions of the bourgeoisie, however, any emotions or drives which do not contribute directly to concord, love, and sociability are despised, distorted, or denied.

When Machiavelli states in his *Discorsi* "that men act right only under compulsion, but from the moment that they have the option and liberty to commit wrong with impunity, they never fail to carry confusion and disorder everywhere,"[7] while in the introduction claiming for himself an inborn "desire . . . to do what may prove for the common benefit of all,"[8] it becomes clear that he does not observe the natural instincts of most human beings simply in a natural-scientific light, but regards them as bad and reprehensible. However distant and unprejudiced his conscious stance toward Christianity may be, on this point he is substantially in agreement with Luther and Calvin. As exponents of similar historical interests, they all break with the Catholic tolerance toward certain modes of human reaction that interfere with the establishment of the new economic order. At the outset of this form of society, as well as in its latest phases, the wretchedness of the individual is asserted. "Luther sees in all clarity," a German treatise states, "that man's will is evil, and this means not that something in man is evil, but that man himself is evil right to the root, that evil is the corrupted nature itself."[9] In contrast with Catholicism, there is here no neutral sphere of instinctual life; on the contrary, the essence of human beings as such is evil and rotten. Similarly, Calvin teaches: "Original sin is the inherited perversion and corruption of our nature in all its parts. . . . Cognitive reason and the heart's will are possessed by sin. From head to foot man is immersed in this flood so that no part of his whole being remains free of sin. Everything he does must be counted as sin, as Paul says (Romans 8:7) that all desires and thoughts of the flesh are enmity to God, and hence death."[10] Rousseau's sharp opposition to this does not refer at all to the condemnation of the "bad" drives and the pleasure in prohibited instinctual goals, but to their ubiquity, their origin and possible change. But it is not only Rousseau and the enthusiasm for everything natural and primitive connected with his name (always evident in a heartfelt style regardless of content), nor only harmony philosophers such as Cumberland and Shaftesbury who, contrary to Hobbes's anthropology, teach an innate morality—the whole tradition of thought that glorifies the natural proves to be identical with its misanthropic counterpart, since it does not at all attack the legitimacy of condemning the allegedly corrupt instincts but only the views on their development and extent.

Turning to the figure of Robespierre, the orthodox disciple of Rousseau, makes sufficiently clear the moral rigorism inherent in this sentimental theory of human beings. His concept of virtue agreed very closely with the Puritan view; condemnation was changed into real persecution under his reign. Political and moral opposition cannot be separated in him. He speaks of the sad consequences of Epicurean thought with the same disgust as a militant theologian.[11] There are two kinds of human behavior according to him: virtue and vice. "Depending on the direction he gives to his passions, Man rises as high as heaven or he plunges into the murky abyss."[12] This separation is exclusive; on the one hand, base, reprehensible pleasure, synonymous with crass selfishness—the doctrines of materialism and atheism run in this direction—and on the other, love of country and self-denial. There are "two kinds of egoism: the one base and cruel, which separates man from his own kind and strives for a solitary well-being purchased with the hardships of others; the other magnanimous and beneficial, which dissolves our personal happiness into the welfare of all while linking our reputation with the fatherland's."[13] Human beings are comprehended in terms of the behavior which society expects of them, and this means that an instinctual disposition that contradicts the principles actually governing social reality is proclaimed as so-called virtue. Religion, metaphysics, and moral declamation fulfilled the task of measuring people by the opposite of what these factors in part led them to necessarily become in the underlying historical world. Apart from the works of a few undaunted writers, the analysis of human beings in the bourgeois epoch was impeded and falsified by this contradiction.

The need for an idealistic morality follows from the bourgeoisie's economic situation. The ever-increasing unleashing of free competition needed certain inhibitions, even according to its own advocates and defenders (apart from a few cynical economists of the last century). Private and criminal law see to it that this play of forces attains a balance, however unstable, guaranteeing a relatively constant functioning of society. In addition, habits and customs likewise keep competition within certain forms and restrict it. But even insofar as the liberal principle is restricted only by these kind of juridical and traditional limits, as was the case during part of the nineteenth century in England, its rule is a special case in economic history. Before and afterward, far-reaching state measures were needed for the social whole to be able to reproduce itself in the given form at all. Social interests that go beyond the horizon of the individual economic subject were recognized, apart from juridical, political-economic, and various other state institutions, by church and private organizations as well as by a philosophically grounded morality. One of the causes of bourgeois morality lies in the social need to restrain the principle of competition that dominated the epoch. Thus, the moralistic view of man contains a rational principle, albeit in mystified, idealistic form.[14] Furthermore, the rejection of antisocial drives is understandable from the severity of social domination. It was less necessary to preach moderation in mutual competition to the poor of recent centuries. For them, morality was supposed to mean submissiveness, resignation, discipline and sacrifice for the whole, i.e., simply the repression of their material claims. Their competition with one another, on the contrary, was desired, and its mitigation through the formation of economic and political associations was made more difficult. The expression of their material interests that morality sought to restrict at this point was not private enterprise but common action: this was fought against ideologically by disparaging those interests.

Both themes, universal social interest and class interest, pervade the critique of egoism. The contradiction contained in morality, stemming from this dual root, gives the bourgeois concept of virtue, as it appears even among progressive thinkers and politicians, its vagueness and ambiguity. Anthropology either sets egoism against a nobler human nature or simply brands it as bestiality. Basically, the charge of egoism does not apply to the striving of the mighty for power, prosperity within sight of misery, or the maintenance of anachronistic and unjust forms of society. Since the bourgeoisie's victory, philosophical morality has devoted ever greater acumen toward maintaining impartiality on this point. The majority of humanity would be better off if it just became accustomed to restraining its own demand for happiness, and to repressing its wish to live as well as that small minority which was quite willing to have its existence be condemned by this useful moral verdict. This sense of bourgeois virtue as a means of domination became increasingly important. In the totalitarian states of the present, where all intellectual life is understood solely from the viewpoint of manipulating the masses, the broader and humanistic elements of morality are intentionally stripped away, and the individual's purposes are declared to be wholly subordinate to whatever the government designates as a common goal. In a few currents of utilitarianism, particularly in liberal political economy, self-interest is proclaimed to be the legitimate root of action, and then reconciled by farfetched constructions and obvious sophistries with the unselfish behavior required of the masses. But those authors who did not merely advocate egoism within conventional bounds—purely "theoretically" and with a knowing wink, as it were[15]—but proclaimed and recommended it openly as the essence of this form of social existence, were suspect and detested. The critique of egoism fits better into this system of egoistic reality than its open defense, for it is based increasingly on the denial of its own nature. Public acceptance of its rule would simultaneously mean its end. However little the average member of the ruling strata may be able, in private, to conceive of any interests except those that are egoistic in the narrowest sense, openly propagating such interests nevertheless evokes the indignation of these very same people. The egoism that has recently been sanctified, the "sacro egoismo" of military states, is for the individuals of the mass rather the exact opposite of self-interest, inducing them to renounce prosperity, security, and freedom. It designates the aggressive tendencies of small groups of society and has nothing to do with the happiness of most individuals. With moral indignation Frederick II of Prussia defended his unprejudiced, egoistic policy against Machiavelli, in spite of the fact that it was first established by the latter; and Mandeville's *Fable of the Bees,* in which the author establishes and propagates egoism as the foundation of present society under the motto "private vices, public benefits," was specifically refuted, characteristically enough, by one of the most representative philosophers of the ascending bourgeoisie.[16] Mandeville himself well knew that the open advocacy of egoism is unwelcome precisely to those who embody it most strongly. Each of them "would have us believe that the pomp and luxury he is served with are as many tiresome plagues to him, and all the grandeur he appears in is an ungrateful burden, which, to his sorrow, is inseparable from the high sphere he moves in, that his noble mind, so much elevated above vulgar capacities, aims at higher ends, and cannot relish such worthless enjoyments, that the highest of his ambition is to promote the public welfare, and his greatest pleasure to see his country flourish, and everybody in it made happy."[17]

What is expressed in philosophy as contempt for instinctual desires turns out in real life to be the practice of their suppression. Every instinct that did not move in predesignated channels, along with every unconditional desire for happiness, was persecuted and repressed in favor of "moral" endeavors related to the "common good." Insofar as this common good contradicted the most immediate interests of most people, the transference of psychic energies into socially permitted forms lacked any rational explanation; consequently, in order to domesticate the masses, society needed education dominated by religion and metaphysics in addition to physical force. In all of history, even in periods which proved to be relatively progressive, excessive self-denial has been demanded of the vast majority. Self-discipline and a conciliatory spirit, both among themselves and toward the rulers, were instilled in them by all means of coercion and persuasion. Individuals were subdued; after all, in official consciousness as well as in their own immediate consciousness, they ultimately were moral beings. Bad desires and passions might slumber at the bottom of their souls, but only those of weak and depraved character fell prey to them. The rulers themselves were forced to act ruthlessly in the hard struggle for existence, but that was one of life's bitter necessities. A real specimen of the privileged bourgeoisie is so strongly indoctrinated with the moral propaganda his class directs at the rest of society that his own ideology does not permit him to enjoy the exploitation and control over people and things, which must instead appear as a duty to the whole, a social accomplishment, the fulfillment of a predesignated career, whereby they may be acknowledged and affirmed. The Renaissance paintings in which wealthy donors with unmerciful and sly faces kneel as humble saints under the cross can be regarded as symbols of this epoch of unchained self-interest.

The struggle against egoism encompasses more than just individual impulses; it applies to emotional life as a whole and ultimately turns against unrationalized, free pleasure which is sought without justification. The assertion of its harmfulness is merely incidental to the arguments made against it. Man as he should be, the model underlying bourgeois anthropology everywhere, has a limited relation to pleasure, because he is oriented toward "higher" values. In the life of the exemplary man, there is little place for pleasure in its most direct form as sexual or, more extensively, material pleasure. The work done by the individual for himself and others is done for the sake of higher ideals that are connected only loosely, if at all, with pleasure. Duty, honor, community, etc., determine the true man and set him apart from animals. In all activity that claims to have cultural value, the greatest emphasis is placed on the absence of pleasure as a motive. This does not mean that joy is rejected openly and fully. On the contrary: in the darkest workplaces, in the most monotonous procedures, under the saddest conditions of existence in a life marked with deprivation, humiliation, and dangers, without prospects of tasting improvement, men are, at all costs, not supposed to be depressed. The more religious consolation loses credibility, the more the cultural apparatus meant to create joy in the common man is refined and expanded. The tavern and festival of the past, the sports and political mass exhibitions of the present, the fostering of a cheerful family life and the modern entertainment industries, both light and serious radio broadcasts—all are designed to evoke a satisfied mood. Nothing makes a person more suspect than the lack of an inner harmony with life as it happens to be. The prescribed joyous temperament, however, is wholly different from orientation toward the pleasures of life or the joy that stems from real satisfaction. In the bourgeois type, happiness does not radiate from pleasurable moments to life as a whole, brightly coloring even those aspects that are not inherently delightful. On the contrary, the capacity for direct pleasure is weakened, coarsened, and in many cases completely lost through the idealistic preaching of improvement and self-denial. The absence of blows of fate and conflicts of conscience—i.e., a relative freedom from external and internal pains and fears, a neutral, often very dismal state in which the soul tends to oscillate between extreme activity and stolid impassivity—is confused with happiness. The tabooing of "common" pleasure has succeeded so well that the average citizen who allows himself any becomes shabby instead of free, crude instead of grateful, stupid instead of clever. In marriage, pleasure retreats before duty, but the social state to which pleasure was always ascribed as its profession has sunk so low and become so despised that it is almost on a level with crime. Pleasure has been banished from the light of cultural consciousness to the sad refuge of small-minded obscenity and prostitution. The individual attained abstract consciousness of itself within a historical process that, in abolishing slavery, ended one form of class society, but not classes themselves; hence this process not only emancipated human beings, it enslaved them internally at the same time.

In the modern age, domination is concealed economically by the superficial independence of economic subjects, as well as philosophically by the idealistic concept of an absolute human freedom; it is internalized by subduing and mortifying all claims to pleasure. This process of civilization admittedly began long before the bourgeois era; nevertheless, this is when the process first gave rise to the formation and consolidation of representative character types and gave social life its stamp.

II

In the quieter periods of the last centuries, it might appear at first
glance that people had adjusted to the moral ideal of love and help-
fulness, or at least were beginning to draw closer to it. The antagonistic mode of production, in which the principle of coldness and enmity
necessarily dominated reality because everyone encountered each other
as competitors, developed positive aspects in comparison to earlier
forms of society. Every further step of realization, even expansion of
competition, brought improvements and provided stronger evidence
that social life could be kept running on the basis of the new principle
of uncontrolled economic activity. But these calmer times, which on
closer inspection were really quite turbulent, were interrupted not
just by wars, famines, and economic crises but also by revolutions and
counterrevolutions, and all these events provide historical material
for the connection between the morality and the practices of the bourgeois individual. This relationship is more clearly apparent in the revolutions than in the counterrevolutions. The temporarily victorious
counterattacks of Catholicism in seventeenth-century England, the rule
of the Bourbons after the fall of Napoleon, and the crushing of the
Paris Commune all took place so exclusively under the sign of revenge that the contradiction under consideration—that between the
morality and the reality of the bourgeois individual, between social
existence and its ideological reflection—cannot come fully into focus.
In the counterrevolutions, reactionary groups of the bourgeoisie
triumphed together with the remnants of feudalism. The kind of historical mechanisms that more typically reproduce the bourgeois character, rather, are movements that are evaluated, at least by more
progressive historians of the bourgeoisie, as positive, i.e., as coincid-
ing with the goals of their class. The smaller revolts of this kind pervade the whole history of Europe: the civil wars in the Italian cities in
the sixteenth century, the Dutch sectarian wars in the seventeenth,
the Spanish uprising in the eighteenth, as well as the small uprisings
in Germany and France led in part by university students during the
first half of the nineteenth century. These examples show that the
major revolutionary events of every country emerge from a background of incessant struggles. The miserable situation of the impoverished population was their cause, and the urban bourgeoisie played

the leading role. The focus here shall be on only a few historical actions that show especially clearly how the peculiar disposition of socially important groups of the bourgeoisie stood in contradiction to their own morality. In the everyday life, trade, and commerce spanning the history of modernity, the particular kind of wickedness and cruelty at work in this epoch is often hidden from those strata that do not experience it personally. During periods in which the social order loosens, however, the causes and essential traits of such phenomena become more clearly visible. The following pages attempt to describe the common structural features of familiar events of modern history. Although the significance of these events for humanity's progress varied greatly—a few are completely local, a few more religious than political—still, at these exceptional moments, the social constellation becomes recognizable together with its most important mediations: the idealistic hierarchy of values, the theoretical condemnation of egoism, and the brutal and cruel streak in the bourgeois type's disposition. Both real human existence and contradictory moral consciousness, as well as their dynamic interaction, result from the social basis. At this juncture, it is necessary to develop a few typical categories in terms of the historical material.

From the episode in which the Romans, under the leadership of Cola di Rienzo, made the untimely attempt to unite Italy under a democratically disguised dictatorship, up to its modern realization on the same soil, the awakening and spread of bourgeois forms of life has been marked with popular revolts. Despite all of the differences in their historical character and of their consequences for social progress, they show common social-psychological features that are especially significant from the vantage point of the present. Savonarola's rise and brief glory in Florence is symptomatic of a whole series of similar tendencies of the century. The struggle against the archaic state of ecclesiastical organization is taken up by clerical leaders who personify the interest of the rising individualistic society. The Reformers, as successors to a series of militant religious figures, achieved the changes that were necessary in the ecclesiastical domain. The English and French revolutions of the next centuries brought about the political form required by the economy. Corresponding tendencies developed in Germany in connection with the wars of liberation and the resistance to the subsequent reaction. The typical course of these bourgeois movements is being repeated in the present; the form is now grotesquely distorted because the progressive function which those past efforts filled in regard to the possible elimination of the prevailing contradictory state of society is today no longer linked with the bourgeoisie's activity, but has passed over to groups dominated by the latter. As the horror at the murderous practices of Chinese and Indian medicine, which had formerly been productive, becomes intensified in light of modern surgery, and the stupid superstition of the native patient who rejects modern medicine only to submit himself to a more primitive one becomes all the more shocking as the gap between the two widens and the disparity becomes increasingly obvious, so the present movements—from the perspective of the interests of the whole society, not those of the national power groups—bear the stamp of futile and ridiculous fanaticism. And as those medical practices, looked at in isolation, have remained the same despite this change, the social movements have maintained their key features, despite the radical change of function.

Their foundation displays a typical structure. The urban bourgeoisie has its particular economic interests; it requires the abolition of all conditions and laws which restrict its industry, whether they be feudal prerogatives, excessively ponderous forms of administration, or social protective measures. It further requires the establishment of large, centrally administered, sovereign economic territories, disciplined armies, the subordination of the whole cultural life under national authorities, the disappearance of all opposing powers, a system of justice oriented toward its needs, and safe and rapid transportation. The proletarianized urban and rural masses always had farther-reaching interests. While the social inequality in those historical stages was a precondition for social progress, the miserable condition of the oppressed corresponded to the utopian wish for equality and justice. The interests of the bourgeoisie regarding the system of ownership did not agree with those of the masses; despite the progressiveness of the system which the bourgeoisie was trying to establish, from the very start it implied a gap between the owners and the majority of society which grew increasingly wide. The spread of this system ultimately meant an improvement for humanity, but by no means for all people living at any particular time. The bourgeoisie's efforts to push through its own demands for a more rational administration against the feudal powers with the help of the desperate popular masses, while simultaneously consolidating its own rule over the masses, combine to account for the peculiar way the struggle for "the people" is carried on in these movements. The people are supposed to recognize that the national movement will, in the long run, bring advantages for them too. Of course no fully carefree existence could commence with the disappearance of the wretched administration whose abuses they previously suffered, as some might have dreamed in mistaken reminiscence of the Mother Church's welfare system; rather, the new freedoms mean greater responsibility of each individual for himself and his family, a responsibility to which each is to be held by educational efforts. A conscience must be made for all. By fighting for bourgeois freedoms, each must at the same time learn to fight against himself. The bourgeois revolution did not lead the masses to the lasting state of joyful existence and universal equality they longed for, but to the hard reality of an individualistic social order instead.

This historical situation determines the character of the bourgeois leader. While his actions conform directly to the interests of particular groups of owners, his behavior and pathos are always vibrant with the misery of the masses. Because he cannot offer them the real satisfaction of their needs and must instead seek to win them over to a policy which stands in variance to their own interests, he can go only so far in winning his followers' allegiance by rational arguments for his goals; an emotional belief in his genius, which inspires exultant enthusiasm, must be at least as strong as reason. The less the policy of the bourgeois leader coincides with the immediate interests of the masses, the more exclusively his greatness must fill the public consciousness, and the more his character must be magnified into a "personality." Formal greatness, greatness regardless of its content, is in general the fetish of the modern concept of history. The pathos of justice accompanied by ascetic severity, the demand for general happiness along with hostility to carefree pleasure, justice embracing rich and poor with the same love, vacillation between partisanship for the upper and for the lower class, rhetorical spite against the benefactors of his own policy, and real blows against the masses that are to help him to victory—all these peculiarities of the leader follow from his historical function in the bourgeois world.

Particular historical phenomena are based on his role, defined by the tension between the interests of the decision makers and those of the masses. To the extent that the leader cannot himself directly influence the masses, he needs subordinate leaders. In the absence of a clear constellation of interests, arguments alone rarely suffice; constantly renewed emotional ties are necessary. The psychological factor in the relationship of leader and followers becomes crucial in these uprisings. The subleaders must in turn idolize the person of the highest leader, for the vagueness of the goals, which results from the divergent interests, extends into the leader's consciousness and limits the significance of substantial political principles to which the subleaders could adhere. In the course of these movements, therefore, personal friendships and rivalries play an outstanding role; important conflicts between social groups are concealed even from their own representatives behind indignation over the personal reprehensibility of competing leaders and their followers. Even the great importance placed on symbols, ceremonies, uniforms, and phrases, which attain the same sanctity as flags and coats-of-arms, follows from the necessity of an irrational bond tying the masses to a policy which is not their own. As crucial as enlightenment and the intellectual education of the masses are to liberating society from obsolete feudal forms, particularly in times of an upward-striving bourgeoisie, it is equally true that the effort to set up a stock of idols, be it in the form of "personalities," things, or concepts, corresponds to the necessity of constantly reconciling the masses to the policies of certain social groups. The more the special interests of these groups become consolidated and at variance with the possibility of a more rational form of society, the more strongly do irrationalist influences on the public consciousness emerge and the less does the effort to raise the public's theoretical level play a role. Whereas, for instance, the concept of nation could stand up to intensive scrutiny at the time of the French Revolution and the subsequent Napoleonic wars due to the general constellation of interests, with the intensification of internal contradictions during the following century such scrutiny took on a more critical function; therefore the category of "nation" has become largely taboo. Even the early bourgeois movements show a vacillating relation and often a strong antipathy toward spirit and reason; only in more recent history does this antihumanistic and barbarizing moment, which lowers the attained intellectual level, become clearly predominant.

The modern uprisings mentioned above clearly display the structural similarities alluded to earlier on. Rienzo's regime obviously asserted the bourgeois demands current at the time. His modern biographer recalls expressly that his tribunate was motivated by the ideas of the reconciliation of nations and world peace, which we associate with names like Leibniz, Rousseau, Kant, Lessing, and Schiller.[18] Freedom, peace, and justice were his slogans.[19] His appointment as papal rector was an act directed against the feudal regime of the Roman barons,[20] and his entire program centered on the struggle against these "tyrants" and for the national Roman-Italian idea. "For I will continue to act impartially as I have done all my life, I am working for the peace and prosperity of all Tuscany and Italy."[21] There is no doubt that the notary public Rienzo came to power essentially due to the support of the property-owning strata in Rome. Gregorovius describes how "citizens of the second estate including prosperous merchants zealously participated"[22] in the conspiracy he led. "The guard he organized was comprised of 390 *cavalerotti*, magnificently equipped burghers on horseback, and a foot militia of thirteen platoons of 100 men each."[23] The "class of *cavalerotti*, i.e., of rich burghers of old patrician houses" represented, according to Gregorovius,[24] the bourgeois upper stratum, a "new nobility" which took up the struggle against the old nobility in Rome together with the various other bourgeois groups, craftsmen, and peasants. Rienzo's first decrees concerned themselves with strict justice against disturbers of public order, the establishment of a people's army, the uniform regulation of pensions and subsidies, state control of tariffs, the protection of merchants and of all transportation, a central administration, and so forth. He stated from the first that he "was willing to sacrifice his life for love of the Pope and to save the people."[25] The Roman bourgeoisie looked to the Pope as the representative of a centralist counterauthority to the arbitrary rule of the aristocrats, and papal power tried to carry out their demands in the centuries following Rienzo's fall, though with extremely varying success. Not long after Rienzo's fall, the Emperor and the Pope in Avignon consulted on how to purge France and Italy of the robbers and companies of freebooters that roamed the countryside threatening trade and traffic. The same cardinal (Albornoz) who years before had brought Cola out of exile back to Rome was assigned to convince the feudal captains to leave Italy and to move instead against the Turks.[26]

Cola's relation to the property owners is clear: he directly represented their interests. His contradictory relation to the masses becomes clear with his fall. The popular uprising to which he falls prey was certainly stirred up by hostile aristocratic families. But the objective cause was "Rienzo's oppressive taxes and unscrupulous financial measures."[27] He needed a great deal of money for the services he rendered to the Pope and the Roman citizens, and it became hard for him to get it. After his banishment, when Roman citizens invited him to return to Rome to rule again, Rienzo asked them to supply him with financial means. "The rich merchants refused,"[28] and their "Tribune" had to obtain funds otherwise. His rule in their interest became more and more clearly a general oppression. The practices on which he had to rely caused the dictatorship to be hated. It was widely known that financial reasons were behind his betrayal of Monreal, whom he ordered executed. The upstart plebeian needed the gang leader's money in order to pay his militia.[29] The Pope and the bourgeoisie benefited from it, but it was Rienzo who fell into general contempt and who became increasingly regarded as a tyrant. Besides the "violent financial exploitation of rich and mighty persons,"[30] he had to rely on all possible methods of financing. His move to increase mandatory taxes on consumer goods (although he had previously reduced others), acceptance of money for the release of prisoners, and terrorist acts of various kinds forced him to take increasingly extensive security measures to protect his own life. "Death to the traitor who introduced the taxes!" was the cry with which the people stormed the Capitol to murder him.[31] The necessity of pleasing the rich citizens and giving more or less ambiguous assurances of devotion and loyalty to their acknowledged patron, the Pope[32] (then far away in Avignon), amounted to subjecting the masses to bourgeois authority. Consequently his rule, despite its great and progressive ideas, assumed an increasingly sinister and servile character. The ambivalent feelings of the masses for such leaders, whom they at first follow enthusiastically, have repeatedly been in evidence in subsequent history. Especially in situations in which the bourgeois goals pursued by such leaders definitely went beyond whatever might be attainable in light of the social powers at the time, it was an easy matter to separate the masses from their leader, since their loyalty on the whole was more emotional than intellectual. As soon as failure became distinctly noticeable—something which a dictatorial apparatus obviously makes extremely difficult—it quickly dispelled the magic surrounding the successful personality who had been magnified to superhuman proportions. The behavior of the masses at the fall of Rienzo, Savonarola, the de Witt brothers, Robespierre, and many other idolized popular leaders is itself part of the cruelty at work in history that is at issue here.

The importance of symbols is clearly evident in Rienzo's early-bourgeois revolt. The importance he set on his own clothing and pageantry is typical.

When going to the cathedral on the feast of St. Peter and St. Paul, he sat on a high battle horse, in green and yellow velvet clothing, a shining steel scepter in his hand, with an escort of fifty spearmen; a Roman held the flag with his coat-of-arms over his head; another carried the sword of justice before him; a knight scattered gold among the people, while a solemn procession of *cavalerotti* and Capitol officials, of commoners and nobility, preceded or followed. Trumpeters blared from silver instruments and musicians played silver hand drums. On the steps of St. Peter's the cardinals greeted Rome's dictator by singing the *Veni Creator Spiritus*. [33]

Drawing on the first biography, later portrayals describe how he returned to Rome in order to meet the papal legates after his campaign against the barons. He "rode with his retinue to St. Peter's, got from the sacristy the precious, pearl-embroidered dalmatic with which the German Emperors were crowned, and put it on over his armor. So with the silver crown of a tribune on his head and scepter in hand, while the trumpets blasted, he entered the papal palace like a Caesar, presenting a half-frightening, half-fantastic sight before the astonished legates, and he scared them into silence with grim, curt questions." [34] The Pope wrote with indignation to the Emperor about Rienzo's pagan inclinations. "Not satisfied with the office of rector, he insolently and unashamedly usurps various titles. . . . In contrast with the mores of the Christian religion and in accordance to pagan customs, he has worn various crowns and diadems and undertaken to pass foolish and illegal laws in the manner of the Caesars." [35] The ceremony on August 1, 1347, in which he had himself knighted and, in the presence of many dignitaries including the papal vicar, cleansed himself of all sins in the ancient bathtub of the Emperor Constantine, certainly had its origins in medieval customs. But on the other hand, Cola presented himself as a man of the people: as a democratic measure he abolished the use of the titles Don and Dominus, which he reserved for the Pope, prohibited the use of aristocratic coats-of-arms on houses, and the like.[36] The tremendous emphasis he placed on symbolism in connection with his own person can therefore not be explained solely in terms of tradition. It was based on the necessity of establishing himself as the new, emotionally recognized authority. Similarly, the handing of flags to delegations was essential to this leader: "On August 2, Cola celebrated the Feast of Italian Unity or the alliance of the cities, at the Capitol. He handed the envoys large and small flags with symbols and put gold rings on their fingers to signify their marriage with Rome."[37]

This symbolism is connected with the endeavor to reintroduce old customs and to refurbish the glory of antiquity in general. However much such leaders portray themselves as revolutionaries and innovators, it is not in their nature to rebel against the existing order and to squeeze from the situation whatever is historically possible for human happiness. They experience themselves as executors of a higher ancient power, and the image that inspires them bears more features of the past than those of a better future. The psychic structure underlying this behavior among leaders and followers has been extensively described by Fromm. "In the name of God, the past, the course of nature, or duty, activity is possible [for this type of character], not for the sake of the unborn, the future, the still powerless, or simply happiness. The authoritarian personality draws his strength for active behavior from reliance on higher powers."[38] The masses which those leaders particularly relied upon due to their miserable situation and their lack of integration into a rational work process evinced a chronically underdeveloped psychological state that was both authoritarian and rebellious,[39] and that bore hardly a trace of independent class consciousness.[40] Despite the leader's efforts to incite the people to rebel against the prevailing conditions, he never intended to destroy the masses' disposition toward mental dependency or their blind faith in authority. The propaganda of the leader does not combine the critique of the authorities that must be toppled with any tendency toward unrestricted rationality. While the old system contained the masses with the help of irrational ties, it is not immediately replaced by a society that truly represents the general interest, though bourgeois ideology asserts as much. The more legitimate authorities are toppled or at least attacked by the spread of freedom, the more strongly the need is felt to glorify the authority of the new rulers with reference to older powers that are untainted by the present dissatisfaction. The living "conjure up anxiously the spirits of the past to their service and borrow from their names, battle cries and costumes in order to present the new scene of world history in this time honored disguise and this borrowed language."[41]

From an early age Cola was attracted to the idea of the old Romans. It is reported how, long before taking power, "a fantastic smile used to play" around his mouth "when he explained ancient statues or reliefs or read inscriptions from marble tablets scattered all around Rome."[42] Later he justified himself to the Pope by asking what harm could be done to faith by his revival of the Roman titles together with the ancient rites.[43] His choice of holidays is based on old dates and celebrations; his entire behavior is guided by the idea of restoring the Roman Empire. He speaks of "Rome's sacred soil,"[44] and seeks to place his entire program, as it were, under the aegis of his nation's glorious past. By thus surrounding himself with the aura of ancient forces, he places himself under the protection of a strong present power. "He feels that he is executer, renewer, deepener, carrier of Boniface VIII's imperial tendencies, and yet—as Clement VI writes— he wants to be just a servant and helper of the Pope and declares himself ready to abdicate immediately, if the Pope so wishes."[45] Cola always professed his loyalty to the Pope and acted in his name. Of course, he also regards himself as commissioned not only by these old and present forces, but directly by God as well. "He believes God has, by calling him, led the Roman people out of the darkness of tyranny, i.e., of the barons, into the light of freedom, peace and justice, and delivered Rome, the *domina gentium, sanctissima urbium* (mistress of the nations, most holy of cities) . . . from tribute, transforming it from a robbers' nest to its original nature."[46] "The people regarded him as a man chosen by God."[47] Although he and his like seek to offer the masses the spectacle of a freedom movement, at the same time they adopt the pathos of absolute obedience to higher truths and thus present the example of a submissiveness which is to be emulated by their followers' loyalty to the leaders and to the bourgeois forms of life. As much as the whole world must tremble before them in fear, they themselves display the image of fear of still higher and supreme beings. Their role in society is revealed in their psychology: they defend the strata of property owners both against old, restrictive privileges that are burdensome to the whole society and against the lower class's demands on the new system. Consequently, their desire for freedom is both abstract and relative. Dependency is merely changed, not abolished. The progressive moment is expressed with greater purity and less restraint in the works of writers who represented the age than among political leaders. Philosophy and poetry reflect both the critique of the present and the more radical desire for a society without oppression; the ambivalent and idolatrous speeches of the politicians evince the brutality of the bourgeois order.

Similarly, Savonarola represented bourgeois demands which brought him into conflict with the masses in the course of the revolt he unleashed. The call for just administration, honest officials, political acumen, respect for privacy, punishment of national unreliability, and above all juridical reform and the conscientious fulfillment of civic duties generally[48]—these are all demands that mark the genuine bourgeois politician. His proposal for the Florentine constitution, which he himself expressly characterized as not just a rehashing but as the product of his own convictions, was drafted on the model of the Venetian Republic.[49] The real enemies against which his proposed political innovations were directed were the great noble families, especially the Medicis, who had attained well-nigh regal privileges and had come into conflict with the very middle classes which had gained strength under their rule. In Florence, unlike Venice, no old aristocracy with a solidly established administration developed gradually into a commercial oligarchy; instead, individual houses which had risen rapidly through the expansion of trade in commodities and money aspired to exclusive dominion. Siding with the majority of the ascending bourgeois and craftsmen meant an antiaristocratic struggle which bore many petit bourgeois traits. Just as Cola 150 years earlier had ranted against the barons, Savonarola assailed the "tyrants." While his treatise on Florence's constitution and government[50] addressed mainly religious reforms, the hatred with which the feudal nobility and its system is discussed recalls Rienzo's drastic style in such matters and occasionally even the literature of the French Revolution.

In the course of the decisive disputes about an oligarchic or democratic form of government, Savonarola advocated popular rule before meetings of 13,000 to 14,000 people;[51] all his life he fought for an orderly bourgeois government. Like Cola, he too was especially concerned that the poor, widows, and orphans should receive assistance, but only insofar as they could not work. "Whoever lets himself be supported, although he can himself take care of his own support, is stealing bread from the poor and is obligated to give back everything he has received beyond his need. Ultimately the poor must prove themselves worthy of the benefits given them by honorable behavior, otherwise they are unworthy of the water they drink."[52] Savonarola spoke up against feudalism and for civil liberties. He spoke for the people. He both maintained and blurred the opposition between the privileged bourgeois groups and the lower strata. He deeply hated riots. "Savonarola pleaded for mercy not only for the small and lowly, but also for the great and prominent. Hardly had he returned from Pisa, when the first word he exclaimed to those burning for revenge against the followers of the fallen government was the exhortation for peace: *Misericordia.* And he repeated this admonition untiringly in the following period." When the people asked whether the wrongdoers should not be punished, he explained: "If God wanted to deal with you according to the justice you are shouting for, not ten of you would be spared. If you ask me however, 'Good, monk, how then do you understand this peace?' I answer you, 'Give up all hatred and resentment and forget and forgive everything that happened before the most recent revolution, but from now on whoever errs against the republic shall be punished.' "[53] In the constitution itself, upon which he had some influence, the bourgeoisie's double front found clear expression: "The lower classes, who did not belong to the guilds, had as little share in the governmental power as the noble families."[54] Membership in the great council was limited according to age and social position. In taxation "precisely the nobility, the large landowners not represented in the guilds, were the ones who . . . were most heavily affected, no less however the lowest circles, since the most necessary foods such as grain, oil, and wine were made considerably more expensive by such taxes."[55]

The differing levels of specificity between Savonarola's and Rienzo's language is due in large measure to the much more developed social conditions that account for the Dominican's efficacy. Although the Florentine citizens could by no means confront the Pope with the same self-assurance as the Venetians they modeled themselves after, the traits of the contemporary ecclesiastical hierarchy that ran counter to bourgeois interests were so fully embodied by Alexander Borgia's court that Savonarola for a time could dare to oppose Borgia openly and not simply behind ambivalent phrases.[56] Although he could not risk a total break with the Pope since Church sanctions would have seriously damaged the city's trade, the enmity between the Florentine bourgeoisie and the corrupt higher and lower clergy including their leader was open and mutual.[57] Savonarola himself appealed not to the current Pope but to the genuine Papacy, the genuine Church, and to Christ himself. He considered Alexander an unbeliever, indeed not even a Christian. Nonetheless, he could not forego protecting his actions by appealing to this most recognized power of the time. He always regarded himself as a representative of higher powers.

Although Savonarola seems to be more clear-headed and rational than Rienzo, he regarded himself as a prophet, or at least as a man gifted with supernatural intuition. As for a series of mystical saints and founders, "the mystical love of God was for the *Frate* too the lofty school of the apostolate and of the ardent love for the Church, the mystical bride of the Savior, which animated him with holy candor to reprimand with relentless severity the undutiful pastors who had surrendered their flock to the rending wolves. The mystic Savonarola was the father of the prophet Savonarola."[58] The description, in his work on the triumph of the cross, of the triumphal carriage pulled by the apostles and preachers, on which Christ with his crown of thorns and stigmata is enthroned, the Holy Scriptures in his right hand and instruments of martyry in his left, with chalice, host, and other objects of worship at his feet—this enthusiastically composed picture[59] recalls Cola's fantastic dreams and allegories. In the case against him, Savonarola was accused of having spoken of his journey to Paradise for his own magnification, and no doubt he had fostered belief in the magical power of his person. Shortly before his fall he had "before an innumerable crowd of people evoked the Redeemer present in the host which he held in his hands to send down fire from heaven and wipe him from the face of the earth if he did not walk in full truth. Never had he left any doubt that God would, if necessary, prove the rightness of his prophetic mission, even by supernatural means." He threatened to his opponent, "You have not yet forced me to perform a miracle; but if I am compelled to, then God will open his hand if his honor demands it, although you have already seen so many miracles that you need no further miracle."[60] But whether he accepted the trial by fire, whose failure marked the beginning of his end, more at the urging of his followers than out of conviction is uncertain. The magnifications of his person by his closest followers and by his own speeches was an indispensable means for his influence upon the masses. This magnification of the personality of the monastic people's tribune has been noted repeatedly in historiography as a principal instrument of his policy. "I find that when Savonarola is spoken of," writes H. Grimm, "his fall is depicted excessively as the result of efforts of his enemies and of papal anger. The most compelling cause for his fall was the decline of his personal power. The people grew tired. He had to stir up their spirits more and more strongly. He succeeded for a time in reviving their slumbering enthusiasm. But while from the outside it seemed to grow, it was really consuming its last energies."[61] Of course, if the petit bourgeois groups that stood behind Savonarola had been capable of establishing an enduring government of their own, then the disproportion between his real qualities and the superhuman image his followers promulgated would not have led to his downfall. The endowment of the leader with magical qualities was a condition for his influence on the masses. His fall resulted from the differences between the ruling groups themselves.

In Savonarola an essential aspect of bourgeois revolts becomes evident. The needs of the mobilized masses are utilized as a motor for the dynamics of the revolutionary process, but the condition toward which the movement tends in terms of the historically attainable balance, i.e., the consolidation of the bourgeois order, can satisfy them only to a very limited degree. This is why it is crucial that the unleashed forces be redirected inwardly and spiritualized [*spiritualisiert*], as it were, and that this deflection already begin in the course of the movement. The process of "internalization" [*Verinnerlichung*], which began as early as the Middle Ages, has one of its roots here. Thode has interpreted the work of the great founders of orders at the beginning of the thirteenth century in this manner. "No power, however great," he writes in the introduction to his book on St. Francis, "can silence the just demands of the third estate which was awakening to self-consciousness, although its goals were too indefinite for the movement to have become unified, independent, and self-regulating. Then, called forth by the eternal laws of logical historical development, Francis of Assisi, in his genial capacity to make and carry out intuitive decisions, found the conciliatory words! He led the impetuous progressive stream into a delimited riverbed and hence rendered the service of having preserved it from an untimely division, gathered its forces, and directed it toward a unified goal. The goal is the spiritualization [*Verinnerlichung*] of the human being."[62] Thode sees Christian doctrine as the "blessedly restrictive riverbed," and he regards the new art as the first product of this process of sublimation. With the development of the contradiction between bourgeois and masses in the centuries after St. Francis, this internalization of social interests changes from an expression of the immaturity of the "third estate" compared to the powers that ruled the world into a practice of this class itself toward the people it dominates. The historical movements we are speaking of here thus increasingly show the translation of individuals' demands on society into moral and religious demands on the dissatisfied individuals themselves. The bourgeois leader tries to idealize and spiritualize the brutal wishes for a better life, the abolition of differences of wealth and the introduction of real community—ideas which have been represented in those centuries by religious populists and theological utopians. Not so much revolt as spiritual renewal, not so much the struggle against the wealth of the privileged as against universal wickedness, not so much external as internal satisfaction are preached to the masses in the course of the revolutionary process. The German reformer hated rioting even when it was directed against the Pope, the devil in human form. As Savonarola had called the people's revolt against the Medici "pharisaic justice . . . that stems from vengefulness"[63] and wished the people would look at their own sins, Luther said of the peasants "that they wanted to punish the authorities for their sins; as if they themselves were completely pure and innocent. Therefore God had to show them the beam in their own eye so that they might forget the splinter in another's."[64]

The common man's temper must be calmed and he must be told to refrain from inordinate desires and words that lead to revolt, and to undertake nothing without command of the authorities or action of the governmental power. . . . But if you say: "What should we then do if the authorities want to do nothing? Should we then endure longer and strengthen their malice?" The answer: "No, you should do none of this: you should do three things. First: recognize your sins, which God's strict justice has inflicted with such ultimate Christian authority. Second: humbly pray against the papal authority. Thirdly: let your mouth be one mouth with the spirit of Christ, of whom St. Paul said: Our Lord will slay him with the mouth of his spirit."[65]

The extremely progressive character of this transformation process is not at issue here. The disciplining of all strata of the population, which resulted from the need to incorporate the masses into the bourgeois mode of production, was affected in turn by the development of this economic form. Without the process of spiritualization and internalization, it is impossible to imagine not only the astonishing development of technology and the simplification of the work process—in short, the increase of human power over nature—but also the human prerequisites for a higher form of society. This cultural process, as well as other aspects of the ideological process that dominate spiritual life in so-called normal times, is merely brought out with particular clarity in the activity of the leaders promoting morality and religiosity. Savonarola's Florence is permeated with a wave of religious and moral enthusiasm, similar to the way cities and countries were gripped by Protestantism. While in the later uprisings the idealistic heroism is expressed mainly as sacrificial zeal for the nation, in the earlier ones religious excitement predominates. "A religious spirit penetrated the redeemed people," Gregorovius states in describing Rienzo's revolt, "like that of the British in Cromwell's time."[66] These centuries witnessed the hypostatization of the belief in a higher freedom and justice: the ideological diremption from the muffled common interests of the masses out of which this belief emerged. Only in later phases of the bourgeois age is this idealistic alienation abolished as the belief in the conscious solidarity of struggling humanity is reasserted. The loud-mouthed and empty heroism that still presumes to be the heir of that formerly progressive idealism has lost all cultural importance and sinks into a vain pose, a common lie.

The leadership which channels the people to particular goals and achieves the internalization of the drives which cannot be satisfied in this period employs a specific instrument: the speech at the mass meeting. The politician in the Greek city-state was also mainly an orator and at times exercised functions very similar to those of the modern leader. But in Greek antiquity the speech is presented in the assembly of freemen; the slaves comprise an element that must merely be dominated, not addressed. As much as these speeches also have enthusiastic traits, they largely lack the internalizing, spiritualizing tendency and the call to turn inward that belongs to the essence of modern rhetoric. Antiquity's rationality is admittedly rigid and constrained. Its logic corresponds to a fixed, self-confident upper class; it aims to convey a particular opinion on the state of affairs, not transform the listening public. The change of function of rhetoric that begins with Socrates already heralds the decline of the city-state. In antiquity and to a great extent in the Middle Ages, the lower class is kept under control by physical coercion and command, by the deterrent example of terrible earthly punishments and, moreover, by the threat of hell. The popular address of modern times, which is half rational argumentation, half an irrational means of domination, belongs to the essence of bourgeois leadership, despite its long prehistory.

The sermon owes its decisive place in religious life to the aforementioned function of the word in the new society. As early as the heresy movements of the twelfth century in Cologne and southern France, the sermon is addressed to the entire people but is promoted mainly by the property-owning classes. Contrary to interpretations that view these early preachers as stemming mainly from the lowest social strata, it turns out "that nobles, rich bourgeois, priests, and monks have often joined the ranks of the wandering heretical preachers and that, at least to their contemporaries, it was precisely this active participation of clergymen, of prominent and wealthy persons in the heretical movement, that was noteworthy."[67] Even in the oldest Franciscan association of preachers, "as far as we know, the very same strata of society are represented, who were everywhere the bearers of the religious poverty movement: rich bourgeois, noblemen, and clergymen."[68] The urban bourgeoisie, from which the new order stemmed, conditioned the development of the sermon as a result of its particular interests. Contrary to theories that are today, though only with relative accuracy, associated with the name of Max Weber, the religious spirit of the modern age, which finds its first expression in the sermonizing popular leaders, is not a primary and independent entity. Humanism and the Reformation are connected with the rise of the bourgeois class, "which with its new views of nature and religion also creates new forms of social life and of ecclesiastical cult."[69] This is clearly expressed in the relation of the mendicant preaching orders to the cities: "The two go . . . hand in hand: The cities became the home of the preaching monks, and the popular religion of the latter becomes the religion of the cities. Each part gives, and each receives."[70] The monks themselves, however, come mostly from the higher social strata, which were beginning to run into conflict with the hierarchy. The religious ideas living in the sermon were as such nothing new. A primary role in the origin of the bourgeois world cannot be ascribed to them; their momentous development through and with the sermon can be understood only in connection with the economically conditioned rise of the bourgeoisie.[71] The internalization of needs and drives of the masses forms an important mediation in this dialectical process. At the beginning of the thirteenth century the Catholic Church itself could not close itself off from the demands of the age; in the Fourth Lateran Council it expressly recognized the necessity of developing the sermon.

Savonarola was a precursor to the Reformers. He was the first to make the church the site of mass meetings, as Cola had similarly done at the Capitol. His magnificent eloquence cannot be praised enough by his contemporaries. "Often he had to leave the chancellery ahead of time, because the people had broken out in tears and loud sobbing and were pleading with God for mercy in deepest contrition; often the scribes, overcome by emotion, could no longer follow his words."[72] The Dominican instructed that a supernatural fire should burn in the preacher. He must be ready to suffer a martyr's death himself. "If, despite the preaching, everything remains the same, and vices grow as luxuriantly as weeds, that is an unmistakable sign that the sermon, like a painted fire, does not ignite."[73] The masses should turn inward, they should become more moral, more unassuming, more resigned.

They should learn to fear God, and the preacher is—this surely applies to Savonarola[74]—the interpreter of the divine will, God's spokesman, his servant, his prophet. The bourgeois virtues, respect for the laws, peaceableness, love of work, obedience to the authorities, willingness to sacrifice for the nation, and the like, are drummed into the people together with fear of God. The language of the sermon is democratic, it is addressed to all, but part of its message is that individuals and whole groups in principle remain outside as the wicked and the obdurate. The appeal to the masses to deny themselves the adequate satisfaction of their drives and turn them inward is accompanied, as a sort of consolation, with the oft-repeated conviction that those who cannot achieve renunciation and exertion are damned and will not escape their terrible penalty. As cruelly and sternly as the clergyman or worldly leader may treat his followers, his brutality does not harm but rather heightens his reputation, since the crowd at least can pretend that they, unlike strangers and enemies, are loved by him. The Reformers' contempt for human beings extended even to their own followers in a manner that was wholly unambiguous. A prominent follower of Calvin, Chauvet, shouts at the end of a sermon: "May the plague, war and famine come over you."[75] Another addresses his listeners as devils.[76] Luther himself spoke the proverb: "Secretly, townspeople and peasants, man and woman, child and servant, princes, officials, and vassals, all are the devil's."[77] This contempt for the masses, which is peculiar to many bourgeois leaders, does not in the least decrease their popularity as long as there are others on the outside who are radically lost. "As friendly, however, and sweet as this sermon is for Christians, who are its pupils, so annoying and intolerable it is for the Jews and their great holy men."[78] There must be such a thing as Jews, Turks, and Papists, who stand outside the community.

While in more peaceful times the school and other educational institutions, together with mass meetings, transmit the internalization effectively and constantly to the successive generations, in revolutionary periods the mass meeting takes on exclusive significance. It is the characteristic form of the manipulation of dangerous social strata and is permeated with irrational elements. In these situations it is crucial to treat the soul of the people mechanically, as is shown by the value set on external format, the songs before and after the speech, and the speaker's solemn appearance. The speech itself is not geared essentially to the rational forces of consciousness, but uses them only to evoke certain reactions. On the other hand, in instances where the real interests of the masses determine a leader, the opposite relation emerges. The speaker's goal then is for the masses to grasp the situation with their own consciousness; the action to be taken then follows from this as a rational consequence. What matters is that things are made clear, for no other interests enter in except those of the audience, and the leader's personality can recede, since it is not itself supposed to act as a directly influencing factor. And like the leader, the masses also change their character. The mass meeting is suitable for the purpose of exerting irrational influence; small groups of individuals with common interests are appropriate for discussions of theory, the analysis of a given historical situation, and the resulting considerations on the policy that should be followed. Movements striving to transcend the bourgeois order can therefore not use the mass meeting with the same exclusiveness and the same success. In the dynamics of history, masses are not simply identical with one another, even if they should in part consist of the same individuals. The appreciable extent to which the mass meeting in the bourgeois revolts must be understood as a psycho-physical influence, as a treatment or cure, is already apparent from its frequency and its compulsory character. Attendance is considered a duty, people are commanded to go, indeed sometimes they are detained there by force. This coercion is reflected clearly in the church regulations passed in the decades after the Reformation. The Saxon General Articles of 1557 state: "Thus, those who miss the sermon on holidays and Sunday morning and afternoon (but especially in the villages) and do not first excuse themselves to the pastors and judges of that place because of necessary business they must perform, shall be punished with a considerable fine, or if they have no fortune, with the pillory at the church or other prison."[79] When under Calvin the Geneva suburb of Gervais did not appear to be entirely reliable at one point, the measures taken went so far as "to station a bailiff and two officers as guards during religious service, so that no member of the congregation could leave the church before the appointed time."[80] Where knowledge is the real concern, assemblies display a completely different structure. Discussions and intellectual progress characterize their course, the analysis of the situation and of practical solutions remains in continuous connection with the developing conscious interests of the participants. No matter how the content of the speeches at the mass meetings may change, it only fulfills a mechanical function by suggesting a certain behavior. The religious as well as the political mass speakers of the bourgeoisie choose their words not so much for their appropriateness to the object as for effect. Any development during the speech itself, or any rational interaction between speaker and participant that goes beyond the purely instinctual, tends not to occur. Subsequent discussions have the same character: they lack the dialectical element. Mass movements do play a role even in nonbourgeois movements. Despite the undeveloped, chaotic nature of their movements, the leaders of the Roman slave uprisings and of rebellious peasants at the beginning of the modern age called their people together, consulted with them, and roused them in tumultuous assemblies. Modern proletarian leaders not only have prepared individual demonstrations in small groups, but have also presented their views and proffered solutions before the masses. But though such gatherings may bear some of the traits just described, just as on the other hand the bourgeois mass meetings at times showed revolutionary features, especially in times of intensified struggle between the third estate and the feudal powers, the fact remains that the irrational, the solemn, and the authoritarian are still predominantly marks of the bourgeois leader's speech.

Despite the differences in social position between Luther and Calvin as reflective of the circumstances in Germany and Geneva, and despite their contrasting personalities as reflective of their origin and educational background, their behavior and even their character display astonishing similarities in virtue of their function as leaders of the masses in the bourgeois era. In the first decades of the sixteenth century "the favored groups of social development" are "the bourgeois patriciate and the territorial princes, the aristocratic strata, the new particular authorities of city and country; the oppressed include the vassals, the masses, the urban proletariat, the peasants, and the small rural nobility, which is connected with the peasants' fate and displays democratic tendencies in its views and its position relative to the newly developed high nobility of the princes."[81] The politics of the property-owning bourgeois circles in Germany, who were the bearers of development at that time, were entirely at the behest of the territorial princes. That Luther subjected himself completely to these princes follows from the nature of his whole life's work. He himself, "with whatever right he called himself a peasant's son, is equally much a product of the city, the mines, and his urban education as a mendicant monk. . . . He certainly did call farming a divine profession and the only livelihood that comes straight from heaven: 'the dear patriarchs also had it.' But he nonetheless wrote the terrible tracts against the peasants and disapproved of the nobility's revolt. Certainly he never hid his antipathy toward the immoral aspects of patrician commercial activities, and to a certain extent he supported the canonical prohibition of usury, but that did not prevent his understanding approval of the quest for capital as business capital; it was just the idea of purely personal credit that he reproved. And certainly he called the princes murderous rascals and God's torturers"; but based on his entire situation, he had to end up "assigning a higher place to the authorities than they had ever occupied in the Christian world."[82]

Originally, the popular leaders [*Volksführer*] made little distinction between the goals of the general public and those of prosperous groups. Only in the course of the movement do the lower classes discover the darker side, and the tension between them and the leader begins. This is true of Calvin in his second reign in Geneva and of the great politicians of the French Revolution. Engels throws this situation into sharp relief in his treatise on the German Peasants' War:

Between 1517 and 1525, Luther had gone through the same transformation as the German constitutionalists between 1846 and 1849. This has been the case with every middle-class party which, having marched for a while at the head of the movement, has been overwhelmed by the plebeian proletarian party pressing from the rear. When in 1517 opposition against the dogmas and the organization of the Catholic church was first raised by Luther, it still had no definite character. Not exceeding the demands of the earlier middle-class heresy, it did not exclude any trend of opinion which went further. It could not do so because the first movement of the struggle demanded that all opposing elements be united, the most aggressive revolutionary energy be utilized, and the totality of the existing heresies fighting the Catholic orthodoxy be represented. . . . This revolutionary order did not last long. . . . The parties became separate from each other, and each found a different spokesman. Luther had to choose between the two. . . . He dropped the popular elements of the movement and joined the train of the middle class, the nobility, and the princes.[83]

In practically no other outstanding popular leader of the bourgeoisie is the moral and religious pathos of the nuances of the various interests he represents as sharply expressed as in Luther's magnificent language. When the Gospel and the real bourgeois interests run into conflict with one another, there can be for Luther no doubt as to what place he concedes to the Gospel on earth.

[What] is needed in the world is a strict, hard, worldly power to force and compel the wicked not to take, nor rob, and to return what they borrow, although a Christian should neither demand it back nor hope to get it back; so that the world not be devastated, peace perish, and the people's commerce and community be destroyed, all of which would happen if one were to rule the world according to the Gospel and not impel and coerce the wicked with laws and might to do and suffer what is right. Therefore, one must keep the streets clean, create peace in the cities and enforce law in the country, and hack away with the sword at violators, as St. Paul teaches in Romans 13:4. . . . No one must think that the world can be ruled without bloodshed; the secular sword should and must be red and bloodthirsty.[84]

However much he may rage against the rebelling peasants, wish that they be "stabbed, struck, and strangled,"[85] castigate mercy toward them as a sin, counsel only that "such mouths have to be answered with the fist so that sweat runs out their nose," and even call for the executioner[86]—still, he is sincerely concerned that among these peasants, who otherwise should and must be mowed down indiscriminately, "there may well be some who went along unwillingly, especially those who were once prosperous." Toward these "fairness must . . . outweigh law. . . . For the rebellion was against the rich as well as against the rulers, and in fairness it can be suspected that no rich person favored the rebellion."[87] And although Luther, for the sake of those elements of the nobility with which he was allied, at times even defended the nobility against the complaints of the merchants they robbed,[88] he nevertheless spoke out unmistakably against those noblemen who, doubtless out of entirely selfish motives, refused to spare the wealthy from the "stabbing and strangling" visited upon peasants. He employs some rather strong language against these "noble people": "Filth also comes from the nobility and it may boast that it comes out of the eagle's body, yet it stinks and is useless. So these too may well be of the nobility. We Germans are Germans and remain Germans, that is, sows and unreasonable beasts."[89] Luther's relation to the parties of his time stands out clearly enough.

Although Calvin in republican Geneva reminds the king of France, protector of the hated Catholic Church, of the avengers "appointed by God's rightful calling to do great deeds and raise the weapons against kings,"[90] we should not believe that this vengeance is assigned to us as private persons: "Nothing is commanded unto us but obedience and suffering."[91] On the other hand, representatives of the people, i.e., the representatives of the upper and prosperous strata, are under certain circumstances thoroughly justified in "restricting the arbitrariness of kings, like the people's tribunes among the Romans, or the estates in our monarchies."[92] He considered an aristocratic and oligarchic form of government to be the best one; like Luther he never tires of repeating that "the civil authority exercises not only its rightful, but exceedingly holy calling, which deserves the highest honor in the whole life of mortals."[93] His love for prominent and wealthy families is well known. "He therefore had to endure hostility and sharp criticism from his enemies for this; he was accused of flattering the rich, and much worse. But such attacks made little impression on him and were the least suited to unnerve him in his principles. And his friends, disciples, and helpers walked in their master's footsteps."[94] He approved the oligarchic constitution of Bern, which moreover varied greatly from Geneva's, as Savonarola had approved Venice's, trying, like his medieval predecessor, to make his and his friends' influence dominant while preserving the aristocratic forms. All these leaders endeavor to anchor their clique in the life of the state and society, if possible for all eternity.

The Reformers' great spiritual achievement consists in the articulation of the idea that salvation does not depend on the sacramental performances of a priestly caste, but on the attitude of the individual's soul. In Calvin, this idea is further strengthened by the doctrine of election, i.e., that each person's eternal destiny is completely separate from the Church's practices. The Reformers thus bestowed upon individuals the independence in ideology to which they were destined by the transformation of reality—an independence, however, that turned out to be abstract and largely imaginary, curtailed in practice by the economy which is kept up but not kept under control by human beings, and in theory by the acts of grace of an inscrutable God who is designed by human beings but regarded as autonomous. The cultural progress of the masses initiated by the Reformers was directly connected with a much more active shaping of individuals than was usual with the old clergy. In light of the new economic tasks, the bourgeoisie had to raise its members to a completely different level of self-discipline, responsibility, and zeal for work than they were accustomed to in the old times of a relatively undynamic economy operating according to fixed rules. Of course, its outstanding representatives such as the old Jacob Fugger embodied the modern attitude toward life even without the Reformation. "It is a very different matter," he replied to his friend who advised him to retire; "he wanted to earn profit as long as he could."[95] The characterological preconditions of this mentality required by the new economy, of being bound to activity and not its content, had to be transmitted universally and continuously to the successive generations of various strata of the bourgeoisie and, with corresponding nuances, also to the ruling classes. This required more than just individual reformers, who were already the first representatives of a new bureaucracy.

Here we come upon another common trait of these historical events. Unlike social revolutions, they do not directly affect the economic base, but tend to develop and enhance the bourgeoisie's position already secured in the economy by opportune changes in the military, political, juridical, religious, and artistic spheres. The most bitter struggles are fought to renew the body of functionaries in these realms, to replace an earlier "elite," an old stratum of bureaucrats and intellectuals, with one better suited to the new tasks and to create more appropriate institutions. Whereas profitable economic activity, the accumulation of wealth by bourgeois economic subjects, is already achieved before and after the uprising and needs only to be freed from the hindering regulations of the old regime, the cultural superstructure must undergo a reorganization. This requires new personnel who are equal to the qualitatively different demands. With the consolidation of a small stratum of monopolists brought about by concentration and centralization, cultural activity takes form more and more exclusively as domination of the masses. Although the culture is addressed just as much to the rulers and is held in especially high esteem by them, they sometimes sense very well that this is its main function in their system. In contradiction to the great artistic and philosophical productions of its own history, therefore, deep contempt and indifference to the spirit is a trait of the ideal type of the modern bourgeois, although this is manifested more in their behavior and instincts than in their views and consciousness, where the opposite scale of values generally prevails. They make religion, ideal values, and sacrifice for the nation into the highest goods of humanity, praise the success of the giants of art and science without any reference to the content of their accomplishments, and characteristically remain atheistic out of intellectual prudery, vulgar materialists incapable of any real pleasure. Pareto blurs the distinction between the key economic groups and their cultural functionaries and replaces it with secondary distinctions such as those between political and nonpolitical functionaries,[96] and in so doing ruins his concept of conflicts among elite groups (which is unhistorically developed in any case) as a potential instrument for understanding the whole age; were it not for this failing, this concept would have otherwise quite usefully lent itself to characterizing these cultural agents of the bourgeoisie and their doings.

While the bourgeoisie itself grows increasingly insensitive toward spiritual existence, at the same time its social situation requires of it an ongoing cultural agility, both in view of the clerical and feudal reaction and in order to incorporate the entire population into its system. The powerful call for inner renewal, into which at certain times the material demands of the masses are transformed, can therefore regularly be drawn into the struggle of the old bureaucracy and intellectuals against one or several competing groups attempting to supplant it. One of the reasons why the princes and the bourgeoisie supported the Reformation, apart from the timely dispatching of cultural issues, was the recognition that the Protestant church organization would not merely halt the flow of money to Rome but would also organize matters with greater thrift. The Catholic clergy had recognized the danger of the heretical preachers' poverty propaganda early on, and its first great advocate, Arnold of Brescia, predecessor of Cola and the Reformers, had fallen victim to an agreement between the Pope and the Emperor at the end of the twelfth century. Since the operation of these reliable and economically efficient new bureaucracies depends on "personalities" to a far higher degree than in the feudal system, in times of transition we see embittered fighting on the part of the leaders and leader cliques who want to rule in the future, not just against the old powers but amongst themselves. Under the growing domination of the performance principle, which applies even to the highest officials and functionaries, they strive with all means available to prove the worth of themselves and the validity of their principles.

Those who did not themselves participate could only be repelled by the quarrels, personal enmities, and unchained passions of domination and revenge which characterize the leading strata of the bourgeoisie in the Renaissance, the Reformation, the French Revolution, and the later bourgeois uprisings. Giordano Bruno formulated well the feeling of a great part of the educated classes of the sixteenth century toward the Reformation. One should just see, he writes,

what a miserable kind of peace and harmony it is that these Reformers preach to the poor people, apparently seeking zealously for nothing more than to have the whole world agree with their sanctimonious and conceited stupidity and concur in their evil, degenerate conscience, while they themselves do not agree on any law, any point of justice, on any doctrine, and everywhere in the rest of the world and in all earlier centuries there never has been such disunity and strife as among them, for among a thousand such pedants hardly one is found who would not have invented his own catechism and, if he has not yet published it, would desire to do so, not one who could bring himself to approve any arrangement other than his own, none who finds anything else in others except what he believes he may condemn, reject, and doubt. Indeed, a great part of them is at odds with themselves, since today they cross out and recant what they wrote and stated yesterday. Let him see what kind of consequences their teachings have, what kind of practical conduct they produce as regards the works of justice and pity, the preservation and increase of the common good, whether among their people and leadership universities, temples, hospitals, schools, and academies of art are founded, or whether these, wherever they have installed themselves, are even simply preserved in the same condition in which they found them, and not instead fallen to ruin or disrepair through their neglect.[97]

To understand the Italian philosopher's repugnance for the Reformation's rule, one need look no further than to the streak of anti-intellectualism which it has in common with many bourgeois uprisings. Even though Catholicism always made a distinction between reason before and after the fall from grace, and even though it was held in even less regard by nominalism, which already displays bourgeois traits in any case, their greatest philosophers nevertheless viewed reason as the pride of humanity. Calvin, however, stresses that "all our effort, our insight, and our understanding is so wrong that in God's sight we can think and plan nothing rightly." The Holy Ghost knows "that all thoughts of the wise are vain, and proclaims clearly that the human heart's every thought and desire is completely evil."[98] In contrast to St. Thomas and his successors, Calvin holds it to be "an indubitable truth which can be shaken by no arts. Man's reason is so completely alienated from God's justice that everything he desires and thinks is impious, wrong, ugly, impure, and sinful; the heart is so deeply immersed in the poison of sin that only a rotten stench can come from it."[99] Luther knows no limits to his obscene denunciations of reason. The doctrine he has received through divine grace, he says, must be preserved in a determined struggle against "the devil's bride, reason, the beautiful strumpet"; for "it is the highest whore the devil has." Luther senses the deep connection between pleasure and intellect and he persecutes both with the same hatred: "What I say of lust, which is a crude sin, must also be understood of reason, for it dishonors and offends God with intellectual offerings, and has far worse whorish ailments than a whore."[100] Though the Reformers personally, within certain limits, esteemed art and science, these were severely hindered as a result of the battle waged against graven images and against the doctrine of good works in the areas under Protestant influence. Above all, there was hostility against everything in art that ran counter to the ethical notions connected with internalization, upon every trace of the erotic, indeed upon luxury in general.

Whoever reads the descriptions of those tumultuous periods of religious and national enthusiasm repeatedly finds references to a wave of bourgeois virtue and morality which, encouraged by the authorities, gripped the people. "A strict police force punished adulterers and gamblers," Gregorovius writes about the Rome of the popular tribunes. Under Savonarola a whole system of informants was organized in order to make all kinds of moral transgressions impossible. The burning of "frivolities" is known. Under his influence and that of his followers, items incompatible with the conversion of the masses were burned: powder boxes, make-up and other cosmetics, as well as chess and other games, harps, etc. On a great bonfire before the Signoria, undesirable books also found a place: "The works of Boccaccio and Petrarch, Morgante and other battle descriptions, as well as magic and other superstitious writings; finally immodest statues and paintings, the pictures of beautiful Florentine ladies from the hand of excellent painters and sculptors and precious foreign fabrics with unchaste depictions."[101] An anti-intellectual tendency asserts itself in all these popular uprisings. This tendency is closely connected with the fact that the masses were not yet capable of an independent political stance that aimed to meet their own interests and had to internalize their wishes by the roundabout way of fetishized persons and ideas. Max Weber stressed the rationalistic trait of the bourgeois mind, but irrationalism is from the start no less associated with its history.

A further phenomenon connected with this irrationalism can be mentioned just briefly. Youth, even children, play a peculiar role in these movements. On the one hand, whenever development is fettered by the powers that be, individual young people side with the oppressed and risk their lives in the struggle against the ruling powers; on the other hand, it was an easy matter in these bourgeois uprisings to get swarms of boys and girls to take the lead in committing acts of violence and denunciations. As yet anther magical element, the so-called purity and idealism of youth promotes the leader's goals and the power of his personality. Farel, Calvin's predecessor and friend, had been mildly reprimanded by the city council on the occasion of the storming of a church. "The Protestant who recorded the incident said that it was none other than God who despised the advice of the wise and who roused the tender youths against the adults' notions. On the afternoon of the very same day 'little children' unexpectedly stormed into the cathedral . . . filling the church with wild shouting. The 'awakening of the children' was the signal for the adults. . . . There followed scenes of the crudest vandalism, incidents such as did not often occur even during the Reformation."[102] Savonarola even had "police children" who helped him exercise moral discipline and carried the conflicts right into individual families.[103] The proletarian children, however, distanced themselves from these moral functions. "The children of the lowest classes of people not only did not belong to Savonarola's groups but on the contrary they showed open hostility toward them and missed no opportunity to play malicious tricks on them. They also vented their spleen on the *Frate* whenever they could."[104] The sentimental glorification of the child as a symbol of purity is one of those expressions of the bourgeois spirit that are both a means and an expression of the compulsory internalization of in stinctual desires. One ascribes to children a freedom from desires in which is effortlessly realized the difficult self-denial expected of one-self.[105] The ideal that youth represents in the bourgeois age is neither as a bearer of theoretical and practical strength nor as a guarantee of the infinite possibilities of humanity, but as a symbol of "purity," "in-nocence," and "childlikeness." The mechanisms alluded to are closely connected with the ideological relation this society has managed to establish not only to children but to nature in general, i.e., the ideali-zation of primitiveness, of "unspoiled" nature, and of the soil and the peasant.

The French Revolution seems, at first sight, to deviate from the structural similarity of bourgeois uprisings sketched here. The bour-geoisie and the propertyless masses had a common interest in remov-ing the ancien régime. Repeated mass uprisings preceded it, and the conditions brought about by the revolution, despite all setbacks, ac-tually led to an improvement in the general situation in both urban and rural areas in the first half of the nineteenth century. In particu-lar, the "democratization of the land" was achieved to a certain extent by the sale of nationalized properties.[106] Despite the relative commu-nity of interest between the wealthy bourgeoisie and the masses, how-ever, contradictions in the overall course of the revolution made themselves felt. From the very beginning, neither the character nor the actions of the great leaders corresponded to a homogeneous in-terest of the general public, an interest that was not realizable at that time; rather, they corresponded to the interest of the bourgeoisie, and although this was a progressive interest, at the same time it led to the exploitation and oppression of large parts of the population. This contradiction is clearly evident in Mathiez's excellent works on the French Revolution, which explain and defend Robespierre's politics in great detail. He traces the economic difficulties at the time of the revolution essentially to the *assignat* economy. All social strata that could not match the declining purchasing power of the *assignats* by raising the price of their own wares fell victim to inflation. They took up the struggle "against the cruelty of 'laissez faire' and 'laissez pas-ser.'" They opposed the right to property with the right to live. Though these urban and rural masses found no significant leaders, in the course of the revolution they finally succeeded in forcing the imposition of general economic controls, most importantly the fixing of maximum prices for grain and other necessary consumer goods. But this regulation, which was wrung from the government only under the strongest mass pressure, also included a wage ceiling. After the bourgeois circles failed in their desperate efforts to maintain a free market situation that was impossible for the poor under inflation, or even a partial market economy, the government fell into a new contradiction with proletarian strata, since it had to impose maximum wages along with maximum prices. Under the given structure of society and the prevailing mode of production, even terror was not enough to foil all the evasions of the food laws. Even though in Paris, for example, at the time when the Hebertists dominated the revolutionary section committees and maximum wages were less rigorously maintained than the laws on food prices, this was out of the question in the cities of the north. "One would be very mistaken," writes Mathiez, "to imagine that the revolutionary offices showed the same zeal everywhere in applying the maximum food prices. Even in the middle of the terror, city administrations that seemed to be mostly Jacobin were in the hands of the owners."[107] But quite apart from these inequities, the government had to alienate the masses by the wage policy forced upon it by circumstances.

Robespierre discovered too late that he could not carry on his revolutionary policy without concessions to the lower classes.

On the eve of his fall, supported by his friends Saint-Just and Couthon, he had convinced the welfare and social security committees in their sessions on 4 and 5 Thermidor finally to implement the Ventôse (February-March) regulations which had until then remained just on paper, through which Saint-Just wanted to expropriate the suspects (the internal enemies) and distribute their property among the poor sans-culottes. This would have created an entirely new class which owed everything to the revolution, because it owed its property to it, and which would defend the revolution. Robespierre had gone beyond democratic policy. He was on the road to a social revolution, and that was one of the reasons for his fall.[108]

These laws, which posed no threat to the bourgeois order in any case, were never implemented. Nevertheless, Robespierre's uneasiness, which led him to revoke them, was justified. He no longer had the workers' support against the wealthy, who were annoyed by the mandatory price limits. In some cases, the authorities had to resort to prohibitions against workers changing their place of employment; in the countryside, people had to be commanded to work the harvest, and laws against association were passed.[109] "On 9 Thermidor, the Parisian workers, dissatisfied with the new tariffs announced by the city authorities in the preceding days, remained indifferent to the political struggle going on before their eyes. Precisely on 9 Thermidor they demonstrated against the wage limits. . . . When Robespierre and his friends were being led to execution, the workers shouted to them as they passed: the devil take the maximum!"[110]

Robespierre is a bourgeois leader. Objectively his policy has a progressive content; the principle of society he represented, however, comprises the contradiction to his idea of universal justice. Blindness to this contradiction stamps his character with an imprint of the fantastic, despite all passionate rationality. His teacher Rousseau was already caught in the same illusions. In Book II of *Emile*[111] he states that the first idea one must give to a child is "less that of freedom than of ownership." The praise of ownership is repeated in many passages. "It is certain," he writes in an article on political economy, "that the right of ownership is the most sacred of all a citizen's rights and in some regards more important than freedom itself."[112] And he deludes himself with the hope that a government without ownership of the means of production could "prevent excessive inequality of wealth,"[113] ward off poverty, or at least make it bearable. Robespierre thinks in exactly the same manner. It was historically impossible for him to understand the immanent laws of the bourgeois economy which were politically anchored in the revolution. Within the system advocated by Robespierre, no government could prevent the intensification of social conflicts against anonymous economic forces. Rousseau and Robespierre's personal world of ideas corresponded directly to the situation of the petite bourgeoisie. They strongly resented large fortunes. The principle of ownership showed them its dark side. For Rousseau, all humanity's unhappiness even begins with it. He nonetheless declares it sacred. "One did not need a revolution," Robespierre said in the National Assembly, when confronted with socialist tendencies, "to teach everyone that excessive inequality of wealth is the source of many evils and crimes, but we are, nevertheless, convinced that equality of property is a chimera."[114] The exclamation "la

propiété; que ce mot n'alarme personne" stands at the beginning of
the same speech. But if ownership is, for the French Revolution, a
human right, still it is part of Robespierre's practice to put his own
moderation and poverty in the right light. In general, he surrounded
his person with the halo of poverty and virtue as diligently as Cola
and Savonarola did theirs with divine grace. When he asserts that he
would rather be the son of Aristides who was raised in the Prytaneum
at Athens's expense than heir to Xerxes's throne,[115] that is not at all
so irrational. But affirmations such as his claim that superfluity was
not merely the price of crime but also its punishment and that he
wanted to be poor in order not to be unhappy[116] are just part of the
bourgeois leader's necessary self-glorification. Such conscious display
of his own ascetic virtues through his own words and way of life was
one of the most important irrational means for magnifying Robespierre's person in the eyes of his followers. Most historians have
portrayed his behavior as a purely psychological fact, without understanding it as one of those practices based on the social function of
these politicians. "What is the secret of his power?" Michelet asks. "The
opinion which he was able to convince everyone of: his incorruptible
honesty and his immutability. With an admirable consistency and astonishing tactics, he succeeded in upholding his reputation for resolute integrity. In the end he maintained it simply by his own assurance.
And his word carried such weight that in the end one denied the
obvious facts in order to recognize Robespierre's assurance as the
highest authority, contrary to reality. . . . Faith in the priest was back
again, immediately after Voltaire. This priest denied nature and made
a nature of his own by his word. And this one was hard compared
with the other."[117] Indeed, Robespierre's ascetic attitude does possess
a magical character. He uses it as a higher legitimation.

He was not able to do without symbols either. They are integral to
his policy and his character. The cockades and flags play a major role
in the revolution. It is reported that Marat, on the eve of the uprising
on August 10, 1792, rode through the streets of Paris with a laurel
wreath on his head,[118] which was certainly not to Robespierre's taste.
He criticized all ostentatious behavior; the feasts of reason celebrated
by the Hebertists, which were a sharp affront to positive religion, especially disgusted him.[119] But his role as bourgeois leader, which requires displays for the masses, forced him to attend the Feast of the

Supreme Being in June 1794, which he presided over and the plans for which he had drawn up with the painter David, or at least approved. When he saw the people in the Tuileries gardens, he cried out enthusiastically: "The whole world is gathered here!"[120] In the course of this ceremony he set fire to the statue of Atheism, which had been erected for this purpose. In the middle of the flame the statue of Wisdom appeared. This defined the symbolic meaning of the event for the organizers and their audience. In truth, the bourgeoisie's struggle against atheism is less indicative of wisdom as a whole than of the wisdom of the government. This society needs a religion as a means of domination because the general interest does not hold it together. The road to the military cemetery, where the National Convention was to listen to hymns[121] and national songs from a mountain built for that purpose, passed in solemn procession. "The legislative assembly proceeded behind a group of old men, mothers, children, and young girls. Robespierre, in his capacity as President, led the way. He wore Nanking trousers, a cornflower-blue jacket, a belt with the national colors, on his head a hat decorated with a tricolor crest, and in his hand, like all his colleagues in office, a bouquet of grain-stalks, blossoms, and fruit."[122] What is distinctive of popular leaders here is not the strangeness of the procession, which is often wrongly stressed by portrayals hostile to the revolution, but the compulsion to have such impressive and symbolic rallies, which even Robespierre could not avoid. At the height of its revolutionary development of power the bourgeoisie recalls its earliest revolts. "The brotherhood festivals of the French Revolution in Paris appear truly to be an imitation of the August festival of the popular tribunes of Rome."[123] As a consequence of the very different political situations in which their class found itself, Rienzo and Robespierre are worlds apart—and yet something in their nature is identical, because the form of society on whose behalf their activity was ultimately brought to bear is one and the same.

Even historians' discussions of these figures display at times a remarkable concurrence. Thus, Cola's modern biographer accuses Gregorovius of "blunders" and "clumsy criticism" for his talk of pathological hypersensitivity, the classical carnival game, the "insane plebeian with his crown of flowers," and so on.[124] Similar statements about Robespierre have frequently provoked the critique of historians. Michelet speaks of the incorruptible man's "pathological imagination,"[125] and has been just as harshly reproved as Gregorovius, with whom he may be compared in regard to his power of depiction and "theatrical pose," as Burdach says of Gregorovius.[126] Michelet and Gregorovius are partly right, partly wrong. Bourgeois leaders are prone to a trace of the fantastic, but this is based less on their psychology than on social conditions. For all of their fantasies, they remain as true to reality as is possible in this contradictory society. The fantastical is a symptom of their profession; almost all of them could have been considered to be manic, at the very least, before or after fulfilling their historical mission. The qualities that make them suited for their role—the oscillation between love for the people, strictness, and cruelty; the combination of a child's gentleness with the rage of a bloody avenger; the obstinacy of the freedom fighter and the submission to the will of higher powers; the intermingling of personal simplicity, bombastic concepts, pomp, and moral severity—whenever the right circumstances bring all of this into evidence, it can be only partly conscious on the leaders' part. This contradictory temperament must surely be inborn, i.e., their character is preformed for their achievement. All these contradictions are contained in the average bourgeois individual as well. The cautious and especially "calculating" businessman, a small-scale model of practicality, precision, and thrift, tends, at least secretly, toward improbable, romantic enterprises, and at times comes up with the most adventurous of ideas. The leader is just the magnified version of this type. His character structure corresponds to that of his followers. Contemporary popular literature contains the same unmediated mishmash of blood craze and virtue, boastfulness and modesty as is worshiped in the leader. In his person, this mixture is "natural." It is told that Prince Colonna at times used to like to invite the notary Rienzo to dinner and have him give a speech. "The prominent gentlemen broke out in laughter once when he said: 'WhenI have become ruler or emperor, I will hang this baron or have that one beheaded,' pointing his finger at the guests. He went about in Rome as a fool. . . . No one suspected that this fool would one day have the terrible power to lop the heads of prominent Romans from their shoulders."[127]

Robespierre shares the Reformers' hostility to erotic culture. The constant exhortations to moral purity and the associated mania to discover filth everywhere is inseparable from his politics. They see physical and moral filth everywhere. They despise idleness, people of loose morals, and attitudes that favor pleasure and happiness. In his letter to d'Alembert, the Genevan Rousseau lashes out at the theater and declares it an "amusement," and that if people cannot do without "amusements" they at least ought to be limited to an absolute minimum: "every unnecessary amusement is an evil for a being whose life is so short and whose time so valuable."[128] When Robespierre's spiritual mentor propagates this hatred of pleasure, he can appeal to illustrious Genevan predecessors. Although Calvin, in contrast with a few of the more radical members of his leadership, was of the opinion that "one must not deprive the people of all delights,"[129] under his rule dance, play, and public and private festivities were either completely forbidden or tied to conditions that virtually amounted to a prohibition.[130] Even theatrical performances with "a good intention"[131] were opposed on grounds of principle by the congregation he headed, even if not by his own initiative. "As could be expected," a modern study of Robespierre says, "he also used his power to enforce universal morality. Maximilien and Couthon, who often ate together at noon, represented a strong puritanical element on the committee. In October they encouraged the Commune in its striving to break the wave of immorality that had inundated Paris. They obtained an order from the committee to arrest the writer and owner of a theater where an indecent play was being performed."[132] Certainly, Robespierre is infinitely more positive toward theory and reason than Luther and his followers, both because of the historical progress which had occurred in the interim and because of his role in the left wing of the bourgeoisie. But it is also true that Robespierre was no less exempt from the rule that bourgeois popular leaders lag behind the knowledge of the writers who prepared the way for them. He was very critical of the Enlightenment. "Virtue and talent are both necessary qualities, but virtue is the most necessary. Virtue without talent can still be useful. Talent without virtue is just a misfortune."[133] In the speech on 18 Floreal 1794, quoted above, he inveighed against the materialism of antiquity and the modern age, especially against the Epicureans and Encyclopedists. After a very idiosyncratic digression into the history of philosophy, he reproaches them for writing against despotism and then accepting pensions from it, and for penning books against the court and dedicating them to kings. Robespierre criticizes the materialist philosophy for "making egoism into a system, and understanding human society as a war of treachery, success as the measure for right and wrong, honesty as a matter of taste and decorum, the world as the property of clever scoundrels."[134] He plays off Rousseau against Voltaire's circle, which of course very much hated the Genevan moralist. But the harsh depiction of the world rejected by Robespierre corresponded more accurately to reality than did his own belief that after the bourgeois order is consolidated, justice will depend on the return to virtue. This idealism, however, is inseparable from Robespierre's historical task. With his fall, this view showed its deficiency compared with the spirit of materialism which he so disdained.

III

In order to illuminate the historical consequences of unrestrained egoism, which, despite the official morality of the modern age, is an essential trait of everyday life, a few non-everyday events were pointed out above. From the key points of its development, the revolutions, a light is cast over the bourgeois spirit as a whole that is also useful in analyzing the normal state. The question arises as to why this historical meditation was necessary at all. The derivation of the psychic and intellectual narrowness of the predominant character seems simple enough. Bourgeois society does not rely upon conscious collaboration for the existence and happiness of its members. Its vital law is a different one. Each person thinks he is working for himself, and must think of his own survival. There is no plan laying out how universal needs are to be met. By everyone producing things which can be exchanged for other things that are needed, production is regulated just enough for society to develop in its given form. The more a better, more rational system becomes technically possible over the course of centuries, the cruder and more clumsy this "fine" instrument, the market, proves to be; it mediates the reproduction of society only with severe losses in human life and goods, and with the advancement of the capitalist economy it is unable to save humanity, despite its growing wealth, from a reversion to barbarity. It is this very state of affairs—that during the epoch that emancipates the individual, each human being experiences itself in the underlying economic sphere as an isolated subject of interests, associated with others only by purchase and sale—that gives rise to otherness [*Fremdheit*] as an anthropological category. The characteristic philosophy of the age understands the human being as a self-contained monad in transcendental loneliness, connected with other monads only by complicated mechanisms independent of their will—this is the bourgeois individual's form of existence expressed in the concepts of metaphysics. Each one is the center of the world, and everyone else is "outside." All communication is an exchange, a transaction between solipsistically constructed realms. The conscious being of these individuals can be reduced to a small number of relations between fixed quantities. The language of logistics is its appropriate expression. Coldness and alienness are the direct result of this basic structure of the epoch: nothing in the essence of the bourgeois individual opposes the repression and annihilation of one's fellow human beings. On the contrary, the circumstance that in this world each becomes the other's competitor, and that even with increasing social wealth there are increasingly too many people, gives the typical individual of the epoch a character of coldness and indifference, one that is satisfied with the most pitiful rationalizations of the most monstrous deeds as long as they correspond to his interest.

The preceding expositions dealt with only a few aspects of the historical realization of the bourgeois principle. In considering the trait of cruelty, they attempted to lend a more concrete form to the purely theoretically derived model of the bourgeois individual than would be possible by means of a purely logical derivation. Though cruelty was not discussed at great length in connection with these uprisings, nothing is more well known about them than this. Certainly the counterrevolutionary reactions were, as a rule, much more bloody, for they lacked even the rapidly disappearing hope of a drastic change, which in bourgeois revolutions works against resentment; the progressive elements are completely helpless and are the main target of terror. The masses are reduced from a particular factor which, though not awakened to complete self-consciousness, nonetheless endeavors to drive the process forward and hence plays a role of its own, to a mere instrument of revenge against the most advanced groups. In the bourgeois revolution the masses, though with changing strength and constant vacillation, are determined by their more conscious wing, and are differentiated and alert. They must constantly be observed, convinced, and taken seriously. They are not a mass in the same sense as in the counterrevolution, where the "mob" tends to appear on the scene. The "mob" is different from the masses in revolutions, down to the psychic structure of its units. The question of whether the uprisings that have taken place in the most recent past in some European states are to be classified more as one or the other kind of historical events—which, moreover, at times have a similar character and are ultimately all phases of a single process and a self-coherent totality—is not as easily answerable as it may appear to be from a liberal perspective. At any rate, what are involved here are not absolutist or clerical reactions but the staging of a bourgeois pseudorevolution with radical populist trappings, wholly contrary to any possible reorganization of society. The forms they take seem to be a bad imitation of the movements previously discussed.

The role of the bourgeois leader as a functionary of the property-owning strata; the surrounding of his person with magic qualities for the masses, his "charisma"; the importance of symbols and holidays; the preponderance of speech over action; the call for inner renewal; the replacement of the old bureaucracy; the personal struggles between aspirants for elite positions; the mostly psychically determined relation of leaders, subleaders, and followers; the religious and national emotionalism; the anchoring of the difference between poor and rich in the eternal essence of the world—all these are expressions of the same dynamic: the masses, set in motion under the slogans of freedom and justice, and with a tremendously vague or clear urge to improve their situation and to attain for themselves a meaningful existence, peace, and happiness, are incorporated into a new phase of class society. Certainly, this is just one side of the whole process. The other is the progress of this selfsame society, which advances in leaps and bounds precisely in these revolutions, in which the preconditions for a higher social order are developed in this way and not otherwise. But as long as the epoch lasts, this negative moment has its own anthropological consequences. Since the egoism of the masses led by the bourgeois leader must not be satisfied, since their demands are repressed as inner purification, obedience, submission, and self-sacrifice, since love and recognition of the individual are deflected toward the leader, who has been magnified to superhuman dimensions, and toward lofty symbols and great concepts, and since one's own being is annihilated along with its claim to existence—idealistic ethics tends to go in this direction—the extraneous [*fremde*] individual is also experienced as a nullity and the individual as such, his pleasure and happiness, is despised and denied.

The feeling of one's own absolute nothingness that dominates the members of the mass corresponds exactly to the puritanical view "that practical success is at the same time the sign and the reward for ethical superiority. . . . The doctrine that misery is a proof of guilt, although it casts a strange light on the life of Christian saints and sages, was always liked among the wealthy." [135] The fact that the poor person is in reality worthless is demonstrated to him anew every day; at bottom, he knows it right from the start. The prevailing ideology does generally contain the opposite thesis, yet a person's deeper psychic layers are not determined by it alone, but equally by the constant experience of contradictory reality. The manifest ideology is just one of the factors that give rise to the personalities typical of the society. The humanism that pervades the history of the new spirit shows a double face. Directly, it signifies the glorification of the human being as the creator of its own destiny. Human dignity lies in the power to determine oneself independently of the powers of blind nature within and without; it lies in one's power to act. In the society in which this humanism spread, however, the power of self-determination is unevenly distributed; for inner energies depend no less on external destiny than it does on them. The more remote the abstract concept of the human being, as glorified by humanism, was from their real situation, the more pitiful the individuals of the masses had to appear to themselves, and the more the idealistic divinization of Man—as manifested in the concepts of the greatness, genius, and grace-endowed personality of the leader, etc.—resulted in the self-abasement and the self-contempt of the concrete individual. Yet the individual is simply reflecting reality. If even the happiest person can, from one moment to the next and without due cause, become like the most miserable and poorest person, not through the blind forces of nature but through causes within human society, and if unhappiness is the only normal and certain condition, then the concrete individual cannot count for very much. Each hour society confirms anew that only circumstances, not persons, actually deserve respect. The Reformation, with its morally depressing antihuman pathos, its hatred for the earthworm's vanity, its dark doctrine of predestination, is not so much the opponent of bourgeois humanism as its other, its misanthropic side. It is humanism for the masses, while humanism itself is the Reformation for the wealthy.

The necessity to move the greatest part of society by spiritual practices to a renunciation which is necessitated not by external nature but by the organization of society into classes gives the whole cultural thinking of the age an ideological character that stands in disproportion to the knowledge possible at this stage of technical development. Even with an organization in which human freedom was restricted solely by external nature that had yet to be mastered and not by social relations, the limits set by nature would compel some portion of external wishes and needs to be internalized, leading to the transformation of energies. To the extent that other goals, satisfactions, and joys would develop, these would completely lack the character of the higher, more noble, and sublime, which today invests all spiritual and all so-called cultural endeavors in contrast to materialistic noninternalized desires. The medicine-man solemnity that, as a consequence of the antagonistic constitution of society, clings to the whole of life in all noneconomic spheres, disappears with the fetishes by means of which the masses are held in check and around whose grounding, cultivation, and propagation this life is centered. The preservation of aesthetic, literary, and philosophical elements of the past epoch does not mean the conservation of the ideological context in which they stood. The affirmative character of culture, according to which the existence of an eternally better world over the real world was asserted, this false idealism is crumbling, but the materialism that is left is not the bourgeois one of indifference and competition; the preconditions of this crude atomistic materialism, which under the sway of that idealism was and is the real religion of practice, will crumble as well. The words "the realm of freedom" do not mean that the fruits borne by culture's present level of development should be extended in a "refined" form to benefit the "whole people," as is usually said. This undialectical view, which naively adopts the bourgeois notion of culture, ascetic scale of priorities, and concept of morality but remains ignorant of its great artistic achievements, has dominated the reform efforts of even the progressive nineteenth-century political parties to this very day, made thinking shallow, and ultimately contributed to defeat. With the increasing hopelessness of the masses' condition, the individual is finally left the choice between two modes of behavior. One is the conscious struggle against the conditions of reality—this retains the positive element of bourgeois morality, the demand for freedom and justice, while annulling its ideological hypostatization. The other is a continued profession of this morality and its corresponding hierarchy—this leads to a secret contempt for one's own concrete existence and to hatred for the happiness of others, to a nihilism[136] which has expressed itself again and again in the history of the modern age as the practical destruction of everything joyful and happy, as barbarity and destruction.

In salient historical moments, this bourgeois nihilism is expressed in the specific form of terror. There have been certain periods in history in which terror was an instrument of the government. But various elements must be distinguished in this. Its rational goal consists in intimidating the opponent. Gruesome acts directed at the enemy are protective measures of domestic and foreign policy. But terror also serves another purpose, one which its originators are not always consciously aware of, and which is even more rarely admitted by them: the satisfaction of their own followers. Insofar as this second element plays a role even in such progressive movements as the French Revolution, it corresponds to the deep contempt, the hatred of happiness itself, that is connected with the morally mediated compulsion to asceticism. The preaching of honorable poverty which accompanies the everyday life of this age, one that has nonetheless made wealth its God, eventually becomes more intense in the course of the uprising and sets the basic tone even of the most liberal bourgeois leader's speech. The deepest instincts of the audience take this to mean that after the return to order, what will begin is not a new, meaningful, and joyous existence that will really put an end to misery—in which case terror would not be required for their satisfaction—but the return to hard work, low pay, and actual subjugation and impotence vis-à-vis those who need make no sacrifices in order to be honest. The equality which the individuals of the mass sense as fair and just at such moments, and which they demand, amounts to a universal abasement to the life of poverty so emphatically commended to them. If pleasure, or even just the capacity for pleasure, which they have had to fight in themselves since their youth, is so ruinous, then those who embody this vice and remind one of it in their whole being, appearance, clothing, and attitude should also be extinguished so that the source of scandal disappears and one's own renunciation is confirmed. The individuals of the mass would have to view the entirety of their lives as misspent if it turned out that pleasure is really worthwhile and that the halo of renunciation exists only in the imagination. Through the clumsy and frenzied attempts to grab whatever is possible, through the imitation of orgies as he imagines them, the little man who one day came to power documents the same inner fear as the obstinately virtuous parvenu of missing the chance of his lifetime. For it is always a question of the soul. Driven by serious curiosity and inextinguishable hatred, people seek the forbidden behind what is alien to them, behind every door which they cannot enter, in harmless clubs and sects, monastery walls and palaces. The concept of the alien becomes synonymous with that of the forbidden and dangerous, and the enmity is all the more fatal since its carriers feel that this forbidden thing is irretrievably lost for themselves by virtue of their own rigid character. Petit bourgeois resentment against the nobility and anti-Semitism have similar psychic functions. Behind the hatred of the courtesan, the contempt for aristocratic existence, the rage over Jewish immorality, over Epicureanism and materialism is hidden a deep erotic resentment which demands the death of their representatives. They must be wiped out, if possible with torments, for the sense of one's own existence is called into question every moment by the existence of the others. In the orgies of the aristocracy, licentiousness in rebellious cities, and bloodthirstiness of the followers of an opposed religion—in the kind of deeds they impute to their victims—virtue betrays its own dream. It is not so much the scarcity of luxury that sets the ideologically dominated masses in motion as it is the very possibility of luxury at all. Luxury is therefore essentially considered impertinent not because there is poverty, but because poverty is taken to be the better of the two. All are equally nothing, and so soon as they believe themselves to be more, they are reduced to nothing. This brutality toward personal destiny, which in the bourgeois world is the law for most, is made plain for all to see by the guillotine, which moreover gives the masses the blissful feeling of omnipotence by virtue of their own principle having attained power. The guillotine symbolizes negative equality, the worst kind of democracy, which is identical with its own opposite: utter contempt for the person. Accordingly, the cruel treatment of suspects in the prisons and tribunals of the bourgeois freedom movements and counterrevolutions is typically accompanied by moral abuse, castigation, and insults. "To make equal" has two meanings: to elevate what is below, to consciously set the highest claim to happiness as the standard of society, or to drag down, to cancel happiness, to bring everything down to the level of the present misery of the masses. Even the rebellions of this era that have been liberating and decisive for humanity harbor elements of this second meaning. Both principles are at work in the masses, and often enough they conflict. Even though only the negative one became operative in the counterrevolutions, it must also be said that the positive one, which points beyond the structure of the epoch, has already predominantly defined the character of a number of historical phenomena.

Nevertheless, one need not read Taine's descriptions, inspired by wild enmity,[137] to recognize this nihilism even in the Terror of the French Revolution. The "philosophical policeman Dutard," whom Mathiez quotes, expresses the significance of terror for the masses more clearly than any listing of terrible incidents. In his report on the execution of twelve condemned men, he makes the following observation:

I must tell you that these executions have the greatest effect in politics, but the most important one consists in calming the people's resentment for the evils they have borne. They exercise their revenge in this way. The wife who has lost her husband, the father who has lost his son, the merchant who no longer has a business, the worker who pays so much for everything that his wage is reduced almost to nothing, can be reconciled with the evils that oppress them only when they see people who are even more unhappy than they are and whom they believe to be enemies.[138]

Marx and Engels did not overlook the contemptible side of the Terror of the French Revolution. "The whole French terrorism," they wrote in the *Neue Rheinische Zeitung*, "was nothing but a plebeian manner of getting even with the enemies of the bourgeoisie: absolutism, feudalism, philistinism."[139] And in 1870 Engels wrote: "*La terreur* amounted to mostly useless cruelties, such as are committed by anxious people for their own reassurance. I am convinced that the guilt for the Reign of Terror of the year 1793 falls almost exclusively on the shoulders of overly anxious bourgeois acting like patriots, the narrow-minded ... petty bourgeois, and the ragged mob [*Lumpenmob*] that made their living from the Terror."[140] Though Engels in this passage understands the Terror mainly as a ridiculous exaggeration of the rational goal, his revulsion toward the petit bourgeois and the ragged mob also points to the socially conditioned sadomasochistic constitution of these strata, who were no less to blame for French terror than the opponents' activity.

In view of the indefinite postponement of a really thorough and lasting improvement for the poor, and of the certainty that the real inequality would continue despite the empty phrase "equality," the leaders hit upon the solution of offering the masses the unhappiness of particular people in place of the happiness of all the people. The beautiful Claire Lacombe played a certain role in the Revolution since the August 10 revolt, in which she had distinguished herself. She was closely affiliated with the radical leftists and had a great deal of influence among revolutionary women. When she came into conflict with Robespierre and his followers, her execution was announced even before her final arrest with the words, "The woman or girl Lacombe is finally in prison and been rendered incapable of doing harm. This bacchantic counterrevolutionary now drinks nothing but water; it is known that she was very fond of wine, no less than she was of good food and men. Proof: the intimate friendship between herself, Jacques Roux, Leclerc, and comrades."[141] Robespierre generally represented this petit bourgeois spirit in his policies. Personally, his ascetic predisposition disposed him to it, but the great progressive significance of the Revolution is also expressed in his character. "The people," he writes in his notes, "what obstacle stands in the way of instructing them? Misery. When will the people, then, be enlightened? When they have bread, and the rich as well as the government stop buying vile pens and tongues to deceive them. When their interest has fused with the people's. When will their interest have fused with the people's? Never."[142] But these sentences actually went beyond the movement he led. He crossed them out in his manuscript. Similarly, Saint-Just had arrived at a great insight. "Happiness is a new idea in Europe."[143] He expressed it in connection with the laws which led to the fall of his government. After Thermidor, it was not happiness but lawless and unrestricted terror that was put on the agenda.

The analysis of the psychic mechanisms by which hatred and cruelty are generated was begun in modern psychology mainly by Freud. The conceptual apparatus which he created in his early works can significantly aide one's understanding of these processes. His original theory shows that social prohibitions, under the given familiar and general social conditions, are suited for arresting people's instinctual development at a sadistic level or reverting them back to this level. His theory of partial drives, of repressions, of ambivalence (a concept he adopted from Bleuler) and so on, are crucial for a psychological understanding of the process under discussion here, even though Freud himself did not pursue this application of his theory in any detail.[144] The transformation of psychic energies that takes place in the process of internalization cannot be understood today without the psychoanalytical perspective. While the Freudian categories originally displayed a dialectical character, in that they related the construction of individual destiny wholly in terms of society and reflected the interaction between external and internal factors, in later years the historical element in his conceptualization retreated in favor of the purely biological. Today it seems as if that dialectical character of his theory had crept into even those early works independent of the positivistically oriented author's will. The more he approaches more comprehensive sociological, historical, or philosophical problems, the more clearly the liberal and ideological cast of his thinking comes to the fore. His theory of narcissism already implies that love would appear to stand in greater need of explanation than hate, which "as a relation to objects, is older than love. It derives from the narcissistic ego's primeval repudiation of the external world with its outpouring of stimuli."[145] Later on, the destruction drive, "the inborn human inclination to 'badness,' to aggressiveness and destructiveness, and so to cruelty as well,"[146] was posited as a basic fact of psychic life that was directly determined by biology. Freud assumes that "besides the instinct to preserve living substance and to join it into ever greater units, there must exist another, contrary instinct seeking to dissolve those units and to bring them back to their primeval, inorganic state. That is to say, as well as Eros, there was an instinct of death."[147] The "meaning of cultural development" is the "struggle between Eros and Death, between the instinct of life and the instinct of destruction, as it works itself out in the human species."[148]

Freud's simple philosophy of history follows from this general model. As a result of "this primary mutual hostility of human beings,"[149] civilization is constantly threatened with disintegration, and a lasting improvement of social conditions is impossible. All manner of coercion and laws, as well as morality and religion, are attempts to counter the effects of the eternal destruction drive. An "elite" will always be needed to hold the destruction-prone masses in check. In history we get the impression that "the idealistic motives served only as an excuse for the destructive appetites; and sometimes—in the case, for instance, of the cruelties of the Inquisition—it seems as though the idealistic motives had pushed themselves forward in consciousness, while the destructive ones lent them an unconscious reinforcement. Both may be true."[150] It is certain, in any case, "that there is no question of getting rid entirely of human aggressive impulses."[151] Although, according to Freud, the life of certain primitive tribes and the doctrine of the Bolsheviks seem to lend substance to such utopian ideas, he nevertheless persists in his skepticism. "That, in my opinion, is an illusion."[152] Above all, one should not think that war can be done away with so soon. "Culturability," i.e., "man's personal capacity for the transformation of the egoistic impulses under the influence of eroticism,"[153] consists of "two parts, one innate and the other acquired in the course of life."[154] We are inclined to overestimate the innate one, and the acquired one is generally held to be of little account. Most people are "hypocrites" as regards their cultivation. Freud does not base his explanation of the cruelty expressed in war, and not only in war, on a transformation of drive-impulses that aim at material goals, nor does he ultimately base it upon the coerced patient endurance of misery. He is inclined to understand the "pressure of culture," so far as it does not concern sexuality, as pressure on the innate destruction drive rather than on the aggregate of needs which the masses must repress contrary to the social possibilities. Like the devil in the Middle Ages, the eternal destruction drive is to be blamed for all evil. Freud, moreover, considers himself especially daring with this view. "We should probably have met with little resistance," he writes as an explanation for the long hesitation of psychoanalysis to accept the death instinct into its doctrine, "if we had wanted to ascribe an instinct with such an aim to animals. But to include it in the human constitution seems sacrilegious; it contradicts too many religious presumptions and social conventions."[155] He does not know how much this new phase of his doctrine and movement merely repeats social and religious convention.

The historical phenomena discussed above should confirm the view that the hostility toward pleasure contained in the modern age's optimistic and pessimistic conception of humanity stems from the social situation of the bourgeoisie. The overstrained human ideal, the simultaneously sentimental and harsh notion of virtue and self-surrender, and the cult of an abstract heroism all share the same roots as individualistic egoism and nihilism, which they simultaneously contradict and interact with. The overcoming of this morality lies not in the positing of a better one, but in the creation of conditions under which their reason for existing is eliminated. The realization of morality, of a state of society and individuals that dignifies humanity, is not merely a psychological but a historical problem. By this insight, Hegel led idealism beyond its original boundaries. Freedom is "itself only a notion—a principle of the mind and heart," but it is destined "to develop into an objective phase." [156] "When a father inquired about the best method of educating his son in ethical conduct, a Pythagorean replied: 'Make him a citizen of a state with good laws.' " [157] Hence the task is not just a spiritual one. At present, it is also not a matter of good guidance and skillful selection. Whether future generations will live in dignity depends on the outcome of a period of struggles whose significance for his own viewpoint Hegel could not yet see. But when Freud scoffs that in certain people's view human brutality, violence, and cruelty are merely temporary and provoked by circumstances, indeed are "perhaps only consequences of the inexpedient social regulations which [man] has hitherto imposed on himself," [158] even though he is summing up a dialectical theory in words that are all too shallow, this contested view—even in its pragmatist rendition—still corresponds to the present condition better than the biologistic metaphysics Freud subscribes to.

In no phenomenon is the relationship between practical ruthlessness and idealistic morality more pregnantly expressed than in the coexistence of the most tender, guileless, and good-natured consideration with hardened cynicism, a combination that is characteristic not only of the individual who gains power but also of the ideal and fantasy figures of this era. At home, the owners of huge fortunes and the politicians whose business entails a terrible ruthlessness are usually sensitive and warm-hearted people. The role of children has already been mentioned. The most gruesome day's work is framed by the friendship and the smile bestowed upon the child. The lower the socially weak must bend, the more the symbol of the naturally weak, of children, and of venerable old men becomes exalted. To date, the impeded intellectual and instinctual development within European society has manifested itself in its blindness to the existence of animals. Their fate in our civilization reflects all of the coldness and callousness of the prevailing human type. Nevertheless, when such individuals consciously resort to especially bloody means, if they have not exactly discovered their love for animals, then they at least tend to assert it. "You call me cruel, even though I can't stand to watch an insect suffer," says Marat, as he recommends the killing of a series of political opponents.[159] Sentimental love for animals is one of the ideological institutions in this society. It is not a universal solidarity that naturally extends itself to encompass these living creatures, but rather an alibi for one's own narcissism and for the public consciousness, a test of one's conformity to the ideal morality, as it were. To acknowledge cruelty, or to admit to enjoying the cruelty one commits, would completely contradict the necessary mood of this age. A government whose most important instruments used each day include that terror in a negative sense, which offers the most terrible sacrifices to the nihilistic disposition of its own followers and shows a calculated indulgence toward their spontaneous participation, would abolish itself if it were to actually admit this. It dismisses nothing more fervently than the inspirational function of cruelty. Indeed, it has long been part of the business of terror, as it were, to trivially or completely deny it. Calvin praised the mildness of the Geneva city council as they were torturing his opponents at his request,[160] then kept silent about the torture in a report meant for the outraged city of Zurich.[161] Voices are heard that in terrorized Geneva "incredible calm" and "harmony among all the good"[162] prevail, and those announcements to the outside world had "no further effects."[163] "The judge is a sublimated executioner," Nietzsche says.[164] If that is true, then this state of affairs would give way if the judge really became conscious of it. Freud is right in saying that for cultural reasons the destruction drive always needs a pretext, a rationalization: the wickedness of the opponent, pedagogical purposefulness, the defense of honor, a war, or some popular uprising. Yet this rationalization does not counteract the degeneration of every human community, but only the present one. The destruction drive, understood to be eternal, was until now continually reproduced by social arrangements and also held in check with the help of ideological practices. Under changed circumstances, the effectiveness and knowledge of common interests can determine the social relations of human beings; the "destruction drive" will no longer disrupt them. In the present epoch egoism has actually become destructive, both the fettered and the diverted egoism of the masses as well as the archaic egoistic principle of the economy, which still shows only its most brutal side. When the latter is overcome, the former can become productive in a new sense. The badness of egoism lies not in itself but in the historical situation; when this changes, its conception will merge with that of the rational society.

Since not only the practical but also the theoretical solution to the anthropological question can be attained only by the progress of society itself, and since the true nature of bourgeois man only becomes completely clear when he has changed, no philosophy and no clever educational methods will be adequate to this problem. The idealistic morality that hampers insight is surely not to be repudiated but historically realized, and hence it is still not to be dismissed even today. The question of how the fate of the universally denounced egoism, of the "destruction and death drive," would be shaped in a more rational reality finds no particular answer. But in recent times there have been signs pointing in one and the same direction for a solution. Some thinkers have, in contrast with the prevailing mentality, neither concealed, nor minimalized, nor accused egoism, but professed it: not that abstract and pitiful fiction, as it appears in the work of some political economists and of Jeremy Bentham, but pleasure, the highest degree of happiness, in which the satisfaction of cruel impulses is also included. They have idealized none of the drives given to them historically as primary; rather, they have stigmatized the distortion of the drives caused by the official ideology. These thinkers, since Aristippus and Epicurus, have been understood in modern history essentially only in terms of their opposition to the prevailing morality, for which they have been either defended or condemned. But there is a peculiar fact about these apologists of unrestricted egoism. When they investigated the despised drives for themselves and raised them to consciousness without rejection or minimalization, these forces lost their demonic power.

These hedonistic psychologists as a rule were portrayed as enemies of humanity, or praised on high by the latter. This happened most to Nietzsche. The superman, the most problematic concept with which the psychologist left the analytical realm Nietzsche had mastered, has been interpreted along the lines of the philistine bourgeois's wildest dreams, and has been confused with Nietzsche himself. The adventurous element seemed so appealing. Greatness, blood, and danger have always been cherished in paintings and monuments. But Nietzsche is the opposite of this inflated sense of power. His error lay in his lack of historical understanding of the present, which led him to bizarre hypotheses where clear theoretical knowledge was possible. He was blind to the historical dynamics of his time and hence to the way to his goal; therefore, even his most magnificent analysis, the genealogy of morals and of Christianity, for all of its subtlety, turns out to be too crude. But this prophet of Epicurean gods and of the pleasurableness of cruelty freed himself from the coercion to rationalize. When the will to cause suffering ceases to act "in the name" of God, "in the name" of justice, morality, honor, or the nation, it loses, by means of insight into itself, the terrible power it exercises so long as it conceals itself from its own carrier on the basis of ideological denial. It is taken up into the economy of real-life conduct for what it is and becomes rationally masterable. What turns it into a culturally destructive force is not the sublation of ideology and its basis, in other words the transition to a better society; rather, it is the unleashing of aggression which is presently reproduced and repressed for social reasons by the bourgeois authorities themselves, for example in war and national mobilization. Nietzsche himself cannot be thought of as an executioner, unlike many of his followers. His inoffensive existence stems from the deepest knowledge of psychic connections that may ever have existed in history. Nietzsche's precursors in the analysis of egoism and cruelty—Mandeville, Helvétius, de Sade—are as free, like himself, of Freud's condescending tolerance toward the destruction drive which "unfortunately" happens to exist, and of his resigned skepticism, as they are of the loving Rousseau's *ressentiment.*

By their own existence these psychologists seem to point out that the liberation from ascetic morality with its nihilistic consequences can bring about a human change in the opposite sense than internalization. This process sublates internalization; it does not cast the people back to the previous psychic stage, as it were, as if that first process had never taken place, but raises them to a higher level of existence. But those thinkers have contributed little to making it a universal reality; that is mainly the task of the historical persons in whom theory and historical practice became a unity. In them the mechanisms of bourgeois psychology, both as determining forces of their life and as theoretical object, are less important than their world-historical mission. Insofar as humanity, with their help, enters a higher form of existence, it will change reality and thereby quickly acquire the freer psychic constitution of which the great number of fighters and martyrs for that general transformation is already possessed without psychological mediation, because the dark ethos of a dying epoch, an ethos that would deny them all happiness, no longer has any power over them.

According to Aristotle's aesthetic theory, the sight of suffering in tragedy causes pleasure.[165] People become purer by satisfying this drive, the pleasure in empathy. The application of Aristotle's theory to the modern age seems to be problematic; it has been reinterpreted and "moralized," even by Lessing, in the sense of idealistic morality. Catharsis through dramatic plays, through play in general, presupposes a changed humanity.

History and Psychology

A Lecture to the Kant Society, Frankfurt am Main

The relationship between history and psychology has been much discussed in recent decades. But you expect from me neither a report on the discussions carried out in the literature, some of which have become quite well known, nor a systematic treatment of the various aspects of the problem today, but rather a characterization of the role of psychology in the context of a theory of history that does justice to the current state of the social sciences. For this purpose, it is necessary to clarify the concept of history which I intend to use. The prevalence of several meanings of "history," associated with heterogeneous intellectual intentions, further complicates agreement regarding questions of detail.

In particular, two logically opposed concepts of history can be identified. The first derives from those systems, whose roots are to be found in Kant, that arose in the latter decades of the nineteenth century in reaction against materialist tendencies in both science and society. Their common denominator lay in the effort to find the meaning of nature, art, and history not from direct immersion in these areas themselves, but rather from an analysis of the knowledge [*Erkenntnis*] corresponding to them. From the fundamental conviction of this philosophy—namely, that the world has a subjective origin—came the attempt to trace the peculiarities of the realms of being back to various characteristics [*Funktionsweisen*] of the knowing subject. The essence of nature was to be illuminated from the systematic elaboration of the constitutive methods of the natural sciences; likewise, history was to be explained on the basis of an analysis of historical methods. The concept of history in this philosophy is thus oriented to the given facts of historical science. In principle this philosophy can relate to historical writing only apologetically, not critically—even at a time when historiography remains behind the current state of knowledge in its methods and approaches.

The philosophy upon which the other concept of history is based maintains no such modesty with respect to the available sciences. It is a part of the contemporary effort to make the so-called ideological [weltanschaulich] questions independent of scientific criteria, and to develop philosophy entirely beyond the realm of empirical research. In contrast to the epistemological view outlined above, the various realms of being are to be made comprehensible not in terms of the sciences but rather in terms of their common root, primordial Being [ursprungliches Sein], to which our age claims a novel access. A new concept of historicity has emerged particularly from the phenomenological school, the fundamental doctrine of which was at first completely ahistorical. In Scheler's attempt during his last years to reconcile the undialectical doctrines of phenomenology with the fact of a revolutionary [umwälzende] history, he essentially understood social and political history under this rubric. For Heidegger, however, "historicity" means a mode of being [Geschehensweise] in the ground of Being [im Seinsgrund]—which latter had itself to be discovered in human beings. History [Geschichte] as a theme of "Historie" would first acquire its meaning from this primordial mode of proceeding. It thus seems appropriate today to begin from this meaning of "history" in any fundamental discussion.

For the topic under consideration here, however, it is no less problematic to premise the concept of inner historicity than it would be to start with the concept of history employed in traditional science. Because existential philosophy in the phenomenological tradition seeks to make itself independent of the results of research in the various spheres, because it is determined to start from the very beginning and strives to determine the meaning of Being without respect to the contemporary state of research, its approach appears too narrow for our problem. According to the notion that history is first to be grasped out of the inner historicity of Dasein,[1] the interweaving of Dasein in the real process of history would have to seem merely external and illusory. Just as engagement with external history illuminates the individual beings [das jeweilige Dasein], however, the analysis of individual existence [das jeweilige Existenzen] conditions the understanding of history. Dasein is indissolubly implicated in external history, and accordingly its analysis cannot lead to the discovery of any ground that moves in itself, independent of all external determination. Real history, then, with its multifaceted, supraindividual structures is not merely a derivative, subsidiary, objectivated realm, as existential philosophy would insist. The theory of human Being [vom Sein im Menschen] is thus transformed—along with all kinds of philosophical anthropology—from a static ontology into the psychology of human beings living in a definite historical epoch.

The difficulties confronted in the application of these concepts of history are multiplied in this context by their negative relation to psychology. I have just described the tendency of contemporary phenomenology to transfer the tasks of psychology to an ontology divorced from scientific criteria. The attitude of Kantianism toward our question has changed little since Fichte's assertion that psychology "is nothing."[2] Rickert, the historical theorist of neo-Kantianism, considers the hopes "that have been placed in an advancement of historical science through psychology or indeed through psychologism" to be evidence of a type of thought "to which the logical essence of history remains completely alien."[3] Instead of proceeding from contemporary philosophy's conception of history, therefore, I would like to proceed from a philosophy of history familiar to you all—namely, the Hegelian. After indicating its relation to psychology, the latter's role in the economic conception of history must be elaborated in some detail. I hope that a discussion of the problem on the basis of this theory may be fruitful even for those among you who see historical questions from the perspective of a subjectivistic philosophy.

Philosophical reflection has to do with insight into the unified dynamic structure of the bewildering multiplicity of events. From Hegel's perspective, this task is impossible without the exact knowledge of the Idea and its moments which derives from dialectical logic, for philosophical consideration of history is nothing but the application to the human world of the conviction that the Idea has the power to realize and develop itself in reality. In this process, philosophers of history acquire from empirical history not merely their raw material, but extensive elements of its historical construction as well. According to Hegel, natural scientists do not merely deliver to philosophers of nature a listing of facts; rather, they approach and anticipate the latter by way of the theoretical formulation of their knowledge. Likewise, *Historie* offers the philosophy of history—beyond mere knowledge of the actual events—basic organizing principles such as the original conditions, the periods, the division of historically acting human beings into races, tribes, and nations. But the periods gain their living meaning only when we grasp them as epochs of the Idea in its self-development. Only when the world-historical nation shows itself to be the bearer of a new, unique principle more adequate to the Idea does it grow from an ordering concept into a meaningful reality; its spirit [*Geist*], the spirit of a people [*Volksgeist*], grows from a collection of peculiarities into a metaphysical power, and the struggles among nations grow from deplorable acts with an arbitrary outcome into a world-historical tribune [*Weltgericht*] realizing itself in the contradictions.

Hegel takes this interplay of empirical *Historie* and philosophy of history quite seriously. He wants neither to interpret empirical history after the fact from a standpoint external to it, nor to measure it against an alien standard. His concept of reason is rather so little abstract that, for instance, the meaning of the moment of freedom as it appears in the *Logic* can only be defined adequately in terms of the bourgeois freedom in the state documented by historians. One can only comprehend freedom in general if one knows that the freedom under examination in the *Logic* is the very same freedom that was realized by a single individual in the oriental despotisms and by only a few Greeks, and which thus stands in contradiction to slavery. The Hegelian system is really a circle; the most abstract ideas of the *Logic* are only realized to the extent that the age is realized—that is, to the extent that the essence of the future is anticipated in the determination of the essence of the present. The exhaustion of a belief in the present—and the intention to undertake its radical transformation—must therefore sublate [*aufheben*] the Hegelian system as a system to which closure was intrinsic, at least in its later form. And this must occur in a manner irreconcilable with the principles of that system.

The significance of psychology for historical knowledge has thus been transformed. For Hegel, as well as for any French Enlightenment thinker, the drives and passions of human beings are the immediate motor of history. Human beings act as their interests determine them to act, and heroes have no more "consciousness of the general Idea" than do the masses.[4] Rather, their own political and other purposes are what count; human beings are determined by their drives. But according to Hegel (and in contrast to the Enlightenment), to pursue the psychic structure of such human beings is unimportant, because the real force that realizes itself in history is comprehensible on the basis of neither the individual psyche nor the mass psyche. Hegel asserts that "great historical men" draw "from a concealed fount—one which has not attained to phenomenal, present existence—from that inner Spirit, still hidden beneath the surface, which, impinging on the outer world as on a shell, bursts it into pieces, because it is another kernel than that which belonged to the shell in question."[5] He refers here not to the unconscious of modern psychology but rather to the Idea itself—that is, that immanent telos of history that can be grasped not through psychology but through philosophy. According to that telos, results are not merely results but testimony to the power of reason; likewise, historical knowledge is not the mere establishment of facts and the most comprehensive possible explanation of events, but knowledge of God.

After the collapse of the Hegelian system, the liberal world view once again assumed partial dominance. It dismissed, along with the belief in the power of an Idea operating in history, the notion of overarching dynamic historical structures, and made self-interested individuals the ultimate independent units in the historical process. Correspondingly, the liberal conception of history is fundamentally psychological. The individuals, with certain eternal drives firmly fixed in their nature, are no longer merely the immediate actors of history, but ultimately the standard against which any theory of processes occurring in social reality must henceforth be measured. Liberalism was of course incapable of solving the problem of how, despite this chaotic foundation of social life, society as a whole could exist—or, of course, of how its life is increasingly damaged by this foundation. The eighteenth-century belief in progress—that the drives of individuals would necessarily lead to the unity of culture once feudal restraints were abolished—was transformed in nineteenth-century liberalism into the dogma of a harmony of interests.

Marx and Engels, however, took up the dialectic in a materialist sense. They remained faithful to Hegel's belief in the existence of supraindividual dynamic structures and tendencies in historical development, but rejected the belief in an independent spiritual power operating in history. According to them, there is nothing at the root of history, and nothing is expressed in history that could be interpreted as comprehensive meaning, as unifying force, as motivating Reason, as immanent telos. The trust in the existence of such a core of history is, in their view, rather the accessory of an inverted idealist philosophy. Thought, and thus concepts and ideas, are modes of functioning of human beings, and not independent forces. There is no comprehensive idea coming to itself in history, for there is no Spirit independent of human beings. Human beings with their consciousness—despite all their knowledge, their memory, their tradition, and their spontaneity, despite their culture and their intellect [Geist]—are transitory; all things come and go.

But this hardly leads Marx to a psychologistic theory of history. According to him, historically acting human beings are never comprehensible simply on the basis of their internal selves, whether of their nature or of some ground of Being to be discovered in themselves. Rather, human beings are bound up in historical formations with dynamics of their own. In methodological terms, Marx here follows Hegel. Hegel had asserted the existence of unique structural principles in each great historical epoch: the principles of the constitutions of the various peoples change in accordance with an inner lawfulness; nations confront each other in the struggles of world history and suffer their fate, without its cause being discernible in the psyche of various individuals or even of a majority of them. While Hegel's dialectic is articulated by way of the logic of absolute Spirit—that is, by way of metaphysics—Marx insists that no insight logically prior to history offers the key to its understanding. Instead, the correct theory derives from consideration of human beings living under definite conditions and sustaining themselves with the aid of specific tools. Such lawfulness as history may reveal is neither an a priori construction nor the registering of facts by a knowing subject conceived as independent;

rather, that lawfulness is produced by thought, itself drawn into historical praxis, as the reflection of the dynamic structure of history.

The economic or materialist conception of history, which grew out of this attitude, thus reveals itself as both the antithesis and the continuation of Hegelian philosophy. In the latter, history is constituted in essence by the struggle for domination among the world-historical empires. For the individuals as well as for peoples and states, the issue is thus not Spirit but their own power. Despite this unconscious quality, the outcome of the struggles is not without spiritual meaning. Hegel thus calls world history the world's court of judgment [*Weltgericht*];[6] this follows from his tenet that the nation [*Volk*] that assumes dominance is always the one whose inner constitution represents a more concrete form of freedom than does that of the defeated people. The extent to which the states have developed toward "the image and actuality of reason"[7] determines their victory. Yet Hegel never explains how this sequence, corresponding to the logic of absolute Spirit, actually realizes itself in acts of war: how, in other words, the people whose state constitutes a more adequate representation of the Idea and its moments must also have the better strategy and superior arms. It appears instead as one of the prestabilized harmonies that necessarily go along with idealist philosophy. Insofar as scientific research into the series of mediating conditions is capable of putting recognized historical connections in the place of merely asserted parallelisms, the myth of the "cunning of reason" (and hence also the metaphysical centerpiece of this philosophy of history) becomes obsolete. We then learn the real reasons why the more differentiated forms of state and society have supplanted the more underdeveloped—that is, in Hegel's terms, the causes of progress in the consciousness of freedom. Knowledge of the real connections dethrones Spirit as the force autonomously shaping history, and installs as the motor of history the dialectic between obsolete forms of society and the various human powers maturing in the struggle with nature.

The economic conception of history completes this shift from metaphysics to scientific theory. That conception holds that the maintenance and reproduction of social life forces upon human beings a definite social order. Conditioning not merely the political and legal institutions but the higher domains of culture, this order is given to human beings through the various functions that must be carried out in the context of the economic process corresponding to the human capacities of a certain period. The fact, for instance, that ancient Roman society was divided into free and slave, the Middle Ages into lords and serfs, the industrial system into entrepreneurs and workers—as well as the differentiation of these relations within states, the cleavage into nations, and the conflicts between national power groups—all of this is explicable in terms neither of good or evil intentions nor of a unitary spiritual principle, but rather in terms of the requirements of the material life process in its various stages of development. Relations of dependency and the corresponding juridical and political apparatuses arise according to the level of technical development of the tools and forms of cooperation among human beings—that is, according to the mode of production. While the growth of human productive capacities may make possible a new mode of production that could serve the whole of society better than the old, the existence of the given social structure with its corresponding institutions and entrenched human dispositions initially inhibits its diffusion as the dominant mode. Thus arise the social tensions that are expressed in historical struggles and that form, so to speak, the basic theme of world history.

This conception of history can be transformed into a closed, dogmatic metaphysics if concrete investigations of the contradiction between growing human capacities and the social structure—which reveals itself in this connection as the motor of history—are replaced by a universal interpretive scheme, or if that contradiction is inflated into a force that shapes the future as a matter of necessity. If, however, this conception of history is understood as the correct theory of the known historical process, though still subordinate to the epistemological problem of theory as such, it constitutes a formulation of historical experience consistent with contemporary knowledge. In attempting to determine its relation to psychology, it becomes clear that—in contrast to the liberal view—this conception is not psychological. To be consistent, liberalism must explain history as the interplay of isolated individuals and their essentially invariant psychical forces: their interests. If, however, history is divided according to the various modes in which the life process of human society takes place, then economic rather than psychological categories are historically fundamental.

Rather than a foundational science, psychology becomes instead an indispensable auxiliary science for history. Its content is influenced by this transformation of function. In the context of this theory, its object loses its unitary quality. Psychology no longer has to do with human beings as such. Rather, it must differentiate within each epoch the total spiritual [*seelische*] powers available within individuals—the strivings at the root of their physical and intellectual efforts, and the spiritual factors that enrich the social and individual life process—from those relatively static psychic characteristics of individuals, groups, classes, races, and nations that are determined by the overall social structure: in short, from their character.

However much the object of psychology may be interwoven with history, the role of individuals may not therefore be dissolved into mere functions of economic relationships. The theory denies the significance neither of world-historical personalities nor of the psychical constitution of the members of different social groups. The replacement of inferior modes of production by ones more differentiated and better adapted to the needs of the people as a whole represents, so to speak, the skeleton of the history that interests us. That insight is the summary expression for human activity. The corresponding claim that culture depends upon the manner in which the life process of a society, its confrontation with nature, takes place—that, indeed, every aspect of culture carries within it the index of those fundamental relationships and that the consciousness of human beings changes along with changes in their economic activity—in no way denies human initiative. Rather, this approach attempts to offer insight into the forms and conditions of its historical efficacy. Human activity must, of course, connect in each case with the exigencies handed down by preceding generations. But the human efforts directed toward both the maintenance and the transformation of given relations have particular qualities that psychology must investigate. It is above all in this sense that the concepts of the economic theory of history distinguish themselves decisively from the metaphysical: they attempt to mirror the historical dynamic in its most definite form, but offer no ultimate view of the totality. To the contrary, they contain points of departure for further investigations, the results of which affect the theory itself.

This is especially true of psychology. The theoretical claim that the historical action of human beings and human groups is determined by the economic process can only be validated in detail by way of the scientific elucidation of the modes of response characteristic of a definite historical stage of development. It remains unknown precisely how structural economic changes that affect the psychic constitution prevailing among the members of different social groups in a given period transform their overall life expressions [*Lebensäusserungen*]. Thus the claim that the latter depends upon the former contains dogmatic elements that seriously undermine its hypothetical value for explaining the present. The disclosure of psychical mediations between economic and cultural development certainly allows us to maintain that radical economic changes precipitate radical cultural changes. Yet it may lead not merely to a critique of the conception of the functional relations between the two, but indeed to a strengthening of the suspicion that the sequence may be changed or reversed in the future. In that case, the priority of economics and psychology with respect to history would have to change. Moreover, it then becomes clear that the conception of history under discussion here considers the hierarchy of the sciences and thus also its own theses—as well as the drives of human beings themselves—as falling within its purview.

The real circumstance, however, that determines the relation of the two sciences at present is reflected in the contemporary form of psychology. That human beings sustain economic relationships which their powers and needs have made obsolete, instead of replacing them with a higher and more rational form of organization, is only possible because the action of numerically significant social strata is determined not by knowledge [*Erkenntnis*] but by a drive structure that leads to false consciousness. Mere ideological machinations are hardly the only roots of this historically crucial moment; this is the type of interpretation one might associate with the rationalistic anthropology of the Enlightenment and its historical situation. Rather, the overall psychic structure of these groups—that is, the character of their members— is continuously renewed in connection with their role in the economic process. Psychology must therefore penetrate to these deeper psychic factors by means of which the economy conditions human beings; it must become largely the psychology of the unconscious. In this form, determined by given social relations, it cannot be applied to the action of the various social strata in the same way. The more the historical action of human beings and groups is motivated by insight, the less the historian needs to revert to psychological explanations. Hegel's contempt for the psychological interpretation of heroes finds its justification here. The less, however, action derives from insight into reality—indeed, the more it contradicts such insight—the more necessary it is to uncover psychologically the irrational powers that determine human compulsions.

The characterization of psychology as an auxiliary science of history is grounded in the fact that every society that has ever held sway on earth is based on a definite level of development of human powers and is thus psychologically codetermined. The functioning of an already-existing society and the maintenance of currently declining forms of organization depend, among other things, upon psychic factors. In the analysis of a historical epoch it is especially important to know the psychic powers and dispositions, the character and mutability of the members of different social groups. Yet psychology does not thus become mass psychology; rather, it gains its insights from the investigation of individuals. "The individual psyche always remains the foundation of social psychology."[8] There exists neither a mass soul nor a mass consciousness. The vulgar concept of the "mass" seems to have been shaped by observations of crowds during tumultuous events. While human beings may react stereotypically when they are part of such accidental groups, comprehension of these reactions is to be sought in the psyche of the individuals constituting them, which is itself determined by the fate of the social group of which they are members. A differentiated group psychology—that is, inquiry into those instinctual mechanisms common to members of the important groups in the production process—takes the place of mass psychology. Above all, this group psychology must investigate the extent to which the function of the individual in the production process is determined by the individual's fate in a certain kind of family, by the effect of socialization at this point in social space, but also by the way in which the individual's own labor in the economy shapes the forms of character and consciousness. It is necessary to investigate the genesis of psychic mechanisms that make it possible to keep latent the tensions between social classes that lead to conflicts on the basis of the economic situation. Though in many discussions of psychology there is much talk of leaders and masses, the loyalty of an unorganized mass to an individual leader is in fact a less significant historical relationship than the trust of social groups in the stability and necessity of the given hierarchy and the social powers-that-be. Psychology has observed that "all successful social organizations, whether democratic or aristocratic, have the effect of bringing a dominant, coherent, individual purpose more purely, less changed and more deeply, more surely, and more directly into the minds of society's members," and that in the absence of such organization the leader of an uprising can never completely command his people, while in contrast the general can almost always do so.[9] But this approach, which takes the relationship between leader and mass as a special problem, remains in need of psychological sophistication.[10] The concept of *"habitude,"* to which French research ascribes an important function in the treatment of social-psychological questions, superbly describes the result of the process of socialization [*Bildungsprozess*]: the strength of the psychological dispositions that lead to the social action demanded of individuals. But this must be pursued more deeply in order to understand the origin of this outcome, its reproduction, and its continuous adaptation to changing social processes. This is only possible on the basis of insights gained from the analysis of individuals.

The adaptability of the members of a social group to their economic situation is especially important among the methodological guidelines of a psychology useful for history. The various psychological mechanisms that continuously make possible this adaptation have themselves developed historically, of course, but they must be assumed as given in the explanation of specific historical events; those mechanisms then constitute part of the psychology of the current epoch. Here must be included, for instance, the capacity of human beings to see the world in such a way that the satisfaction of the interests deriving from a group's economic situation is in harmony with the essence of things—in other words, to see the world as rooted in an objective morality [*Moral*]. Such an orientation need not develop so rationally that distortion and lying are necessary. On the basis of their psychical apparatus, human beings tend to take account of the world in such a way that their action can accord with their knowledge. In his discussion of "schematism," the essential achievement of which consists in the overall preformation of our impressions before their assimilation into empirical consciousness, Kant spoke of a hidden art in the depths of the human soul "whose real modes of activity nature is hardly likely ever to allow us to discover, and to have open to our gaze."[11] Psychology must explain that particular preformation, however, which has as its consequence the harmony of world views with the action demanded by the economy; it is even possible that something of the "schematism" referred to by Kant might be discerned in the process. For its function of bringing the world into consciousness in such a manner that the world is subsequently absorbed by the mathematical and mechanical categories of natural science appears to be a historically conditioned psychical effect—irrespective of how such categories are determined.

The grounding of some psychological systems in a rationalistic utilitarianism has justifiably contributed to the mistrust with which many historians approach psychology in the first place. According to this perspective, human beings supposedly act exclusively on the basis of their material advantage. Such psychological considerations have been decisive for liberal political economy [*Nationalökonomie*], not only in the sense of working hypotheses, but predominantly so. To be sure, private interests play in the societies of certain periods a role that can hardly be overestimated. But the analogue to this psychological abstraction in real, active human beings—namely economic egoism—is historically conditioned and subject to radical change, just like the social situation that this principle is supposed to explain. The proponents as well as the opponents of an egoistic theory of human nature are incorrect to hinge their arguments concerning the possibility of a nonindividualistic economic order on the general validity of such a problematic principle. Modern psychology has long since identified the error of asserting that the human instinct of self-preservation is "natural," as well as of introducing so-called "central" factors to derive from it manifestly unrelated individual and social deeds. Human beings—and probably animals as well—are hardly so psychologically individualistic that all their instinctual impulses are necessarily founded in immediate desire for material gratifications. Human beings may, for instance, experience a sort of happiness in the solidarity with like-minded souls that makes it possible for them to assume the risk of suffering and death. Wars and revolutions offer the most tangible example here. Nonegoistic instinctual impulses have existed during all periods, and are not denied factually by any serious psychology; at worst, problematic attempts have been made to trace them back to

individualistic motives. In the face of this economistic misrepresenta-
tion of the theory of human nature by certain psychological and
philosophical tendencies, some sociologists have tried to come up with
their own theory of instincts. In contrast to the utilitarian theory, which
attempts to explain everything on the basis of one point, however,
these approaches tend to draw up great lists of instincts and drives
which are seen as equiprimordial, and to neglect the specifically psychological relations.[12]

In any case, the actions of human beings derive not simply from
their striving for physical self-preservation, nor simply from their immediate sexual drive, but rather also from the needs to employ their
aggressive powers, to gain recognition and affirmation as persons, to
find security in a collectivity, and from other drives as well. Modern
psychology (Freud) has shown that such demands are distinguished
from hunger, which requires a more direct and more continuous satisfaction, while the others admit of being delayed, reshaped, and satisfied in fantasy. Connections exist, however, between the two types
of instinctual impulses—the immutable and the "plastic"—that are of
great importance in historical development. Despite their greater ur-
gency, inadequate satisfaction of the immediately physical needs can
partially and temporarily be replaced by satisfying other kinds of desires. *Circenses* of all kinds have in many historical situations taken the
place of *panis,* and the study of the psychological mechanisms that
make this possible—along with their skilled application to the explanation of the concrete historical process—is an urgent task that psychology must fulfill in the context of historical research.

In this effort, the economistic principle could only cause damage. The participation of lower social strata in actions of the larger
society from which they can expect no economic improvement (such
as wars) might thus mistakenly be explained, via theoretical legerde-
main, on the basis of material aims. Such an explanation misses the
great psychic meaning for human beings of membership in a respected and powerful collectivity, where their upbringing has taught
them to desire personal efficacy, mobility, and a secure existence, and
where the realization of these values has been made impossible by
their social situation. Satisfying work that raises self-respect allows
physical sacrifices to be borne more lightly, and even the simple
awareness of success can largely compensate for the unpleasantness

of inadequate nutrition. To the extent that human beings are denied this compensation for an oppressive material existence, the identification in fantasy with a supraindividual collectivity that affords respect and success becomes profoundly important. Our understanding of a variety of world-historical phenomena would be much enhanced if psychology could demonstrate that the satisfaction of these needs is a psychical reality no less intense than that of material gratifications.

I offer another example of the role of psychology in the context of the theory of history. The differentiated processes and conflicts in the consciousness of refined individuals—the phenomena of their consciences—are a product of the economic division of labor to the extent that those individuals are removed from the crude tasks necessary for the reproduction of society. Although their lives as they lead them depend upon the existence of prisons and slaughterhouses and the execution of a whole series of labors whose performance under current arrangements is unthinkable without brutality, they can repress these processes from their consciousness due to their social distance from the coarser aspects of the life process. Their mental apparatus is capable of reacting in such a refined manner that an insignificant moral conflict in their own lives can result in the greatest upsets. Both their conscious reaction and difficulties and the mechanism of repression must be grasped by psychology; the condition of existence of these phenomena, however, is economic. The economic appears as the comprehensive and primary category, but recognizing its conditionedness, investigating the mediating processes themselves, and thus also grasping the results depend upon psychological work.

The rejection of a psychology rooted in economistic prejudices should not distract us, however, from the fact that the economic situation affects the most minute aspects of human inner life. The strength as well as the content of the eruptions of the psychic apparatus are economically conditioned. In the face of the slightest annoyance or of an insignificant but pleasant change of pace, certain relationships give rise to mood swings of an intensity hardly comprehensible to the outside observer. Reduction of one's life to a restricted sphere leads to a corresponding distribution of love and desire that reacts back upon and qualitatively influences character. In contrast, more favorable situations in the production process, such as the management of large industries, afford so broad an overview that pleasures and distresses that would entail great shifts in the lives of other human beings become irrelevant. Moral conceptions and world views, held rigidly by and determining the lives of those for whom social connections are not visible, are surveyed from the vantage of high economic positions in their conditioning and vicissitudes, so that their rigid character dissolves. Even if we assume that inborn psychic differences are extremely great, the structure of fundamental interests stamped upon individuals from childhood onward by their fate—the horizon prescribed to them by their function in society—only rarely permits the uninterrupted development of those original differences. The chances for such development themselves vary according to the social stratum to which the individual belongs. Above all, intelligence and a series of other talents may develop more easily if their situation in life puts fewer hindrances in their way from the very beginning. The present is characterized more by the unrecognized effect of economic relationships on the overall shaping of a life than it is by conscious economic motives.

To Dilthey we owe the honor of having made the relation between psychology and history the object of philosophical discussion. In the course of his work he repeatedly returned to this problem. He demanded a new psychology that would accommodate the needs of the human sciences and overcome the weakness of academic psychology. In his view, the development of the individual human sciences is bound up with the development of psychology; without the psychic [seelische] context in which their objects are grounded, the human sciences constitute "an aggregate, a bundle, [but] not a system."[13] "This is so," he writes, "and no departmentalization can prevent it; the systems of culture, commerce, law, religion, art, and scholarship and the outer organization of society in family, community, church, and state originated from the living context of the human mind and, ultimately, can only be understood through it. Mental facts form their most important constituents so they cannot be grasped without psychological analysis."[14] Even though for Dilthey psychology functions as an auxiliary science to history, the latter is itself in essence a means to understanding human beings. It is his firm conviction that the unitary human essence originally given in every individual unfolds itself in its various aspects in the great historical cultures; the representative personalities of each epoch are for him only the best expressions of each of these various aspects. "Races, nations, social classes, occupations, historical stages, individualities: all these are . . . distinctions of the individual aspects within a uniform human nature"[15] that reveals itself in a particular way in each epoch.

However justified Dilthey's research into a psychology adequate to the needs of historical scholarship, it hardly seems correct that the cultural systems of an epoch are rooted in a unified mental context, and that this thoroughly understandable [*verständliche*] context represents an aspect of a human essence that first gains expression in the overall development of history. This unity of cultural systems in a single epoch and in all epochs must be in essence an intellectual [*geistige*] unity, for otherwise its expressions could not be asserted to be comprehensible and accessible to the methods of an interpretive psychology. The psychology demanded by Dilthey is indeed an interpretive psychology [*Psychologie des Verstehens*], and history is thus transformed in his philosophy essentially into intellectual history. As I have argued in the foregoing, neither an epoch nor so-called world history, indeed not even the history of the individual spheres of culture, can be understood in terms of such a unity, even if some elements of, say, the history of philosophy—perhaps as a legacy of the pre-Socratics—may be characterized by a unitary intellectual thread. Historical transformations are drenched with the mental and the intellectual; individuals in their groups and within variously conditioned social antagonisms are mental entities, and history thus needs psychology. But it would be a grave error to seek to grasp any facet of history on the basis of some unitary mental life of a universal human nature.

An understanding of history as the history of ideas tends also to be bound up with the belief that human beings are essentially identical to that which they themselves see, feel, judge—in short, with their consciousness of themselves. This confusion of the task of the cultural scientist [*Geisteswissenschaftler*] with that of the economist, the sociologist, the psychologist, the physiologist, and others derives from an idealist tradition, but constitutes a narrowing of the historical horizon that can hardly be squared with the status of contemporary knowledge. What is true of individuals is also true of humanity in general: if one wishes to know what they are, one cannot believe what they think of themselves.

I have only been able to offer here a few remarks concerning the logical place of psychology in a theory of history adequate to the contemporary situation. Despite the orientation to the economic conception, this approach could hardly be outlined satisfactorily. Still, the question of the general significance of detailed psychological work for historical research is important, because psychological problems are in principle ignored by many sociologists and historians, and above all because a primitive psychology may thus play an uncontrolled role in much historical writing. Psychology also has a special significance in the current period—a significance which may, however, prove ephemeral. With the quickening of economic development, changes in the modes of human response that are immediately conditioned by the economy—that is, the habits, fashions, and moral and aesthetic notions emerging directly from economic life—can shift so rapidly that they do not have the time to establish themselves and become fully developed characteristics of human beings. Under these circumstances, the relatively permanent elements in the mental structure— and thus general psychology—gain greater weight. In more stable periods, the mere differentiation of social character types seems to suffice; at present, psychology tends to become the most important source for learning something about human modes of being. In critical moments, therefore, the psyche becomes a more decisive factor than is usually the case—for economic factors alone do not dictate whether and in what sense the moral constitution of the members of different social classes in the period just surpassed is maintained or changed.

The meaning of neither problems nor theories is independent of the historical situation and of the role an individual plays in it. This is also true of the economic conception of history: there may be individuals to whom history turns another side, or for whom it seems to have no structure whatsoever. In that case, it is difficult to achieve consensus in these questions, and not merely because of the variety of material interests, but rather because, despite the parallelism, theoretical interests also lead in different directions. But this concerns the difficulty of agreement, not the unity of truth. The great variety of interests notwithstanding, the subjective element in human beings that must be understood is not their arbitrariness. Instead, it is their capacities, their upbringing, their labor—in short, their own history—which must be grasped in connection with the history of society.

A New Concept of Ideology?

With the incorporation of the teachings of Karl Marx into contemporary social science, the intention of his basic concepts is being transformed into its opposite. Their usefulness consists essentially in the unified explanation of social movements in terms of the class relationships determined by economic development. The aim of his theoretical work was the transformation of specific social conditions, not knowledge of a "totality" or of a total and absolute truth. In this connection, Marx criticized philosophy as well, but he put no new metaphysics in place of the old.

The discussion of Marxist theory in Germany has taken on substantial proportions in the past several decades. A recent, particularly acute attempt to include some of its concepts in a purely philosophical investigation is to be found in the works of Karl Mannheim, especially in his book *Ideology and Utopia*.[1] The book has justifiably met with broad critical acclaim, for it offers a particularly astute example of how these increasingly explosive questions are being treated today. I would like here to contribute to this effort by analyzing Mannheim's concept of ideology.

According to Mannheim, the task of the sociology of knowledge is to transform the theory of ideology from the "intellectual armament of a party" into a "sociological history of thought" above parties (78). In his interpretation, the achievement of the concept of ideology thus far has been to discredit the views of one's political opponents by reference to their social determination. But now that one can no longer avoid recognition of the "situational determination" of one's own intellectual standpoint, the concept has become a general tool of knowledge according to which the past can be investigated anew, and with which the crisis-ridden intellectual situation of the present can be assessed. The science of the social ascription of ideas which thus emerges, he argues, constitutes the only way out of the intellectual crisis of our time—a time in which faith in the unconditional validity of the various world views has been fundamentally shaken (98–99, n. 32).

At the beginning of this new sociology of knowledge stands a new concept of ideology, the history of which Mannheim sets out to describe. A "metaphysical orientation" developed, probably in political praxis, which suspects that the individual ideas of one's opponents are deceptions that serve their interest. In time, according to Mannheim, this suspicion becomes pervasive. It concerns not the form but only the contents of the opposing thought, which he explains psychologically in terms of self-interest. If the accusation of "ideology" extends no further than asserting that "this or that interest is the cause of a given deception or lie," Mannheim calls it "particular." In comparison with this "particular" concept of ideology, the "total" concept, which calls into question "the opponent's total *Weltanschauung* (including his conceptual apparatus)," constitutes an important advance (56ff.). According to Kant, in whose philosophy of consciousness this new concept is said to be grounded theoretically, the whole of our experience is formed by the active application of the elements of our understanding, and is not the mirror of an independently existing world. In this sense, the total concept of ideology also asserts that the structure of a world view is dependent upon the subject. But the subject no longer perceives unconditionally and generally, as with Kant; rather, the subject's entire perceptual apparatus and all categories and forms of perception are determined by historical and sociological conditions. Not just certain contents but indeed a definite way of knowing—and, accordingly, of judging and acting—are said to "correspond" with the situation of a social group. In contrast to the particular concept of ideology, in which real human beings with their interests are examined for the explanation of their ideas, the total concept refers to an "ascribed subject" [*Zurechnungssubjekt*], that is, an ideal mode of perception that belongs according to its meaning to the position of a given group in a society (59).[2] If the originally philosophical intention of the total concept of ideology is joined to the political intention of the particular concept, it is no longer isolated ideas that come under attack; instead, the charge of false consciousness is decisively generalized.

Previously, one's adversary, as the representative of a certain political-social position, was accused of conscious or unconscious falsification. Now, however, the critique is more thoroughgoing in that, having discredited the total structure of his consciousness, we consider him no longer capable of thinking correctly. This simple observation means, in the light of a structural analysis of thought, that in earlier attempts to discover the sources of error, distortion was uncovered only on the psychological plane by pointing out the personal roots of intellectual bias. The annihilation is now more thoroughgoing since the attack is made on the noological level and the validity of the adversary's theories is undermined by showing that they are merely a function of the generally prevailing social situation (69).

According to Mannheim, the total concept of ideology makes its first appearance as the concept of class consciousness in Marxism. But, he claims, it is only now that the courage has been found to think it through to its conclusions. As long as class-bound false thought is sought only in the camp of the opposition, and one's own position is not recognized as ideological, the problem of ideology has not been put consistently, but instead has been restricted unjustifiably. Accordingly, Mannheim wants to oppose a "general" version of the total concept of ideology to the "special" version beyond which Marxism has not reached. Because not only bourgeois consciousness but that of *every* social group is dependent upon social circumstances in its content and form, not even Marxism may lay claim to unrestricted validity (77).

The application of the general total concept of ideology, which is of fundamental importance for Mannheim's sociology of knowledge, is said not to entail philosophical relativism (for reasons to be discussed below). The concept is only meant to show that all thought is "situationally determined," that is, that it is "rooted" in a definite social situation. To every group there conforms a cognitive totality, the various aspects of which relate thoroughly to one another and to its historical foundation. This fundamental "reference of all elements of meaning in a given situation to one another and the fact that they derive their significance from this reciprocal interrelationship in a given frame of thought [M.]" Mannheim calls "relationism" (86). Sociologists of knowledge can investigate these relationships in their historical rise and decline without having to take sides for one or the other of the systems of thought and judgment. They may be content with considering the history of the various views which laid claim to truth and with showing how, "in the whole history of thought, certain intellectual standpoints are connected with certain forms of experience, and with tracing the intimate connection between the two in the course of social and intellectual change [M.]" (81).

According to Mannheim, this "value-free" application of the developed concept of ideology pushes beyond itself dialectically and leads to a new division of systems of thought with respect to their truth content. Whereas philosophy had previously distinguished a certain view from all others as the true theory of reality as a whole, Mannheim is convinced that, in consequence of the continuous transformation of reality, a system valid in the past could become a fateful falsehood. Research in the sociology of knowledge, he claims, has shown that forms of consciousness may persist when the social situation to which they were appropriate has changed. Given this lack of correspondence between the existential foundations and the life span of the systems of thought ascribed to them, there are at any given time various ways of interpreting the world. Some of these are appropriate to the social reality and prove themselves therein, others are obsolete, and still others (as "utopias") outdistance that reality (83ff.). The degree of this lack of correspondence provides sociologists of knowledge with a standard according to which they can distinguish "the true from the untrue, the genuine from the spurious among the norms, modes of thought, and patterns of behavior that exist *alongside one another in a given historical period*" (94).[3]

Thus those demands that are precisely attainable would be true or genuine "in ethical terms"; in "the moral interpretation of one's own action," true or genuine would be an attitude which neither obscures nor prevents the "adjustment and transformation of man"; in theoretical terms, true or genuine would be those views with which one could orient oneself in the given reality. In essence, then, *false* consciousness is to be distinguished from correct consciousness in that its norms and modes of thought are "antiquated" and that it "conceal[s] the actual meaning of conduct rather than . . . revealing it" (95). Since according to this theory the truth content of every consciousness is measured against a reality that never remains the same, the concept of ideology attains a more dynamic character at this level.

The "crisis" of the present is said to consist in the fact that each of the "systems of life that struggle against one another but that exist side by side" are to be grasped as "particular." To be sure, all of them claim to interpret adequately the whole of the world and of life—that is, to be definitively valid truths. But in reality, each and every one is a "situationally determined" partial view. This is not to be understood as saying that they deal with fundamentally different objects; in this case, one could simply combine together the most progressive among them into an overall theory. According to Mannheim, however, the diversity results from the circumstance that the facts are experienced in a given "context of life and thought," which differs according to the individual's social standpoint. The way in which something is experienced, the questioning and the mastery of a problem is said everywhere to contain a metaphysical presupposition, a "vital and intellectual commitment [M.]" (102), that corresponds to one of the many conflicting existential foundations in our fragmented present. If it is really true "that we hardly live in the same world of thought, that there are competing systems of thought which in the end no longer experience the same reality" (99), however, it becomes questionable to what extent one can speak of a common reality. Our peculiar predicament consists in the fact that we have access to an infinite number of scientific methods and individual observations—even if the crisis is said to have "penetrated even into the heart of empirical research" (102)—and yet, in the "questions of totality," we have completely lost the "somnambulistic certainty of more stable times" (102) due to the discovery of the "particularity" of all standpoints. The sociology of knowledge seeks to protect us from misunderstanding this reality; indeed, it strives to intensify this shattering of "values and contents" through the consistent application of its new concept of ideology to all past and present beliefs. But precisely in its unmasking of the dependence of all "styles of thought" on a mutable historical situation, it recognizes the spark "that should serve as an impetus to the type of thought required by the present situation" (99, n. 32). The sociology of knowledge refuses to allow any system of thought which understands itself as unconditional to exist in isolation. Instead, it comprehends each system on the basis of its historical presuppositions, thus practicing "sociological diagnosis of the times." The sociology of knowledge thus believes itself to be on the only plausible path to the "totality." According to Mannheim's philosophical conviction, the latter is to be grasped neither as the quintessence of all that is nor as a completely comprehensive theory. Rather, totality means "both the assimilation and transcendence of the limitations of particular points of view. It represents the continuous process of the expansion of knowledge, and has as its goal not achievement of a supra-temporally valid conclusion but the broadest possible extension of our horizon of vision" (106). The objective of the sociology of knowledge is to advance the cause of freeing human beings from their dependence on ephemeral certainties, and thus to disclose to them with the aid of history the evolution of their own being through a "situational report [M.]," which is to be based on intellectual history and which must constantly be revised.

In the context of the sociology of knowledge, the modern concept of ideology is put at the service of a task which contradicts the theory from which it derives. Marx wanted to transform philosophy into positive science and praxis; the sociology of knowledge pursues an ultimately *philosophical* intention. The sociology of knowledge is preoccupied with the problem of absolute truth, its form and its content; it sees its mission in the illumination of that problem. The effort to achieve ever deeper insight into the evolution of all metaphysical decisions with which human beings attempt to comprehend the world in its totality becomes itself a metaphysical undertaking. The possibility of gradually disclosing the essence of things gives this approach its sanctity. Those who were disappointed by the older metaphysics need not despair. To be sure, we have no final conception of truth valid for all times and for all human beings, but the sociological investigation of the fate of the world views that have emerged historically yields at each higher level a richer perspective on "reality" (103). Reality is to be understood principally as "the ascent of human beings." This process takes place and "becomes intelligible in the course of the variation in the norms, the forms, and the works of mankind, in the course of the change in institutions and collective aims, in the course of its changing assumptions and points of view, in terms of which each social-historical subject becomes aware of himself and acquires an appreciation of his past" (92). In the changing course of intellectual conceptions, in other words, the essence of humanity gradually reveals itself to the sociologist of knowledge.

In Mannheim's hands, the sociology of knowledge connects up with important aspects of Dilthey's philosophy of history. Dilthey, too, argues that there is no philosophical system that grasps the essence of the world in a generally valid way. Nonetheless, through investigation of the modes of conduct and systems which have arisen historically in all areas of culture, we can recognize ever more clearly the essence of humanity that expresses itself therein. He characterizes it as a "position close to my own" that one "can study the infinite content of human nature only in its development in history."[4] "Man knows himself only in history, never through introspection; indeed, we all seek him in history. . . . The individual always realizes only one of the possibilities in his development, which could always have taken a different turning whenever he had to make an important decision. Man is only given to us at all in terms of his realized possibilities. In the cultural systems, too, we seek an anthropologically determined structure in which an 'X' realizes himself. We call this human nature."[5]

Mannheim, however, expresses himself much less clearly than Dilthey, and argues only that "all the systems of meaning which constitute a given world are simply a historically determined and continuously shifting curtain, and that the development of humanity takes place either within or behind them [M.]" (85). At the same time, he also gives expression to the notion that the meaning to be discovered in history, which "imparts to the historical and the social its impetus [M.]" (92), is really the development of "humanity."

In Dilthey, this philosophy of history is entirely consistent with the rest of his doctrines. He is convinced that the development of the intellectual realms of culture is rooted not merely in society but equally "in the individual as such."[6] According to him, the deeds and creations of human beings of all times, peoples, and classes emanate from one and the same human "being," the essence of which all existing persons carry within themselves. He emphatically opposes a sociology which seeks the basis of the forms of spirit in the social life process; instead, philosophy, art, and religiosity are to be traced back to an ultimate creative principle. "If one could imagine a lone individual on earth, it would, given a life span of sufficient length, develop these functions in complete isolation."[7] During his time, psychology had only investigated humanity on the basis of its experimental subjects and reconstructed the whole of culture from the spiritual elements discerned thereby. In contrast, Dilthey's achievement consists in the fact that he made the history of ideas an important means for studying humanity.

This philosophical conviction seems appropriate to Dilthey's individualistic mode of thought; it is difficult to understand how Mannheim, as a sociologist, can speak of the "essence" of humanity, the development of which takes place behind or in cultural forms. Mannheim cannot possibly mean, as with Dilthey, that all human beings at all times have the same essence, that all individuals contain the same components and functions. Any such assertion which referred to the definite object "humanity" would certainly stand condemned before the tribunal of the "total, general, and dynamic" concept of ideology. However imprecisely Mannheim himself may express this view of the philosophy of history, his version indicates that research in the sociology of knowledge yields experience of an essence of humanity not determined by history. For him, too, genuine historical research is supposed to lead to knowledge of our own essence. Thus, like Dilthey's human science, Mannheim's sociology of knowledge reveals itself as an heir of classical idealist philosophy. The latter posited as the result of real, recorded history the self-knowing subject, which constituted for it the sole true, self-sufficient essence, and thus the "totality." But the idealist credo—according to which the subject, the essence "humanity," or some other real or ideal entity intrinsic to humanity is said to have absolute or exclusive priority over all else—comports no better with the comprehensive theory of ideology than any other "self-hypostatization." If we take Mannheim's theory of ideology seriously, then there is no adequate justification for claiming that, in a thoroughly conditioned and mutable reality, the "development of humanity" alone should occupy this exceptional position. Nor is it convincing to argue that, of all kinds of knowledge, the anthropological is not ideological. From a standpoint which claims "to discover the ideological element in all thinking" (84), Dilthey's belief in a "humanity" which unfolds in the course of history—the most progressive form of the idealist philosophy of history—must appear as the mere "absolutization" of a single situationally determined perception.

While the characterization of "the development of humanity" as the metaphysical reality to which the sociology of knowledge affords access is inadequate according to its own premises, the general claim remains that there exists a foundation of history outside history. This claim includes the corresponding notion that the true cause of human activity is a "realm beyond history," rather than mutable society (92). The denial in this claim is illuminating. All processes of which real history reports, all nations and classes with their deeds and fates, the famines, wars, economic crises, and revolutions, are not the "real" things toward which our investigations are directed. According to Mannheim, it would be mistaken to seek the true cause of these processes in the realm of the positive, or even in that of the determinately expressible. All factual matters are already determined by a "conceptual apparatus" which itself is determined and mutable. To imbue experience with validity as the true reality is said to be impossible because the standpoint from which we have these experiences prohibits, due to its inherent limitations, assertions of definitive truth—claims about reality "as such." Were we to attempt to disclose "reality" nonetheless, we would thus have to seek the traces of the extrahistorical in mundane history. Mannheim is thinking of this "essence," without the expectation of which "history is mute and meaningless," when he states that "something of profound significance does transpire in the realm of the historical" (93). If one disregards its metaphysics of "humanity" as such, the central idea of this sociology remains the dubious belief that all "standpoints and contents . . . are part of a meaningful overall process."[8]

Despite its indeterminacy, this meaning of history is more closely defined. It is the "ineffable element at which the mystics aim" (92)—in other words, if we understand correctly, the divine. One cannot name it or express it "directly," but it must "necessarily bear some relation" to that which actually takes place.

Mannheim himself speaks in this respect of a "point of view which is based without doubt on a particular attitude toward historical and social reality" (92). In any case, history is metaphysically transfigured by this attitude. Mannheim disputed like few other philosophers the possibility of an eternal essence sufficient unto itself; according to him, all meaning is bound to practice. But in this secularization of the sacred, it is not only in the language that the reference to metaphysical foundations remains. For the revolutionary idea that no standpoint can claim the certainty of eternal validity is qualified by the assertion that the ontological decisions according to which we experience and analyze facts increasingly reveal an overarching meaning.[9] Mannheim fails to reject the concepts of a metaphysics that transfigures the overall movement of history; indeed, despite all the criticism, he retains them in an unclear and vague form. This is hardly reconcilable with his own total concept of ideology. The assertion of a unified and at the same time positively evaluated meaning of history, which plays a decisive role in the construction of Mannheim's central concepts, connects his view with contemporary philosophy yet, like the latter, is rooted in Europe in Christian theology. But given Mannheim's sociology, can unity have a greater ontological probability than multiplicity—indeed, than chaos? Can the divine be more likely than the diabolical (such as Schopenhauer's blind world motive [Weltwille])? Why should that which we perceive from our restricted standpoint as the divine meaning not also prove to be a deceptive myth? This decisive question could be convincingly answered on the foundations of a theistic or pantheistic theology, which of course would have to reject the application of the concept of ideology to its own contents. Yet all of the terms with which Mannheim attempts either directly or indirectly to describe the "essence" belong to metaphysical systems whose validity it is precisely the intention of his theory of ideology to dispute. Whether the terms used to distinguish that essence from "a mere X" are "the ascent of human beings," "the ecstatic element in human experience which . . . is never directly revealed or expressed" (92), "the whole" (106), or "unity and meaning" (92), he is unable to reconcile them with his basic conception.

This revolutionary sociology, which dissolves everything "dynamically," requires the support of a dogmatic metaphysics. On the contrary, it sublates [aufhebt] the destruction of all philosophical investigation of absolute meaning by recommending itself as the latter's most progressive form. At the price of unfailing consistency—which he maintains in all other respects—Mannheim privileges the task of the metaphysician. Marx tried to overthrow the prestige of metaphysics with his concept of ideology. Insofar as the concept is not merely applied but deepened, generalized, and thought through to its conclusions and made more flexible, this new sociology seeks to reconcile it with that form of thought whose validity it was supposed to undermine. Marx correctly sought to do away with the conviction that there is some essence of being which pervades all epochs and societies and lends them their meaning. It was precisely this element of Hegelian philosophy that appeared to him to be an idealist illusion. Only human beings themselves—not the "essence" of humanity, but the real human beings in a definite historical moment, dependent upon each other and upon outer and inner nature—are the acting and suffering subjects of history. Only earthly creatures have a "fate"; one cannot sensibly say of either "spirit" or of any "essence" that the fates of "the historical and social . . . are somehow its fates as well" (92). Because the fates of human beings are extremely unequal and reveal no unified context of meaning either in different times or at the same time, indeed within the same people, Marx's theory calls it "ideology" to mitigate the real sufferings of economically underprivileged classes by asserting such a context.

Indeed, history as a whole cannot possibly be the expression of some meaningful whole. For history is the recapitulation of processes that arise from the contradictory relationships of human society. These processes reveal no spiritual or intellectual unity; they are not the effect of struggles between mere attitudes, positions, styles of thought, and systems. Instead, completely unequal human and extrahuman forces influence their development. Insofar as history does not emerge from the conscious direction of human beings determining it according to a plan, it has none. One can attempt to comprehend the various driving forces of a certain epoch under laws, but the assertion of a comprehensible meaning behind these facticities is founded upon philosophical poesy—whether it is really elaborated, as it is by Hegel, or merely asserted, as it is by Mannheim. It is central to Marxian materialism to give expression to the unsatisfactory condition of earthly reality as true being, and not to permit vague ideas of humanity to be hypostatized as Being in a higher sense. Materialism is the sworn enemy of every attempt to understand reality on the basis of some idealist paradise or of any purely intellectual order. After Marx, we are forbidden any such consolation about the world.

With Mannheim, by contrast, such a consoling idealist belief is not merely the central idea of his sociology, but the highest concern of all intellectual effort. Correspondingly, he repeatedly seeks to defend his theory against the charge of relativism. In contemporary logic, the charge was originally leveled against an epistemology that sought to derive logical principles from individual facts. Later, this accusation was extended to that theory which refuses to ascribe eternal truth to judgments about factual matters. In this broad form, the charge is only comprehensible from the standpoint of a static ontology, and it rests on an overextended concept of truth which maintains the universality of factual judgments—that is, their independence from the perceiving subject. In the meantime, this idea, too, has fallen into disrepute in philosophy.[10] Static ontology and a universalistic concept of truth have become untenable. For it is just as certain that all our ideas— the true ones as well as the false—depend upon conditions that may change, and that the notion of an eternal truth which outlives all perceiving subjects is unattainable. None of this affects the validity of science. For example, the statement that a definite form of nature would exist after the death of all human beings remains binding for us, and it would be equally false to imagine this nature in terms other than those of the logical and mathematical laws that we recognize from our determinate standpoint. Such statements, whose content concerns something that reaches beyond the lifetime of humanity, certainly express something about the relationship of humanity and nature on the basis of our theory of objective time, but nothing about the relation of truth and being in general. In other words, they are in no way connected with the fate of the overextended concept of truth. Those in science concerned with the accuracy of their judgments about spiritual matters, whether about the time until their death or about a later time, have nothing to hope for and nothing to fear from a fundamental decision concerning the problem of absolute truth. But Mannheim attempts to rescue his theory of ideology from the objection to this untenable concept of truth, which is intrinsic to his own view of the overarching meaning of history. He interprets the charge of relativism as itself relative before the judgment of eternal truth, and therefore as missing the mark. That epistemology which would characterize as relativistic an understanding of all standpoints as "particular," he argues, is itself merely particular.

The concept of particularity, which plays a central role in Mannheim's work, refers quite simply to the relationship of any given standpoint to eternal truth. It claims that every statement is inadequate to the latter due to the conditioned character of the speaker.

But the notion that the "situational determination" of any judgment should have any influence on its truth content is incoherent: why is the insight not just as situationally determined as the error? The sociology of knowledge—like every metaphysics—characterizes every standpoint *sub specie aeternitatis*. It claims not yet to have taken possession of eternal truth; rather, it considers itself merely on the way to its attainment.

When Mannheim evaluates beliefs according to their practical applicability, the undertaking is only loosely connected with this overextended concept of truth. This concern with pragmatic evaluation is also intended to parry the charge of relativism. But it is obvious that such an assessment of truth, which understands itself as determined, is inadequate to a philosophy for which relativism in this sense constitutes an accusation. This pragmatic conception, which confuses the contradiction between true and false with that of genuine and spurious (94), is reminiscent of *Lebensphilosophie*; the latter, however, shares "the at present widespread fear of relativism"[11] much less than does Mannheim himself.

Mannheim treats the most important aspects of the metamorphosis of his concept of ideology, as they have been set out above, as stages of a development that have led to a deepening and radicalization of the concept. There is indeed no doubt that he has "thought it out to its conclusions." The concept has become so generalized that it has gained the authority to deal with "questions of totality" in Mannheim's sense, but at the same time it has forfeited its determinate content. To think out a concept does not necessarily lead to making it a more refined tool of knowledge; if this were the case, the widespread contemporary practice of transforming concepts that have been fruitful in specific areas into world-embracing theories would have had greater success.

The determinate meaning of the concept of ideology is damaged by the first step that removes it from the realm of political critique. As we have seen, this step leads from the "particular" to the "total" ideology. It is easy to see how the "particular" concept of ideology contributes to the criticism of ideas. Wherever nations or classes have secured their domination through moral, metaphysical, or religious ideas rather than with mere force, these notions were ultimately vulnerable to attack by the dominated. The struggle against the cultural props of social conditions tends to engender and accompany political opposition in such a way that the distribution of the parties in the intellectual struggle corresponds to the political-economic interest situation. Accordingly, the discrediting of certain ideas, upon which an odious situation is based, supported, and mystified, is as old as these struggles themselves. Such an attack is characterized less by the Renaissance maxim advanced by Mannheim—that one thinks differently *in piazza* than *in palazzo*—than by the speech which Machiavelli puts in the mouth of the leader of a rebellion of the underclasses in his history of Florence: "If you will take note of the mode of proceeding of men, you will see that all those who come to great riches and great power have obtained them either by fraud or by force; and afterwards, to hide the ugliness of acquisition, they make it decent by applying the false title of earnings to things they have usurped by deceit or by violence."[12]

The total concept of ideology leaves behind isolated theories and evaluations of one's political opponents, dealing instead with their entire consciousness, "including their conceptual apparatus" (57). Our whole life context, everything we know, even if it influences our thought without being recognized as an "option," the smallest tidbits as well as the grand aspects of the context, ultimately the perceiving subject in its "totality," its entire "world motive" [*Weltwollen*], as Mannheim puts it, should be declared "ideological." It is asserted that every consciousness "corresponds to" a definite situation in history and in society, and thus its truth is to be doubted. Mannheim asserts that the attack is "radicalized" in that one disputes one's opponent's "capacity for correct thought." In reality, the attack is thus transformed from a determinate accusation into the unenlightening speech of a dogmatic philosopher. Neither interest nor any empirical facts whatsoever are supposed to serve as an explanation for the emergence and consolidation of a person's overall perspective; instead, an unadorned, unmediated "correspondence" is asserted. The fact that such a perspective represents a false consciousness must thus appear as fateful providence, as mystical destiny.

In this connection, Mannheim must reject not merely the old-style psychology of interest but contemporary psychology as well, insofar as the latter inherits the attempt to explain intellectual processes ultimately in terms of external necessity. He wants to replace

psychological findings with "an analysis of the correspondence between the situation to be known and the forms of knowledge" (58).
What he means by this is never clearly expressed.[13] As far as we understand him, the systems of *Weltanschauungen*—that is, the intellectual totalities—do not develop out of the actual life situation of human
beings, but rather are bound to definite social strata. To these systems
of *Weltanschauungen* belong a definite "economic motive" [*Wirtschafts-
wollen*], as well as a style of art, a style of thought, etc. According to
Mannheim, it would be incorrect to attempt to investigate the cognitive totality or its individual parts by reference to the social situation
conditioning its carriers. Rather, he seeks "correspondences of form"
between the social situation and the totality of a *Weltanschauung*, conceived in terms of an "ideal type." On the basis of certain peculiarities
of a style of thought or judgment, the consciousness of an individual
is ascribed to one of the ideal-typical "world postulates" [*Weltwollun-
gen*]. Finally, and once again on the basis of very vague considerations,
its origin in a social situation is "reconstructed." Even in Mannheim's
work, the concept of ideology has something to do with the problem
of truth; what can such "constructions" say about the truth, falsity, or
problematic nature of a consciousness?

Whether this "total" concept of ideology is supposed to comprehend the perceiving subject or a dubious ideal "world postulate," it
proves in every case to be an idealistic overextension, not unlike eternal truth and "the meaning of history." This overextension is rooted
in the notion of a "totality" of consciousness. When the total concept
of ideology refers to such a totality, it refers not to a mere sum but to
the totality in the sense of a superficial concept of the whole. Just as it
is said that all parts of an organism carry in themselves the mark of
the living being, the parts of consciousness are supposed to contain
the characteristics of the totality to which they belong. On the basis of
such formal elements as the "style" of thought and judgment, we are
supposed to be able to construct an ideal totality to which it is bound
by inner necessity. But the notion of consciousness as a unified whole
completely contradicts its unique character. The concept of totality,
conceived in terms regularly misunderstood outside the realm of Gestalt research, has proven fruitful in recent biology, and especially in
"Gestalt psychology." Here it has been possible to identify real events
that are governed by Gestalt laws. But the consciousness of a human

being and the historical "systems of *Weltanschauungen*" have no such characteristic. A simple perception and a complex scientific theory, an isolated emotion and the enduring attitude toward one's fellow human beings, are bound up with the particular relations under which they appear. To these relations belong not only the instinctual structure of the individual but the influence of the dead and the living environment as well. Changes in the environment of individuals do not take place on the basis of the same conditions as their personal development (which is, of course, influenced by those changes). Thus conscious experience necessarily emerges in any given situation, but it is the result of quite multifarious causes. On the basis of psychological experience—that is, given some understanding of how a certain kind of entity tends to react in certain situations—we can certainly hold well-founded expectations about what will take place in its consciousness in this or that case. But without particular attention to the relations of noncognitive reality, it is impossible to construct a unified "world motive" [*Weltwollen*] on the basis of knowledge concerning certain parts of consciousness, and from which one would be able to comprehend these parts as deriving from a unifying principle. The notion that one could understand a *Weltanschauung* purely on the basis of investigations of intellectual constructs, without consideration of the material conditions of their emergence and existence, is an idealist illusion. Surely it is not difficult to recognize an idea as part of those views in the context of which it is typically found. Surely research in the most various areas has come so far as to be able to establish on the basis of apparently insignificant characteristics the society and the epoch from which an intellectual construct derives. Surely, alongside many discontinuities, elements of purely intellectual "affinity" are to be found in the ideas and more generally in the modes of individual and social life of a given epoch. But the leap from this pedestrian historian's knowledge, so to speak, to the assertion of a "total psychic-spiritual structured context belonging to the social and historical reality of a specific epoch"[14] is a leap from empirical science to Hegel's theory of the *Volksgeister,* which are resurrected as "world postulates" or "objective structural contexts."

Despite Mannheim's repeated insistence that these cognitive unities are closely bound up with the fate of the classes "committed" to their existence, his idealist project of conceiving intellectual processes as

unsullied by the raw power struggles of real human beings is so strong
that the vague relationship between being and consciousness appears
as a merely external juxtaposition, indeed as a predestined arrangement. For him, there exist the mundane struggles of everyday historical life, and *next to them also* the conflicts of the "systems of
Weltanschauungen." What is curious here is that each of the contending groups has laid claim to and persists in advocating one of these
systems—but one knows not why: "We find in a given stage of history
not only antagonistic groups with different social interests, but also
with them at the same time a conflict of opposed world postulates." Just
as the gods associated with the warring Greeks and Trojans warred
among themselves above the troops, according to this modern sociology one is supposed to see "worlds . . . against worlds" struggling above
the social classes.[15]

If the transformation of the concept of ideology from the particular
to the total shifts our attention from real events upward to the misty
regions of contending "world postulates," its further development takes
the ground out from under our feet. For on the level of the total
concept of ideology, upon which Marx is supposed to have stood, the
"ideological character" of an overall perspective was at least judged
from the standpoint of a theory understood as itself nonideological.
With the removal of this restriction on the total concept of ideology—
that is, with its transformation into the general concept—this distinction falls away, and "the thought of all parties in all epochs" is branded
as "ideology" (77). Herewith the concept of ideology is cleansed of the
residues of its accusatory meaning, and its integration into the philosophy of mind is complete. If all thought as such is to be characterized
as ideological, it becomes apparent that ideology, just like "particularity," signifies nothing other than inadequacy to eternal truth. There
may, of course, be certain differences in the genuineness or obsoles-
cence of given ideas, but they are all fundamentally "ideological" because they are "situationally determined."

A consistent application of the general concept of ideology would
have to call into question one's own theories about "being," about the
structure of *Weltanschauungen,* and about the connection between the
two if one is to speak—in contrast with the foregoing—in a determinate sense about the ideas, about their "correspondence," and about
"being." With the "special" conception of the concept of ideology, it

appeared as if a definite theory was considered compelling—namely, the Marxist analysis of society as classes in conflict. In the substantive portions of Mannheim's sociology of knowledge, this being is characterized among other things as "class society,"[16] as aristocracy, bureaucracy, and bourgeoisie. Now that it is recognized that Marxism's "own position is subject to the same criticism" (105)—now that it is emphatically demanded that Marxism reflect upon itself and recognize its own ideological character—this basic element of Marx's theory must also fall into disrepute. What is to constitute the fundamental sociological idea with respect to the categorization of various modes of thought, if not precisely this or some other specific theory of social structure? Without such a theory, the term "situationally determined" completely lacks content and draws dangerously close to the concept of being at the beginning of Hegel's *Logic,* where it has the dialectical tendency to transform itself into that of nothingness. The ground is really pulled out from under us. "Being," upon which all ideas are said to be dependent, retains in Mannheim's usage a certain relevance to social groups. But because the theory which offers an analysis of these groups is essentially only introduced in order to call it into question, we remain completely in the dark about the actual meaning of "situational determination." It can be interpreted by Marxists as categorization into social classes divided according to ownership relations, and by the declared enemies of the materialist conception of history, with Mannheim's agreement, as dependence upon a "particular mentality."[17] When, in the central parts of this sociology of knowledge, reference is made to a very general notion of connection "to the actually existing social situation" (78) or merely to "situational determination," Troeltsch's discussion of the concept of the social is particularly appropriate: "It is impossible to speak of society, as the essence of all large and small sociological circles and their mutual interpenetration and influence, as something comprehensible and scientifically useful. In the infinitude of its construction and of the arbitrary connection of phenomena from any given perspective, society is something quite unimaginable: an abstraction, like culture and history more generally, about which only the dilettantes talk in terms of their totality."[18] According to Troeltsch, the concept of "social" being "can only mean society organized according to its division of

labor, its social classes, its production of goods, and its exchange on
the basis of economic need, together with its manifold complications."[19] Clearly, such determinate concepts of society would not just
bring Mannheim's theory of the situational determination of all thought
closer to the historical materialism which he declares to be ideological;
they would entail an expansion of Marxism itself into adventurism.
For one would go well beyond Marx if one were to assert that to each
determinate class situation there belongs an entire *Weltanschauung*,
with form and content, including all judgments and "subconscious"
metaphysical decisions. In this specific version, the untenability of the
general, total concept of ideology becomes completely clear. With the
empty concept of "being" that appears in the central parts of the sociology of knowledge, in contrast, one can include in this assertion all
theories—including one's own—as well as God and the world. The
sociology of knowledge is scientifically meaningless, and has significance at best in the context of an absolute philosophy of quite dubious
value.

The question of the correctness or falsity of equally situationally
determined ideologies can only be put in terms of a judgment of their
appropriateness for their time. The fundamentally spiritualistic attitude of this sociology emerges nowhere more clearly than in such an
examination. The sociology of knowledge must remain arbitrary and
unreliable because the determination of what is appropriate for the
time and what is obsolete is not made on the basis of an explicit, scientific theory of society. Beyond that, however, this sociology takes to
the limit its intention of substituting considerations of the history of
ideas for investigation of the actual conditions which determine the
relations between the real struggles of human beings and their ideas.
Mannheim characterizes as an example of false (because antiquated)
consciousness "a landed proprietor whose estate has already become
a capitalistic undertaking, but who still attempts to explain his relations to his laborers and his own function in the undertaking by means
of categories reminiscent of the patriarchal order" (96). In this case,
Mannheim measures inappropriateness in terms of a theory which,
like every natural-scientific theory, must raise the claim of "nonideological" correctness, and which declares on the basis of numerous observations that the relationship of the landowner to his workers is

"capitalistic," and thus cannot be comprehended in feudal terms. To base one's commitment to this theory on the grounds of its appropriateness to the epoch, which is precisely the basis upon which the theory is to be judged, would be circular. It is not this logical inadequacy that is characteristic of such efforts, however, but rather its fundamental restriction to the cognitive realm. What concerns Mannheim in this example is the fact that the landowner "fails epistemologically in comprehending the actual world [M.]" (96). Whether this "failure" in the intersubjective reality—in this case, in the actual relationship between landowner and agricultural laborer—also constitutes a shortcoming, or indeed whether this failure inevitably shapes that relationship, is never considered. The most important task of a sociology of knowledge, however, would be to investigate the extent to which the nature of such relationships affects adherence to the old way of thinking and, vice versa, what effect the latter has on the former. In Mannheim's work, attention is diverted from the social function of the "ideology" to exclusively intellectual considerations.

Throughout Mannheim, the sociological concepts are so attenuated that, in the end, they are no longer useful for understanding social life. A "diagnosis of the time" that operates primarily with the imprecise, idealist notions of this sociology of knowledge must yield an extremely one-sided picture. To be sure, it raises the claim of "analyzing . . . a cross-section of the total intellectual and social situation of our time" (93), but this cross-section leaves untouched the most important parts of social reality. In its "situational report" on the present, no real misery appears under the terms "need" and "crisis"; the "curiously appalling trend of modern thought" (87) refers essentially to the fate of the "category of the absolute." The "profound disquietude which we feel in our present intellectual situation" derives not from the condition of reality, but rather from the "notion of the possibility of a totally false consciousness [M.]" (70). And the "profound dilemma from which all our questions arise can be summed up in the single question: How can human beings still think and live at all in an epoch in which the problem of ideology and utopia has once been stated in radical terms and thought out to its conclusions?"[20]

Even in its application to well-defined, concrete subjects—such as in the investigations of "conservative thought,"[21] which are explicitly characterized as "sociological contributions to the development of political-historical thought in Germany"—there are only scant references to the connections between social reality and the group of ideas branded as "conservative." The historical relations of the carriers of this thought, their relationship to other social strata, and the overall political situation are only occasionally touched upon, as if the constellation of "conservative" ideas could possibly be understood without careful discussion of these matters. The entire work is restricted almost exclusively to "the phenomenological-logical analysis of style," "immanent analysis of *Weltanschauung*," analysis of "experience," analysis of the confluence of various styles of thought, and similar dissections of cognitive constructs.

According to its own convictions, the sociology of knowledge represents a form of thought "which moves at the forefront of the real problematic of an epoch, and which is capable of seeing beyond any particular controversy [M.]". In the process, it employs an extremely "radical" terminology and Marxist modes of thinking. With its attempt to restore these tools of thought to the service of a philosophy of spirit from whose Hegelian form Marx had dissolved them, however, the sociology of knowledge ultimately leads to the idealist reinterpretation of existing contradictions as mere oppositions of ideas, "styles of thought," and "systems of *Weltanschauung*." Whereas Marx was concerned to distinguish real insights from the mystifying cloak of ideology, for Mannheim everything amounts to a question of the contradictions between finite and infinite truth. Ultimately, Mannheim distinguishes himself from those irresponsible philosophers whose blindness he claims is caused by their persistence in a " 'higher' realm" (104) only in that he returns there himself with a few weapons from the arsenal of Marxism.

Remarks on Philosophical Anthropology

The conviction that each epoch in history expresses one facet of human nature or even that history as a whole reveals this nature stems from a point of view that is all too harmonious. It may be granted that individuals belonging to a particular historical period do indeed share certain psychological characteristics. One can justifiably speak of an Athenian citizen of the fifth century, or of a French *grand seigneur* of the ancien régime. However, such typologies designate only particular social groups. In Greece there existed not only citizens but also slaves; in France, not just *grands seigneurs* but also peasants, the bourgeoisie, and the urban proletariat. The members of one class provided the foundation for the social forms just as much as did the members of any other. Furthermore, although individual cultural monuments stem exclusively from certain social groups, their content is determined by the history of tensions and conflicts between the classes. To the symmetry and natural beauty of Greek statues belongs not only the freedom of a hero's life but also the other freedom, which consisted in his emancipation from oppressive labor and poverty. It is impossible to understand these cultural products without considering the dynamic of such conflicts.

However, it is not only the relationship between social classes that prevents us from maintaining that a constant and unchanging human nature functions as the foundation for an epoch. Research into periods in European history reveals that, when old economic forms persist even after new means of production are introduced, earlier modes of conceptualization and of psychological response remain in existence as well. Contemporary research vacillates on the question of whether certain personalities and historical trends belong to the Middle Ages or to the bourgeois world. The reason for this lies in the fact that in the Renaissance, and even into the seventeenth century, very few groups, and in fact only a few traits of the groups' members, could be shown to have represented the birth of new social relationships. Huge masses of people persisted materially and, more importantly, intellectually, within the old forms while their wretched lives and dire psychological constitution played a decisive role in the new developments.

Of course, human beings have been similar to one another in every epoch as well as in the entire history of mankind. They not only have certain practical needs in common, but they coincide in their beliefs and perceptions. Moral and religious systems tend to benefit social groups in highly diverse ways, and they fulfill extremely varied functions in the psychological household of their members: the idea of God or of eternity can serve as a justification for guilt or can provide hope to desperate people. These same ideas are often applied in a superficial way. Nevertheless, these similarities among various groups are not the result of a consistency in human nature. The social life process in which they emerge involves both human and suprahuman factors. This process consists not simply in the representation or expression of human nature in general, but rather in a continuous struggle of individual human beings with nature. Furthermore, the character of every individual within a group originates not only in the dynamic that pertains to him in his capacity as a representative product of human nature, but in his individual fate within society as well. The relationships among social groups arise from the changing constellations between society and nature. These relationships are determining factors in the creation of the spiritual and psychological makeup of individuals, while this resulting character in turn affects the social structure. Human nature is thus continuously influenced and changed by a manifold of circumstances. One could even understand the existence of a human nature that is invariable in time as a result of processes that continuously renew themselves, processes in which human beings form an inextricable part. However, one cannot understand it as the expression of a person in and for itself. Moreover, new forms of behavior and characters emerge which by no means existed from the beginning. The task that Max Scheler assigned to anthropology is unrealistic. For him, anthropology was to show precisely how "all the specific achievements and works of man—language, conscience, tools, weapons, ideas of right and wrong, the state, leadership, the representational function of art, myths, religion, science, history and social life—arise from the basic structure of human existence."[1] This task is impossible to fulfill. Regardless of how much the notions of change and progression are integrated into the idea of man, this way of stating the problem assumes a fixed, abstract hierarchy. It contradicts the dialectical character of historical events, in which the foundational structure of individual existence is always interwoven with that of the group, and can lead, at best, to paradigms not unlike those of the natural sciences.

There is no formula that defines the relationship among individuals, society, and nature for all time. Even if we are not justified in interpreting history as the unfolding of a consistent, unchanging human nature, the contrary and fatalistic formulation—that of a necessity that is independent of human beings and that governs the course of things—would be just as naive. The dependence is neither one-dimensional nor always structured in the same way. Rather, social development necessitates that particular groups and personalities be better prepared for changes and reformation in social processes than others, who in their thought and action function chiefly as products of the given circumstances. To be sure, conscious historical action is linked in its temporal circumstances and its content to certain preconditions. Yet this is different from the way in which reactive behavior and an existence that is completely dependent on present historical conditions are bound up with current social circumstances. The more these factors gain force, the more the psychology of unconscious mechanisms finds appropriate ways of explaining them. Direct understanding of the motives suffices the more historical action is undertaken independent of the authority of actual states of affairs and the more it is based on an accurate theory. Not the rational and emancipatory activity of theoretically educated human beings, but rather the intractability and helplessness of underdeveloped groups, constitutes the proper object for depth psychology.

Modern philosophical anthropology stems from precisely the same need that the idealistic philosophy of the bourgeois era tried to satisfy from its inception: namely the need to lay down new, absolute principles that provide the rationale for action. These principles were especially needed after the collapse of the medieval order and its tradition of unconditional authority. The most important tasks of idealistic philosophy consisted in delineating abstract principles that provided the foundation for a meaningful existence and in bringing spiritual endeavors—the fate of the individual and of all of humanity—in harmony with an eternal purpose. This philosophical school arose above all from the contradictory circumstance that while the modern age proclaimed the spiritual and personal independence of man, the preconditions had not yet been realized for autonomy and rationally structured communal work within society. Under the prevailing conditions, the processes of the production and reproduction of social life—the "law of value"—emerge not as a result of human labor and of the way in which labor is executed. Instead, economic mechanisms make themselves felt blindly, and thus appear as sovereign powers of nature. The necessary character of the forms in which society develops and renews itself, and within which the entire existence of individuals unfolds, remains obscure. On the other hand, individuals have learned to demand justification for social life forms which they maintain by means of their daily activity and, when necessary, defend. That is, they demand justification for the distribution of functions in labor, for the form of produced goods, for property relationships, for forms of justice, for relations between nations, etc. They want to know why they should act in one way and not in another, and they insist on an overarching rationale. The role of philosophy is to give meaning and direction to this bewilderment. Instead of satisfying the individual's demand for meaning by uncovering social contradictions and by providing a means of overcoming them, philosophy confounds the needs of the present age by analyzing only the possibility of "real" life or even of "real" death, and by attempting to cloak existence with a deeper meaning.

Overcoming the conflict between an advanced form of rationality and blind reproduction of social processes presupposes that one recognize the incongruity between social needs and powers on the one side and their entire technical and cultural organization on the other. The particular predicament of the present age and the fight for its termination stem from this growing tension. The goal of the struggle is to bring social life into conformity with the needs of all. This would result in a social form in which individuals organize their labor with a view to their own interests and goals and are thus always prepared to adjust to new forms. Only a transparent and adequate relationship between individual action and the life of the society can provide a foundation for individual existence. The rationality of this relationship gives meaning to labor. When this relationship is realized, and when a manifold of seemingly free activity among individuals is replaced by a society that unfolds and protects its life against threatening natural forces, then it is impossible to provide a deeper foundation for the activity of free human beings. The notion of social life as a willful product of collective individual labor does not originate from the free recognition of an eternal purpose or fulfill any purpose whatsoever. Human beings satisfy their changing needs and desires and defend themselves from death not because they believe that by doing so they are fulfilling an absolute imperative, but rather because they cannot escape from the longing for happiness and the fear of death. The notion of a protective power outside of humanity will disappear in the future. As the belief in this consolation declines, awareness of its unreliability will intervene in human relationships, and so these relationships will become more immediate. When the relationship of human beings toward their work is recognized and fashioned like their relationships to one another, moral commandments will be "sublated." The precondition of these commandments was the fragmentation of interests in earlier forms of society. It is not as if the anxiety regarding the finite nature of individuals and of humanity has lost its validity. However, since energy has been sapped from this anxiety, metaphysics, this abstract pretense of security, can no longer provide protection from it. Rather, the actual social battle for real security against suffering and death assumes responsibility for the elimination of this emotion. However, the sorrow that necessarily remains preserves its own form and cannot be eliminated by any system. The application of thought to the goal of creating absolute principles, a futile undertaking that has dominated European philosophy since Descartes, is a manifestation of the strange confusion prevalent in the bourgeois age.

The project of modern philosophical anthropology consists in finding a norm that will provide meaning to an individual's life in the world as it currently exists. Since religious revelation has lost its authority, and the deduction of moral axioms, typical of philosophy from the seventeenth century to the period of neo-Kantianism, has proven futile, metaphysics has sought to show that the true conception of man lay in the goal toward which his actions were directed. Certain doctrines press spiritual and intellectual energies, whether for purposes of mere show or of analysis, into the service of a higher justification and assurance that are nonetheless impossible and confusing. One such doctrine decrees that a particular form of human behavior, for example devotion to state and nation, constitutes the only true model of human existence. However, even the more liberal doctrines of human nature that fail to establish a particular teleology for human action, and that thus assimilate a notion of "risk" into their system, do the same. Anthropology differs from a utopia in the same way that a profound interpretation of a particular state of affairs differs from a univocal will to a happier future, insofar as this will is certain of the endpoint but not of the way to reach it. The meaning of human action can be interpreted on a quite general level in anthropology, for example by portraying the telos of history as itself consisting in the unfolding and development of mankind. This philosophy strives for "security, even such a one that makes risks possible and leads to risks."[2] "It is precisely absolute insecurity that cripples humans.... Their crippling itself is, however, a consequence of the fact that these humans can no longer conceive of themselves in such a way that a uniform, comprehensive meaning and an overall purpose by which one can and must take risks, will ensue." Landsberg thus touches upon the conscious impulse of the entire philosophical enterprise from which modern anthropology and existentialism emerged. The desire to provide a foundation for action by way of insights into human nature has motivated phenomenology since its beginnings.

In this respect, it contradicts the theory of society. According to this theory, the formulation of the closest and the representation of the most distant goals develop in a continuous relationship with cognition. However, this theory does not provide the grounds for meaning and an eternal purpose. Rather, human needs play a role in determining goals. Thus these goals do not include a vision of the future; they originate purely from need. They mockingly transform the order of things into distorted relationships. A theory free from illusions can only conceive of human purpose negatively, and reveals the inherent contradiction between the conditions of existence and everything that the great philosophies have postulated as a purpose. The unfolding of human powers, which these days have atrophied, is thus a motif that goes back even further than the humanism of the Renaissance. However, this motif does not need to assume the mystical character of an absolute principle. The corresponding will to the realization of a better society finds an endless number of stimuli in contemporary conditions. Whether it is consistent with an ostensible human purpose or not, whether in an absolute sense it is better or worse than its opposite—these questions have meaning only when one presupposes that God exists. Toward the end of his life, Scheler, the founder of modern philosophical anthropology, began to deny this "presupposition of theism: a spiritual, personal God omnipotent in his spirituality."[3] He consequently had to declare that absolute Being as a means of "support for human beings"[4] was impossible. He thereby repudiated the strongest impulse to metaphysics. This step leads in the direction of a materialistic theory. It denies not objective Being, but rather an absolute meaning that, despite all the philosophies of life and other pantheistic trends of the present age, can in fact never be separated from that theistic precondition.

A theory derived from the classical and the French Enlightenments, which, in contrast to the idealistic conception, holds that the world contains no inherent meaning, has consequences for the concept of self-consciousness that follows from it. Whoever accepts this theory does not link its corresponding existential demands with an eternal, spiritual being. The hope that there is something beyond space and time appears futile to him. When things are going well, later generations will remember the martyrs who died for freedom. However, this will mean about as much for these martyrs and their convictions as it did for the three hundred men of Leonidas who died in battle long before this wanderer came to Sparta and proclaimed that he saw them lying dead, as the law required him to do. That is, it will mean absolutely nothing. However, this knowledge in no way provides action with a narrower horizon. The idea of helping other individuals become freer and happier can always boost the self-esteem of a particular human being. As long as the goals that determine his own life do not crumble along with him, but rather can be pursued in society after his death, he may cherish the hope that his death will not mean the end of his will. The goal of self-realization is not, for him, contingent on his status as an individual, but rather is dependent on the development of humanity, and the end does not appear to him merely as destruction. The attainment of his goals does not depend exclusively on his personal existence. He can be independent and brave.

This self-concept is, for various reasons, superior to other forms of courage that involve living in harmony with a truth that is immediately attainable. Simple belief, however, can provide consolation that is just as profound. Those who believe in a particular religion have even stronger views regarding a beyond or an inexhaustible, divine realm of life. The student of the Enlightenment, however, is convinced that the future generations for which he is fighting are irrevocably transitory and that, in the end, nothingness is victorious over joy. Certainly he is inspired by the notion of a higher form of society and of a brighter existence for all human beings. However, the reason why he prefers personal engagement to conformity toward existing reality and a career lies not in a commandment or an inner voice pregnant with promises, but rather only in his wishes and desires, which will one day disappear. It may appear a noble goal for humans to live on this earth more happily and wisely than they did under the bloody and stultifying conditions that tend to designate the end of social life forms. However, the future generations will die out anyway, and the earth will continue its course as if nothing had happened. Skepticism and nihilism are speaking here. In reality, a sincere consciousness and honest action begin in the place where this simple truth gains ground and is resolutely retained.

The difference between anthropological philosophy and materialism has nothing to do with the principle of recognition of values and goals. This difference, however, encompasses the structure of every theory, especially when that theory is supposed to be free from certain interests and values. The unconditional duty of science toward truth and its alleged freedom from values, which of course play an immense role in the positivism of the present age, are irreconcilable. Reflection thus constitutes an important element in how a doctrine is understood. It allows the life situation, that is, individual interests, to find expression and to determine the direction of thoughts. This process can occur only in the acts of generalization that lead to the doctrine's fundamental concepts, and in the gradual steps that lead to the comprehension of concrete developmental processes. The theory may otherwise bring valuable results to light and fulfill an immediate goal, but it dispenses with philosophical truth. This truth requires that consciousness think in social terms, since its thought processes are comprehensible only in terms of the reality in which they have meaning. Consciousness requires clarity concerning the historical context in which it evolves and the praxis within which it emerges, takes effect, and is changed. No seemingly practical, disinterested, unfocused analysis will fulfill the demand of this dialectic, since there is no such thing as merely intellectual cognition. The value of concrete thinking and of self-criticism is contingent on their relationship to praxis. Correct ideas in themselves can be absolutely trivial even if they are concerned with "society." There are innumerable possible assessments and analyses. When the interests of humanity and the historical conditions that give rise to them do not emerge from these analyses, then either a private conformity or the flight from reality is hiding beneath them. Anthropology shares with dialectical thinking a rejection of the notion that one can be absolutely free from values. Scheler's doctrine that cognition has moral preconditions seems like a conclusion derived from the current state of affairs. Even consciousness of one's own historicity forms a principal theme in modern anthropology: "The historical context of every philosophical anthropology, even ours, . . . cannot, in principle, be sublated and is in no way to be negatively valorized."[5] The principle that follows from this, that the particular, constantly changing association between theory and practice is to be made conscious in each individual, comes close to including anthropology in a dialectical theory of history. However, this demand is not likely to be fulfilled.

The actual difference lies not in an affirmation of values generally but in their function in thinking. The metaphysician derives an ideal "ought" from these values. This need not happen deductively. According to Scheler, the order of rank of values must "be comprehended only through the acts of preferring and placing after. There exists here an *intuitive 'evidence of preference.'* "[6] When a conviction is free from illusions, action that is associated with this conviction cannot be brought into a transparent connection with clear and essential conditions. Rather, this action emerges from the longing for happiness and freedom, which does not need to be further legitimated but only historically explained. When an image of the man of the future is contained in this vision it is not represented as a prototype, but is instead perceived by its representatives as having been determined by current conditions and goals that are as ephemeral as they themselves are. On the other hand, anthropology finds itself in danger of striving for too much or too little. It asks for and seeks a definition of human nature that extends from prehistory to the end of humanity, and it avoids the anthropological question par excellence, namely: how can we overcome an inhumane reality (since all human capacities that we love suffocate and decay within it)? Insofar as the first question can be posed meaningfully, its answer depends not only practically but also theoretically on every advance made in the second.

Skepticism and nihilism, as well as the selfish and anarchistic attitudes that spring from them, belong to that philosophical mode of thought that demands absolute justification, poses final questions, and is completely radical. The skeptics want to bring their deeds into harmony with a metaphysical authority just as other dogmatic philosophers do. According to them, values ought to be realized only when they can be proved to be binding and univocal. Skeptics derive the core of their existence from the conviction that this is an impossibility, and their principles result from their confusion. They thus give themselves over to the narrow, individualistic impulses that come naturally to them, and they consider every other motive a rationalization or a lie. However, some human beings hold fast to their goals without considering them unconditionally binding or suprahistorical. A particular bond seems to exist between egoistical structures of desire and metaphysical interpretations of action. While solidarity with struggling, suffering human beings obviously tends to make one apathetic toward metaphysical assurances, a particular notion appears to reside in the passionate effort not merely to seek meaning in the world, but to contend that such a thing exists. According to this notion, all human beings who do not believe in such a meaning become purely egoistical, know nothing other than what is to their own advantage, and become simply base. A coarsely materialistic conception of man thus lurks in metaphysical systems, in contrast to materialism. This is the same anthropological pessimism that is expressed not so much by Machiavelli as by the theories of state of all restoration periods:

"l'homme en général, s'il est réduit à lui-même, est trop méchant pour être libre."[7]

If history has as its foundation a concept of human nature that is neither uniform nor undeviating (a notion, moreover, that is rejected by modern anthropology), this concept can hardly serve as a way of lending meaning to history. Anthropological studies therefore do not need to dispose of the concept of value; they can extend and refine the understanding of historical tendencies. They would then be concerned with historically determined human beings and groups of human beings instead of with man as such, and would seek to understand their existence and development not as isolated individuals but rather as integral parts of the life of society. This notion is here structured in a manner different from that in modern philosophy. If the concept of man developed by modern philosophy is supposed to serve as a foundation for the humanistic disciplines, then, looked at systematically and realistically, secondary nuances would come into play. Here we are not emphasizing the traits that separate man from plants and animals on the one hand and from God on the other—passionate interest in such all-encompassing concepts must ultimately be explained by recourse to the need for metaphysical orientation in the present. Rather, we want to stress the existence and transformation of characteristics that may well determine the actual course of history. The concept of man here appears not as uniform, but as consisting in characteristics that designate certain groups. These characteristics arise together with the social life process, are transmitted from one class to another, and under certain circumstances are either absorbed by the entire society and given new meaning or else disappear. Every feature of the present age should be understood as a factor in a historical dynamic and not as a manifestation of an eternal being. The motivation for such studies lies not so much in the questionable belief of anthropology itself that "at no time in his history has man been so much of a problem to himself as he is now"[8]—a condition that, even if true, would not appear to us as especially worrisome. Rather, their impetus must arise from the realization that real sufferings must be eliminated. It may indeed be true that the images of eternal life are losing their force and that the forms of the temporal are dispensing completely with the notion of harmony. However, this in no way implies that the time has arrived for new acts of theological fantasy.

As a consequence of metaphysical radicalism and of the breadth of its questioning, a questioning that is not undertaken by any theory that deals with historical tendencies, it is difficult to comment upon particular views in philosophical anthropology and to criticize them productively. Individual anthropological concepts tend to be both correct and incorrect, since they set the contents that are abstracted from history into an idea and elevate them to the level of "true" conditions of existence. This holds not just for modern but also for the most recent anthropology. In the question of the individual, which is a primary theme of anthropology in the bourgeois age, a contradictory relationship to truth is especially pronounced. Here, Hobbes's notion of civil justice is predominant and, with its irrational denial of mechanistic foundations, is more viable today than it may appear to be. Hobbes considers humans to be selfish and fearful. The egoistical drives appear to him to be just as ultimate and unchangeable as the mechanistic powers of matter. The individual is by nature completely isolated and concerned only with his own advantage. Society is founded so that each individual tacitly enters into and acknowledges a contract by virtue of the fact of his existence in the state. By means of this contract each person gives himself over once and for all to any individual power and to its arbitrariness. Despite his selfishness the individual is supposed to be capable of keeping promises. This contradiction, which Hobbes himself did not see as such, is not without its foundations in reality. Neither is it written in stone, however. It emerged in history, and will disappear in it as well. There is no simple yes or no to this anthropological conception, according to which the isolated individual steps out of his loneliness through promises and contracts. In the present moment of transition its manifest simplicity appears together with its relative, theoretical and practical justification. We shall attempt to show this briefly.

The ability to make promises has become second nature to human beings in the course of history. They have learned to believe that a declaration made in the present will be fulfilled in the future. The validity of these categories was a condition of production. It contributed to making life calculable, and belongs to the development of civilization in the past two thousands years. It forms a constitutive element of the civil bourgeois world.

Although promises were not only given but also kept with regularity, egoistical drives gave rise to a new condition: the highly developed legislative apparatus with the entire power of the dominating class as its basis. It became more advantageous to keep one's promise than to break it. From the beginning, both business life and the entire community were in fact based on a promise of each and every individual in the truest sense of the word, as long as unbridled slavery did not come into question. As a member of this community I abide by its provisions; I shall neither steal nor murder, nor think badly of those in power. In commerce between peoples, the conditionality of promises was even more important than among states. Contracts concerning the rights of peoples appear consistently to have formulated only power relationships. As soon as the latter changed in any significant way, the contracts and promises lost their substance. "For to trust too much in words and promises, no matter how good they sound, is impossible in the storms of world history. The great powers push ahead on their own until they find resistance."[9] Frederick II of Prussia himself confirmed that, in the contracts among princes, "in truth, only deception and infidelity constitute the oath," and in the end one sees oneself compelled "to choose between the horrendous necessity of betraying one's work or one's subjects."[10]

Nevertheless, humanity has learned in the past millennia to attribute meaning to promises independently of power. "Furthermore, he that is tied by contract is trusted; for faith only is the bond of contracts."[11] Regardless of whether the one to whom it is given has effective social interests, he must hold to his word, and it actually happens that the promise is fulfilled without the threat of disadvantages. Whoever pledges to carry out a promise voluntarily puts his self-consciousness at risk. This is possible only because the fulfillment of promises has already come to be understood as a moral imperative. The social necessity of fidelity in commerce and business has come to be regarded as a moral value. It is based not merely on circumstances that bear directly on the future. Everything that in the modern age is termed "conviction" [Gesinnung], the affirmation of certain goals, includes a form of resolution that is identical to a promise. If the predictability of modern life is in part contingent upon the consistency of individual drive structures, that is, upon what we commonly call "character" (with hunger and penitentiaries in the background, of course), then it belongs to our concept of man, as it has been historically formed, that he too—independent of established character traits and of the fear of punishment, indeed against the entire world and thus against selfishness—stands by his own word and confession.

This moral resolve has nothing to do with the incapacity for spiritual development. It implies the incessant unfolding of all powers in order to protect the unity of purpose in the continuous differentiation of perception, in the changes involved in social life, and the varying demands of the situation. The capacity for this is closely linked with all values for which the bourgeoisie has sharpened its senses. Freedom means enforcing a value even against natural and social powers, standing by it, and retaining it in consciousness, such that it regulates both theoretical and practical ways of behavior and can be perceived as a nuance in even the most irrelevant thoughts and deeds. Justice requires that we not change our standards under all circumstances and situations, or organize reality in such a way that people must suffer without a significant reason. For it is not happiness but rather misery that requires justification in a world of reason.

During the last few centuries, promises were kept without continuous application of force, and this has helped to maintain commerce. With the continuous accumulation of capital, however, the possibility for this has become slighter. The ruling class no longer consists of countless subjects who sign contracts, but rather of large power groups controlled by a few people who compete with each other on the world market. They have transformed huge areas of Europe into immense work camps by the use of iron discipline. The more competition on the world market turns into a sheer power struggle, the more tightly organized and strictly structured these power groups become internally and externally. The economic foundation for meaning and promises thus becomes narrower every day. For it is no longer the contract but rather the power to command and to demand obedience that now increasingly characterizes domestic commerce.

The social relationships involved in economic processes affect the entire spiritual and intellectual world and thus the constitution of human nature. In earlier periods of history, power was considered immoral when it came into conflict with contracts. Today, a contract violates morality when it runs counter to power relationships. Everyone who has anything to do with such matters knows this, and for that reason contracts must occasionally be drawn up rather hastily, and they must be settled more quickly now than ever. Their importance remains indisputable: they are binding *praemissis praemittendis,* they travel cursorily around the atlas of interests in a particular historical moment. However, if power is now to become established as the true legislative authority whereas, before the advent of Christianity, it ruled only de facto and did not have a differentiated moral consciousness as its advocate, may Nietzsche not triumph! The power of which we are here speaking runs counter to human traits that are directed toward the future. Even by its own standards it is "decadent." Nietzsche wanted to give to the history "of the entire past a goal," [12] and stressed the possibility of higher forms of life. He thought that contemporary expressions of power arose from the laziness and anxiety of the masses and had nothing else to claim for itself. Even the dialectical principle of the masses did not escape him: "To help the common masses to rule is of course the only means of making their kind noble: however, one must hope for this first as one who himself rules, not in a battle for the rule." [13] The notion that those who are against power and for the masses are not identical to these masses is revealed in Nietzsche's view that one must force the masses to use their own faculty of reason and realize their own advantage. This maxim holds not only for those who rule but for their opponents as well. However, because Nietzsche kept the masses firmly separate from the superman without developing that dialectical principle, he remained vulnerable to the misuse that he despised, and was considered a herald for those who were ruling at the time. He understood everything that concerned the present except its inner nexus. Had he recognized and applied dialectic not just in his capacity as a classical philologist but rather in its contemporary form, he would have better understood those who considered the masses an atavism and who were striving to overcome the condition of their existence, the constant resurgence of poverty. It is unscientific to think of the superman merely as a biological type. This concept designates the higher stages of a future society that originates from the struggles in the present. The superman is either a social-theoretical concept or the utopian dream of a philosopher. The masses can only be contemned as long as the actual power that rules over them veils itself in a fictitious image of power. This is, of course, the distinguishing mark of rule over the masses in all previous periods of history. As soon as the masses transform themselves through their correct use of power, then power itself loses its "decadence" and becomes an effect of the uniform and thus "superhuman" force of society. The bridge to the future is not erected by lonely individuals, as Nietzsche had held, but rather by organized efforts, in which his opinions regarding eugenics play only an insignificant role and the will to a freer humanity is fused with an explicit and highly developed theory of society.

One facet of the independence of the human being who has this goal in mind consists in revealing and employing the qualities that have been promulgated by classical idealism, namely human autonomy and resolution, against its own epigones. This is particularly true in a period in which the petit bourgeois masses unconditionally learn to affirm the state power as an expression of "honor." The ideas under which the society of Fichte and Kant became universal have long ago turned into charades. If they were now to be discarded it would not mean a great deal historically. Despite its deplorable nature, this condition at least has the advantage that the truth becomes clearly manifest. Whoever has no power in this world has few rights and seldom a foundation on which to build anything. Any law that is supposed to be to his advantage loses force. Justice stops when he makes a claim on it, and this surprises no one. The human type that corresponds to contemporary conditions acknowledges everything that serves power. The great aspects of what occurs and is in force constitute for him the norm of the world. As a smaller version of Aristotle, every average man of today sees more perfection in a matter the more real it is. As a smaller version of Schiller, he considers world history to be the world court. Above us stand those who are in a position to strike; everything that is below is not yet low enough. "What is falling, we should still push!"[14]

The conduct of the struggling individual is not the simple contrast to this type of human being; the former is not opposed to power in general. However, his nature consists in remaining resolute irrespective of his conditions, for he lives an idea that has yet to be realized. The average member of groups left behind by historical processes represents a function of the ruling power; he has no opinions of his own. Those who want to subdue him have one goal to fulfill: they must protect the status of their word and their self-respect. Instead of violating them for reasons of selfishness, they fulfill them in order to sublate their selfishness. The human trait of fidelity to oneself and to one's given word has achieved the status of a moral imperative in a long, historical process. In the age of self-interest that is now reaching its end, it constitutes an element in the compulsion that has been internalized as a conscience. In the present period, in which these relationships are becoming transparent, resolution that is founded on cognition turns into a forward-looking praxis as the will to a more humane future. This resolution is no longer clothed in mythic illusions concerning its origins, nor is it connected to the pomp of self-satisfied integrity or with the pathos of duty.

Hobbes's anthropology was ahead of its time. It stands as an important advance in the founding of the political science of the bourgeoisie.[15] This interest is today having no productive effect. The difficulty of knowing which stance to take toward this anthropology, which became obvious in the fragmentary reflection upon one of its isolated characteristics, exists to no less a degree in other theories. The conception of man that is derived from the real, historical situation of the present does not apply to the problems inherent in anthropology. In this respect, anthropology does not guarantee continuity. Thus what there is often irrelevant appears here as meaningful, and what there is of utmost importance is here worthless. The theoretical outlines are accentuated in many different ways. Another difference consists in the fact that philosophical anthropology considers every facet of its system a lasting possession, insofar as this facet is arrived at according to its principles and shows no signs of being in error. According to Husserl, philosophy is, like science, "a title standing for absolute, timeless values. Every such value, once discovered, belongs thereafter to the treasure trove of all succeeding humanity and obviously determines likewise the material content of the idea of culture, wisdom, Weltanschauung."[16] Dialectical thinking, on the other hand, considers the interests and goals that consciously and unconsciously enter into the preformation and the processing of material as conditioned and transient, and tends to understand its own effects more in the sense of a social driving force than as an eternal possession. This does no harm to the consciousness of the actual truth, for the relationship among duration, certainty, and truth is not as stable and uniform as it may appear to dogmatism on the one hand and to skepticism on the other.

Whatever holds for such special traits as faithfulness to a contract and resoluteness holds as well for the characteristics of the image of man. These characteristics are the focus of traditional anthropological interests: instead of seeking simple approval or immediate correction of philosophical doctrines, enlightened thinking attempts to bring the definition of "man" into association with groups and phases of the social life process and to overcome metaphysics by means of theory. In Greece there existed a famous distinction in anthropology. The view that human capabilities were determined at birth was opposed by the notion that inequality was a product of social relationships and individual fate. According to Aristotle, it was a commonplace notion that humans were born with the qualifications either of mastery or of slavery.[17] In Democritus on the other hand we read: "More men become good through practice than by nature."[18] He holds that nature and education are similar to one another, for education transforms human nature and by this means creates a second nature.[19] In the modern age, these anthropological concepts have been used for the justification of political systems. Aristotle's view is an integral component of conservative doctrines that incline toward feudalism and the Middle Ages; Democritus's notion belongs to the ideology of the aspiring bourgeoisie. The belief in human equality and in nobility by birth stood irreconcilably side by side. In the present age, there exists no conclusive settlement for either of these convictions. Each of them reflects a period of social reality, but naturally in a false, distorted form, and both represent a self-concept of man on two different levels. Just so, the modified position of current progressive groups toward both images of man reflects a future reality. The criticism of the distortions that each of these images contains, as well as the recognition of their relative truth, play a role in the historical praxis that looks ahead to the future. The new form of existence, which is superior to any that is reflected in past anthropological principles, is already embodied by its pioneers. Only an opinion regarding the distinction drawn by the ancient Greek thinkers, in which actual historical tendencies find expression, can really lead beyond them. Both sides are correct in a limited way.

In the Middle Ages, power and status were determined by birth. Poverty was accordingly a misfortune, but was not a source of guilt. The modern age has obliterated these notions. Hegel "may therefore say, 'Never has innocence suffered; every suffering is guilt.' "[20] Power has become negotiable because it is incarnated in money. Money is easily moved, and as a rule it is subject to an accountant's manipulations. Anyone can attain money if only he performs. Earlier bourgeois thinkers, Machiavelli, Spinoza, the Enlightenment philosophers, all denounced power that was derived solely from birth and held that only those positions earned from work were a criterion of status.

As we know, with this notion the responsibility of humans toward one another ceased to exist. Each individual was supposed to be concerned only with himself. Each person was supposed to work. Everyone considered himself a competitor for prizes that could be won by achievement. People had to prove their capabilities, and when they were capable of nothing or had bad luck, they went to the dogs. This is the context in which each person observes others. A benefactor of humanity can become a nothing overnight simply because of vacillations in the stock exchange. The hopelessly indigent ceases to be a subject. In the best case scenario, he becomes an object of social policy. He becomes a burden.

The totalitarian state has, in a certain way, introduced once again the status of power as derived from birth or, more precisely, from innate qualities of leadership. In earlier periods, the Christian neighbor had a right to be helped; now it is the "comrade of the people" who has. This, however, is merely the impossible repetition of the past. The entire epoch that followed the Renaissance was not in vain. The principle of achievement is basically correct. In these difficult centuries humanity learned the difficult lesson that pleasure is not contingent on the gods, but rather on one's own labor. However, in the end the acuity of human understanding led people to attack the concept of the individual and to discover that this concept, in both its form and its content, is determined by the dynamic of the entire society. Everything that this individual achieves, whether through his innate ability or from the content of his labor, is an effect not only of his youth and education but also of the entire economic system, the legal relationships and conditions of dependence within his society, and his own past and potential failures and chances. In each individual act, subjective and objective elements are inextricably interwoven. It cannot be said of any human characteristic that it existed in embryo exactly as it exists now, and that it simply attained full growth directly from this embryo.

The achievement of the individual does not depend on him alone but on society as well. Society itself, the people or the nation, is of course not an entity in relation to which all individuals are nothing. Individuals belong to the dynamic of the society in the same way in which they developed in history. In every moment, they have a fully particular existence. The genesis of capabilities and of the labor of each human being is to be sought not in this individual human being but rather in the fate of the entire society. This society regulates personal development by means of both long-lasting relationships and intermittent and small events or catastrophes. It is true that everything depends on whether or not each person applies and cultivates his individual powers. However, this word "his" does not designate a relationship between fixed entities. "His" actions refer to effects, in whose prehistory the character of the individual need only constitute a relatively inconsequential moment.

We are here concerned not with mythological elements of the origin, but with labor that is derived from reason, and with pleasure as its benefit. This consciousness of the present will enter into considerations of a future society. However, its meaning will have changed. The category of the individual will be stripped of its metaphysical isolation, if not completely rejected. The extent to which each individual is alone and unique depends on the condition of society and the degree to which it can govern and control nature, and on the individual's inner character. Achievement will be recognized as a function of the whole in which each individual participates. However, birth will once again confer a certain kind of power, namely, that of being a member of a truly human society. In the Middle Ages, the principle of birth was identical to the rule of chance, for no one was at fault in determining it. In the age of the bourgeoisie, this concept of chance was repudiated, and the natural equality of all human beings was proclaimed. Achievement, not birth, was now the decisive element. In reality, however, chance reasserted itself, since the conditions for labor and for pleasure were contingent on class. We have now reached the point at which mere admission into the world means luck, not through the power over others but rather through the dominion of man over nature. The man who is noble by birth appears again when his opposite, the man who is equal by nature, is transformed from an ideology into a truth. The preconditions for this lie neither in the state constitution and legislature—this was the illusion of the French Revolution—nor in the souls of human beings—this was German idealism—but rather in the foundational structures of the social life process, in which both elements are tightly interwoven.

The meaning of all anthropological categories is changed in their very foundations concomitantly with great historical transformations. This occurs without any interruption in historical continuity. If one analyzes the meaning of the concept "equality" in two distinct historical phases, one sees that the notion has a different significance in each. Positivism and its contemporary scientific and logical progeny, which emphasize exact definitions, reject the possibility of speaking of a transformation within one and the same concept. However, they do allow for the possibility of one meaning taking the place of another, and of various new linguistic signs being established. They rightly demand that distinct meanings not be confused and that what should be kept separate be so. This rule, so central to mathematics and natural sciences, is opposed by another that finds its expression in historical studies and according to which elements flow into one another and form a structural unity. These are to be reconstructed as a unity and reflected precisely as such. If the meaning and the object themselves are changed, we cannot decide whether or not the same name is to be preserved on the basis of the claim that the concepts themselves remain the same. We must instead determine whether the name designates something that has continuity or not. The function of a name in the course of history, in which the transformation in meaning occurs, can entail that the name must remain the same whether or not the majority of all of its representational meanings have changed. On the other hand, when only a nuanced change in the meaning occurs, then we can, under certain circumstances, introduce a new name. This nuance can be strong enough that it requires a change of linguistic sign so that its significance becomes sufficiently clear. The revolts of the Roman slaves were quite different from the battles against the feudal power organizations of the eighteenth century. However, the goals of both were designated by the same name: freedom. In turn, English economists and jurists unjustly invoked this same word a century ago when, after the fall of absolutism, they demolished the remains of social support networks that could have been reminiscent of absolutism. The relationship between the name, the representation, and the object is extremely complex, and everything that is evil exploits this complexity as a means of confusion. In the theoretical application of a name, arbitrariness must be avoided. However, there exists no recipe for doing this. The period of transition to the monopolistic phase of economic systems is characterized by a change in human beings. The names remain the same, but the anthropological realities are altered. Love, understanding, and sympathy, for example, assume such differing functions today in the relationships between human beings that the corresponding phenomena have been changed accordingly. These processes do not occur in an independent and isolated fashion, but rather in connection with transformations in the society as a whole.

In the bourgeois age, when one was incapable of looking after others, he was termed inferior. The lack of influence and understanding associated with certain individuals vis-à-vis other group members commonly originates in their inability to love someone and their ability only to brood over their own concerns. Because such people never communicate their anxieties or express their joy to someone, they ultimately forfeit their place in their milieu and become failures. Economic development has progressed to a point where even successful advancement within society is contingent on the ability to show interest in the concerns of others. In a free market economy, other things being equal, the salesman who shows such concern for his customers has a distinct advantage over his competitor. Besides the participation of the bourgeoisie in the government, each citizen is bound by the necessities of taking pains for customers, of showing them what is to their advantage, and of guessing and influencing their inclinations. These exigencies counteract purely selfish dispositions and develop the capacity for compassion toward others. This interpersonal understanding, which even in its more sublime manifestations bears the mark of its relationship with trade and commerce, is not equivalent to the spontaneous feeling of unity in prebourgeois forms of community or to unconditional solidarity. Nevertheless, bourgeois commerce in conjunction with egoism has nurtured its own negation: altruism. Classes that were left behind in economic development—for example, a segment of the farmers in certain parts of a country—appear to the more refined, bourgeois consciousness as emotional cripples, not least because of their concern only with themselves.

However, just like other economic mechanisms that originally facilitated the unfolding of human qualities but that have now lost their meaning or come to mean their opposite, hate and mistrust gain the upper hand in human relationships in times of growing economic crisis. One of the most important tasks of the latest *Weltanschauung* consists in channeling the huge amounts of aggression, which are emerging in a climate of destitution, either into self-sacrificial devotion against each particular individual or into a spirit of battle against potential national enemies. This deflection of an originally positive side of bourgeois man into destructive aims becomes more and more difficult under worsening economic conditions and requires an increasingly complicated apparatus. At the same time, however, contempt for an all too individualistic character loses its relevance. The staunchly zealous person who succeeds in steering his hatred and his love in the prescribed direction has nothing on the narrow egoist who has only his own interests at heart. In a society in which everyone is alike, the analysis of which is immediately useful, the relationship to unfamiliar individuals is no longer mediated by an understanding of their particular individuality. Love and hate originate here from commands, not from insight. Precisely because of this, there exists less that can be objectively understood. Under these conditions the individual sinks to the level of an element of the masses that ultimately looks similar to all other elements. This form of equality does not entail that each person is able to survey the whole and find his own goals sublated in it on the basis of a rationalization of the labor process. Rather, it implies only negative equality before the law, which recognizes no differences. Not everyone has the same freedom to develop his or her potentials. Rather, each person must sacrifice them equally.

It is axiomatic that those who fail because of their lack of participation in society surface again and again. However, they are difficult to identify for two reasons. First, the majority of human beings regard success as a legend whose main sources are revealed in the biographies of heroes and leaders. Second, under the conditions of current economic trends, increasingly questionable human qualities are coming to form the criteria for building a hierarchy. The virtues that decide whether or not one climbs socially are these days more often than not connected with ruthlessness. In the age of the totalitarian state, competition has become wilder and more unscrupulous not only on the world market but also among peoples. The bad elements of liberalism are proliferating madly at present, while the good ones have come under censure.

The attempt to conceive of human beings either as a fixed or as an evolving unity is futile. Anthropology assumes "that the complex of questions regarding human beings represents a matter that is closed in itself and, in a manner of speaking, primary. Modern developments lead us increasingly to destroy this unity and to challenge the claim of man in the questions that he poses to himself in order to find something original."[21] Human characteristics are inextricably linked to the course of history, and history itself is in no way marked by a uniform will. Like the object of anthropological studies, even history itself represents no autonomous entity. Our own concept of history is structured by both theoretical and practical considerations of the present. The reconciliation of theory with its object, which in fact constitutes intellectual progress, does not mean that knowledge and existence will ever be in accord, for as the function of knowledge in society changes, so too does its meaning and the reality on which it is based. When knowledge loses this insight into itself, it becomes a fetish that finds expression in philosophy and in the battle of skepticism against philosophy. The foregoing remarks challenge the notion of a uniform definition of man, since history up to now has shown us that the fate of human beings is infinitely varied. The argument that has been advanced against any concept of historically necessary transformations, namely that such a concept is contrary to human nature, must be put to rest once and for all. It may be true that the more liberal philosophical anthropologists are in fact not subject to this criticism and explicitly teach that we cannot predict what potentials mankind has yet to fulfill. However, their undialectical method has, at least for the social pessimism that emerges from allegedly conflicting experience, made their appeal to essence and determination seem "plebeian" and has distorted the actual state of affairs. The denial of an unchanging, constant human nature should, on the other hand, not be taken as an absolute to the extent that the belief in a universal human nature appears only as a slight error. One must also recognize that happiness and misery run constantly through history; that human beings as they are have their limits and deserve consideration; and that there is a price to be paid for overlooking those limits.

On the Problem of Truth

The philosophic thought of recent decades, shot through with contradictions, has also been divided on the problem of truth. Two opposing and unreconciled views exist side by side in public life and, not
infrequently, in the behavior of the same individual. According to
one, cognition never has more than limited validity. This is rooted in
objective fact as well as in the knower. Every thing and every relation
of things changes with time, and thus every judgment as to real situations must lose its truth with time. "Every particular entity is given
to us in time, occupies a definite place in time, and is perceived as
lasting for a length of time and during this time developing changing
activities and possibly altering its properties. Thus all our judgments
on the essence, properties, activities, and relations of particular things
are necessarily involved with the relationship to time, and every judgment of this sort can only be valid for a certain time."[1] Subjectively,
too, truth is viewed as necessarily circumscribed. Perception is shaped
not only by the object but by the individual and generic characteristics
of human beings. It is particularly this subjective moment to which
the modern science of mind has given its attention. Depth psychology
seemed to destroy the illusion of absolutely valid truth by pointing
out that the function of consciousness only made its appearance together with unconscious psychic processes, while sociology made a
philosophically developed discipline out of the doctrine that every idea
belongs to an intellectual pattern bound up with a social group, a
"standpoint." Present-day relativism, in particular, has subjectivist
characteristics, but it is by no means the sole representative of this

period's intellectual attitude toward truth. Rather, it is opposed by the impulse to blind faith, to absolute submission, which has always been necessarily linked with relativism as its opposite, and is once again characteristic of the cultural situation today. Since the metaphysical reworking of the concept of the intuition of essence, which at first had been understood in the strictest sense, a new dogmatism has developed within philosophy. This development in the history of ideas reflects the historical circumstance that the social totality to which the liberal, democratic, and progressive tendencies of the dominant culture belonged also contained from its beginning their opposite compulsion, chance and the rule of primal nature. By the system's own dynamic, this eventually threatens to wipe out all its positive characteristics. The role of human autonomy in the preservation and renewal of social life is completely subordinated to the effort to hold together mechanically a dissolving order. The public mind is increasingly dominated by some rigid judgments and a few postulated concepts.

The appearance of this contradiction in our time repeats in distorted form a discord which has always permeated the philosophy of the bourgeois era. Its prototype in the history of philosophy is the linkage of Descartes's universal methodical doubt with his devout Catholicism. It extends to the details of his system. It reveals itself not only in the unreconciled juxtaposition of faith and contradictory knowledge, but in the theory of cognition itself. The doctrine of a solid *res cogitans,* a self-contained ego independent of the body, which serves as an absolute resolution of the attempt at doubt and is preserved immutable in the metaphysics of Descartes and his idealistic successors, reveals itself as an illusion corresponding to the situation of the bourgeois individual and present before the inquiry rather than based on it. The independent existence of individual souls, the principle which for Descartes makes the world philosophically intelligible, is no easier to reconcile with the criteria and the whole spirit of the analytic geometry which he himself invented than is his proclamation of empty space as the sole physical substance with the theological dogma of transubstantiation. Complete doubt as to the reality of material truth, the constant emphasis on the uncertainty, conditional character, and finiteness of all definite knowledge, immediately next to ostensible

insights into eternal truths and the fetishization of individual categories and modes of being—this duality permeates the Cartesian philosophy.

It finds its classic expression in Kant. The critical method was supposed to perform the task of differentiating the purely conditional
and empirical from "pure" knowledge and reached the conclusion
that pure knowledge was possible only in regard to the conditions of
the conditional. The system of the necessary subjective conditions of
human knowledge is the exclusive goal of transcendental philosophy.
To Hume's skepticism, Kant opposes nothing but the sensory and
conceptual forms of knowledge and what can be deduced therefrom.
But what comes into existence on the basis of these conditions, the
theory of our actual world and not a merely possible one, knowledge
of actual nature and existing human society, lacks for Kant the criteria of genuine truth and is only relative. Everything that we know of
reality, of conditions in space and time, relates according to him only
to appearances, and of these he claims to have shown "that they are
not things (but only a form of representation), and that they are not
qualities inherently belonging to the things in themselves."[2] In regard
to knowledge of the world, he is no less a skeptical relativist than the
"mystical" and "dreaming" idealists whom he combats. In the latest
phase of transcendental philosophy, this subjective relativism is clearly
formulated: "In the last analysis, all being is relative (as opposed to
the false ideal of an absolute Being and its absolute truth), and is
nevertheless *relative in some customary sense to the transcendental subjectivity*. But this subjectivity alone is 'in and for itself.' "[3] Along with the
careful and differentiated theoretical philosophy, which did indeed
keep thought rooted in the ahistorical sphere of transcendental subjectivity, there are in Kant the postulates of practical reason and—
linked to them by conclusions which are in part extremely questionable—the transformation into absolutes of the existing property relations under prevalent public and private law. In the *Critique of Practical
Reason,* which fetishizes the concept of duty, he did not in any way
overcome the need for an immovable intellectual foundation but merely
met it in a way more fitting to the time than that of the rationalist
ontology of the period. The theoretical philosophy itself assumes that
there is absolute knowledge, independent of any sensory experience,

and indeed that this alone deserves the name of truth. Even the *Critique of Pure Reason* depends on the assumption that pure concepts and judgments exist "a priori" in the consciousness, and that metaphysics not only has always existed but will of right exist for all eternity. Kant's work embraces in itself the contradiction between the German and English schools of philosophy. The resolution of the contradictions it produces, the mediation between critique and dogmatic system, between a mechanistic concept of science and the doctrine of intelligible freedom, between belief in an eternal order and a theory isolated from practice, increasingly and vainly occupied his own thought till the last years of his life: this is the mark of his greatness. Analysis carried through to the end and skeptical distrust of all theory on the one hand and readiness to believe naively in detached fixed principles on the other, these are characteristic of the bourgeois mind. It appears in its most highly developed form in Kant's philosophy.

This dual relationship to truth is again mirrored in the failure of the progressive methods of the scholar to influence his attitude toward the most important problems of the time, the combination of notable knowledge in the natural sciences with childlike faith in the Bible. The association of that particularly strict tendency in modern philosophy, positivism, with the crudest superstition has already been noted in this journal.[4] Auguste Comte not merely laid the groundwork for a whimsical cult, but prided himself on his understanding of the various theories of the beyond. William James turned to mysticism and even mediumism.[5] The brain appears to him not so much to promote as to obstruct the enlightening intuitions which exist "ready-made in the transcendental world" and come through as telepathic experiences as soon as the brain's activity is "abnormally" reduced. "The word 'influx' used in Swedenborgian circles" describes the phenomenon very well.[6] The pragmatist F. C. S. Schiller, whom James quotes, declares on this point, "Matter is not that which produces consciousness but that which limits it," and he conceives of the body as "a mechanism for inhibiting consciousness."[7] This inclination to spiritualism can be followed through the later history of positivism. In Germany, it seems to have reached its culmination in the philosophy of Hans Driesch, in which a scientism carried to extremes goes together with unconcealed occultism in all questions of this world and the beyond. In this, the occultist dilemma finds a grotesque expression in his logic and theory of knowledge through intentional formalism and rigidity and through the monomaniacal reference of all the problems of the world to some few biological experiments. On the other side, the misconception of a self-sufficient science independent of history appears through the pseudoscientific dress of his barbarous errors in religion and practice.

Only in the decline of the contemporary epoch has it become the typical behavior of scholars to develop high critical faculties in a specific branch of science while remaining on the level of backward groups regarding questions of social life and echoing the most ignorant phrases. In the beginning of the bourgeois order, the turn to specific juristic and scientific studies without regard to social and religious demands immediately produced a moment of liberation from the theological tutelage of thought. But as a result of the alteration of the social structure, this sort of production without regard to the rational relation to the whole has become regressive and obstructive in all fields—in science just as in industry and agriculture. This abstractness and ostensible independence of the bourgeois science industry shows itself in the mass of isolated individual empirical studies, not related to any sort of theory and practice by clear terminology and subject matter. It is likewise visible in the efforts of scientists, without any significant reason, to divest their concepts of all empirical material, and especially in the inordinate mathematization of many intellectual disciplines. The conventional attitude of the scholar to the dominant questions of the period and the confinement of his critical attention to his professional specialty were formerly factors in the improvement of the general situation. Thinkers ceased to be concerned exclusively with the welfare of their immortal souls, or to make concern for it their guide in all theoretical matters. But subsequently this attitude has taken on another meaning: instead of being a sign of necessary courage and independence, the withdrawal of intellectual energies from general cultural and social questions, the placing of actual historical interests and struggles in a parenthesis, is more a sign of anxiety and incapacity for rational activity than of an inclination to the true tasks of science. The substance underlying intellectual phenomena changes with the social totality.

It is not the intention here to go into detail in regard to the historical causes of this dual relationship to truth. The competition within the bourgeois economy, in the context of which the forces of this society unfolded, produced a critical spirit which not only was able to liberate itself from the bureaucracies of church and absolutism but, driven by the dynamic of the economic apparatus, can to a fantastic degree place nature at its service. But this power only seems to be its own. The methods for the production of social wealth are available, the conditions for the production of useful natural effects are largely known, and the human will can bring them about. But this spirit and will themselves exist in false and distorted form. The concept of having power over something includes deciding for oneself and making use of it for one's own purposes. But domination over nature is not exercised according to a unified plan and purpose, but merely serves as an instrument for individuals, groups, and nations which use it in their struggle against one another and, as they develop it, at the same time reciprocally circumscribe it and bend it to destructive ends. Thus, the bearers of this spirit, with their critical capacity and their developed thinking, do not really become masters but are driven by the changing constellations of the general struggle which, even though summoned up by men themselves, face them as incalculable forces of destiny. This seemingly necessary dependence, which increasingly bears fruit in disruptive tensions and crises, general misery and decline, becomes for the greatest part of humanity an incomprehensible fate. But to the extent that the alteration of basic relationships is excluded in practice, a need arises for an interpretation based purely on faith. The conviction that a constricting and painful constellation is essentially unalterable prods the mind to give it a profound interpretation so as to be able to come to terms with it without despairing. Death as the inevitable end was always the basis of the religious and metaphysical illusion. The metaphysical need which permeates the history of this period stems from the fact that the inner mechanism of this society, which produces insecurity and continuous pressure, does not emerge into clear consciousness and is put up with as something necessary and eternal, rather than as an object of effective change. The firm faith which was part of the mortar of the medieval social structure has disappeared. The great systems of European philosophy were always intended only for an educated upper crust and fail completely in the face of the psychic needs of the impoverished and socially continually sinking sections of the citizenry and peasantry, who are nevertheless completely tied to this form of society by upbringing, work, and hope and cannot believe it to be transitory. This is why the intellectual situation has for decades been dominated by the craving to bring an eternal meaning into a life which offers no way out, by philosophical practices such as the direct intellectual or intuitive apprehension of truth, and finally by blind submission to a personality, be it an anthroposophic prophet, a poet, or a politician. To the extent to which individual activity is circumscribed and the capacity for it eventually stunted, there exists the readiness to find security in the protective shelter of a faith or person taken as the vessel and incarnation of the truth. In particular periods of the rise of contemporary society, the expectation of steady progress within its own framework reduced the need for an interpretation that would transfigure reality, and the rational and critical faculties achieved greater influence in private and public thought. But as this form of social organization becomes increasingly crisis-prone and insecure, all those who regard its characteristics as eternal are sacrificed to the institutions which are intended as substitutes for the lost religion.

This is, to be sure, only one aspect of the social situation out of which the shaky relationship to truth in modern times arises. A fundamental analysis of the fallacious bourgeois self-perception, which preserves the ideology of complete inner freedom in the face of the dependence and insecurity of its bearers, could show that the liberal validation of alien ideas (the mark of relativism) has a common root with the fear of making one's own decisions, which leads to belief in a rigid absolute truth: the abstract, reified concept of the individual which inescapably dominates thought in this economic system. But here the question is less one of the derivation of the phenomenon than of its practical significance. Is there really only the choice between acceptance of a final truth, as proclaimed in religions and idealistic schools of philosophy, and the view that every thesis and every theory is always merely "subjective," i.e., true and valid for a person or a group or a time or human beings as a species, but lacking objective validity? In developing the dialectical method, bourgeois thought itself has made the most ambitious attempt to transcend this antinomy. Here the goal of philosophy no longer appears, as in Kant, to be merely the system of the subjective factors of cognition; perceived truth is no longer so empty that in practice one must take refuge in the solidity of faith.

While the concrete content is perceived as conditional and dependent and every "final" truth is just as decisively "negated" as in Kant, it does not for Hegel simply fall through the sieve in the sifting out of pure knowledge. Recognition of the conditional character of every isolated view and rejection of its absolute claim to truth does not destroy this conditional knowledge; rather, it is incorporated into the system of truth at any given time as a conditional, one-sided, and isolated view. Through nothing but this continuous delimitation and correction of partial truths, the process itself evolves its proper content as knowledge of limited insights in their limits and connection.

To skepticism, Hegel opposes the concept of determinate negation. The progressive recognition of partial truths, the advance from one isolated definition to another, certainly does not mean for him a mere lining up of attributes but a description which follows the actual subject matter in all particulars. This critique of every concept and every complex of concepts by progressive incorporation into the more complete picture of the whole does not eliminate the individual aspects, nor does it leave them undisturbed in subsequent thought, but every negated insight is preserved as a moment of truth in the progress of cognition, forms a determining factor in it, and is further defined and transformed with every new step. Precisely because of this, the methodological form of thesis, antithesis, and synthesis is not to be applied as a "lifeless schema."[8] If at any given time the antithesis expresses the critical and relativizing impetus in opposition to the assimilation and establishment of a pattern of thought, thesis and antithesis together immediately form a new insight, a synthesis, because the negation has not simply rejected the original insight but has deepened and defined it. Hegel does not end up with the bare assurance that all definite knowledge is transitory and unreal, that what we know is only appearance in contrast to an unknowable thing in itself or an intuitively perceived essence. If for Hegel the true is the whole, the whole is not something distinct from the parts in its determinate structure, but is the entire pattern of thought which at a given time embraces in itself all limited conceptions in the consciousness of their limitation.

Since the dialectical method does not rest with showing that a thing is conditioned but takes the conditioned thing seriously, it escapes the relativistic formalism of the Kantian philosophy. Hegel therefore does not need to make a fetish out of an isolated concept like that of duty. He recognizes the vain effort of all idealistic philosophy before him to make the whole content of the world disappear in some conceptual generalization and declare all specific differences unreal as opposed to such attributes as the infinite, will, experience, absolute indifference, consciousness, etc. The second-rate thought to which the world always appears as a mysterious presentation in which only the initiate knows what goes on behind the scenes, which sets philosophy to solving an ostensible riddle in order to know once and for all or even to despair that such a key is not to be found—this sort of dogmatism does not exist in Hegel. Rather, the dialectical method quickly led him to become aware of the stupidity of such philosophical work and to see in development and flux what presents itself as absolute and eternal.

But insofar as this method, in Hegel, still belongs to an idealistic system, he has not freed his thought from the old contradiction. His philosophy shares relativism's indifference to particular perceptions, ideas, and goals. It is also marked by its hypostatization of conceptual structures and by the inability to take theoretical and practical account of the dogmatism and historical genesis of his own thought. Its dogmatic side has been especially often attacked in the critique of cognition since the middle of the nineteenth century. In place of those doctrines that made an abstract concept into substance, that is, that made this limited aspect identical with Being by dirempting it from history and that thus degenerate into naive faith, Hegel puts the hypostatization of his own system. In his polemic against skepticism and relativism, he himself says, "But the *goal* is as necessarily fixed for knowledge as the serial progression; it is the point where knowledge no longer needs to go beyond itself, where Notion corresponds to object and object to Notion. Hence the progress towards this goal is also unhalting, and short of it no satisfaction is to be found at any of the stations on the way."[9] Hegel believes that he guarantees this satisfaction through the whole of his thought. For him, philosophy has the same absolute content as religion, the complete unity of subject and object, a final and eternally valid knowledge.

What mankind, pressed on all sides by the boundaries of his purely terrestrial life, in fact requires is that region of more essential reality, in which every opposition and contradiction is overcome, and freedom can finally claim to be wholly at peace with itself. And this is, of course, nothing other than absolute Truth itself, no merely relative truth. In the Truth, according to its highest notion, all must be brought home to one unity. In it there can be no more opposition between freedom and necessity, Spirit and Nature, knowledge and the object of knowledge, law and impulse, between whatever form, in fact, the opposition of these contradictory phenomena of human experience may assume. . . . Our ordinary conscious life fails to overcome this contradiction, and either plunges desperately into the same, or thrusts it on one side and makes its escape from it in some other way. Philosophy will, however, so address itself to the two determinating factors of the contradiction as to show that they are apprehended as isolate from each other in abstraction, not according to their concrete notion; and by the grasp of this latter it will demonstrate the one-sidedness in its relative character, placing these opposing aspects in the fuller union and harmony which is truth. It is the function of philosophy to grasp and formulate this notion of truth. . . . Philosophy has no other object than God. In its substance it is in fact rational theology, and in its service of the truth a continual service of God.[10]

According to Hegel himself, the doctrine of an absolute self-contained truth has the purpose of harmonizing in a higher spiritual region the "oppositions and contradictions" not resolved in the world. Especially in his later lectures and writings, he stresses that "the sphere of truth, freedom, and . . . satisfaction"[11] is to be found not in the mechanism of reality but in the spiritual spheres of art, religion, and philosophy. He opposes this peace and satisfaction in thought not only to skeptical despair but to the active attitude which tries to overcome the incompleteness of existing conditions "in some other way."

This dogmatic narrow-mindedness is not some sort of an accidental defect of his doctrine which one can strip off without changing anything essential. Rather, it is inextricably bound up with the idealistic character of his thought and enters into all the details of his application of the dialectic. Hegel cannot be reproached for the role in his thought played by external observation, which as Trendelenburg points out in his criticism[12] gives rise to the basic concept of the dialectic: movement. He himself emphasized the importance of experience for philosophy. Rather, in contemplating his own system, Hegel forgets one very definite side of the empirical situation. The belief that this system is the completion of truth hides from him the significance of the temporally conditioned interest which plays a role in the details of the dialectical presentation through the direction of thought, the choice of material content, and the use of names and words, and diverts attention from the fact that his conscious and unconscious partisanship in regard to the problems of life must necessarily have its effect as a constituent element of his philosophy. Thus, his conceptions of nation and freedom, which form the backbone of many parts of his work, are not perceived in terms of their temporal presuppositions and their transitory character; on the contrary, as conceptual realities and forces, they are made the basis of the historical developments from which they are abstracted. Because Hegel does not recognize and consistently embrace the specific historical tendencies which find expression in his own work, but presents himself as absolute Spirit through his philosophizing and accordingly preserves on ostensible distance and impartiality, many parts of his work lack clarity and, in spite of the revolutionary sharpness and flexibility of the method, take on the arbitrary and pedantic character that was so closely bound up with the political conditions of his time. In the idealistic thought to which it owes its existence, dialectic is beset by dogmatism. Since the abstractions at which the method arrives are supposed to be moments in a system in which thought "no longer needs to go beyond itself," the relationships comprehended by it are also regarded as unalterable and eternal. If a great deal may happen in history yet to come, even if other peoples, e.g., the Slavs,[13] should take over leadership from those nations which have in the past been decisive, nevertheless no new principle of social organization will become dominant and no decisive change will take place in the organization of humanity. No historical change which brought about a new form of human association could leave the concepts of society, freedom, right, etc., unaltered. The interconnection of all categories, even the most abstract, would be affected thereby. Hence, Hegel's belief that his thought comprehended the essential characteristics of all being—the unity of which remained as it appeared in the system, a complete hierarchy and totality undisturbed by the becoming and passing of individuals—represented the conceptual eternalization of the earthly relationships on which it was based. Dialectic takes on a transfiguring function. The laws of life, in which according to Hegel domination and servitude as well as poverty and misery have their eternal place, are sanctioned by the fact that the conceptual interconnection in which they are included is regarded as something higher, divine and absolute. Just as religion and the deification of a race or state or the worship of nature offer the suffering individual an immortal and eternal essence, so Hegel believes he has revealed an eternal meaning in the contemplation of which the individual should feel sheltered from all personal misery. This is the dogmatic, metaphysical, naive aspect of his theory.

Its relativism is directly bound up with this. The dogmatic assertion that all the particular views which have ever entered the lists against one another in real historical combat, all the creeds of particular groups, all attempts at reform are now transcended and canceled out, the notion of the all-embracing thought which is to apportion its partial rightness and final limitation to every point of view without consciously taking sides with any one against the others and deciding between them—this is the very soul of bourgeois relativism. The attempt to afford justification to every idea and every historical person and to assign the heroes of past revolutions their place in the pantheon of history next to the victorious generals of the counterrevolution, this ostensibly free-floating objectivity conditioned by the bourgeoisie's stand on two fronts against absolutist restoration and against the proletariat, has acquired validity in the Hegelian system along with the idealistic pathos of absolute knowledge. It is self-evident that tolerance toward all views that belong to the past and are recognized as conditioned is no less relativistic than negativist skepticism. The more the age demands unsparing outspokenness and defense of particular truths and rights, the more unequivocally such tolerance reveals its inherent inhumanity. If, in spite of the lack of a conscious relationship between his philosophy and any particular practical principle, Hegel was guided in detail not simply by the conservative Prussian spirit but also by progressive interests, his dogmatism nevertheless prevented his recognizing and defending these tendencies that found expression in his science as his own purposes and progressive interests. He seems to speak of himself when he describes how "consciousness drops like a discarded cloak its idea of a good that exists [only] in principle, but has as yet no actual existence."[14] In Hegel, as in Goethe, the progressive impulses enter secretly into the viewpoint which ostensibly comprehends and harmonizes everything real impartially. Later relativism, in contrast, directs its demonstration of limiting conditionality mainly against the progressive ideas themselves, which it thereby seeks to flatten, that is, to equate with everything already past. In its conceptual projections, the new as well as the old easily appear as simple rationalizing and ideology. Since the recognition of the truth of particular ideas disappears behind the display of conditions, the coordination with historical unities, this impartial relativism reveals itself as the friend of what exists at any given time. The dogmatism concealed within it is the affirmation of the existing power, what is coming into being needs conscious decision in its struggle, while the limitation to mere understanding and contemplation serves what is already in existence. That impartial partisanship and indiscriminate objectivity represent a subjective viewpoint is a dialectical proposition that indeed takes relativism beyond itself.

In materialism, dialectic is not regarded as a closed system. Understanding that the prevalent circumstances are conditioned and transitory is not here immediately equated with transcending them and canceling them out. Hegel declares: "No one knows, or even feels, that anything is a limit or defect, until he is at the same time above and beyond it. . . . A very little consideration might show that to call a thing finite or limited proves by implication the very presence of the infinite and unlimited, and that our knowledge of a limit can only be when the unlimited is *on this side* in consciousness." [15] This view has as its presupposition the basic postulate of idealism that concept and being are in truth the same, and therefore that all fulfillment can take place in the pure medium of the spirit. Inner renewal and exaltation, reformation and spiritual elevation were always the solution to which he pointed. Insofar as dealing with and changing the external world was regarded as at all fundamental, it appeared as a mere consequence of this. Materialism, on the other hand, insists that objective reality is not identical with man's thought and can never be merged into it. As much as thought in its own element seeks to copy the life of the object and adapt itself to it, thought is never simultaneously the object thought about, unless in self-observation and reflection—and not even there. To conceptualize a defect is therefore not to transcend it; concepts and theories constitute one moment of its rectification, a prerequisite to the proper procedure, which as it progresses is constantly redefined, adapted, and improved.

An isolated and conclusive theory of reality is completely unthinkable. If one takes seriously the formal definition of truth which runs through the whole history of logic as the correspondence of cognition

with its object,[16] there follows from it the contradiction to the dogmatic interpretation of thought. This correspondence is neither a simple
datum, an immediate fact, as it appears in the doctrine of intuitive,
immediate certainty and in mysticism, nor does it take place in the
pure sphere of spiritual immanence, as it seems to in Hegel's metaphysical legend. Rather, it is always established by real events and
human activity. Already in the investigation and determination of facts,
and even more in the verification of theories, a role is played by the
direction of attention, the refinement of methods, the categorical
structure of the subject matter—in short, by human activity corresponding to the given social period. (The discussion here will not deal
with the question of how far all connection with such activity is avoided
by Husserl's "formal ontology" which refers "to any possible world in
empty generality"[17] or by formal apophantic, which likewise relates
to all possible statements in empty generality, or by other parts of
pure logic and mathematics, nor with how far they possess real cognitive value without regard to such a connection.)

If certain philosophical interpretations of mathematics correctly stress
its a priori character, that is, the independence of mathematical constructions from all empirical observation, the mathematical models of
theoretical physics in which the cognitive value of mathematics finally
shows itself are, in any case, structured with reference to the events
that can be brought about and verified on the basis of the current
level of development of the technical apparatus. As little as mathematics needs to trouble itself about this relationship in its deductions,
its form at any given time is nevertheless as much conditioned by the
increase in the technical capacity of humanity as the latter is by the
development of mathematics. The verification and corroboration [Be-
währung][18] of ideas relating to humanity and society, however, consist
not merely in laboratory experiments or the examination of documents, but in historical struggles in which conviction itself plays an
essential role. The false view that the present social order is essentially
harmonious serves as an impetus to the renewal of disharmony and
decline and becomes a factor in its own practical refutation. The correct theory of the prevalent conditions, the doctrine of the deepening
of crises and the approach of catastrophes, does, to be sure, find continuous confirmation [bestätigt] in all particulars. But the picture of a
better world that is intrinsic to this theory and guides the assertion of

the badness of the present, the idea of men and their capabilities immanent in it, finds its definition, correction, and confirmation in the course of historical struggles. Hence, activity is not to be regarded as an appendix, as merely what comes after thought, but enters into theory at every point and is inseparable from it. Just for this reason pure thought does not here give the satisfaction of having sure and certain grasp of the question and being at one with it. It is certainly impossible to speak too highly of the conquests of the human spirit as a factor in the liberation from the domination of nature and in improving the pattern of relationships. Social groups and possessors of power who fought against it, all propagandists of every sort of obscurantism, had their shady reasons and always led men into misery and servitude. But if in particular historical situations knowledge can, by its mere presence, obstruct evil and become power, the effort to make it in isolation the highest purpose and means of salvation rests on a philosophical misunderstanding. It cannot be said in general and a priori what meaning and value some particular knowledge has. That depends on social conditions as a whole at the particular time, on the concrete situation to which it belongs. Thoughts which, taken in isolation, are identical in content can at one time be unripe and fantastical and at another outdated and unimportant, yet in a particular historical moment can form factors of a force that changes the world.

There is no eternal riddle of the world, no world secret whose penetration once and for all is the mission of thought. This narrow-minded view, which ignores the constant alteration in knowing human beings along with the objects of their knowledge as well as the insurmountable tension between concept and objective reality, corresponds today to the narrow horizon of groups and individuals who, from their felt inability to change the world through rational work, grasp at and compulsively hold to universal recipes which they memorize and monotonously repeat. When dialectic is freed of its connection with the exaggerated concept of isolated thought, self-determining and complete in itself, the theory defined by it necessarily loses the metaphysical character of final validity, the sanctity of a revelation, and becomes an element, itself transitory, intertwined in the fate of human beings.

But by ceasing to be a closed system, dialectic does not lose the stamp of truth. In fact, the disclosure of conditional and one-sided aspects of others' thought and of one's own constitutes an important part of the intellectual process. Hegel and his materialist followers were correct in always stressing that this critical and relativizing characteristic is a necessary part of cognition. But being certain of one's own conviction and acting upon it do not require the assertion that concept and object are now one, and thought can rest. To the degree that the knowledge gained from perception and inference, methodical inquiry and historical events, daily work and political struggle, meets the test of the available means of cognition, it is the truth. The abstract proposition that once a critique is justified from its own standpoint it will show itself open to correction expresses itself for the materialists not in liberality toward opposing views or skeptical indecision, but in alertness to their own errors and flexibility of thought. They are no less "objective" than pure logic when it teaches that the relativistic "talk of a subjective truth which is this for one and the opposite for another must rate as nonsense."[19] Since that extrahistorical and hence exaggerated concept of truth is impossible which stems from the idea of a pure infinite mind and thus in the last analysis from the concept of God, it no longer makes any sense to orient the knowledge that we have to this impossibility and in this sense call it relative. The theory which we regard as correct may disappear because the practical and scientific interests which played a role in the formation of its concepts, and above all the facts and circumstances to which it referred, have disappeared. Then this truth is in fact irrecoverably gone, since there is no superhuman essence to preserve the present-day relationship between the content of ideas and their objects in its all-embracing spirit when the actual human beings have changed or even when humanity has died out. Only when measured against an extraterrestrial, unchanging existence does human truth appear to be of an inferior quality. At the same time as it nevertheless necessarily remains inconclusive and to that extent "relative," it is also absolute, since later correction does not mean that a former truth was formerly untrue. In the progress of knowledge, to be sure, much incorrectly regarded as true will prove wrong. Nevertheless, the overturning of categories stems from the fact that the relationship of concept and reality is affected and altered as a whole and in all its parts by the historical changes in forces and tasks. To a large extent the direction and outcome of the historical struggle depends on the decisiveness with which people draw the consequences of what they know, their readiness to test their theories against reality and refine them, in short by the uncompromising application of the insight recognized as true. The correction and further definition of the truth is not taken care of by History, so that all the cognizant subject has to do is passively observe, conscious that even his particular truth, which contains the others negated in it, is not the whole. Rather, the truth is advanced because the human beings who possess it stand by it unbendingly, apply it and carry it through, act according to it, and bring it to power against the resistance of reactionary, narrow, one-sided points of view. The process of cognition includes real historical will and action just as much as it does learning from experience and intellectual comprehension. The latter cannot progress without the former.

Freed from idealistic illusion, dialectic overcomes the contradiction between relativism and dogmatism. As it does not imagine the progress of criticism and definition to have ended with its own point of view and consequently does not hypostatize the latter, it by no means abandons the conviction that, in the whole context to which its judgments and concepts refer, its insights are valid not only for particular individuals and groups but in general—that is, that the opposing theory is wrong. Dialectical logic includes the principle of contradiction, but in materialism it has completely stripped off its metaphysical character, because here a static system of propositions about reality, indeed any relation of concept and object not historically mediated, no longer appears meaningful as an idea. Dialectical logic in no way invalidates the rules of understanding. While it has as its subject the forms of movement of the advancing cognitive process, the breaking up and restructuring of fixed systems and categories also belongs within its scope along with the coordination of all intellectual forces as an impetus to human practice in general. In an era which in its hopelessness tries to make everything into a fetish, even the abstract business of understanding, and would like thereby to replace the lost divine support, so that its philosophers rejoice in ostensibly atemporal relations between isolated concepts and propositions as the timeless truth, dialectical logic points out both the questionable character of the interest in such "rigor" and the existence of a truth apart from it that it in no way denies. If it is true that a person has tuberculosis, this concept may indeed be transformed in the development of medicine or lose its meaning entirely. But whoever makes a contrary diagnosis today with the same concept, not in terms of a higher insight which includes identifying this man's tuberculosis but simply denying the finding from the same medical standpoint, is wrong. The truth is also valid for whomever contradicts it, ignores it, or declares it unimportant. Truth is decided not by individuals' beliefs and opinions, not by the subject in itself, but by the relation of the propositions to reality, and when someone imagines himself the messenger of God or the rescuer of a people, the matter is not decided by him or even by the majority of his fellows, but by the relation of his assertions and acts to the objective facts of the rescue. The conditions to which those opinions point must really occur and be present in the course of events. There are at present various opposed views of society. According to one, the present wretched physical and psychological state of the masses and the critical condition of society as a whole, in the face of the developed state of the productive apparatus and technology, necessarily follow from the continued existence of an obsolete principle of social organization. According to the others, the problem is not the principle but interference with it or carrying it too far or a matter of spiritual, religious, or purely biological factors. They are not all true, only that theory is true which can grasp the historical process so deeply that it is possible to develop from it the closest approximation to the structure and tendency of social life in the various spheres of culture. It too is no exception to the rule that it is conditioned like every thought and every intellectual content, but the circumstance that it corresponds to a specific social class and is tied up with the horizon and the interests of certain groups does not in any way change the fact that it is also valid for the others who deny and suppress its truth and must nevertheless eventually experience it for themselves.

This is the place to define the concept of corroboration which dominates the logic of many otherwise opposed tendencies. Epicurus says: "Just as we desire the knowledge of the physician not for the sake of its technical perfection itself but for the sake of good health, and the skill of the helmsman possesses its value not for its own perfection but because it masters the methods of correct navigation, so wisdom, which must be perceived in skill in life, would not be sought after if it did not accomplish something."[20] The motif of accomplishment and corroboration as a criterion of science and truth has never disappeared in the subsequent history of philosophy. Goethe's line "What is fruitful is alone true" and the sentence "I have noticed that I regard as true that idea which is fruitful for me, fits in with the rest of my thought, and at the same time benefits me"[21] appear to imply a pragmatic theory of cognition. Many phrases of Nietzsche suggest a similar interpretation. "The criterion of truth lies in the enhancement of the feeling of power. . . . *What is truth? that* hypothesis which brings satisfaction, the smallest expense of intellectual strength, etc."[22] "True means 'useful for the existence of human beings.' But since we know the conditions for the existence of human beings only very imprecisely, the decision as to true and untrue can, strictly speaking, only be based on success."[23]

With Goethe and Nietzsche, such views, to which contradictions exist in their own writing, must be placed in the context of their entire thought in order to comprehend their meaning properly. But a special school of professional philosophy has grown up since the middle of the nineteenth century which places the pragmatic concept of truth in the center of its system. It has developed principally in America, where pragmatism has become the distinctive philosophical tendency through William James and subsequently John Dewey. According to this view, the truth of theories is decided by what one accomplishes with them. Their power to produce desired effects for the spiritual and physical existence of human beings is also their criterion. The furtherance of life is the meaning and measure of every science. "Our account of truth is an account of truths in the plural, of processes of leading realized *in rebus,* and having only this quality in common, that they pay."[24] If two theories are equally well fitted to produce a particular desired effect, it is at most still necessary to ask whether more intellectual energy is required with one than with the other. The corroboration of thoughts in practice is identical with their truth, and indeed pragmatism, especially in its most recent development, places the principal emphasis not so much on the mere confirmation of a judgment by the occurrence of the predicted factual situation, as on the promotion of human activity, liberation from all sorts of internal restraints, and the growth of personality and social life.

If ideas, meanings, conceptions, notions, theories, systems are instrumental to an active reorganization of the given environment, to a removal of some specific trouble and perplexity, then the test of their validity and value lies in accomplishing this work. If they succeed in their office, they are reliable, sound, valid, good, true. If they fail to clear up confusion, to eliminate defects, if they increase confusion, uncertainty and evil when they are acted upon, then are they false. Confirmation, corroboration, verification lie in works, consequences. . . . That which guides us truly is true—demonstrated capacity for such guidance is precisely what is meant by truth.[25]

This view is closely related to positivism in France. If Bergson had not taken over the pragmatically restricted concept of science from Comte, it would be impossible to understand the need for a separate, supplementary, vitalistic metaphysics. The isolated intuition is the wishful dream of objective truth to which the acceptance of the pragmatic theory of cognition must give rise in a contemplative existence. The pragmatic concept of truth in its exclusive form, without any contradictory metaphysics to supplement it, corresponds to limitless trust in the existing world. If the goodness of every idea is given time and opportunity to come to light, if the success of the truth—even if after struggle and resistance—is in the long run certain, if the idea of a dangerous, explosive truth cannot come into the field of vision, then the present social structure is consecrated and—to the extent that it warns of harm—capable of unlimited development. In pragmatism there lies embedded the belief in the existence and advantages of free competition. Where in regard to the present it is shaken by a feeling of the dominant injustice, as in the far-reaching pragmatic philosophy of Ernst Mach, the problem of necessary change forms a personal commitment, a utopian supplement with a merely external connection to the other part, rather than a principle for the development of theory. It is therefore easy to separate that ideal from the empirico-critical way of thinking without doing it violence.

There are various elements contained in the concept of corroboration that are not always differentiated from one another in pragmatist literature. An opinion can be completely validated because the objective relationships whose existence it asserts are confirmed on the basis of experience and observation with unobjectionable instruments and logical conclusions, and it can moreover be of practical use to its holder or other people. Even with the first of these relationships, a need arises for intellectual organization and orientation. In this connection, James speaks of a "function of guidance, which repays the effort."[26]

He sees that this theoretical corroboration, the agreement between idea and reality, delineation, often means nothing more than "that nothing contradictory from the quarter of that reality comes to interfere with the way in which our ideas guide us elsewhere."[27] If the difference between this theoretical verification of truth and its practical meaning, the "furtherance of life," is nevertheless often eliminated in a given moment of history, there comes into existence that idea of a strictly parallel progress of science and humanity which was philosophically established by positivism and has become a general illusion in liberalism. But the more a given social order moves from the promotion of the creative cultural forces to their restriction, the greater the conflict between the verifiable truth and the interests bound up with this form, bringing the advocates of truth into contradiction with the existing reality. Insofar as it affects the general public rather than their own existence, individuals have reason, despite the fact that proclaiming the truth can endanger them, to sharpen it and carry it forward, because the result of their struggle and the realization of better principles of society is decisively dependent on theoretical clarity. Pragmatism overlooks the fact that the same theory can be an annihilating force for other interests in the degree to which it heightens the activity of the progressive forces and makes it more effective. The epistemological doctrine that the truth promotes life, or rather that all thought that "pays" must also be true, contains a harmonistic illusion if this theory of cognition does not belong to a whole in which the tendencies working toward a better, life-promoting situation really find expression. Separated from a particular theory of society as a whole, every theory of cognition remains formalistic and abstract. Not only expressions like *life* and *promotion* but also terms seemingly specific to cognitive theory such as *verification, confirmation, corroboration,* etc. remain vague and indefinite, despite the most scrupulous definition and transference to a language of mathematical formulae, if they do not stand in relation to real history and receive their definition by being part of a comprehensive theoretical unity. The dialectical proposition is valid here too that every concept possesses real validity only as a part of the theoretical whole and arrives at its real significance only when, by its interconnection with other concepts, a theoretical unity has been reached and its role in this is known. What is the life promoted by the ideas to which the predicate of truth is to be attributed? In what does promotion consist in the present period? Is the idea to be considered valid when the individual who has comprehended it goes down while the society, the class, the public interest for which he fights strides forward? What does confirmation mean? Is the power of the slanderers and scoundrels to serve as confirmation of the assertions with whose help they attained it? Cannot the crudest superstition, the most miserable perversion of the truth about world, society, justice, religion, and history grip whole peoples and prove most excellent for its author and his clique? In contrast, does the defeat of the forces of freedom signify the disproof of their theory?

The concept of corroboration also plays a role in the materialistic way of thinking. Above all, it is a weapon against every form of mysticism because of its significance in the criticism of the acceptance of a transcendent and superhuman truth which is reserved for revelation and the insight of the elect, instead of being basically accessible to experience and practice. Yet as much as theory and practice are linked to history, there is no preestablished harmony between them. What is seen as theoretically correct is not therefore simultaneously realized. Human activity is no unambiguous function of insight, but rather a process which at every moment is likewise determined by other factors and resistances. This clearly follows from the present state of the theory of history. A number of social tendencies in their reciprocal action are described there theoretically: the agglomeration of great amounts of capital as against the declining share of the average individual in relation to the wealth of society as a whole, the increase of unemployment interrupted by ever shorter periods of a relative prosperity, the growing discrepancy between the apportionment of social labor to the various types of goods and the general needs, the diversion of productivity from constructive to destructive purposes, the sharpening of contradictions within states and among them. All these processes were shown by Marx to be necessary at a time when they could only be studied in a few advanced countries and in embryo, and the prospect of a liberal organization of the world still seemed excellent. But from the beginning, this view of history, now in fact confirmed, understood these developments in a particular way, that is, as tendencies which could be prevented from leading to a relapse into barbarism by the effort of people guided by this theory. This theory, confirmed by the course of history, was thought of not only as theory but as a moment of a liberating practice, bound up with the whole impatience of threatened humanity. The corroboration of the unswerving faith involved in this struggle is closely connected with the confirmation of the predicted tendencies that has already taken place, but the two aspects of the verification are not immediately identical; rather, they are mediated by the actual struggle, the solution of concrete historical problems based on theory substantiated by experience. Continuously in this process partial views may prove incorrect, timetables be disproved, corrections become necessary; historical factors which were overlooked reveal themselves; many a vigorously defended and cherished thesis proves to be an error. Yet the connection with the theory as a whole is in no way lost in this application. Adherence to its confirmed doctrines and to the interests and goals shaping and permeating it is the prerequisite for effective correction of errors. Unswerving loyalty to what is recognized as true is as much a moment of theoretical progress as openness to new tasks and situations and the corresponding refocusing of ideas.

The possibility must be considered of whether, in such a process of corroboration, the individuals and groups struggling for more rational conditions might succumb completely and human society develop retrogressively, a conceivable possibility which any view of history that has not degenerated into fatalism must formally take into account. This would refute the trust in the future which is not merely an external supplement to the theory but belongs to it as a force shaping its concepts. But the frivolous comments of well-meaning critics who use every premature claim, every incorrect analysis of a momentary situation by the adherents of the cause of freedom as evidence against their theory as a whole, indeed against theory in general, are nevertheless unjustified. The defeats of a great cause, which run counter to the hope for its early victory, are mainly due to mistakes which do not damage the theoretical content of the conception as a whole, however far-reaching the consequences they have. The direction and content of activity, along with its success, are more closely related to their theory for the historically progressive groups than is the case with the representatives of naked power. The talk of the latter is related to their rise only as a mechanical aid, and their speech merely supplements open and secret force with craft and treachery, even when the sound of the words resembles truth. But the knowledge of the falling fighter, insofar as it reflects the structure of the present epoch and the basic possibility of a better one, is not dishonored because humanity succumbs to bombs and poison gases. The concept of corroboration as the criterion of truth must not be interpreted so simply. The truth is a moment of correct practice. But whoever identifies it directly with success passes over history and makes himself an apologist for the reality dominant at any given time. Misunderstanding the irremovable difference between concept and reality, he reverts to idealism, spiritualism, and mysticism.

One can find in Marxist literature formulations close to pragmatist doctrine. Max Adler writes: "Theory turns directly into practice because, as Marxism has taught us to understand, nothing can be right which does not work in practice; the social theory is nevertheless only the recapitulation of the practice itself."[28] In regard to the identity of theory and practice, however, their difference is not to be forgotten. While it is the duty of everyone who acts responsibly to learn from setbacks in practice, these can nevertheless not destroy the confirmed basic structure of the theory, in terms of which they are to be understood only as setbacks. According to pragmatism, the corroboration of ideas and their truth merge. According to materialism, corroboration, the demonstration that ideas and objective reality correspond, is itself a historical occurrence that can be obstructed and interrupted. This viewpoint has no place for a basically closed and unknowable truth or for the existence of ideas not requiring any reality, but neither does it conceptually equate a conviction with untruth because a given constellation of the world cuts it off from corroboration and success. This also holds true for historical conflicts. The possibility of a more rational form of human association has been sufficiently demonstrated to be obvious. Its full demonstration requires universal success; this depends on historical developments. The fact that meanwhile misery continues and terror spreads—the terrible force which suppresses that general demonstration—has no probative force for the contrary.

The contradictions appear plainly in Max Scheler's extensive refutation of pragmatism in postwar Germany. Scheler did not fail to recognize the relative truths of pragmatism: "So-called 'knowledge for knowledge's sake' . . . exists nowhere and cannot and also 'should' not

exist, and has never existed anywhere in the world. When pragmatism attributes to the positive, exact sciences a primary purpose of
control, it is certainly not wrong. Rather, it is vain foolishness to consider positive science too 'good' or too 'grand' to give men freedom
and power, to guide and lead the world."[29] He also understood that
the criteria for practical work in this doctrine were modeled exclusively on the inorganic natural sciences and then mechanically transferred unchanged to knowledge as a whole. Had he analyzed the
concept of practice itself, it would have been evident that this is by no
means as clear and simple as it seems in pragmatism, where it reduces
and impoverishes truth. The meaning of the criterion is indeed not
developed in experiments in natural science. Its essence consists in
neatly isolating assertion, object, and verification. The undefined
and questionable aspect of the situation lies in the unarticulated relationship between the specific scientific activity and the life of the individuals involved and people in general, in the ostensible natural and
self-evident character of the theoretical act. The unresolved and
problematical aspect of its relationship to the concrete historical life
with which it is obviously interwoven appears as soon as one more
closely investigates the controlling categories and the choice of objects
and methods. Practice as corroboration itself leads to a critique of
positivist philosophy's hypostatization of natural science and its basic
concepts. The help of metaphysics is not required. However much
the problems of natural science are soluble within its boundaries and
with its specific means, independent of anything else, technical knowledge is in itself abstract and acquires its full truth only in the theory
which comprehends natural science in this particular historical situation as an aspect of society's development as a whole. If, in addition,
practice is understood as the criterion not merely in the special case
of physical science and the technique based on it but in the theory of
history, then it becomes clear without further ado that it embraces the
whole situation of society at any given moment. It takes more than
attention to isolated events or groups of events, or reference to general concepts such as that of progress, to apply the criterion of practice in deciding such questions as whether one or another judgment
of the contemporary authoritarian states is correct; whether they can
develop only in politically backward countries with strong remnants

of a landed aristocracy or whether they should be regarded as an adequate state form for the present economic phase, hence necessarily to be expected in other areas; whether this or that theory of colonial expansion applies; whether, to come to more abstract problems, the progressive technical sealing off and mathematization of logic and economics is more suited to their present situation than sticking to the development of concepts reflecting the historical situation. For this one needs a definite theory of society as a whole, which is itself only to be thought of in terms of particular interests and tasks with one's own point of view and activity.

Scheler does not pursue this conceptual movement in which it becomes clear that practice as an abstract criterion of truth changes into the concrete theory of society and casts off the formalism lent to it by the undialectical thought of the pragmatic school as such. He does not push this category to consequences that contradict the system of bourgeois thought in which it is firmly frozen. Instead, he opposes to the knowledge which can be verified and criticized through practice other forms of knowledge which according to him exist along with it and unconnected to it. He fails to recognize, in the elevation of mechanical natural science to a philosophical absolute, the ideological reflection of bourgeois society which was able greatly to increase reason and thereby human "power and freedom" in the technology of material production, and yet must block the ever more urgently necessary reorganization of human relations in production in accordance with its own principle. Thus it negates and destroys the same criteria of reason, power, and freedom which in cognitive theory it recognizes in isolated areas. Nor does he relate the bourgeois reality and science which he combats to their own ideas and standards, thus showing both society and ideas in their one-sidedness and abstraction and contributing to their supersession. Instead, like Bergson and other philosophers of this period, he goes on to proclaim his own special higher forms of cognition. In the face of the deepening contradictions between use in science and use for humanity, between use for privileged groups and for society as a whole, use for facilitating production and for easing life, the criterion of utility has become a dubious principle. Scheler does not further pursue the dialectic sketched out in his work, but rather places useful science at the very bottom in his ranking of knowledge. Turning back to earlier stages of human development, he advocates in opposition to "mastery or production knowledge" the two types of "cultural knowledge" and "redemption knowledge." He declares himself in complete agreement with the "new sub-bourgeois class" in the pragmatist interpretation of "the pretentious rationalist metaphysics of the bourgeois entrepreneurs,"[30] attacking most sharply classic German idealism and the historical materialism which issued from it. For him it is nonsense "that the human spirit and the ideal factors could ever control the real factors according to a positive plan. What J. G. Fichte, Hegel ('Age of Reason') and—following them, only postponed to a future point in time—Karl Marx, with his doctrine of the 'leap into freedom,' have dreamed will remain a mere dream for all time."[31] In contrast to this freedom, in which science would in fact have an important role to play, Scheler prophesied that the world should and could expect the rise of noble and spiritually elevated groups. If bourgeoisie and proletariat are "completely uncreative of all cultural knowledge and redemptive knowledge,"[32] this will be remedied from now on by the fact "that growing and advancing capitalism will gradually again be able to produce a whole class of purely cognitive people, and likewise of such people who have broken with the authoritative class doctrines, with bourgeois and proletarian metaphysics—that is, with the absolute mechanistic view and philosophical pragmatism. In this elite and its hands alone rests the future development of human knowledge. . . . But the future will have a new independent rise of the genuine philosophical and metaphysical spirit."[33] In connection with the passage previously cited, Epicurus defines the goal of knowledge and wisdom as the happiness and good fortune of humanity. Scheler's view and the present heralded by him are in irreconcilable opposition to this materialistic pragmatism.

In the analysis of the concept of corroboration and its role in open-ended, dialectical thought, it is shown that the decision on particular truths depends on still uncompleted historical processes. Progress in theory and practice is conditioned by the fact that, in contrast to relativistic neutrality, a definite theory corresponding to the highest available level of knowledge is adhered to and applied. This application reacts on the form of the theory and the meaning of its concepts. This is not merely a question of the correction of errors. Categories such as history, society, progress, science, and so on experience a change of function in the course of time. They are not independent essences but aspects of the whole body of knowledge at a given time, which is developed by human beings in interaction with one another and with nature and is never identical with reality. This also applies to dialectic itself. It is the sum total of the methods and laws which thought adheres to in order to copy reality as exactly as possible and to correspond as far as possible with the formal principles of real events.

What are the characteristics of dialectical thought? It relativizes every many-sided but isolated definition in the consciousness of the alteration of subject and object as well as their relationship. (What results in idealism from a postulated absolute takes place in materialism on the basis of developing experience.)[34] Instead of ranging attributes alongside one another, it seeks to show, by analysis of each general characteristic in respect to the particular object, that this generalization taken by itself simultaneously contradicts the object, and that in order to be properly comprehended it must be related to the contrary property and finally to the whole system of knowledge. From this follows the principle that every insight is to be regarded as true only in connection with the whole body of theory, and hence is so to be understood conceptually that in its formulation the connection with the structural principles and practical tendencies governing the theory is preserved. Bound up with this is the rule that, while maintaining unswerving fidelity to the key ideas and goals and the historical tasks of the epoch, the style of presentation should be characterized more by "as well as" than by "either-or." A basic principle is the inseparability of the regressive and progressive moments, the preserving and decomposing, the good and bad sides of particular situations in nature and human history. Instead of accepting the legitimate analyses and abstractions of professional science but turning to metaphysics and religion for an understanding of concrete reality, it tries to place the analytically achieved concepts in relation to one another and reconstruct reality through them. These and all the other characteristics of dialectical reason correspond to the form of a complicated reality, constantly changing in all its details.

Such very general intellectual laws of motion, which are abstracted from previous history and which form the content of dialectical logic in general, seem relatively constant and also extremely empty. But the special dialectical forms of description of a particular subject matter correspond to its characteristics and lose their validity as forms of the theory when their bases change. The critique of political economy comprehends the present form of society. In a purely intellectual construction, the concept of value is derived from the basic concept of the commodity. From this concept of value Marx develops the categories of money and capital in a closed system. All the historical tendencies of this form of economy—the concentration of capital, the falling rate of profit, unemployment and crises—are placed in relation to this concept and deduced in strict succession. At least in terms of the theoretical intention, a close intellectual relationship should exist between the first and most general concept, whose abstractness is further transcended with every theoretical step, and the unique historical event, in which every thesis necessarily follows from the first postulate, the concept of free exchange of commodities. According to the theoretical intention, whose success will not be examined here, knowledge of all social processes in the economic, political, and all other cultural fields will be mediated by that initial cognition. This attempt to carry the theory through to the end in the closed form of an inherently necessary succession of ideas has an objective significance. The theoretical necessity mirrors the real compulsiveness with which the production and reproduction of human life goes on in this epoch, the autonomy which the economic forces have acquired in respect to humanity, the dependence of all social groups on the self-regulation of the economic apparatus. That men cannot shape their labor according to their common will but, under a principle which sets them against one another individually and in groups, produce with their labor not security and freedom but general insecurity and dependence, that they fall into misery, war, and destruction instead of using the immeasurably increased social wealth for their happiness, and are the slaves instead of the masters of their fate—this finds expression in the form of logical necessity, proper to the true theory of contemporary society. It would therefore be wrong to think that events in a future society could be deduced according to the same principles and with the same necessity as the lines of development of the present one.

The meaning of the categories will change along with the structure of the society from which they are drawn and in whose description they play a role. The concept of historical tendency loses the compulsive character that it had in the present historical period while preserving a relation to the category of natural necessity, which may indeed be narrowed but can never be transcended completely. The concept of the individual will lose the character of an isolated monad and simultaneously the unconditionally central place it has held in the system of thought and feeling in recent centuries at the moment when individual and general goals really coincide and are supported in the whole society, when each person no longer merely imagines himself or herself to embody absolute self-determination but is in reality a member of a freely self-determining society. With the ending of the situation in which the contradiction between particular and general purposes necessarily follows from the economic structure, and in which the idea that the individualistic principle has been fully transcended rests partly on conscious deception and partly on impotent dreaming, the concept of the I loses its function of controlling the entire relation to the world and acquires another meaning. As long as the life of society flows not from cooperative work but from the destructive competition of individuals whose relationship is essentially conducted through the exchange of commodities, the I, possession, the mine and not-mine play a fundamental role in experience, in speech and thought, in all cultural expressions, characterizing and dominating all particulars in a decisive way. In this period, the world disintegrates into I and not-I as in Fichte's transcendental philosophy, and one's own death means absolute annihilation insofar as this relationship is not alleviated by metaphysical or religious faith. Like the categories of tendency and the individual, all other social concepts will be affected by the alteration of reality. The more formal categories such as the lawful nature of society, causality, necessity, science, etc., as well as the more material ones such as value, price, profit, class, family, and nation, acquire a different look in the theoretical structures which correspond to a new situation.

In traditional logic, this alteration of concepts is interpreted in such a way that the original divisions in the system of classification of a field of knowledge are made more specific by subdivisions. The general concept of tendency then includes the historical tendencies of the present society as well as the possible tendencies of a different sort in a future society. In spite of all historical changes, Aristotle's definition of the polis—composed of individuals and groups and differing not only quantitatively but qualitatively from its elements—can be absorbed into a supreme formal category of society, valid for all forms of society, and thus preserved in its general validity. For Aristotle himself slavery belonged to this highest category, while in later conceptual systems it is only one of the subcategories of society, contrasted to other definite types. The conceptual realism which dominates Platonic and in part medieval philosophy, and whose remnants have by no means yet been surmounted in modern logic (for instance, in modern phenomenology), has the character of discursive logic. It interprets all changes as mere additions of new subtypes under the universal types, made absolute and subsumed under the metaphysical view that all change is to be understood as the incarnation or emanation of permanent ideas and essences in ever-new particulars and exemplars. Thus, the essential would always remain in the old, there would be an eternal realm of unalterable ideas, and all change would affect only the lower levels of being. Indeed, it would not be genuinely real and would only exist for the dull senses of men. Since the Hegelian system hypostatizes the categories dealt with within its framework, it still preserves something of this realism and falls into the dualism of essence and appearance which it opposed so vigorously. The given fate of historically determined individuals and the changing circumstances of present and future history become null and void in comparison with the ideas which are supposed to underlie the past. The discursive logic of "understanding" is only limited inside Hegel's system; in the sense of a metaphysical legend, it retains its reifying power over his philosophy as a whole. The logic of the Understanding abstracts from the fact that in the face of the changed content of concepts, lumping them indiscriminately with those which formerly went under the same headings can become distortion, and a new definition, a new ordering and hierarchy of concepts can become necessary. Perhaps the category of tendency later becomes so restructured as to revolutionize its relation to the concept of systematic purpose on the one hand and that of the power of nature on the other. The concept of the state alters its relation to the categories of will, domination, force, society, etc. Such definite perspectives do not flow from observation of today's valid system of classification of social phenomena, but from the theory of historical development itself, of which the former is only an ordered, abstract inventory. The connection between the concrete movement of thought, as it develops in constant interrelation with the life of society, and the systems organized by the Understanding is not examined in detail by traditional logic, which relegates it to a separate discipline as the subject of the history of science or culture. It itself deals with the relations of unchanging concepts: how one passes from one to another judiciously and conclusively and how one develops from each what it contains. Traditional logic is "a science of the necessary laws of thought, without which no employment of understanding and the reason takes place, which consequently are the conditions under which alone the understanding can and should be consistent with itself—the necessary laws and conditions of its right use."[35] Their function is *"to make clear concepts distinct."*[36] This proceeds analytically, drawing out of the concept what is in it. The concept itself "remains the same; only the form is changed. . . . Just as by mere illumination of a map nothing is added to it, so by the mere clearing up of a given concept by analysis of its attributes this concept itself is not in the least degree enlarged."[37]

Traditional logic has nothing to do with the alteration of the "map" and the construction of new systems of classification. But if concepts are used without being strictly tied in to the existing system of reference, in which all previous discoveries of the branch concerned have been arranged, if they are used without that correct reading of the "map" which is required by the laws of logic, every intellectual outline remains blurred, or rather meaningless. The accurate description of the object results from the methodical collaboration of all cognitive forces in the theoretical construction. Aside from the "table of contents" for this content, which it does not itself produce, "the understanding in its pigeon-holing process" also gives conceptual material.[38] From time to time "the empirical sciences," investigation and analysis, "are able to meet" dialectical description "with materials prepared for it, in the shape of general uniformities, i.e. laws, and classifications of the phenomena."[39] The real significance of this work, the cognitive value of understanding, rests on the fact that reality knows not only constant change but also relatively static structures. Because development proceeds not gradually but in leaps, there are between these junctures, leaps, and revolutions periods in which the tensions and contradictions trying to break through appear as elements of a relatively closed and fixed totality, until the particular form of being turns into another. This determinate and organized state is therefore a necessary condition of truth but not its real form, movement, and progress.

Thus, traditional logic is inadequate for, and comprehends only individual aspects of, the historically conditioned alteration of the fundamental categories and every thought process about the subject matter. Since a concept plays a determinate role in the dialectical construction of an event, it becomes a nonautonomous aspect of a conceptual whole which has other qualities than the sum of all the concepts included in it. This whole, the construction of the particular object, can indeed only come into existence in a way appropriate to the existing knowledge if the concepts are interpreted in the sense that belongs to them in the systems of the individual sciences, in the systematic inventory of scientifically based definitions, insofar as it is a question of concepts for which special branches of science exist. In *Capital*, Marx introduces the basic concepts of classical English political economy— value, price, labor time, etc.—in accordance with their precise definitions. All the most progressive definitions drawn from scientific practice at that time are employed. Nevertheless, these categories acquire new functions in the course of the presentation. They contribute to a theoretical whole, the character of which contradicts the static views in connection with which they came into being, in particular their uncritical use in isolation. Materialist economics as a whole is placed in opposition to the classical system, yet individual concepts are taken over. The dialectical forms of the movement of thought show themselves to be the same as those of reality. A hydrogen atom observed in isolation has its specific characteristics, acquires new ones in molecular combination with other elements, and displays the old ones again as soon as it is freed from the combination. Concepts behave in the same way; considered individually, they preserve their definitions, while in combination they become aspects of new units of meaning.[40] The movement of reality is mirrored in the "fluidity" of concepts.

The open-ended materialistic dialectic does not regard the "rational" as completed at any point in history and does not expect to bring about the resolution of contradictions and tensions, the end of the historic dynamic, by the full development of mere ideas and their simple consequences. It lacks the aspect of the idealistic dialectic which Hegel described as "speculative" and at the same time as "mystical," namely, the idea of knowing the ostensibly unconditioned and thereby being oneself unconditioned.[41] It does not hypostatize any such universal system of categories. To attain the "positively rational," it does not suffice to resolve and transcend contradictions in thought. It requires the historical struggle whose guiding ideas and theoretical prerequisites are indeed given in the consciousness of the combatants. But the outcome cannot be predicted on a purely theoretical basis. It will be determined not by any firmly outlined unity such as the "course of history," the principles of which could be established indivisibly for all time, but by human beings interacting with one another and with nature, who enter into new relationships and structures and thereby change themselves. The resolution of contradictions in subjective thought and the overcoming of objective antagonisms can be closely intertwined, but they are in no way identical. In a particular historical period, a free society in the sense of the free development of the individual and in the sense of free enterprise on the basis of inequality will be conceptually and actually full of contradictions. The resolution in terms of ideas occurs through the concept of a differentiated higher form of freedom. It has a decisive voice in the real overcoming, but in no way coincides with it and predicts the future only abstractly and inexactly. Since the logic of the open-ended dialectic allows for the possibility that change will affect the entire present content of the categories, without therefore considering the theory formed from it as any less true, it corresponds exactly to the Hegelian conception of the difference between dialectic and understanding without overlaying it with a new dogmatism. "The Understanding stops short at concepts in their fixed determinateness and difference from one another; dialectic exhibits them in their transition and dissolution."[42] To be sure, the first is immanent in the second; without the definition and organization of concepts, without understanding, there is no thought and also no dialectic. But the understanding becomes metaphysical as soon as it absolutizes its function of preserving and expanding existing knowledge, of confirming, organizing, and drawing conclusions from it, or the results of that function as the existence and progress of truth. The revolutionizing, disintegration, and restructuring of knowledge, its changing relation to reality, its changes of function resulting from its intertwinement with history, fall outside the thought processes which traditional logic, whose theme is understanding, comprehends. Taken by itself, it leads to the erroneous concept of a detached thought with fixed, eternal, and autonomous results. Nietzsche said that a great truth "wants to be criticized, not worshiped."[43] This is valid for truth in general. He might have added that criticism includes not only the negative and skeptical moment but also the inner independence that does not let the truth fall but remains firm in its application even if it may sometime pass away. In the individual, the process of cognition includes not only intelligence but also character; for a group, not merely adaptation to changing reality but the strength to declare and put into practice its own views and ideas.

The division in the bourgeois spirit with regard to truth, in contrast to dialectical thought, finds especially clear expression in the attitude toward religion. In the face of the primitive materialism which dominates economic life, religion has become more and more internalized. The practice of general competition which characterizes contemporary reality was pitiless from the beginning, and with the exception of a few periods has become increasingly inhuman. Its means and consequences, which at particular historical moments have led to domination by small economic groups, the abandonment of power to the most culturally backward elements of society, and the extermination of minorities, notoriously contradict the basic teachings of Christianity. In a period in which, despite great resistance, reading and writing had to become common skills for economic reasons, and the contents of the Bible could not remain a permanent secret from the masses, it had long been inevitable that the opposing principle of Christianity would be openly sacrificed to reality, and the vulgar positivism of bare facts along with the worship of success, immanent in this lifestyle, would be propagated as the exclusive and highest truth. But the gross contradiction that existed was really understood within the bourgeoisie only by religious outsiders such as Kierkegaard and Tolstoy. The monistic propaganda of Strauss and Haeckel, who proclaimed it on the basis of scientific research, saw only the difference which it implied between natural science by itself and revelation and misunderstood both the spirit of the Gospels and historical reality. These materialists on the basis of natural science had to remain sectarians, for religion was indispensable for the social groups to which they belonged. The predominant intellectual attitude in recent centuries was not that of exposing the split. Instead, religion was so robbed of any clear and definite content, formalized, adapted, spiritualized, relegated to the innermost subjectivity, that it was compatible with every activity and every public practice that existed in this atheistic reality.

Since individuals began to think more independently, that is, since the rise of the new economic order, philosophy in all fields has ever more clearly fulfilled the function of erasing the contradiction between the dominant way of life and Christian or Christian-oriented theoretical and practical doctrines and ideas. The reason for this coincides with the root of bourgeois dogmatism in general. The isolated individual, who is simultaneously regarded as free and responsible, is in the present epoch necessarily dominated by anxiety and uncertainty. In addition to this inner need, which is directly grounded in the atomistic principles of the existing order, the external concern for social peace has led to great efforts to gloss over the irreconcilability of modern science and the way people conduct their lives with the religious views on the origin and structure of the world as well as the ideas of love for one's neighbor, justice, and the goodness of God. Troeltsch, a typical philosopher of religion in prewar Germany, openly states what he fears:

To anyone even moderately acquainted with human beings, it will be inconceivable that divine authority could ever disappear without damage to the moral law, that the generally coarse-thinking average person could do without this supplement to the motivation of morality. The abstraction of a self-validating law will be forever unrealizable for him; in connection with law, he will always have to think of the lawgiver and watcher. He may think of this a bit coarsely, but not so irrationally. . . . Where atheistic morality has undone divine authority among the masses, experience shows that there is little sense of that law left. A fierce hatred of all authority and an unbounded unchaining of selfishness as the most obvious thing in the world has been, with few exceptions, the easily comprehensible logical consequence.[44]

A social situation in which there would be no "watcher," either in the form of a transcendent being or "a self-validating law," to hold the "unbounded" selfishness of the masses in check is something Troeltsch cannot conceive of. Dogmatic adherence to the inherited conceptual world seems to him a self-evident proposition, a *thema probandum*. Nevertheless, he also sees

that the Protestant confessional axiom must be self-revised and more freely interpreted; that its accomplishments must find a broader, more general basis and make themselves far more independent of immediate clerical reality; that its style must leave room for detailed historical research and the definitive results of natural science, and be constantly prepared for new revisions on the basis of this work. Indeed, the possibility exists that eventually Christianity itself will cease to be axiomatic.[45]

The axioms to which earlier liberal theology could reach back have meanwhile been overturned. "Kant and Schleiermacher, Goethe and Hegel still lived under the influence of an axiomatic validation which no longer exists."[46] He therefore recommends resorting to Kant's critical philosophy "which undertakes to discover the ultimate presuppositions in the organization of consciousness instead of metaphysics."[47] He seeks refuge in a "critique of religious consciousness"[48] and hopes

to find a firm footing through a general theory of religion and its historical development. But this theory itself would have to be rooted in a transcendental theory of consciousness and to answer, from this ultimate basis of all scientific thinking, this ultimate and correct presupposition, two questions: the question of the justification of religion in general, and that of the difference in value between its historical forms. Theology is thereby referred to the philosophy of religion. On this basis only will it be able so to construe the essence and validity of Christianity as to satisfy the modern spirit of taking nothing for granted. The ultimate presuppositions lie in the philosophy of transcendentalism.[49]

According to this, the "justification of religion in general" and even the advantages of Christianity are still the question, and the whole uncertainty, the relativistic readiness for concessions not to the selfishness of the masses but to ostensibly nonaxiomatic science, becomes clear. Only one thing is preserved at any cost: "In all change there must be a permanent truth. This is a requirement of that ideal faith, to renounce which would be to renounce the meaning of the world."[50] If this so necessary faith only remains attached to an eternal meaning, one can come to terms with idealistic philosophy, Judaism, Islam, Confucianism, Brahmin and Buddhist ideas of salvation.[51]

This ambiguous relationship to religion characterizes the whole period, and only finds a particularly clear ideological expression in phenomena like Troeltsch. It is one aspect of the objective dishonesty which, despite the good conscience of the participants, dominated the spiritual atmosphere. If one looks closely at previous history, the fact that in many areas of public discussion the crude and obvious lie is now treated with honor represents no incomprehensible change. The situation of the bourgeoisie has resulted in the setting aside of intellectual development in moral and religious questions and the keeping in twilight of central areas, as if by tacit agreement. The religious philosophy of the Middle Ages outlines the spiritual horizon which corresponded to society at the time. Its most important results therefore form historical evidence of obvious greatness. Since the irreligion immanent in modern natural science and technology, these specifically bourgeois achievements, has found no corresponding place in the general consciousness, and the conflicts that this involves have not been arbitrated, official spirituality is characterized by hypocrisy and indulgence toward particular forms of error and injustice, and this has eventually spread over the cultural life of entire peoples. The only great spirit who, in the face of the gross thickening of this fog which has taken place since the middle of the last century, has achieved the freedom from illusion and the comprehensive view which are possible from the standpoint of the haute bourgeoisie, is Nietzsche. It must indeed have escaped him that the intellectual honesty with which he was concerned did not fit in with this social standpoint. The reason for the foulness against which he fought lies neither in individual nor national character but in the structure of society as a whole, which includes both. Since as a true bourgeois philosopher he made psychology, even if the most profound that exists today, the fundamental science of history, he misunderstood the origin of spiritual decay and the way out, and the fate which befell his own work was therefore inevitable. ("Who among my friends would have seen more in it than an impermissible presumption, completely indifferent to happiness?")[52]

The philosophically mediated dishonesty in questions of religion cannot be eliminated by psychological or other explanations. Whereas Nietzsche makes the religious question and Christian morality negatively central and thereby makes an ideologue of himself, this aspect of the existing situation also can only be eliminated by transcending it through higher forms of society. In dialectical thought, religious phenomena too are related to knowledge as a whole and judged at any given time in connection with the analysis of the whole historical situation. As important as it is to see the incompatibility of the religious content with advanced knowledge, the present shows that making religious questions central to the whole cultural problem can be foolish. One can find more penetrating analysis of bourgeois society in the literature of the Catholic counterrevolution in France, in Bonald and de Maistre and the writings of the Catholic royalist Balzac, than in the critics of religion in Germany at the same period. The devout Victor Hugo and Tolstoy have more nobly depicted and more vigorously fought the horrors of existing conditions than the enlightened Gutzkow and Friedrich Theodor Vischer. In the practical questions of daily life, efforts guided by dialectical thought can lead to temporary collaboration with religiously motivated groups and tendencies and radical opposition to antireligious ones. The complex of historical tasks which is decisive for an illusion-free and progressive attitude today does not divide people primarily on the basis of their religious preference. Groups and individuals may be characterized more quickly today on the basis of their particular interest (theoretically explicable, to be sure) or lack of interest in just conditions which promote the free development of human beings, in the abolition of conditions of oppression which are dangerous to and unworthy of humanity, than by their relation to religion. It follows from the differing cultural levels of social groups, the miserable state of education on social problems, and other factors, that religion can mean altogether different things for different classes and different ways of life. It requires not merely experience and theoretical education but a particular fate in society to avoid either inflating thought into the creation of idols or devaluing it as the sum total of mere illusions, making it an absolute lawgiver and unambiguous guide for action or separating it from the practical goals and tasks with which it interacts. It is a utopian illusion to expect that the strength to live with the sober truth will become general until the causes of untruth are removed.

The Rationalism Debate in Contemporary Philosophy

In the historiography of modern philosophy, rationalism is understood as that orientation which began with Descartes. One of its main doctrines consists in the division of the world into two independent realms, that of mental or spiritual substance and that of corporeal or extended substance. If, in Descartes's thought itself, this fundamental notion seems to be transgressed for theological reasons by the occasional assertion of a connection of the two separated parts at a certain point in the human brain, subsequent developments have eliminated this inconsistency: from now on, mental substance is to be regarded as completely independent of bodily reality.

Cartesian rationalism, which has dominated philosophical discussion since the seventeenth century, acquired its uniqueness from this fundamental division. According to it, the mind—which is separated from matter and is only externally coupled with it in the human being—is capable of producing valid knowledge out of itself. Its true activity consists in pure thought. In consequence of the fundamental separation of mind and matter, the experiences of the senses can in no way be considered as effects of, and thus as testimony to, the external world; they amount to murky, mutable, confused foundations of the life of the mind, not to sources of knowledge. The isolated ego discovers the eternally valid truths about God and the world through its application of mind to itself, through reflection on its own essence. In this exclusive recognition of pure thought, a static structure of the world is predetermined: its outlines must be absorbed in firm conceptual frameworks. As with all of idealist philosophy, rationalism thus presupposes a constant relationship between concept and reality, independent of human praxis.

The philosophical opponents of rationalism have not attacked its foundations. The well-known objections of the English empiricists to Continental rationalism were almost all directed toward its underestimation of the facts of experience in favor of conceptual construction. The questions of the justification and the reach of conceptual thought in general stood in the forefront of the rationalistic systems of the seventeenth century. But the increasing development of the bourgeois mode of production made necessary an orientation to this new world by means of experience. The general problem of shaping and dominating nature and society, which pervades Continental ontology and philosophy of law, developed on English soil into the concern of individuals to orient themselves quickly. The intellectual achievement that must have seemed increasingly important to the leading social groups was that of drawing conclusions from the observation of human beings and things in commercial life. From Locke to John Stuart Mill, English philosophy is largely characterized by the theory of thought processes of this type, though of course such problems did not necessarily constitute the conscious motivation of the individual philosophers. In the process, significant epistemological discoveries emerged, but the aforementioned assumptions of Cartesian philosophy remained untouched. Even among those French and German heirs of Descartes who denied one of the two halves of the world—namely, the material—the consequences of the division were retained to the extent that they continued to consider the part they did recognize as pure, isolated mind, as monad. Among them, however, this detached ego is preoccupied not with the self-actuated production of thought, but rather above all with the establishment and connection of sensuous impressions. Just like the Cartesians, the English empiricists view human existence as comprised of individual processes of consciousness, of *cogitationes*.

In both philosophical approaches, truth consists in judgments whose concepts are related to individual sense data as the general is to the particular. According to the empiricists, these concepts arise from the sensuous material and are derived by a process of progressive omission of substantive differences—that is, through abstraction. According to the rationalists, in contrast, they are fundamental unities inherent

in reason. As the Cartesians assert, the truths concerning the processes of reality exist a priori in each individual; each individual cognition must in principle be developed by deduction from the highest
judgments given to every rational being.

Similarly, empiricism asserts that each monad is capable of knowing
reality on the basis of pure processes of consciousness. Knowledge is
independent of forces external to or fundamentally different from
consciousness. Its relation to the object, its task, the limits of its capacity, indeed its most important contents may be determined or at least
classified once and for all. A firm world view can be outlined, however
skeptical it may be, because one can be certain of that which is essential for all future time. The emphasis on our ignorance, as it is to be
found in positivist writings since Hume—the assurance that "the essence of the mind [is] equally unknown to us with that of external
bodies"[1]—is every bit as much a dogmatic metaphysics as the eternal
truths of Cartesianism. From its analysis of consciousness positivism
arrives at an agnostic world view, Cartesian rationalism at a substantively more determinate one. Both hold that we must subject ourselves to the business of metaphysics, "in order to live at ease ever
after."[2] Hume wishes to relax contentedly when "we have arrived at
the utmost extent of human reason,"[3] and establishes this limit on the
basis of the self-reflection of consciousness. Kant unites the notion of
innate concepts with Hume's more modest belief in the limits of our
knowledge, and then likewise promulgates the outcome of the reflection of consciousness upon itself as the content of an immutable, universal theory. In these controversies of modern philosophy, the closed
individual consciousness is set on a par with human existence. According to the rationalist tendency, all problems were resolved when
the individual had gained a clear and concrete concept of itself; according to the empiricist, the matter depends more on bringing order
to the panoply of given experiences. In both cases, truth is supposed
to emerge from the introspection of the rational individual. Action is
judged essentially in terms of the degree to which it is the correct
consequence of this truth. Once the intellectual tasks that all individuals are capable of conducting in their own consciousness are carried
out on the basis of competent clarification of the matter at hand, practical execution appears to take care of itself; it is regarded as a mere
consequence of reflection. The well-being of each individual—or

at least the fulfillment of each individual's destiny—depends therefore upon the adequate functioning of his or her intellectual apparatus.

Early on, however, not just Cartesianism but the whole of modern philosophy came to be associated with the term *rationalism*. The role ascribed to thought by both Cartesianism and empiricism was an expression of the attitude of enlightened bourgeois strata which hoped to put all questions of life under their own control. Still, attacks on the Cartesian-empiricist philosophy of consciousness have gained ground in certain periods among those social groups that opposed the further diffusion of bourgeois dominance, and which indeed had serious apprehensions concerning its consequences for the bourgeoisie itself. Here we refer not so much to such phenomena as the opposition among German academic youth to a rationalism grown increasingly pedantic (especially in theology) during the first half of the nineteenth century. Rationalism appeared here more in its original connection with the first phase of the bourgeois era, the absolutist regime, and came into conflict with the second, liberal phase. In particular, the disinclination to abolish traditional, "historically developed"—but in reality obsolescent—institutions in favor of more functional forms had an antirationalist character. Since the French Revolution, this opposition blithely counterposed the "historical" and "organic" conception to the "rationalistic" passion for renewal, especially in Germany. The rationalism they wished to oppose consisted essentially in the resolve to judge views and relations not according to their venerability, but instead in terms of their adequacy to the needs of human society. This interpretation of the term in Germany from the era of Metternich acquired such common usage so early that even Helmholtz spoke occasionally of the "tendency of the French to throw overboard everything of historical development to suit some rationalistic theory."[4] Hegel made himself into a defender of this besieged rationalism when he wrote:

Age has nothing to do with what "old rights" and "constitution" mean or with whether they are good or bad. Even the abolition of human sacrifice, slavery, feudal despotism, and countless [other] infamies was in every case the cancellation of something that was an "old right." It has often been repeated that rights cannot be lost, that a century cannot make wrong into right, but we should add: "even if this century-old wrong has been called right all the time," and further that an actual positive right a hundred years old rightly perishes if the basis conditioning its existence disappears.[5]

Moreover, the modern struggle against rationalism carried on since 1900 in philosophy and other cultural realms is hardly directed exclusively at Cartesianism. To be sure, antirationalism criticizes theories that have precise meaning only in terms of the latter; for instance, it rejects "pure" thought, itself a variation on the concept of autonomous reason that was attacked with equal fervor by the empiricists. Today, however, there is a facile tendency to ascribe these traits to the entire philosophy of consciousness without paying too much attention to nuances. In the most varied academic disciplines and realms of life, rationalism is viewed as a posture that must be eliminated. Just as the meaning connected with the term has grown vague and has come to include the most diverse contents, the most disparate motives and aims are at work in this antirationalist movement. The rejection of rationalism that has steadily risen in the last decades—and that seems already to have passed its zenith—reflects the history of the transition from the liberal to the monopoly capitalist period of the bourgeois order. The development from what was at first a relatively progressive antirationalism into a universalistic version closely associated with a totalitarian theory of the state shares numerous similarities with the course of romanticism during the "restoration period," as Troeltsch has characterized it.[6]

The turn against rationalism in impressionist literature and painting, as well as the philosophy of Nietzsche and Bergson, already offered insight into the insecurity of the bourgeoisie in its humanistic tradition; at the same time, however, this tendency expresses a protest against the fettering of individual life by the increasing concentration of capital. In contrast, the contemporary versions of irrationalism have completely broken with those traditions. In them, too, the suffering of individuals is reflected in an order which has become irrational, but this reflection is distorted, so to speak, for this irrationality and the individual suffering that flows from it are accepted as necessity and transformed in thought into a positive good. The lives of the masses of the petite bourgeoisie in town and country, excluded from any part in economic power, are reduced to pawns in the inner and outer aims of the dominant groups, to being a mere means. Adaptation to this situation occurs, as always, by way of ideological mystification. The sign that a social stratum has accepted its lot is the consciousness of its members of the metaphysical meaning of this form of existence. The glorification of the duty-conscious but simultaneously autonomous person, as it appears in rationalistic philosophy from Leibniz to Fichte, becomes (with Max Scheler, for instance) the song of praise for the meaning of suffering. Self-abnegation and the readiness to sacrifice, which in the end must be recognized as the virtues of obedience and the denial of one's own interests, become a general sentiment and reveal the adjustment of a large part of society to its contemporary circumstances. The human being no longer constitutes an end in itself, but only a means. "Autonomous individuality no longer exists."[7] Life and "service" coincide. "Every attitude which has a true relationship to power can be identified by the fact that it conceives the human being not as an end but as a means, as the bearer of power as well as freedom. The human being develops its highest power, develops domination wherever it serves."[8]

The point here is not to indicate the extremely varied motifs and arguments that come together in the contemporary rejection of rationalism, along with their social roots. Rather, it is exclusively to discuss the relation of materialist philosophy to certain elements of the controversy over rationalism. Describing this relation may facilitate a substantive clarification of the problems to the extent that the commonalities—as well as the differences—between rationalism and irrationalism must be discussed. For both tendencies are in many respects to be contrasted with materialism: both the philosophy of consciousness—Cartesian rationalism and English empiricism—and the modern irrationalist world view bear an idealist character. The spiritual [seelische] forces to which the various irrationalist doctrines refer are supposed to offer human beings insight into the permanent essence or the foundation of the world, just as the rationalistic systems expect this result from conceptual efforts. Powers of the soul or of the mind are supposed to reveal an eternal truth. The contemporary debate concerning rationalist and antirationalist thought leaves untouched the idealist notion that human beings can gain access to the primordial ground of being in the world—and can thus derive the norm of their actions—through internal capacities. Indeed, the debate plays itself out on the basis of this conviction, and stands to that extent over against materialism.

This proposition has also been criticized in idealist philosophy; because it belongs to the essence of idealism, however, this must lead to the denial either of the very possibility of philosophy or at least of its idealist foundations. The former was the case with Hume's skepticism and in modern historicism; they rejected theoretical truth. The second alternative occurred with those philosophers who proceeded from idealist notions to a materialist mode of thought. This was the case for those among the French Enlightenment who treated universal ontological questions with complete open-mindedness while observing actual historical praxis with extreme rigor; it was especially true of Hegel's dialectical method, which explodes his starting point in identity philosophy as well as his closed system. In any case, the idealist character intrinsic to both rationalism and irrationalism as ideological [weltanschauliche] tendencies constitutes one of the most decisive contradictions between them and materialism.

According to materialism, neither pure thought, nor abstraction in the sense of the philosophy of consciousness, nor intuition in the sense of irrationalism, is capable of creating a connection between the individual and the permanent structure of being. The individual within itself is incapable of discovering either the deepest foundations or the highest essence; nor can it discern supposedly ultimate elements of being. Such final determinations of thought and its object, which disregard the historical situation and the theoretical tasks created by it, lie at the basis of the whole of idealist philosophy. They all contain a dogmatic concept of totality. All questions based on that concept are alien to materialism. The attitude of the latter toward the individual arguments involved in the current controversy over rationalism is not simple: it sides with neither of the contending parties. The philosophical positions within irrationalism are extremely varied; essential to it is their rapid change, and the fact that much of what yesterday was characteristic of this standpoint today appears worthy of condemnation, even to its previous adherents. In his attempt "to construct the 'hidden philosophy' of the historical school as a context of meaning,"[9] Rothacker appropriates Wilhelm Scherer's characterization of the contradiction. It reads:

In contrast to cosmopolitanism, nationality; in contrast to factitious cultivation, the power of nature; to centralization, autonomous forces; to benevolence from above, self-government; to the omnipotence of the state, individual freedom; to the constructed ideal, the supremacy of history; to the pursuit of novelty, veneration of the old; to the willfully created, pure development; to understanding and evaluation, mood and perception; to the mathematical form, the organic; to the abstract, the sensuous; to the rule, the inborn power of creation; to the mechanical, the "living." [10]

These antitheses are viewed from the perspective of irrationalism. A number of them still retain their validity; those concerning the state have been turned around in several countries. Here, only two of the main traits of the irrationalist critique are to be treated: the attack on thought itself, and that on the individualism of the liberal era.

The first objection relates to the claim that the Understanding [*der Verstand*] is not universal but applicable only to a limited realm of issues. Before many—indeed, the most important—aspects of life, the conceptual approach fails: more still, it destroys its objects. This assertion of the deadening effect of thought, whose unconstrained application constituted one of the principles of the bourgeoisie during its entire ascent, touches a fundamental attitude of the liberal era. As *Lebensphilosophie*—above all, Bergson—raised this accusation against thought, the social order developed by the bourgeoisie with the help of its science and technology had already become intolerable for a large part of that group. As *Lebensphilosophie* took up cudgels—in the name of the unfolding of life—against that thought which originally helped to liberate precisely this life from the fetters of an obsolete feudal order, it revealed in its sphere the deepening contradiction between the bourgeois order and the founding ideas of the bourgeoisie. The untrammeled application to all life's problems of a reason liberated from its medieval tutelage, the free rein of each individual's intellectual powers promised the unconstrained ascendance of society and the steady increase of the general welfare. The irrationalist restriction of thought to individual domains contained from the outset two contradictory elements: the protest against a social order gone sour, and the rejection of the possibility of transforming that order with the aid of the application of theoretical thought to the problem of society as a whole. *Lebensphilosophie* declared from the very beginning that all great human questions elude the power of thought, and that they can only be hopelessly distorted by the Understanding.

According to this perspective, not merely the metaphysical ground of events, the creative life, and the inner conditions of the individual, but all creations of intellectual culture are closed to thought in their true essence. Neither love for the individual or the community nor a religion nor a work of art are said to be accessible to conceptual judgment. The intellectual dismemberment of these phenomena would lead to the identification of a series of abstract characteristics; it would be an illusion to believe that the original meaningful content from which they were derived analytically could be reconstructed from these pieces. Those who subject value-laden phenomena to conceptual analysis will destroy their object and, in the end, replace it with an impoverished distortion. According to them, the only possibility for understanding consists not in critical judgment but in surrendering oneself to the living content. Originally, *Lebensphilosophie* held onto the theoretical character of understanding [*Einsicht*] to the extent that the effort of intuition, which was to move one into the center of living events, was not necessarily identical with taking up a specific practical position. As early as Max Scheler's notion that philosophical knowledge is bound to certain ethical presuppositions (among which he includes love and humility),[11] the opinion gained ground that engagement, emotion, and the deepest devotion belong to the knowledge of genuine essences. In the end, subordination became the precondition of understanding. Today it seems to be taken for granted that theoretical comprehension of the dominant powers must be replaced by the inspiration of those subjected to them.

The successors to the old rationalism and empiricism have countered the growing slander of thought with penetrating arguments; indeed, certain among them have indicated some of the social functions of irrationalism. Rickert thus characterizes Scheler's "genius of war," which "serves to justify war as the zenith of the state's efficacy,"[12] as entirely consistent with the meaning of *Lebensphilosophie*. "Those who see more than mere growth in natural, vital life, those who also glimpse in this biologistic 'law' a norm for all cultural life, must, in fact, think like Scheler."[13] Despite the logical subtlety of the arguments that rationalism marshals against *Lebensphilosophie*, however, it is incapable of wounding irrationalism decisively. It is as correct in its critique of rationalism as the latter is of it. The devaluation of conceptual thought in favor of a mere surrendering to experience is, of course, an antiin-tellectual and thus simply a regressive standpoint, and indeed contra-dicts the philosophical work of *Lebensphilosophie* itself. "Where the will to conceptual mastery has disappeared, the best that can emerge is holy passivity—and we are then near to Schlegel's laziness as the last remnant of the divine."[14] This objection to the romantic and mystical element of *Lebensphilosophie* is quite justified. At the same time, the representation of thought in the philosophy of consciousness has be-come manifestly untenable. According to the latter, the task of con-ceptual work is to let something formed or structured emerge from the world, which in itself is a mere confusion of facticities. In the rationalistic systems, it remains for the most part unclear whether thought is to be ascribed to a given individual subject or to a general, anonymous consciousness. Nonetheless, thought—as an active yet completely empty form—is supposed to bring forth "the world" from the sensuous material of knowledge. Even Rickert distinguishes him-self from the older rationalism in essence only by way of the recogni-tion of an irrational, "if one will, empirical" moment:[15] "For those engaged in theoretical pursuits who remain pure of all extrascientific evaluations, the world is, at the outset of their investigations—that is, independent of any conception whatsoever—not a 'world' at all in the sense of a cosmos or an ordered whole, but rather a chaotic confusion, the recounting of which is . . . factually impossible."[16]

This rigid juxtaposition of the two principles, out of whose combi-nation the world is supposed to emerge, is every bit as much a mystical legend as irrationalist metaphysics itself. Despite all caution, it must lead to the nonsensical assertion of a suprahistorical dynamic, since it itself claims that history arises only from the process in which thought and empirical material play a role.

Lebensphilosophie and its related tendencies in philosophy and psy-chology have carried the day against this rationalistic myth. One of the most important means here was the demonstration that the struc-tures found in the material were not brought in by the thinking and observing subject, but rather were objectively grounded. The belief that there exists originally a chaos of sensuous elements from which only the concept creates an ordered world can be refuted both by the description of that which is intuitively given [*des anschaulich Gegebenen*] and by the study of acts of the intellect. Gestalt theory,[17] in particular, demonstrated the structured quality of the given, and uncovered through painstaking investigations the mythological character of the notion of independent intellectual factors. To be sure, *Lebensphiloso-phie*'s critique of rationalism goes beyond this. For it is always tempted to confuse the correct assertion of the unique structure of the given—and the corresponding rejection of the notion that all order in the world is produced by thought—with the false belief in an unmediated truth. It overlooks the fact that all knowledge is codetermined by the people who bring it about. Lacking insight into the indissoluble tension between knowledge and object, it takes on the character of an identity philosophy that remains every bit as ahistorical as the doctrine it criticizes.

Rationalism and irrationalism mutually negate each other's metaphysical claim; thought exerts upon them both its destructive effect, and something can certainly be done away with in consequence of the criticism they level at one another. For irrationalism, this would be the philosophical form as a whole: that is, irrationalism itself as well as its opponent, rationalism. Even if the controversy, here only sketched roughly, were to be related in detail, the philosophical doctrines they criticize would still remain. Contrary to the irrationalist theory, these doctrines could in principle be reconstructed by one's opponent on the basis of the relevant documents. The achievements attained in connection with both metaphysical tendencies in a number of individual fields of knowledge remain completely untouched. To the extent that it is unjustifiably raised, only the claim to truth is destroyed, not the statements through which it acquires validity. No one who considers those statements with the assistance of contemporary resources of knowledge can continue to believe in them. Yet thought by itself is incapable of achieving even this result. For every step on the road to knowledge depends upon more than purely logical considerations. The objective falsity of assertions is merely a necessary, not a sufficient condition of their rejection, especially if the false view belongs to the reigning intellectual mood. The direction of the individual steps that lead to acceptance or rejection is by no means determined only by the desire to discover the truth, but rather by the overall psychic constitution of the personality, and this derives from the fate of the knowing subject in the social environment. Even mathematics, which as an abstract science particularly removed from social struggles was able to isolate its intellectual functions and to develop through signally autonomous processes, is hardly as free from atheoretical influences as is often assumed. The discovery of truths, furthermore, says little about whether others can assimilate them. Due to their role in the production process, a psychic constitution is produced among broad social strata that diverts them from insight into the most important questions of life, and thus also from their own true interests. In all previous history, only certain groups were driven to recognize the reigning intellectual mood as limited, and to develop new ideas by way of confrontation with the old perspectives. For the other parts of society, it was relatively insignificant whether a certain matter should be considered true given the current state of knowledge. There are large social groups for whom theoretical clarity would only constitute a hindrance for adjustment to their situation, a cause for inner conflict for the individual. The interest in the decisive truth of a given historical moment emerges under circumstances which point human beings to the transformation of the existing, and which force them to go to the root of social and thus also of metaphysical and religious questions. These preconditions exist only in certain strata and certain periods. Generally speaking, conceptual thought alone is incapable of destroying even the darkest superstition if this sort of thinking performs an important function in the dynamics of a moderately stable social structure.

There are, of course, situations in which the historical significance of thought increases. The skeptical attitude that it is necessarily powerless is just as false as the assertion of its overpowering force. The historical significance of certain ideas [*Erkenntnisse*] depends upon the social struggles of the periods involved. For instance, the theory that the earth moves, which was calmly discussed along with other questions in the High Middle Ages, assumed revolutionary force during the Renaissance. In the present, as during other critical epochs, ideas gain greater historical significance than in the centuries of stability. The ideology of progress, which facilitated the adaptation of the bourgeois middle class and the higher strata of the working class, crumbles during economic crisis, and threatens to clear the way for a deeper understanding of the social process. The philosophical defense of the oldest prejudices and of crude superstition has moved in to check the spread of this understanding, the effects of which are unpredictable. The coarse denigration of thought as such, the admonition concerning its deadening effect, is an element in this struggle. The *Lebensphilosophie* of Bergson, Simmel, and Dilthey, which has yet to deliver the arguments for the denigration of thought, nonetheless includes progressive aspects; among other things, these find expression in the relation of their concept of intuition to the history of rationalism, and in particular to the philosophy of Spinoza. In contrast, the popular sloganeering against thought as such, according to which it is primarily a tool of destruction, has mostly been propagated by dilettantes. Their talent lies more in the grandeur of their facades than in their capacity for theoretical truth. They no longer confine themselves to the limitation of science, but instead contest thought as the manifestation of decline:

Scientific worlds are superficial worlds, practical, soulless and purely extensive worlds. The ideas of Buddhism, of Stoicism, and of Socialism alike rest upon them. Life is no longer to be lived as something self-evident—hardly a matter of consciousness, let alone choice—or to be accepted as God-willed destiny, but is to be treated as a problem, presented as the intellect sees it, judged by "utilitarian" or "rational" criteria. This, at the back, is what all three mean. . . . Culture-men live unconsciously, Civilization-men [*Tatsachen-menschen*] consciously.[18]

As a rule, the farmer is considered to be the "culture-man"; Spengler warns us against the urban dweller, the worker. "The Cosmopolis itself, the supreme Inorganic, is there, settled in the midst of the Culture-landscape, whose men it is uprooting, drawing into itself and using up."[19] Similarly, Klages takes up arms for superstition and against science and a scientific praxis:

The Understanding supplants plenitude with "order," extracts from the ocean of images the indissoluble rigidity of objects, replaces the innate with lifeless things for which time becomes a gnawing tooth and events the maelstrom of destruction; in short, it deprives the world of its reality and leaves behind a mere mechanism. . . . The clouds cease to be tempestuous hordes of demons once one becomes aware of the law of the expulsion of steam, which—dead though it may be—follows the regular vacillations of air pressure.[20]

Recognition is denied all experiment or practical demonstration of theory. The confirmation of science by technology, of thought by action, is considered impossible.

Proof on the basis of hypotheses and machinism [*Machinalismus*] is a gross self-deception! The machine—itself also nature, but a nature outwitted and forced to prostitute itself—can destroy life, to be sure, but it can never create it! The "unreality" of the physical world does not inhibit mind [*Geist*] from using concepts drawn from that world to create the tool with which to kill reality.[21]

The fact—certainly true of the current social situation—that human beings increasingly use the means and methods of production they create for the purpose of conflict with one another and for their own decline, is promulgated quite naively as an eternal law. The machine can "destroy life"; that it might also contribute to maintaining, easing, and promoting it never occurs to Klages. This distinction between fantasy and correct theory seems not to matter. The more retrograde, the more primitive the consciousness, the better.

As far as "superstition" and the "fantastic" are concerned, one should not forget that being free of them only constitutes the dubious preference of the "educated" [*der 'Gebildeten'*], whereas we have delved ever more deeply into both the further we descend to the level of folk consciousness [*Volksbewusstsein*], where alone the strands of human prehistory come together.[22]

Today, the strivings of progressive social groups toward the realization of a more rational society appear to have been brought to a standstill for some time to come. The forms of social life have largely been adapted to the requirements of the monopoly economy. This embittered successor of *Lebensphilosophie* is thus no longer characteristic of the current intellectual temperament. It is increasingly contested precisely in those countries that have progressed furthest in this adaptation. This defeatist posture stands opposed to the form of domination under which the return to domestic social stability takes place. The ideological inclusion of broad masses of workers into the "*Volksgemeinschaft*" and the compulsion, in connection with the external contradictions, to increase continuously the efficiency of the entire population and to elicit their intensive participation in national politics yields a new overall social situation that carries within it its own dialectic. Forces that were unleashed with the aim of suppressing—

indeed, of eradicating—progressive tendencies, and of forcibly preserving obsolete forms of life, now promote elements which, due to social contradictions, lead to the dissolution of the order they protect. Among these contradictions, in addition to raising great masses of the urban and rural middle class to a more up-to-date existence, are the development of their rational thought and thus their awakening from vocational and political lethargy. Despite the artificial rejuvenation of a dying form of the family that must be promoted to sustain the reproduction of the indispensable psychic constitution of the masses, a number of old customs and prejudices—including the residues of the feudal spirit of caste—are being abolished. Irrationalism is now being constrained, just as it once constrained science. Reason and technology are no longer simply laid open to vilification; now only certain matters are kept beyond the reach of conceptual thought by "banishing [them] to the sanctuary of the irrational."[23] These matters are grouped above all around the concept of sacrifice. In wide areas, however, the new attitude acclimates human beings to a rational conduct of life. Concrete thought is promoted to a greater extent than before, and technology affirmed. The ethos of work, which includes this positive relation to rational forces, is itself of course irrational. Technology is not understood as an aid to human beings and brought clearly into connection with their happiness; this would indeed contradict its role in contemporary society. Instead, technology undergoes an ethical and aesthetic mystification. Spengler celebrates it as an expression of Faustian striving; for Dacque, the construction of a machine signifies "a glimpse and a realization of an eternal idea, if we view this activity as the physical realization of a primal image through an act of the mind"; "what is [a machine] but a true homage to the ideal meaning of iron, which receives life through our spirit, so to speak, and which thus symbolically shows us its inner countenance."[24] Ernst Jünger declares "that technology itself is of cultic origins, that it disposes over peculiar symbols, and that behind its processes is hidden a struggle between forms [Gestalten]."[25] Rationality is affirmed—though in an irrational, distorted form—to the extent that it contributes to the competitiveness of the dominant powers in war and peace. However, thought is accused of being destructive wherever it runs counter to the glorification of power and its various ends.

In reality, reason is capable only of destroying falsehood. The claim that correct thought obliterates the object is self-contradictory. The truth or falsity of many general beliefs eludes verification in principle: to that extent, however, they lack meaning, for every assertion makes a claim to truth, and every truth has a basis in knowledge. The groundless convictions of an epoch are not destroyed by thought alone; as long as they are maintained by powerful social forces, knowledge may run riot over them, but the fetish stands while witnesses against it meet their demise. "La révélation de la verité n'est funeste qu'à celui qui la dit."[26] Thought, which uncovers the groundlessness of certain ideas, only remains victorious if the forces that sustain an ideology lose their effectiveness for other reasons as well. Theory is only *one* element in the historical process, and its significance can be determined only in connection with a circumscribed historical situation. Liberal idealism, which expects salvation from the mere unfettering of thought in every human being (just as it claims that general prosperity will emerge from the unfettering of the private pursuit of profit), overlooks historical distinctions. In the eighteenth century, the promotion of the private freedom of conscience and of entrepreneurial initiative had another meaning than under contemporary conditions, for freedom of expression essentially serves to hasten its own elimination in those places where it still exists. The power of thought in history cannot be established once and for all, any more than can its decisive categories or its structure.

In *Lebensphilosophie*, thought—which it accuses of being destructive—is understood in a particular form, namely as conceptually dissecting, comparative, explanatory, generalizing thought: in short, as analysis. To that extent, the critique has a certain justification, for a number of rationalistic systems have in fact confused this type of thought with intellectual activity *tout court*. As *Lebensphilosophie* correctly emphasizes, abstract features of the object are characterized with concepts. Regardless of whether the conceptual apparatus is developed through abstraction, in accordance with the old empiricist theory, or through "essential intuiting" [*Wesensschau*] as phenomenology recommends, concepts refer—to the extent that they are more than mere names—not to the object in its full concretion, but to individual traits that it shares with other objects. Science depends largely upon distinguishing and grasping such traits, in order then to discern connections between them. To the extent that each of these traits can be found not just in one but in principle in an unlimited number of these objects, these connections are general and have the significance of laws. Their category is causality. Certain scientists consider as their objects of investigation individual abstract elements of reality. Physicists are concerned with the mass and movement of bodies; a concrete process that occurs at a certain place and time concerns them only to the extent that something can be learned about these general processes. Chemists investigate the changes in substances generally, physiologists the bodily processes of living things. The needs of human society have determined the development and division of the sciences in accordance with the necessary investigation of such abstract qualities. Descartes even believed that one could get along with the thorough study of one single feature, namely the spatial relations of bodies; all other features, including the entire sensuous world, were thus declared insignificant, mere appearance. In his time, however, it was less the rationalist confusion of an abstract quality with the whole of reality than trust in self-conscious human beings and their rational powers that helped win recognition for this theory, which reduced the world to calculable relations. Later, to mathematics as the only science was added a physics differentiated from it, and then the chemistry developed by the English. Ultimately, the system or the sum of a whole series of scientific disciplines came to be viewed as the very image of reality. This conception of science as the aggregate of fixed relationships of abstract elements sufficed for the needs of the nascent bourgeois world, when the socially necessary intellectual tasks consisted primarily in the progress of the arts of government, in the growth of technology, and in the diffusion of a minimum of industrially indispensable background knowledge. The equation of knowledge with a stable system of general axioms or with a plethora of individual investigations grew inadequate and regressive once the developmental tendency of the society as a whole became the decisive practical and thus also the decisive theoretical topic.

Lebensphilosophie emphasizes that the abstract elements derived from conceptual analysis cannot be added up to reconstruct the living object. The sum of the strokes in a drawing is hardly the same as the picture. The enumeration of human instinctual impulses does not represent an episode in an individual's inner life.

Psychology [writes Bergson], in fact, proceeds like all the other sciences by analysis. It resolves the self, which has been given to it at first in a simple intuition, into sensations, feelings, ideas, etc., which it studies separately. It substitutes, then, for the self a series of elements which form the facts of psychology. But are these *elements* really *parts?* . . . The very idea of reconstituting a thing by operations practised on symbolic elements alone implies such an absurdity that it would never occur to any one if they recollected that they were not dealing with fragments of the thing, but only, as it were, with fragments of its symbol.[27]

What is asserted here concerning the psychology of the individual human being is also true of history as a whole. The belief that the infinite specialized studies collected in libraries, from the most varied national and personal viewpoints, could yield a picture of the true course of events was indeed an illusion of the liberal era. It constituted part of the general conviction that the diligent activity of the individual in all realms of life must come together in a harmonious whole. *Lebensphilosophie* rejects root and branch the value of the painstaking work of analysis. The act of intuition that is supposedly only possible in certain moments is for *Lebensphilosophie* the only means of philosophical knowledge. Its methodology is radical.

The materialism schooled in Hegel's logic has always been aware that the abstract elements derived from analysis cannot be simply added up to coincide with the original phenomena. Abstraction and analysis are transformative activities. Their effect must be sublated again in the act of knowing, by taking into consideration the various peculiarities of the analysis in the process of reconstruction. Even if this precept can never be completely fulfilled, every dialectical exposition is based on the attempt to take it into account.

Cognition, it is often said, can never do more than separate the given concrete objects into their abstract elements, and then consider these elements in their isolation. It is, however, at once apparent that this turns things upside down, and that cognition, if its purpose be to take things as they are, thereby falls into contradiction with itself. Thus the chemist e.g. places a piece of flesh in his retort, tortures it in many ways, and then informs us that it consists of nitrogen, carbon, hydrogen, etc. True: but these abstract matters have ceased to be flesh. The same defect occurs in the reasoning of an empirical psychologist when he analyses an action into the various aspects which it presents, and then sticks to these aspects in their separation. The object which is subjected to analysis is treated as a sort of onion from which one coat is peeled off after another.[28]

From the circumstance that analysis distances thought from the original object, however, *Lebensphilosophie* concludes that knowledge mediated by concepts is entirely useless for the discovery of truth. It seeks to replace the effort of comprehension in the pursuit of truth by mere intuition, by immediate perception, or indeed by sympathetic inspiration [*zustimmende Begeisterung*]. In so doing, it regresses well behind the Hegelian logic.

The dialectical method is the quintessence of all intellectual tools for making fruitful the abstract elements derived from the analytic Understanding [*trennendes Verstand*] for the representation of the living object. There are no universal rules for this purpose. Even within a particular science such as individual psychology, observation of almost every individual human being demands a different form of theoretical construction. The psychologist must attempt to understand the actual psychic situation with its peculiar dynamic on the basis of the fundamental analytic concepts—developed from the observation of innumerable cases and comprising the general understanding of the typical evolution of the individual psyche—and the data obtained by the special analysis of an individual's history. The data as well as the manner of the dialectical construction are different in each case; the meaning of the general concepts that go into them are never exactly the same from one individual to another. If, for instance, the categories of resentment or of the instinct of self-preservation are taken up into a description, they receive in this whole a different meaning in each case. The function and thus also the content of the concepts applied are affected by every step in the representation of a living process. Conceptual realism—that is, the doctrine of the reality of the general concepts themselves—is just as incorrect as its nominalist opposite, according to which general concepts are mere names. Or, rather, both doctrines are correct. General concepts have real meaning, but this is only determined in the overall representation of a concrete object, which has its own principles appropriate to the object. Aristotle's axiom—that general concepts exist only to the same extent as the individual objects that fall under them—was transformed by Hegelian philosophy into the axiom that the *meaning* of concepts changes according to the individual object in which they are realized. This entails that a definite meaning be ascribed to each conceptual term. In thought, it is not permissible to use a symbol arbitrarily to mean this now and something else later. As soon as a concept is thought out in isolation, it has a firm meaning; if, however, it goes into a complex intellectual construction, it acquires in this whole a particular function. Thus, for example, the instinct of self-preservation can be unambiguously defined to the extent that it is considered in isolation; in the total picture of a particular human being, as the instinct of self-preservation of a concrete, living person, it is affected in its content by other psychic characteristics. The fact that chemical compounds consist of certain elements and can be separated back into them does not mean that these elements retain the same characteristics in compound as they had before their inclusion in the whole. Neither is it true that the strict definability of abstract concepts precludes them from being affected by their involvement in the mental image of a concrete whole. When concepts are realized, they become elements in complete theoretical constructs, and are no longer isolated symbols.

Hegel's doctrine that true thought contains contradictions is grounded in this simple insight. Concepts derived from abstraction change their meaning as soon as they come into relation with each other in the representation of a concrete whole; at the same time, they remain identical to themselves to the extent that they retain their established definitions. The principles of traditional logic, the "logic of the Understanding"—above all the principle of identity, but the other rules of analytic thought as well—are by no means simply expunged in dialectical logic. The abstract conceptual elements and their fixed relationships, which are investigated in specialized scientific research, constitute the material for the theoretical reconstruction of living processes. *Lebensphilosophie* and the other irrationalist tendencies are thus incorrect to claim that insight into true being has nothing to do with analysis, and that thoughtless "surrender" must replace it. The product of the analysis, the abstract concepts and rules, are not, of course, identical with knowledge of events in reality. The individual disciplines yield only the elements of the theoretical construction of the historical process, and these do not remain what they were in the individual disciplines but acquire new meanings. All true thought is thus to be understood as a continuous critique of abstract determinations; it contains a critical or—as Hegel put it—a skeptical moment. The dialectical side of logic is at the same time "that of negative reason."[29] If, however, concept formation in physics, the definitions of organic processes in biology, the general description of an instinctual impulse, the characterization of the typical mechanism of inflation or of capital accumulation, and other results of the individual sciences constitute not the representation of real events in nature living and dead but only their presuppositions, the research has abstracted these concepts and judgments from real phenomena. They are thus already distinguished from fantasy images and arbitrary constructions; they stand in a positive relationship to reality by their origin and their applicability. The faithfulness of the mental reflection of reality depends upon the precision of the results of analysis.

Analysis proceeds from the particular to the general. It suffices to the extent that thought has only to isolate from actual events that which repeats itself. Science thus fulfills its true task for those activities that depend upon the relative immutability of natural and social relations. In the liberal period, miracles were expected from the mere development of specialized research, because the foundations of the current form of society were considered static. The mechanistic approach fails, however, in the effort to understand history. Here, the issue is to understand the dominant tendencies of incomplete, unique processes. To be sure, analytic knowledge must be brought to bear, but the task demands going beyond such knowledge. The process of discovery and that of representation are here fundamentally different. In the reconstruction of the tendencies of society as a whole, quite different psychic functions play a role than in the development of the individual science; even "intuition" is included among them. "Empiricism," writes Hegel, "prepares the empirical material" for the dialectical Notion, "so that the latter can then receive it ready for its use. . . . [The] process of the origination of science is different from its process in itself when it is complete, just as is the process of the history of Philosophy and that of Philosophy itself. . . . The working out of the empirical side has really become the conditioning of the Idea, so that this last may reach its full development and determination."[30] Research "has to appropriate the material in detail, to analyse its different forms of development, to trace out their inner connexion. Only after this work is done, can the actual movement be adequately described" (Marx).[31]

Irrationalism understands that analysis "really transforms the concrete into an abstract."[32] It fails to grasp, however, that "that division must take place" if comprehension is to be possible at all. This failure in the realm of the positive is characteristic not only of the attack on rationalist thought but of the contemporary struggle against liberal forms of life in all spheres. The representatives of the reigning intellectual mood are, to be sure, largely correct in their critique of an obsolete culture, but they are incapable of deriving progressive conclusions from that critique. They would prefer to return to a precapitalist form of society. To the overspecialized and ultimately empty life of the more recent era, they offer only articles of faith; blind obedience is supposed to take the place of an analytic thought which is nonetheless rich with nuance. The spirit is thus renewed regressively rather than progressively. The vacuous intellectual work in many disciplines is not abolished in favor of the application of all intellectual forces of production to the true interests of human beings; instead, thought is merely simplified. The requirements of progressive economic development lend to most contemporary political, social, and cultural tendencies a dual character of which its bearers are not necessarily aware: the violent simplification of thought goes hand in hand with its diffusion among the masses. The same holds for the other elements of the irrationalist world view. Among broad segments of the bourgeois strata, the denial of the individual in favor of a merely imagined community [Gemeinschaft] replaces the false consciousness of their supposed individual autonomy with incipient social considerations: the glorification of a social order which breeds poverty and the constant danger of war despite a wealth of raw materials and means of production—and the ferocious struggle against every effort to improve that order—unintentionally contain the admission that this house of humanity is actually a prison. The regression conditioned by the general hostility toward thought embodies the revision of a form of progress that had already reversed itself and turned into the opposite of progress.

Rather than denying it, materialism proceeds to the correct application of analytic thought—which, like other aids to society, is transformed under contemporary conditions from a productive force into a constraint. As a result, however, analytic thought plays a different role in materialism than elsewhere in philosophy. The materialist dialectic is also to be fundamentally distinguished from the Hegelian. With his development of dialectical principles, and even more through his dialectical representations [*Darstellungen*], Hegel showed in detail how analytically derived concepts could be made fruitful for the intellectual reconstruction of living processes. In Hegel's thought, however, there is in truth only one great process that contains in itself all concepts as its moments, and the philosopher can grasp and represent this process—this "concrete," this "one"—once and for all. The individual stages of this representation are thus considered to be eternal relations not just in logic but in the philosophy of nature and of spirit as well. All relationships in the completed system are conceived as immutable. Thus morality—which in Hegel is determined in a particular sense by the Good and by conscience—appears together with abstract bourgeois law [*Recht*] as an eternal moment of ethical life; in that realm, the state also has a fixed meaning that comprehends and supersedes family and society in a particular fashion. The abstract categories of all parts of the system—both those of pure logic (such as quantity and quality) and those of individual realms of culture (such as art and religion)—are to be put together in an enduring image of concrete Being. Whoever wishes, at any given time, to grasp the real meaning of any category will have to construct the same image of Being, driven by the inner logic of the object. Until its completion, the entire conceptual material is in movement in the minds of those who reconstruct it, because the meaning of the individual categories is only fulfilled in the whole. As moments of the mental unity, which for Hegel is not merely a pure reflection but is itself the Absolute, they are supposed to have immutable validity, however. "Accordingly, logic is to be understood as the system of pure reason, as the realm of pure thought. This realm is truth as it is without veil and in its own absolute nature. It can therefore be said that this content is the exposition of God as he is in his eternal essence before the creation of nature and a finite mind."[33] However, the logic contains *in nuce* the entire system. The complete theory itself is, in Hegel, no longer drawn into history; it yields an all-comprehending thought, the product of which is no longer abstract and transient. The dialectic is closed.

The materialist cannot have faith in such certainty. There is no conclusive image of reality, either in essence or in appearance. Even the proposition of a suprahistorical subject which alone could grasp reality is a delusion. Furthermore, the overcoming of the one-sidedness of abstract concepts through the art of dialectical construction does not lead to absolute truth, as Hegel claims. That process always takes place in the thought of definite, historical human beings. "It is man who thinks, not the ego, not reason."[34] Materialist philosophy "therefore regards as its *epistemological principle*, as its *subject, not the ego, not the absolute*—i.e., abstract spirit, *in short, not reason for itself alone*—but the *real* and the *whole essence of man*."[35] If this essence were immutably the same, as the early materialists including Feuerbach still believed, its mental constructions would at least have had one and the same subjective foundation. These constructions would have been theoretical projections of that essence concerning the entire world with which it was confronted. Dilthey, too, understood the intellectual culture of humanity in the same way. Dialectical materialism, however, understands the subject of thought not as itself another abstraction such as the essence "humanity," but rather as human beings of a definite historical epoch. Moreover, these human beings are not hypostatized as isolated units, closed off from one another and from the world; their entire being and thus also their consciousness depend upon their natural endowments every bit as much as upon the overall social relations that have taken shape in their time. According to materialism, therefore, the theory of the social life process is on the one hand the most comprehensive mental construction to which analytic research in all areas contributes; on the other hand, this theory is necessarily aimed at the intellectual and material situation, and the impulses deriving from it, that are characteristic for one of the various social classes. Many viewpoints, of course, are determined less by the psychic structure of a certain group in the production process than by the private peculiarities of their originators. Such opinions, however, either tend not to acquire social significance or receive a more or less unambiguous reinterpretation in the understanding of a certain class.

Since especially in the present historical period the solution of the decisive, real problems from which humanity suffers depends upon the outcome of struggles between social groups, a theory's significance is determined above all by the extent to which its principle of construction is codetermined by the tasks of such a group rather than by the private situation of its author. According to Hegel, the course of the universal dialectic is established by the immanent dynamic of the concepts; for materialism, in contrast, every dialectical construction is a product that human beings develop in their confrontation with their social and natural environment. The entire process of developing such a construction, therefore, is guided not merely by the object but by the level of intellectual development and the conscious and unconscious strivings of the subjects as well. The formal criterion of truth does not alone decide the value of a theory. (How many investigations have been conducted during just the most recent past which fail to further knowledge one bit, but which may nonetheless claim to be true! How many writings have their *raison d'être* merely in their function of diverting attention from the decisive problems, despite the fact that they could not be accused of logical errors!) The value of a theory is decided by its connection to the tasks that have been taken in hand by the most progressive social forces in a given historical moment, and a theory is valuable not for the whole of humanity directly, but only for the group with an interest in those tasks. The fact that thought has in many cases distanced itself from the questions of a strife-ridden humanity is one of the reasons underlying mistrust toward intellectuals. The criterion for this distancing is not the unsophisticated consciousness; that criterion can only be the actual demonstration that the connection to the decisive questions has been lost. This accusation against an apparently free-floating [*unbedingte*] intelligentsia—which is linked with that against rationalism—is nonetheless correct to the extent that the disconnected character of thought does not signify freedom of judgment, but rather the insufficient control of thought with respect to its own motives. The surrender of a historically determined terminology, the constant coining of new concepts and the philosophers' starting-from-square-one, the preoccupation with neutral expressions and the search for originality are all manifestations of this tendency. The fault lies not with the intelligentsia itself, however, but with its insufficient connection to the relevant historical problems. The most abstract thought processes can have a more real meaning than an apparently concrete approach to a problem couched in the most everyday, commonplace terms. The craft and agrarian sphere are given preference here. The more the conscious connection to historical struggles is lost, the more strongly the philosophers insist that their thought stands on and is rooted in solid ground—a notion whose untenability makes that inadequacy completely clear.

Concepts, judgments, and theories are phenomena that develop in the confrontations of human beings with each other and with nature. Utility is by no means the criterion of knowledge, as the pragmatists would have it; knowledge in the various realms of science and life can be distinguished in many ways. The claim that all knowledge is useful—that is, that it must lead directly to the satisfaction of a practical need—is false. But the theoretical need itself, the interest in truth, is determined by the situation of the knowers. If their fate, in which material and psychic factors are interwoven, leads to penetration of their intellectual labors by the needs of humanity rather than merely by private whims, those efforts can take on historical significance. A god is incapable of knowing anything because it has no needs. Thought processes are hardly guided in detail by the demands imposed directly by the material situation, but just as much by unconscious instinctual impulses which themselves ultimately comprise individuals' reactions to their situation in society. Regardless of its correctness or falsity, the need for self-affirmation that remains unsatisfied in real life can be expressed in a theory. Such irrational factors play a smaller role in the intellectual life of a group the less their situation drives them toward repressions; the intellectual task itself and the means to its resolution derive, however, from the demands placed upon specific people in a specific situation.

Even the establishment of truth according to the relevant criteria—whether through mere psychic processes (such as memory), through experiments, or through events independent of the subject—has, as a procedure in the real world, historical conditions. The correspondence between judgment and the true facts of the matter is never given directly; there is no identity between the two. The problem that thought must solve, the manner of this thinking, and the relation of judgment to object are all transient. Nonetheless, in every given case there remains a distinction between true and false. The relativistic denial of this distinction contradicts itself. It is, for instance, quite possible to decide which of the many theories of the economic crisis is correct. True and false are distinguishable characteristics of theoretical constructs; they have to do with their relationship to the object. Human beings in the process of making distinctions by no means create this relationship arbitrarily; it is, however, mediated, and without this mediation there would be no truth. Theory is thus not a fact of nature separable from human beings. One cannot reflect upon oneself or indeed upon humanity as if one were a subject freed of definite historical conditions. To be sure, individuals may choose to disregard

certain personal interests, to tune out all possible peculiarities conditioned by their own fate; nonetheless, every step of a thought process
will be the reaction of a specific human being from a specific social
class in a specific period. This is certainly obvious on its face, but the
whole of idealist philosophy runs contrary to this manifest truth. In
idealism, philosophical thought is understood—either explicitly (as in
classical German idealism) or implicitly (as in Berkeley)—as something that appears to be carried out by empirical human beings, but
which in reality is the timeless precondition of these empirical human
beings, or at least a process independent of them. In the bourgeois
age, idealist philosophy has largely replaced revelation, at least among
the enlightened bourgeoisie. Comprehensive meaning, insight into the
foundations of the world, is no longer promulgated from on high;
instead, it is discovered or even brought forth by spiritual powers
dwelling in each individual. The world view of idealism, like the affirmative content of religion, is supposed to bear not the traits of the
socialized human beings who brought it about but the pure reflection
of eternal orders. The irrationalist currents in idealism have nothing
on the rationalists in this respect. To be sure, they replace analytic
thought with intuition or other transient stimuli, such as feeling, joy,
boredom, anxiety, credulousness, or fellow feeling, as the conditions
of insight.[36] But the essence of which the individual becomes aware
in this mood—whether it be life, existence, or communion [*Volkheit*]—
is considered the standard to which one can hold unconditionally,
even if this consists only in the command always to call into question
one's own principles and actions, or to affirm freely the place in which
given individuals find themselves as a result of their fate. The solemnity accorded to certain positions and aims by idealist philosophy necessarily goes along with the incoherent notion of a timeless subject.
By uncovering this connection, materialism dethrones the deified spirit
more fundamentally than irrationalism, which rejects analysis in order to deliver itself over to blind faith.

Dialectical materialism recognizes the justification in the critique of
merely analytical thought. Old and new philosophical doctrines that
hypostatize the results of analysis and posit the products of abstraction as the foundation or the elements of being are one-sided and
limited. The reified categories of irrationalist philosophy such as life
and existence—however much they may be held to be spiritually

motivated, historical, and concrete—are no less abstract than the ontological principles of tendencies attacked as rationalist, such as the
ego, the absolute idea, and the sum of sense impressions. Where the
process from which they are derived is forgotten or considered insignificant, all these isolated unities today fulfill the ideological functions
of fundamental metaphysical concepts. In contrast to irrationalism,
materialism attempts to transcend the one-sidedness of analytic thought
without dismissing it altogether. Dialectical theory itself has, of course,
an abstract character. For despite the efforts to reflect the object in its
various forms of development, the very act of observing it—as well as
every step of those developmental processes—depends upon specific
historical conditions. Knowledge of the totality is a self-contradictory
concept. Consciousness of one's own conditionedness, which distinguishes materialist thought, is identical in the current state of theory
with an understanding of the social conditionedness of individuals.
Just as the notion of the autonomy and self-sufficiency of thought is
intrinsic to the concept of the closed, monadic individual, the notion
that every individual is caught up in the overall social life process
belongs to the materialist view of the finitude of thought. In materialism, as in Hegel, the overcoming of the errors of abstract thought
takes place through the attempt to grasp the individual categories as
dependent upon the process that creates them. In materialism, however, this process itself is not viewed as intellectual in nature; its result
is not the self-comprehending and thus infinite Idea. Rather, according to materialism, individuals with all their categories depend upon
social development; this is laid out in the economic theory of history.
Subject and object never entirely coincide here; rather, they find
themselves in a variable tension according to the role which theory
plays in society, and to the level of domination of human beings over
each other and over nonhuman nature.

While society by no means comprises the totality of the conditions
determining individual fates, and though individuals' membership in
a certain social group does not necessarily entail that they must have
the capacities and views typical of this group, such conditioning goes
much further than is commonly assumed in philosophy and psychology, which are predominantly oriented to the individual. In addition
to the fact that the factors determining the action of the members of
a class, despite great variation among them, tend to be much more

unitary than they appear to the superficial observer, the genuine variations should not be considered simply "natural." As we now know, character differences derive not merely from conscious educational processes but even more from childhood experiences. The inventory of these experiences and their various causes are determined for the individual by the peculiarities of the family as they have developed in various social classes in the course of history, as well as by the particular fate of each family. Each personality has its own nature, but this nature is socially determined in ways not yet comprehended scientifically.

From this materialist conception of the individual derives not just materialism's critical stance toward the hypostatization of analytic thought (indeed, toward that of dialectical thought as well). Rather, this conception also constitutes the basis for materialism's attitude toward individualism, the second major criticism directed today at rationalist approaches in philosophy. To be sure, the actions and, more importantly, the happiness of individuals have always been functions of society. Yet in some epochs, above all in the early periods of capitalist development, individuals (socially determined, to be sure) in broad social strata were in a position to improve their situation through their own particular calculations, decisions, and undertakings. Due to economic conditions, the lives of human beings even in the most highly developed countries are, with ever fewer exceptions, dominated by factors that are not at all subject to their will. All their calculations of individual advantage are ineffectual with respect to great social events, such as economic crises and the wars so closely related to them. Indeed, the temporary successes of an individual or indeed an entirely successful life—insofar as the resolute individual does not belong to the small circle of the economically powerful or their immediate servants—seems like a mistake, one of the minor inaccuracies in the apparatus that can never be completely eliminated. In earlier periods, materialism justifiably exhorted human beings to look after their individual well-being; today it clearly grasps the nearly complete hopelessness of such activity. Attention to personal fate has been widely transformed into participation in social struggles. This should not be misunderstood in a mechanistic fashion. Those who work on social tasks in the sense of materialist theory do not seek to pursue, on the basis of abstract considerations, their own well-being via social change.

This would indeed be an extremely one-sided kind of thought that would prove vain simply due to the time span of social change. The transition from individualistic thought to knowledge of the social situation is characterized less by individual subjects changing their views than by correct theory being taken up by social strata especially prepared for this by their position in the production process. In the contemporary social order, great masses repress for long periods their understanding of the hopelessness of individualistic striving, no matter how clearly this may be demonstrated to them practically and theoretically. The conditions of socialization to be found among most social groups contribute to the steady reproduction of psychic mechanisms through which this knowledge is perceived as intolerable and processed accordingly. Such knowledge, so painful from the perspective of the immediate interests of the individual, is suffered only when individualistic values are no longer felt to be the highest—either in the sense of a good personal life or of individual mobility. The type of person in whom the clear knowledge of the contemporary situation of society really gains force transforms the meaning which this knowledge had in the skeptical reflection of the disappointed bourgeois. In this type of person, knowledge constitutes a progressive force. For all those who are condemned to a hopeless existence by the maintenance of obsolete forms of social life, it points toward a goal that can only be attained through solidarity: the transformation of this society into a form adequate to the needs of the whole society. In this solidarity, self-interest is not utterly rejected, for—as insight into the hopelessness of individual striving in the world as it is—it constitutes a constant stimulus to activity. But self-interest loses the character intrinsic to it in the bourgeois era—namely, its contradiction to the interest of society at large.

The irrationalist concept of "decomposition" ["*Zersetzung*"] connects the objection that thought destroys the object with the accusation that it is also individualistic. This concept aims not only at the attitude of human beings who, incapable of surrendering to the great matters of life, conceptually pick apart the experiences others find inspiring. It also asserts that the analytic devaluation of everything significant takes place in the service of an individual preoccupied only with self-preservation and indifferent to the rest of society. Rationalist critique is attacked not only because it exposes religious, metaphysical, or other ideological doctrines to thought and thus to the danger of a just demise, but also because it measures norms and values against individualistic ends. Cartesian rationalism was indeed individualistic to the extent that it viewed the contradiction involved in judgments against innate human reason as the criterion of the falsity of those judgments. Increasingly, the standard for norms and theories became an individual posited as absolute, and the various ends of the monadic ego were hypostatized. Contrary to the axiom of the equality of human beings, which the bourgeoisie transformed from a demand into an assertion after its ascension to power, individuals are historically determined. The socially conditioned differences are great enough. In contemporary irrationalism, these differences are mystified as "natural" and God-given just as they were during the time of slavery; in the liberal period they were dogmatically denied. An individual exclusively oriented to economic advantage appeared as the prototype of the human being. Its *ratio* became *ratio* as such; purposive activity was reduced to concurrence with its ends and, ultimately, with the ends of a social enterprise following its own dynamic. The foundation of this development lay in the principle of the free commodity economy—the same one which, after promoting the whole of social life, has today become a fetter. In it, the law of economic utility dominates the psychic reactions of human beings like a natural law. Irrationalism discards the type of thought that corresponds to this law. It opposes self-interest every bit as much as it opposes the Understanding.

The rationalist division of the individual into the two independent halves of body and mind had withdrawn all unconscious and half-conscious psychic activity from scientific theory. With a few exceptions in French psychology (especially La Rochefoucauld and Vauvenargues) and German philosophy (especially in Goethe's theoretical writings and in romanticism), the genuinely emotional part of human life received attention only in literature. Nonindividualistic impulses were thus withdrawn from the attention of rationalism; its psychology become the theory of "self-interest."[37] Modern irrationalism is to be credited for attacking this deficiency. At least initially, Freudian theory, which belongs according to its structure to the liberal period, understood the individual as the product of a conflict between conscious and unconscious, a dialectic between the ego and the id that plays itself out under the compulsions of the social environment.

Irrationalism, however, began to deify the unconscious. It dogmatically singles out individual factors that are quite vague theoretically, such as the unconscious influence of historical rootedness, race, or landscape, and puts them directly in place of individual rational thought, which it denigrates. But it is just as great a mistake to reduce the conditioned quality of thought, which is guided by the entire life situation as well as by the object, to allegedly eternal individual factors, as it is to deny this conditioned quality in the rationalist manner.

The laying bare of pure egoistic reflection, of "self-interest"—like that of analytic thought—contains a correct insight in incorrect form. Action oriented only to individual values is today futile for the great majority of humanity. The concentration of all concerns on mere survival, the greatest possible accommodation of one's own life to given circumstances, the constant measurement of all events against one's own well-being and that of one's immediate group constitutes the appropriate form of reaction of enlightened individuals in a declining economic situation. To the extent that it has exclusively this quality, thought is indeed not rational but rationalistic. But if it is true that the individual is dependent upon the whole of society, and attention to the whole has to stand today above blind devotion to individual interests, the foundation of this truth lies in the fact that society in its current form stands in contradiction to the self-interests of most people. According to materialist theory, the task is not the suppression of those interests but the overcoming of this contradiction, which can be resolved only by a definite transformation of the relations of production, the basis of the entire social order. In contrast, irrationalism denies the right to individual self-preservation and sees the whole as the meaning and aim of all human activity, as if the interest in the whole were mediated by unconditional subordination rather than by the interests of the individuals for themselves and their kind. Just as it wishes to derive the image of living processes from immediate experience rather than through intellectual reconstruction from the results of analysis, participation in social and political events is supposed to take place not with respect to the real needs of human beings but rather through the individual's unreserved surrender to the whole as it is. In both respects, irrationalism makes itself the servant of the powers that be. As demonstrated above, hostility to thought protects only untruth—namely, the false contents of metaphysics and religion. Surrender to the whole, to the "common good," is an especially welcome principle to a bad form of rule. As long as the whole is not constantly judged against the standard of human happiness, the notion of the "common good" is just as dogmatic as that of self-interest. Without the fulfillment of the Hegelian dictum that the "end [of the state] is the universal interest as such and the conservation therein of particular interests since the universal interest is the substance of these,"[38] the demand of total surrender to the interests of the state remains mere dogmatism.

From the point of view of world history, the pressure exerted upon large backward strata in town and country to learn to repress their own narrow interests may be a treatment that would be unavoidable in other circumstances as well. Corresponding to their obsolete mode of production is an intellectual attitude which makes possible only an assimilation to the contemporary state of knowledge mediated by authority, not a rational one. The demand of a sacrifice of one's own interests, the call to discipline and heroism, and the praise of poverty are directed primarily to the progressive social groups, however, which have the universal interest much more "as their substance" than is the case with the various "totalities" in the name of which that demand is raised. As with its attack on thought, therefore, irrationalism falls well behind liberalism in its otherwise correct critique of individualism. It is a "countermovement." In criticism, in destruction—which it detests in principle—it remains successful. In "creation" ["*Aufbau*"]—which it affirms as a principle—in the conquest of new realms of life, it is capable of achieving anything only to the extent that the elements opposed to irrationalism necessarily come to effect in it: with the aid of thought and of the motor of particular interests.

The striving for mere self-preservation, the purely egoistic aim next to which other instinctual impulses pale, typifies today's miserable life. If this insight is transformed from a theoretical reflection into a principle of domination, it takes on a particular ideological function. The philosophical irrationalism of Nietzsche and Bergson had challenged the dominant strata themselves to resist their economically conditioned inner impoverishment by reminding them of their own possibilities, the possibilities of "life." When the dominant invoke the same challenge vis-à-vis the larger society without offering a rational justification connected to individual self-interest, it becomes a convenient rationalization for demanding that these people suffer patiently the life of privation they must lead under prevailing conditions. It entails the denial of accountability. While rational thought cannot be narrowed—as extreme liberal ideology would have it—to the standard of egoistic ends, rational justification of any action can ultimately be related only to the happiness of human beings. A government that scorns any demonstration that its actions have this significance for the governed is mere despotism. Despotism need not be necessarily bad or even retrograde; the zenith is long since past of those theories of the state that treat the forms of government while ignoring their content, and that devote more attention to the representation of interests than to their fulfillment. There exists such a thing as an enlightened, indeed a revolutionary despotism. Its character is determined by its relation to the real interests of the masses subject to it. There is no unconditional standard against which to judge this relation in various periods, if for no other reason than that the harshness and injustice of despotism is to be explained not alone in terms of its rule, but also with respect to the general level of development of the subjugated masses. Nonetheless, during the whole of the modern period their social function, their progressive or reactionary significance, is determined by the extent to which their exercise of power corresponds to either general or particular social interests. Even if one were to consider the most gruesome periods of human history only teleologically—that is, with respect to their evolution, their development toward a stage in which they kept in mind "a few basic requirements of communal living"[39]—the aim of this development can only be defined in terms of specific human interests. At present, the contradiction between the life interests of human beings and the maintenance of forms of life that run counter to these interests dominates all historical events. By denying the individual interests of the masses via the demand of thoughtless obedience and blind sacrifice—instead of transforming them through reflection on the foundations of the social process and raising them above the mere pursuit of advantage—irrationalism today unconsciously serves the particular, indeed unconcealed interests of the dominant, who continue to benefit from the persistence of the given in its old form.

The logical error here lies in the undialectical usage of the concepts "whole" and "part." To be sure, in contrast to the positivist methodology of liberalism, the whole is correctly understood as not simply more than but something entirely different from the sum of its parts—or, better, the sum is a limiting case of the whole. This insight was already present in the irrationalist critique of abstract thought. In the exclusive emphasis on the independence of the whole, it expresses "only the tautology that *the whole as whole* is equal not to the parts, but to *the whole*."[40] From this perspective it appears that the relationship between whole and part is one-sided, so that the part in the whole seems to be determined by the latter alone and not at all by itself. The simplistic truth that the whole is nothing without the parts—to which the positivist theory of knowledge holds one-sidedly—plays a subordinate role in the irrationalist theory of totality. It must be understood, however, that the dynamics of every whole, each in its own way, are determined just as much by its elements as by its own peculiar structure. Indeed, in human history, the point is precisely that even the structure of the whole, the forms of social life, fall under the control of their elements, namely the human beings living in them.

In the liberal period, and certainly in that following it as well, society and its institutions, the whole of cultural life, were only apparently governed by human beings. They imagined that they made the important decisions themselves—whether in their social undertakings, in parliaments, or in the person of their political leaders—while precisely the sphere that ultimately determines the course of history, namely the economic sphere, was withdrawn from any rational control. The necessities that arose from it, the genuine questions of human survival, thus operated blindly—that is, with the unnecessary development of social deprivation, wars, and regressions to barbaric social conditions. Because the human productive process lacks any true organization or control despite all the monopolies—indeed, because, as isolated attempts at organization, modern monopolies multiply the general disorganization—the whole of social life, which in the end depends upon economic factors, is withdrawn from human will. It confronts individuals as an alien power of fate, as nature. Chance and death rule over life, however, precisely to the extent that conscious beings are determined by blind nature, and to the extent that the realm of freedom is limited by that of necessity. It is therefore crucial that the social whole not just apparently but actually comes under the control of its parts. At the same time, these parts will continue to be dominated to a certain degree by the whole, for what they create must in turn influence them. This is obvious; it is an axiom that holds for all living processes.

The undynamic use of the concepts "whole" and "part" lies at the root of the irrationalist conception of individual and community [Gemeinschaft]. At present, this usage is especially prominent in the universalistic philosophy deriving from Othmar Spann. Two particular methodological errors dominate contemporary talk about the individual and the community. First, the unique character of the process being investigated, in which the totality and the elementary factors determine each other in different ways, is inadequately considered in the one-sided determination of the relationship. This error finds expression in conclusions that can hardly be surpassed in their metaphysical primitiveness, but which are therefore easily comprehensible. For example, it is said of the assertion "The whole precedes the parts"[41] that this does not refer to a causal relationship, but only to logical priority; causal reasoning has "no place in thinking about society."[42] It quickly becomes clear, however, that only terminological and not substantive significance is imputed to this position, for the assertion—meaningless in purely logical terms, to be sure—is blithely related to genetic problems of reality. Its application to social questions is entirely mechanical:

Once the fact is recognized that spiritual community or totality [geistige Gemeinschaft oder Ganzheit] constitutes the foundation and essence of all social phenomena, it becomes obvious that the quintessential reality lies in "society," and that the individual emerges derivatively (as a part) from it. The individual reveals itself now not as self-generative (autarkic), but as a member; society not as an agglomeration, but as a totality that divides itself up.[43]

Thus emerge two characteristics: (a) the whole, society, is the true reality; and (b) the whole is the primary (conceptually prior); the individual exists so to speak only as constituent part, as a member of it, and is thus derivative.[44]

Most contemporary philosophical and sociological discussions of the individual and community tend to be based on equally loose perspectives. They are in no way superior to their individualistic opponents, who maintain the reverse thesis—namely, the logical and ontological priority of the parts over the whole. Indeed, these are nearer the truth to the extent that their doctrine is accurate for the mechanical natural sciences, at least superficially, and to the extent that, in sociology, individuals have priority at least in the sense of the pursuit of control over society as discussed above. Neither party sees that the exclusive emphasis on one side of the relation is "an empty abstraction"; they both fall into pure metaphysics.

The contemporary discussion concerning the relation between the individual and the community contains still another error, however. The problem tends to be stated not in conscious connection to the real needs of specific groups of people—that is, in terms of historical praxis—but rather as if active human beings had to orient themselves forever in the same way toward the universally valid answer to the philosophical problem of whole and part, individual and community. Philosophical conclusions are taken as eternal norms that give meaning and aims to action, instead of as a moment in the mastery of the tasks of human beings which, to be sure, has its own effect. Philosophers believe that they determine the aims of human beings and, due to a lack of clarity about the implication of thought in the real needs and struggles of those human beings, fall into blind dependence upon the powers that be. Investigation of the relation between whole and part in the abstract realm of logic, or a fundamental examination of the individual and the community, may play a minor role even in the theory involved in the struggle for an improvement of contemporary society. But rigid norms derived from such investigations can only perform extrascientific functions. Recourse to such distant problems, conceived as eternal—like the return to a supposedly original, actual, or genuine (in any case, prehistorical) essence of human being—have an ideological function insofar as they are undertaken with respect to a goal for which they are unsatisfactory in principle: namely, the attainment or justification of a certain behavior demanded of human beings consisting in passive subordination. The notion rarely arises that ontology, anthropology, folklore, or psychology are mere derivatives from the past and not models for the future. Indeed, not only the prehistory of humanity but extrahuman nature as well are supposed to serve as ideals. If a misbehaving child wanted to point to its "nature" or a petty trickster to the pursuit of power as a primal human drive, one would certainly point out to them that human beings are supposed to outgrow such impulses. The philosophers, however, serve up the most tasteless comparisons from theories of plants, races, and evolution as justification for the miserable condition of the world today. Such considerations from distant areas of knowledge—and, even more, of ignorance—can only confuse human ends. These certainly depend in various respects upon the current state of scientific knowledge. Max Weber's radical separation of ends and science is untenable. But even an advanced science—not to mention contemporary philosophical biology[45]—is incapable of prescribing the ends, or of grounding or justifying them by itself alone. Rather, in the struggle for a better order, the refinement of theory plays an important role as a critical, corrective, forward-driving, and strengthening element. If one presses contemporary science and philosophy for an abstract demonstration that the community is always everything and the individual nothing (with the exception of a few heroes), these efforts have little to do with the progressive function of science. They belong to the history of ideological methods of domination, not to that of human knowledge.

Irrationalism does not surmount merely individualistic thought with the aid of the insight that the vast majority of humanity has a common interest in the rational organization of society. On the contrary, it demands the renunciation of individual happiness in favor of metaphysical essences. Knowledge of the causes of mass misery—which consists in the current poverty, and in the prospect of a painful demise in the wars connected with this system—would facilitate a change in humanity not just with respect to its consciousness, but indeed to its entire psychic essence. The straightforward preoccupation with personal gain, the exclusive orientation to economic advantage, and "rational" compulsions have taken on a life of their own in the course of the bourgeois era. They have reduced the human beings of those strata that still think they have a chance in the current system to automata of individual self-preservation. The impossibility of adequately satisfying the individualistic instincts denies the real individual as the meaning of life, and the given community is thus put in its place as the true self. Accordingly, these individuals divert their unfulfilled desire for upward mobility in part toward the collectivity to which they belong, and in their thoughts and feelings ascribe directly to the state those individualistic values that the liberal epoch had instilled in them. They satisfy their own desires, as socially prescribed, through representative individuals. Individualistic thought is thereby hardly overcome but simply transferred. Correspondingly, rationalistic considerations that are supposed to be negated in the individual are viewed as highly legitimate. With respect to the state, thought can hardly be egoistic enough. In contrast, the rational concept of community rests on the recognition of common life interests. These interests bind together those dominated groups who, as a consequence of the contemporary social order (which is promoted, even eternalized by irrationalism), must injure each other in peace and destroy each other in war. The apparent but also partially real conflict of interest among human beings divided into nations—with which the world view of irrationalist philosophy may with some rational justification connect in its call for the subordination of the individual to the whole—derives from the retrograde organization and division of the world. At one time, this meant the advancement of life; its persistence today is in the interest only of a tiny portion of humanity, which must transform this conflict of interest or face its demise.

By ideologically [weltanschaulich] glorifying the economically determined denial of instinct, irrationalism contributes to reconciling human beings to such denial. Irrationalism facilitates the adaptation of the masses to their current situation and, through the psychic satisfaction that it offers, puts in the service of the dominant politics forces otherwise unavailable to it. The notion that the immediate gratification of the physical needs of the masses can, at least partially and temporarily, be replaced with substitute satisfactions is an important social-psychological axiom. The mental attitude that arises everywhere on the basis of the adaptation to poor conditions of existence with the aid of contemporary irrationalism is a certain kind of willingness to sacrifice. Human beings are just as fixated upon individualistic values in this ascetic attitude as they are in the most brutal egoism. Here, however, these values are transferred positively to the whole, and appear in the individual itself with reversed premises: in place of personal power stands only obedience; in place of wealth, poverty; in place of libertinism, chastity.

In a life that transcends the bourgeois forms of existence in a progressive sense, individualistic values are neither opposed nor suppressed, but recede behind the aims decisive for the entire society.

The morality of sacrifice and self-abnegation derives, in contrast, from the adaptation of egoistic beings to a situation which makes impossible the adequate satisfaction of their instincts. In this case, individuals only change the manifestation of their drives, and even with this transformation at least a portion of the egoistic drive [*Triebmasse*] remains. Next to their asceticism, therefore, a bit of wild self-interest, ambition, and striving for social power tends to live on in the hearts of those ready to sacrifice, and finds expression wherever reality allows it a little room. The fact that denial is exercised consciously for the sake of the existing community in no way entails that the capacity for love supersedes the instinct for self-preservation in the character of these human beings. In such a case, the notion of sacrifice would certainly not play so important a role in their attitudes, and their attitude toward the world would hardly have the "tragic" cast upon which contemporary literature puts so much value. Nor does the concept of community at issue here rest upon insight into the common sources of one's own impoverishment and that of others; if this were the case, it is primarily impoverishment that would be perceived as shared, and community as the mark of social life would appear not as real but rather as something that still remained to be achieved. The community to which sacrifice is related is simply posited from above as an essence to be venerated. It can be promulgated as something apparently existing because its realization is not merely distinct from the fulfillment of material demands, but has nothing to do with them. It is a symbol by means of which individualistic drives are reversed and reconciled with things as they are. Psychic forces which otherwise could have been directed toward changing that reality now operate in the service of maintaining a system that runs counter to the interests of most individuals. To the extent that this system sustains and renews the life of the society—despite the accidental character and the tremendous losses with which it does so—surrender to the existing, taking action in the interest of this bad reality, is not completely without a positive, rational foundation. At the same time, the struggle for its transformation must at first cripple some of the forces toward whose liberation that struggle aims. All activity in this contradictory reality has itself a contradictory character. The renunciation of individual interests and their transferrence to the symbol of the community may therefore be relatively useful and rational not only for the most economically powerful, but for a time for other strata and indeed for the majority within a given structure of power as well. From the perspective of the theory as a whole, however, this rationality appears in its limited nature. The small advantage that human beings within one of the contending power groups might gain at the expense of another by throwing into the scales their claim to happiness—indeed, their very lives—is purchased not merely at this cost, but indeed with a prolongation and exacerbation of the senseless misery, and with the injustice and barbarism in the entire world. The implications of this condition must ultimately affect those who originally had the advantage. Irrationalism retains this awareness of the senselessness of sacrifice for the individuals who make it; indeed, this awareness belongs to its essence. In its eyes, therefore, the victims of our era "must be the more highly esteemed as they have been brought to the edge of senselessness."[46]

The psychological mechanism through which the transformation [*Vorzeichenänderung*] of instincts takes place has been widely studied in psychology. With the concepts of ambivalence and reaction formation, Freud described the fundamental characteristics of psychic life.[47] It was above all Nietzsche, however, who understood the social significance of the psychic capacity for making a virtue of necessity by way of a reinterpretation of powerlessness. According to him, the ascetic ideal is "a dodge for the preservation of life."[48] He has studied in detail the psychic means by which the underclass resists the depressive effects of the economic sacrifice demanded of it. In addition to the "hypnotic damping of the sensibilities," he mentions "mechanical activity, with its numerous implications (regular performance, punctual and automatic obedience, unvarying routine, a sanctioning, even an enjoining of impersonality, self-oblivion)."[49] Of course, Nietzsche's analysis relates in the first instance to the priest. He describes the priest's technique, however, in a manner quite appropriate to recent irrationalism:

All he has to do, especially when dealing with sufferers of the lower classes, slaves or prisoners (or women, who as a rule are both things), has been to exercise a little art of name changing in order to make them see as blessings things which hitherto they had abominated. The dissatisfaction of the slave with his lot has not, at any rate, been an invention of the priest.—An even more highly prized specific against depression has been the ministration of small pleasures, which are readily accessible and can be made routine. This form of medication is frequently associated with the preceding one.[50]

Social development since Nietzsche has, however, in many ways outpaced his investigation, which referred primarily to the practice of Christianity and which only captured some of its historical functions. Though in the modern period religion had assumed certain humanistic traits, it now adapts itself to changed circumstances by its broad forfeiture of these traits, and has moved strongly in the direction of the biological side of Nietzsche's philosophy. Furthermore, in its efforts to overcome dissatisfaction, it has been substantially supplemented by new socializing forces. Despite its inadequacies, however, Nietzsche's "revaluation" also retains its significance for these new social functions. Symbolic categories of another order replace religious concepts, or they are both valid together. That which in religion is demanded for the sake of God now takes place for the whole, for the community. The true life—which was once to be achieved through grace—is now supposed to emerge from a vital connection to nature, from the powers of blood and soil [*Blut und Boden*]. Contrary to a declining rationalism, it is correct to say that the Understanding is not wholly created of itself, and that intellectual powers are an expression of the overall human condition. This view is unjustifiably hypostatized, however, where the differences in this condition among individuals and peoples are conceived as directly posited by nature, and not as the result of a developmental process including both social and extrasocial factors. Nature is thus arbitrarily given evaluative accents according to which group is referred to—one's own or one's opponents. Occasionally, it is confused with God or, indeed, deified.

Materialist thought cannot offer a view of the problem of sacrifice that is valid once and for all; it is not radical in the manner of metaphysics. The historical tendencies with which it is connected are co-determined by the threat to individual happiness and life, but it is not oriented merely to the self-preservation of the individual. For materialism, existence is by no means the highest or the only end. The sacrifice of one's existence can unquestionably be demanded in the course of historical practice, and exclusive preoccupation with existence can completely debase the individual. The motives with which the individual participates in this practice are certainly not rooted in the intellect alone; they derive from the overall character of the acting subject. But without the correct theory of society as a whole, social action—however clever it might be in technical details—is abandoned to mere accident. It only pretends to serve its own ends; in truth, it serves a constellation of interests unknown to the actor. Rational action is oriented to a theory of society that—as elaborated above—is no mere summation of abstract conceptual elements. Rather, it is the attempt, with the aid of all the various disciplines, to reconstruct an image of the social life process that can assist in understanding the critical condition of the world and the possibilities for a more rational order. This theory is based on analysis, and the dogmatic concept of community has a great deal to fear from it. What contradicts materialism is not the engagement of life as such, but its engagement for antihuman interests—that sacrifice that presupposes the *sacrificium intellectus,* or at least a dearth of intellect. The demand to stay at the forefront of available knowledge is not "rationalism" for the most progressive social groups; rather, it derives of necessity from their life situation. To be sure, knowledge in itself means little to them. Like the action it informs, knowledge first gains significance in connection with the struggles concerning a humanization of life. Cut adrift from all need and hope, even the genuine thoughts of human beings have little value for them.

But doesn't the struggle for the realization of a dignified human order itself have a deeper meaning? Is there not some determination of history, perhaps hidden to individuals, so that those who intervene in their specific situation serve a higher, unknowable, and yet venerable aim? Rationalism and irrationalism have both given a number of positive answers to these questions. They thus fall prey to an optimistic metaphysics, and make even easier their current social pessimism. Materialism knows no second reality, whether above us or below us. The happiness and peace that human beings do not receive on earth is not just apparently but actually lost to them, and for all eternity— for death is not peace, but truly leads to nothingness. Love of one's fellow human beings, as materialism understands it, has nothing to do with beings that find eternal security after their death, but with individuals that are quite literally ephemeral.

The escape hatch of modern philosophy—which, given the demise of the hope of an afterlife, posits death as "the necessary fulfillment of the meaning of life"[51]—is a specific attempt to make an intellectual accommodation to a senseless reality; it cannot stand up before the materialist view. The latter lacks any trace of an ideological [*weltanschaulich*] optimism, and thus has a more difficult time reconciling itself to the course of world history. It diverts all energies, even the most desperate, toward this world, and thus exposes to disappointment the only belief that it permits: the hope for the earthly possibilities of humanity. In contrast, metaphysical and religious optimism is not forced to clutch at even the tiniest prospects for human beings in this world and hold onto them energetically.

The future of humanity is extremely endangered and the regression to barbarism seems to threaten directly that part of the world most promising for the development of cultural potentials. In times like these, materialism's unconditional rejection of any possibility of an ideal harmonization comes to the fore in an especially striking way. All the various conclusions imparted in the gloomiest moments by rationalism and irrationalism as branches of idealist metaphysics—the eternal ideas and inexhaustible life, the autonomous ego and the true meaning of existence, the indestructible core of personality and the mission of one's own people—prove to be abstract concepts in which are immortalized the reflection of a transitory reality. Rationalism and irrationalism have both assumed the function of accommodating human beings to things as they are. Rationalism bestowed upon the liberal period the conviction that the future is anticipated in the reason of the individual. World history was, so to speak, the unfolding of the rational essence that each individual carried in its core; in its substance, the individual could feel itself immortal. The rationalist belief in progress was not merely an expression of respect for the unlimited possibilities of the development of human powers and the moral desire for a better human future. It was at the same time a narcissistic projection of the individual, timebound ego into all eternity. In monopoly capitalism, which holds most people in its thrall as mere elements of a mass, irrationalism passes along the theory that the essence of these individuals exists in the overarching historical unity to which they belong. And, as long as they are obedient, they have nothing to be concerned about: their better selves will be sublated in the community after their deaths. Thus rationalism and irrationalism both provide the service of mystification.

That materialism should entirely lack this quality seems to contradict its historical origins. To ban fear and despair from the soul through thought was the stated fundamental motive of Epicurean philosophy; it ascribed to theory the power to heal.[52] But in contrast to idealist philosophy, materialism never provided this psychological service, even in antiquity, by pointing to the eternal and creating for human beings a home to which they could hope to return, as had Plato in the immortal concepts or the Stoics in a deified nature. By unmasking the metaphysical idols which have long constituted a centerpiece of its theory, materialism directed the human capacity for love away from the products of fantasy, away from the mere symbols and reflections, and toward real living beings. For many of them, a greater composure may emerge not only from their solidarity with one another but from a clarity of consciousness. The simple establishment of commonality in suffering and the description of oppressive relations, which tend to be hidden from the light of consciousness by the ideological apparatus, can be liberating.

Neither is it simply thought as such that can acquire such signficance, but rather the structure in which the various ideas stand to each other and toward reality. However differentiated and meticulous, thought in itself means little to materialism. What matters is that a few insights stand at the center of knowledge, capable of illuminating the reality of a particular historical moment. The mere quantity of knowledge plays a decidedly subsidiary role. Whereas at various periods in antiquity—and even then only for certain ruling strata—a precise concept of matter and liberation from fear of the gods were of decisive significance, correct knowledge in the Renaissance was centered around a progressive anthropology and cosmology. At that time, men [Männer] and ideas were characterized by subtle differences of opinion concerning matters which in other times may have been irrelevant for the character of philosophical theories and that of their adherents. At present, certain fundamental insights into the essence of society are more decisive for the truth of an overall view than the possession or lack of extensive specialized knowledge. In these fundamental insights themselves, the most apparently trivial shadings are crucial. The boundary that one could draw today between human beings with respect to the weight of their knowledge would thus be oriented less to the extent of their academic training than to certain features of their behavior, in which are expressed their stance toward social struggles. When it becomes necessary, those who have the decisive insights can acquire the knowledge developed in other areas; beginning from an anachronistically structured education, however, the path to such knowledge can be strewn with serious obstacles. It is sometimes but a short stop from the limited individual discipline to superstition: some representatives of such sciences, themselves outstanding contributors to their fields, prove this as soon as they discuss things that cut close for all human beings. The mass of specialized knowledge, which is certainly extremely important for the overall society as a means of production, means less today for the individual than it had in the positivist period of science because, since Hegel's dialectic, the view gained sway that the progress of knowledge no longer takes place through the summation of data. It is not the growth of facts and theories but the spasmodic reconfiguration of the basic categories that characterizes the stages of science. Of course, that is preceded by the progressive revision of specialized knowledge; this takes place necessarily with respect to the highest system principles, which supply the standards for correction. The revolutionizing of the fundamental categories, which are only prepared in this way, raises knowledge as a whole to a higher level and affects its entire structure. Thus, next to its historical role as a weapon in social struggles, materialist thought may exert a liberating and affirming effect on the individual and thereby constitute a psychic aid. If it does so, this is not only because it values highly the possession of knowledge irrespective of all practical tasks and aims, but because some psychic fetters under which human beings suffer today burst when the right word is sounded, and because this word can to a great extent dissolve the tremendous isolation of human beings from one another peculiar to the current period. This force is characteristic of truth, though truth not only rejects all ideological consolation but is indeed intent upon destroying it.

Materialism supports neither side in the controversy between rationalism and irrationalism. Since the Cartesian isolation of mental substance from all spatial reality, rationalism has absolutized a specific form of thought—namely, the discovery of abstract concepts and the establishment of purely statistical relationships among them—as the

highest human activity. In the process, it has clung to an intellectu-
alistic psychology and explained human actions exclusively on the basis of their conscious motives. Its anthropology was determined from
the very beginning by a concept of isolated mental substance, by the
monad, which expresses faithfully the one-sidedness of human beings
in the bourgeois epoch. Because this anthropology overlooks the individual's dependence upon the total social life process, however, either
the claims of the social whole were seen only as a furtherance or an
obstacle to egoistic purposes, or these claims were mythologized as
conscience or divine commandments. "When irrationalism, as the
counterplay to rationalism, talks about the things to which rationalism
is blind, it does so only with a squint." [53] With its concept of the community, it pushes unresolved problems off into the "sanctuary of the
irrational." It has its logical genesis in the failure of rationalism in the
face of social problems. Its power stems from the current decline of a
society of self-conscious individuals. The false rationalist concept of
equality—which is grounded logically in the hypostatization of the capacity for abstract thought, and transformed from a demand for the
rational ordering of relations into a metaphysical doctrine—today flies
in the face of truth. Given the emerging laws of the economy, only
very small groups emerge truly victorious from the competitive struggle among bourgeois individuals concerned solely with their own interests. The vast majority of people lose their individuality and become
a mass capable only of acting heteronomously, even if their own interests must, for better or worse, to a certain extent be incorporated
in the ends that are set for them. Irrationalism correctly grasps the
bankruptcy of rationalism, but draws from it the wrong conclusion. It
does not criticize one-sided thought and egoistic interest in favor of a
construction of the world according to the powers available to humanity. Instead, it leaves untouched the essentials of the economic laws
that have ushered in the contemporary situation, and serves the ends
of the economically powerful people who are merely the executors of
those economic forces. It promotes blind affirmation of them with its
precept of subordination to an allegedly universal whole. It is an obstacle to the reorganization of society in that it apparently acknowledges the necessity of such a reorganization but limits that process to
an inner conversion and mere spiritual renewal. It makes a primitive

pedagogical issue of a complicated social problem, which may suffice for the regressive strata that stand in intimate relation to this philosophy. The negative character of irrationalism derives from the peculiarities of the period in which it plays a role, just as the positive character of rationalism is connected to the great creative achievements of the bourgeoisie. In the present, rationalism becomes easy prey for its opponent; history has long since left behind the era of rationalistic systems. The reason inherent in rationalism lives on today in the theory whose method was developed by rationalism itself under the rubric of dialectics.

Montaigne and the Function of Skepticism

Philosophical skepticism has had outstanding representatives in two periods of European history: at the end of antiquity and in the Renaissance. Despite the deep differences between the economic forms of the Greek polis and of those city-states that heralded the emergence of modern nation-states, the transitional phenomena nonetheless reveal certain similarities. In both instances, social struggles and social reorganization take place on the terrain of an older urban culture. Centrally organized forces set about the task of assuming a leading historical role. Highly developed individuals from the urban bourgeoisie see the world caught up in a process of political development that calls into question the values of an ordered life: long-term efficacy, personal security, cooperation of parties, the cultivation of commerce, art, and science. In both instances, the process extended over centuries. The order had already been threatened earlier; now the unrest becomes permanent. Economic progress alternates with deep crises; wealthy bourgeois penetrate into the old patrician strata and even dispossess them; all social contradictions become differentiated and intensify. The urban boom lasted long enough, however, that the refinement of needs and capacities proceeded apace with the division of labor; there were human beings who knew what happiness was, and who had an education too thorough to flee into religious and metaphysical illusions in the face of the transformations that constantly called that happiness into question.

The birth of Pyrrhus, the founder of ancient skepticism, occurred during the epoch of the victories and of the death of Epaminondas. As Burckhardt writes:

After Epaminondas threw one more spasm into these miserable times, it gradually becomes dark in this nation; the definitive destruction of the polis follows. While the cities of the lands under the Diadochi[1] at least led a tranquil economic existence and only the largest rose up in occasional revolts, the ground shook constantly in a great number of the old Greek polises. . . . And now, next to the development of factions among Macedonians, Achaeans, and Aetolians, the degeneration of the state into the latest forms of tyranny goes relentlessly forward with a terrifying military economy and in violent oligarchies and democracies, which distinguish themselves by butchery, expulsions, and the partitioning of land. The unavoidable final consequence of all democracy—strife over property—leads to a true purgatory; communism emerges again and again, both parties enter into every alliance that contributes to the goal, and they allow themselves any means whatsoever. With everything that happened falling into worse and worse hands, the bankruptcy of the Greek idea of the state—which essentially had begun with that senseless upward-striving of the bourgeoisie—became complete. The genuinely Greek feature amidst all this was that delight could be taken in a conspiracy prepared with all due subtlety, whereas one would become quite unsettled if one were to consider the internal solidity of advancing Rome, where individuals were not yet spiritually separated from the state, and cooperated with rather than persecuted one another. If one were unaware of what had happened before and later, Polybius' accounts of the last twenty years of the third century would lead one to believe that the greatest loss of life struck the nation at that time.[2]

Montaigne must be considered the founder of modern skepticism. His life spanned the stormy years of a rising absolutism. In 1533, the year of his birth, the relatively peaceful period into which France had entered at the end of the Hundred Years' War came to an end. An elevated bourgeoisie had emerged.

It consists of people who have made their fortunes in such branches of commerce as meat butchering, cloth trading, and goldsmithing; of shipowners; and especially of financiers with currency-trading firms or who grew rich as civil servants of the king or of the great fiefdoms. These wealthy bourgeois buy up country real estate and even large demesnes, and thus invade the ranks of the nobility. The incumbents of royal offices also often receive patents of nobility. . . . Thus begins a social transformation that would spread dramatically in the course of the sixteenth century.[3]

The means of circulation are multiplied by the extension of trade, inflation ruins the old nobility, and the lower social strata suffer widespread impoverishment. Workers' wages sink tremendously with the currency devaluation. Naturally, the entire rise in prices is blamed on the rise in wages, which lag pathetically behind the rapid price increases. The authorities rush to the aid of the employers, establish wage ceilings, hinder proletarian organization, and forbid strikes. Popular rebellions animated by poverty follow one another in the cities; plagues and famines become the order of the day.[4]

The class struggles between bourgeoisie and proletariat were complicated by those among the ruling strata. Reinforced by the financial disarray of the feudal nobility, the court under the last Valois vacillates between alliance with the old powers—the Church and an aristocracy oriented toward Spain—on the one hand, and with progressive bourgeois and the Reformation on the other. The religious civil wars are largely traceable directly to the economic conflicts among the ruling groups. The impoverishment of the masses served as a lever to mobilize them for the various purposes of these parties. The mob was an especially useful tool in the hands of the clergy. Michelet sees the origins of the St. Bartholomew's Day massacre in the proposal, made in Paris in 1561, that the goods of the clergy be sold. "From the day when the church beheld the king wavering, and tempted by the hopes of that booty, she turned hastily, violently towards the people, and employed every means in her power, by preaching, by alms, by different influences, and by her immense connection, her converts, tradespeople, and mendicants, to organize the massacre."[5] The condition of France after the civil wars mirrors that of the German Empire during the Thirty Years' War. The peasants, for whom military and other bands prepared a gruesome fate,[6] surged into the cities, whose tasks became insoluble.

Pressed by the poor, whose numbers had been multiplied by unemployment and the decline of business among their bourgeois, [the cities] watched with growing concern as people from the flatlands streamed to their gates. Hungry mouths, hands without work, demoralization, infectious diseases, treason, insurrection—all of these could be expected from them. The gates were closed to them, but they circumvented the sentries and snuck into the cities individually, or forced their way in *en masse*, partially with permission and partially by force. They were repulsed by citizens deputized for the task with the telling name of "rogue-chasers" [*chasse-coquins*] or they were pressed into concentration camps for excavation or demolition work, in which they wore distinguishing marks. Plague and starvation came periodically, and decimated an urban population weakened by poverty.[7]

The miserable condition of the roads, the innumerable tolls and duties everywhere one passed on land or on the waterways, and the hordes
of wolves and bandits made the insecurity so great that in many areas
trade was completely paralyzed.[8] Plunder was the order of the day. "I
have a thousand times gone to bed in my own house," writes Montaigne, "with an apprehension that I should be betrayed and struck
dead that same night."[9]

In the face of the horrors of the transition to modernity, Montaigne
flees no more than the ancient skeptics into a strong faith. He scorns
the illusion of unconditional certainty. There are far too many who
consider their views absolute, whether theoretically or morally, and
who mutually contradict one another. One need only peruse literature and the world in order to see that. No one can sit in judgment
and determine which of the authorities, so certain of their opinions,
is correct. In essence they are simply uneducated. The senses themselves are uncertain, not to speak of concepts. To pledge oneself to a
theory is always limited. The wise person sees the mass of unconditionally certain judgments—the one overthrowing the other—and
smiles. Such a person notes the appearance of a new doctrine with the
thought that it was preceded by another, once equally prevalent, and
that yet another will come to replace it. Human beings tend to acquire
their so-called convictions through custom, socialization, material interest, or other circumstances. They drift

without judgment and without choice, nay, most often before the age of dis-
cretion. . . . Is there not some advantage in being free from the necessity that
curbs others? Is it not better to remain in suspense, than to be entangled in
the many errors that the human imagination has brought forth? Is it not
better to suspend one's conviction than to get mixed up with those seditious
and wrangling divisions? . . . Take the most reputed school theory, it will
never be so sure but that, in order to defend it, you will be obliged to attack
and combat hundreds of contrary theories. Is it not better to keep out of this
scuffle?[10]

Montaigne's reaction to these frightful circumstances is to retreat from
any kind of unconditional certainty to a moderate self-interest. Pyrrhus was quite correct.

He had no wish to make himself a stock or stone; he wished to be a living, dis-
coursing and reasoning being, enjoying all natural pleasures and amenities,

using and bringing all his bodily and spiritual gifts into play, in right and orderly fashion. The fantastic, imaginary and unreal privileges which man has usurped of lording it, of laying down the law and setting up the truth, he honestly renounced and abandoned.[11]

Montaigne also shows himself a rejuvenator of the old skepticism through his knowledge of the world and his statesmanlike abilities. Pyrrhus went to India with Alexander's army.[12] Carneades, the most significant representative of academic skepticism, participated in the mission of Greek philosophers to Rome and had great success due to his adroit behavior.[13] By character, Montaigne was a diplomat. He belonged to the new nobility arising from the bourgeoisie, and thus considered himself fully a noble. Though as a conservative he was a strict adherent of the state religion, Catholicism, and declared during the religious conflicts that it is "neither handsome nor honorable to be a wobbler and a hybrid, to be unmoved in one's affections and to incline to neither side,"[14] he saw his role essentially as that of a nego-tiator rather than an antagonist. As mayor of Bourdeaux, he showed exemplary objectivity. His moderate position in general questions cor-responds to that of the party of the "politicians" who believed it dan-gerous to exchange Catholicism for the fanatical Protestantism of Calvin as the state religion, but who also did not want to enter into alliance with a retrograde Spain. The motto "one faith, one law, one king" hardly appeared to them beyond question. They began to assert that "between the intolerance of Rome and that of Geneva, two religions exist in one state."[15] Montaigne did not put it so explicitly, but he held talks with both parties, the Parisian court and the Huguenots. The representative of the Inquisition promised him his favor, and the Protestant majesty from Navarre was a guest in his quarters. Goethe admired that "a knight loyally and enthusiastically devoted to the Ro-man Church as well as to the monarchy . . . could conduct animated, open discussions with Catholic as well as Protestant clerics and school-teachers in Germany concerning divergent faiths and opinions."[16] As with the ancients, philosophical skepticism presupposes a broad ho-rizon. It is the opposite of narrow-mindedness. Its style is that of de-scription, not theory. "I don't teach, I tell stories," says Montaigne, and Goethe repeats it enthusiastically.[17]

The relativism of the Greek skeptics had already been accused of making action impossible. They replied that in order to act, one does not need knowledge; probability suffices.[18] Human beings act not on the basis of absolutes, which do not exist, but primarily out of prejudice and habit. Since no opinion is better than any other, it is never advisable to contravene existing customs and institutions. According to Zeller, Carneades "acted like a true Sceptic. He expressed doubts as to whether anything could be known about God, but for practical purposes he accepted the belief in God as an opinion more or less probable and useful."[19] In practice, skepticism means a sympathetic stance toward the traditional and mistrust toward all utopias. If there is no such thing as truth, it makes little sense to stick up for it. At times, of course, even the display of reserve can be dangerous. There are times in which the state fails to guarantee even the freedom to consider the dominant ideology as merely probable, even though one obeys it. In such periods, skepticism tends to blossom in silence, for struggle—even that concerning its development as a particular doctrine—is not its element. Where conflicts arise and the skeptics prove themselves courageous, they are driven not so much by their philosophy; even the liberality and tolerance occasionally connected with it is insufficient for that. At times like these, a militant love of humanity comes to the fore which can slumber behind a skeptical attitude and take hold of the individual. The skeptic typically lets experience and healthy, sensuous common sense reign. To be sure, our senses are a paltry thread; even the animals have sharper and perhaps more numerous ones than we. Nonetheless, science—which has not yet come very far—begins and ends with the senses; "they are our masters."[20]

The skeptics are of one mind with respect to sensualism. They have consistently opposed those schools that gave an independent role to thought, and particularly to constructive theory. If it is completely vain—indeed meaningless—to speak of the essence of a thing, there remain observation and the connection of phenomena with conjectures regarding their repetition. The basis of practical skills and occupations is experience, against which there is no objection. But the skeptic loathes as dogmatism and speculation all thought that goes beyond given appearances, any kind of judgment that contradicts the plausible. Immediate perception and reflection, natural need, laws and tradition, honed dexterity and customary knowledge are considered the norms of action.[21] The firmly grounded order with its relative freedom, which belongs to the presuppositions of bourgeois commerce, has become a decisive personal need for the representatives of the skeptical attitude. The diffusion of economic relations advances itself through these representatives by means of their enthusiasm for general practical and theoretical refinement [*Bildung*]. Social life appears to them only as the reproduction of the given. They do not seriously attack the practical and intellectual activities associated with reproduction. However, the thought or the deed that calls the whole thing in question, which they come to know in transitional periods in the form of civil and international wars, is a horror for them. Philosophical skepticism is the exact opposite of destruction, which it occasionally appears to be to its adherents and opponents. It is in essence conservative.

The conservative traits emerge more strongly in Montaigne than in the ancients with whom he links up. In Alexander's empire or under the Roman emperors, no new forms of life arose that offered optimism to the educated individual. Hopelessness and emptiness are characteristic of the skeptical philosophy of antiquity; there was no rational worldly content in the power of the *Imperatores* before which it bowed. There is no reasonable prospect for the individual to find contentment in the world. Ancient skepticism prepared the way for mystical Neoplatonism and Christian asceticism. In contrast, Montaigne sees a rising absolutism with which he can identify because it guarantees the conservation of bourgeois property. Despite the horrors of the civil wars, he knows that life goes on and that this, too, shall pass. The national state will protect the new bourgeoisie and establish calm. Montaigne's stoical indifference [*Ataraxie*]²² consists in the contented ordering of the inner spirit, in which one recovers from any inequity. The reservation of judgment, the *Epoché*, here becomes the retreat into private interiority, in which one can replenish oneself, freed from the compulsions of occupational duties. Interiority plays in individual life the role that falls to churches, museums, and places of entertainment—to leisure generally—in social life. In the bourgeois era, the cultural spheres are separated from the economy, in the individual as well as in the social whole. Outside, in work and the economy, duty and the economic law of value arising from the competitive struggle call the tune. In the realm of culture, however, eternal harmony reigns.

The skeptics assure us that no particular mode of action follows from philosophy. With them, the consequences of thought appear only in their being good, loyal citizens. Montaigne chides the Stoics and Christians, "who [are] slaves to themselves, lie hard, put out [their] eyes, throw [their] riches into the river, court pain (either, as some do, to win the beatitude of another life by torturing [themselves] in this, or, like others, to be safe from falling anew by standing on the lowest step)."[23] He himself practices another method. "It is enough for me, while under Fortune's favours, to prepare for her disfavours, and to picture to myself, whilst I am well off, the ill that is to come, as far as my imagination can reach: just as we exercise ourselves in jousts and tournaments, and mimic wars, in the midst of peace."[24] That is the Stoicism of the rich. According to Pascal, Montaigne "preserve[s] a happy moderation in [his] deportment; [he does] as other people do; and what they do, in a mistaken fancy that they are pursuing true happiness, [he does] from a different principle, which is, that—probabilities on both sides being balanced—example and convenience are the counterpoises of [his] conduct."[25] In short, he acts not so much according to what he thinks, as according to what he has. He describes his independence characteristically:

We should have wife, children, worldly goods, and, above all, health, if we can; but not be so strongly attached to them that our happiness depends on them. We must reserve a little back-shop, all our own, entirely free, wherein to establish our true liberty and principal retreat and solitude. In this retreat we should keep up our ordinary converse with ourselves, and so private, that no acquaintance or outside communication may find a place there; there to talk and laugh, as if we had neither wife, nor children, nor worldly goods, retinue or servants: to the end that, should we happen to lose them, it may be no new thing to do without them.[26]

He retreats into his inner sanctum, such as into his castle Montaigne (and there into his library) or when he travels. Life decomposes into one's responsibilities, on the one hand, and diversion, edification, and so on, on the other. One's responsibilities also include taking care of the family and the duties of citizenship. Beyond this begins the passing of time. Responsible thought belongs exclusively to those realistic spheres; seriousness is exhausted in them, and otherwise one wants to let go. "To those who ask me why I travel I usually reply, 'I know well what I am fleeing from, but not what I am in search of.' "[27] That is, I travel "pour mon plaisir."[28] In modern skepticism, both diversion and a relationless and comfortably appointed interiority arise from stoical indifference. Worldly enjoyment and retreat into interiority are identical for Montaigne. Those who sit in their libraries or who take a pleasant trip rest contentedly by themselves. The social stratum in France to which he belonged had the means to create a pleasurable private life.

At the same time, a kind of interiority developed among the masses that had nothing to do with restfulness. The collapse of the feudal [*ständische*] order drove the poor into unaccustomed and arduous work in manufactures. Unemployment and the rising price of food compelled people to hire themselves out at every opportunity. A new labor discipline became necessary. The comfortable mode of work still dominant in France in the sixteenth century was less and less compatible with modern competition. The many holidays, indeed leisure in general, had to be cut down; work itself had to be made more intensive. The process began whereby workers were forced into ever greater responsibility and increasing output, on the one hand, and sustained deprivation, on the other. The adaptation of the masses to this situation took place with the renewal of Christianity, in Protestantism and also in Catholicism after the Council of Trent. One side of Protestantism corresponds exactly with skepticism: we are incapable of perceiving a meaningful order in the world. The lower strata should no longer look to the higher, nor individuals to God in the expectation that the powerful will take care of the powerless. Such hopes are silly and reprehensible. Individuals must make demands not on the higher-ups but on themselves. They must take themselves in hand. Their material needs are directed inward as so many indictments of their own wretchedness. If therefore the individuals of the mass withdraw into their interiority, they find there no such pleasurable relaxation as the cultivated bourgeois of the transition period, but rather their own strict conscience, which accuses them of sin, explores their mistakes and oversights, and drives them to further work. An interiority hostile to enjoyment and opposed to the person becomes increasingly widespread in subsequent centuries. The wealth and education Montaigne received were the fruits of a declining feudal order. In the nascent bourgeois order, culture exists only on the basis of the capitalist form of labor.

Just as the mystical religiosity of antiquity bore skeptical traits,[29] Protestantism is in agreement with Montaigne's critique of knowledge. Luther's attack on reason and science distinguishes itself from skeptical irony only by virtue of its coarseness of expression. He sees in reason a whore raped and insulted by God.[30] According to Calvin, all thoughts of the wise person are vain. They cannot condemn theoretical thought enough. Human beings should submit to God's word and to authority, and should not think themselves capable of coming up with a better understanding of the truth and with a standard for His actions. Montaigne goes still further. The most famous chapter of the *Essais* is devoted to a defense of Raymond Sebond's *Natural Theology*, which, in accordance with Thomist tradition, did not wish to do without the light of reason in spiritual matters—indeed, sought to ground faith in it. Sebond's defender, however, denies reason any value whatsoever, and not merely in theology but in the realm of science as well.[31] In genuine Reformation style, he says, "Is it possible to imagine anything more ridiculous than that this miserable and puny creature, who is not so much as master of himself, exposed to shocks on all sides, should call himself Master and Emperor of the universe, of which it is not in his power to know the smallest part, much less to command it?"[32] Among the opinions of the ancients, Montaigne prizes most highly "those that are most contemptuous, most humiliating and most crushing. To me Philosophy never seems to have so easy a game as when she attacks our presumption and vanity, when she sincerely admits her own indecision, weakness, and ignorance."[33] Not Luther but the humanistically schooled Calvin thought more highly of reason. To be sure, according to him, "The dulness of the human mind renders it incapable of pursuing the right way of investigating the truth . . . ; thus, in its search after truth, it betrays its incapacity to seek and find it. . . . Yet its attempts are not always so fruitless, but that it makes some discoveries, particularly when it applies itself to inferior things."[34] Montaigne is more definitive. "The conviction of wisdom is the plague of man."[35] "The things that come to us from heaven have alone the right and authority to persuade, they alone have the stamp of truth, which also we do not see with our own eyes, nor receive by our own powers. That great and holy image could not remain in so mean a habitation, unless God prepared it for that purpose, unless God repaired and strengthened it with his particular and supernatural grace and favour."[36] Human reason is not simply weak; it is harmful and dangerous. "People who judge and find fault with their judges never submit to them as they should. How much more docile and tractable, both to the laws of religion and to the civil laws, are simple and incurious minds, than those wits who supervise and pedantically hold forth on divine and human causes!"[37]

If human beings were to assume the skeptical viewpoint, they would see themselves as

naked and empty, confessing their natural weakness and ready to receive from on high some power not their own; stripped bare of human knowledge, and all the more fit to harbour within themselves divine knowledge; suppressing their own judgement to leave more room for faith; neither disbelieving nor setting up any teaching contrary to the common observances; humble, obedient, docile, zealous, a sworn enemy to heresy and consequently free from the vain and irreligious beliefs introduced by the false sects. They are blank tablets prepared to take from the finger of God such forms as he shall be pleased to engrave upon them.[38]

The attack on the sects here is undoubtedly directed at the Huguenots—though not at their faith but at their claim as a French party, which would threaten the steady advance of national power. This attack is consistent with the attitude of a triumphant Protestantism. Even Calvin excused and promoted political thought and activity against the Papists; in the Republic of Geneva, however, humility was preferred to vanity, and faith was more important than science. As he put it in the *Institutio,*

To every noble mind it appears very absurd to submit to an unjust and imperious despotism, if it be possible by any means to resist it. A uniform decision of human reason is, that it is the mark of a servile and abject disposition patiently to bear it, and of an honest and ingenuous mind to shake it off. Nor is the revenging of injuries esteemed a vice among the philosophers. But the Lord, condemning such excessive haughtiness of mind, prescribes to his people that patience which is deemed dishonourable among men.[39]

The reasoning of private persons is idle and vain with respect to the form of the state.[40] Luther imposes complete passivity on human beings. In contrast to his opinion concerning the arrogance of human reason, Montaigne's skeptical *Epoché* appears feeble, and Calvin looks like a crass Catholic. "Like a cripple, with limp hands and feet, the human being must beseech mercy as the taskmistress of action."[41] We must, he says, "return to the point at which we know nothing, desire nothing, are nothing. That is a short path, a *Via Crucis* (Way of the Cross), upon which we shall attain life most readily."[42] Human beings "sin though they do what they can [to stop themselves], for of themselves they are capable neither of desiring nor of thinking."[43] In other words, Montaigne shares with the Protestants the doctrine of the feebleness of human reason. To be sure, both reject thought only insofar as it comes into contradiction with the given legal order, but they do not reject science as such. Calvin, too, had a sense for Montaigne's ancient philosophers.

Now, shall we deny the light of truth to the ancient lawyers, who have delivered such just principles of civil order and polity? Shall we say that the philosophers were blind in their exquisite contemplation and in their scientific description of nature? Shall we say that those, who by the art of logic have taught us to speak in a manner consistent with reason, were destitute of understanding themselves? . . . On the contrary, we shall not be able even to read the writings of the ancients on these subjects without great admiration.[44]

Melanchthon moderates Luther's bluntness on this point. The mind is bad only as critical theory and practice; to the extent that it falls in line and subordinates itself—as custom, bourgeois efficiency, practical understanding, and cultural works—it is tolerated in Protestantism as well as in skepticism.

In contrast to the Protestant Reformers' attitude, however, Montaigne considers the highest virtue to be moderation, not absolute self-abnegation. He views the antagonistic parties from the standpoint of an enlightened diplomat; for him, freedom of conscience is the precondition of peace. According to him, no one is in the right; indeed, there is no such thing as "the right," only order and disorder. From his discussions with German Protestants he drew the conclusion that the religious question amounts to a semantic debate. Luther interprets the Bible differently than the Papists. Luther formed a faction; factions then form concerning how to interpret Luther.[45] Montaigne regards Protestantism as dangerous in France for political, not religious reasons; he fears civil unrest.

For the common people, lacking the power to weigh things by themselves, and being easily misled by chance appearances, when once they have become possessed with the temerity to despise and criticize the beliefs they once held in the utmost reverence, such as those on which depends their salvation; and when once certain articles of their religion have been called in question and placed in the scales, they will soon be ready to throw into a like uncertainty all the other articles of their faith, which had no more authority or foundation in their eyes than those which are already shattered; and will shake off . . . all the impressions they once received from the authority of the laws or the reverence of ancient usage; "for, once too dreaded, with more greedy zest/trampled beneath the rabble heel" (Lucretius); resolved henceforth to accept nothing to which they have not applied their judgement and given their special sanction.[46]

To be sure, the orthodox Catholics are not much better. The alliance of the Church, Spain, the house of Guise and the whole decaying aristocracy defended the feudal forms of life in which the partners' parasitic existence was still possible. According to Montaigne, they too stir up the people, and not only "out of true zeal to their religion and a godly desire to maintain the peace and the present state of their country,"[47] but for the sake of their own personal advantage. Neither the common man in the army nor the leaders take religion so seriously. Indeed, when the Dukes of Guise moved against the Calvinists, even the Lutherans were acceptable to them.[48] According to Montaigne, the Catholics' legitimate concern "is only there as an ornament and a cloak: it is indeed alleged, but is neither received nor harboured nor espoused. It is there as on the lips of an advocate, not as in the heart or affection of a suitor."[49] Montaigne's position corresponds to that of his contemporary Bodin, who recommended to the king "the mildest and most holy ways" in the treatment of the Protestants,[50] and who opposed the violent repression of Protestantism for the same reason Montaigne opposed its expansion. Otherwise, says Bodin,

they which are destitute of the exercise of their religion, and withall distasted of the religion of the other, shall become altogether Atheists (as wee daily see) and so after that they have once lost the feare of God, tread also underfoot both the lawes and magistrats, and so inure themselves to all kinds of impieties and villainies, such as is impossible by mans lawes to be redressed. . . . For as the greatest tyranny is nothing so miserable as an Anarchie, . . . [s]o the greatest superstition that is, is not by much anything so detestable as Atheisme.[51]

The inclination to remain personally neutral in religious questions, to subordinate religion to reasons of state, to turn to the strong state as the guarantor of secure trade and commerce corresponds to the conditions of existence of a moneyed bourgeoisie and its alliance with the absolute monarchy. That alliance had its happiest period in France under Henry IV and, however much against its will, came to an end only at the close of the eighteenth century.

Important aspects of the bourgeois spirit are expressed in Montaigne's attitude. Representative thinkers of other countries—Machiavelli in Italy, Spinoza in Holland, Hobbes in England—have asserted the irrelevance of the content of religion in comparison with the interests of state. The tendency to subordinate the truth to power did not first emerge with fascism; irrationalism, just as deeply rooted in the economic situation of the bourgeoisie as the liberal traits, pervades the entire history of the modern era and limits its concept of reason. Religious ideas—indeed, universal aims as such—recede behind the exigencies of capital accumulation. Yet Montaigne introduced a characteristic development with respect not only to religion but to science as well. His thought stands closer to the classical rationalists Descartes and Leibniz than it might appear. It does not contradict the science they founded, only alchemy and the other kinds of charlatanry that he saw before him. Montaigne's influence on Cartesian doubt, and thus on the critical attitude of modern natural science [*Naturerkenntnis*], is regularly emphasized. Many passages in the *Essais* seem to point to Kant. Human beings "are right in setting up the strictest possible barriers for the human mind. In study, as in all else, its steps should be counted and regulated; its hunting rights should be artificially prescribed."[52] Montaigne's project of describing himself, to which his entire oeuvre is devoted, was significant for the genesis of the great French psychology. The unsystematic form of representation found adherents even among the systematic philosophers. It has been remarked that Descartes first expressed his doctrines in essay form.[53] The *Discourse on Method* contains a biographical sketch. Like Montaigne, Descartes announces his ideas as personal views. In England, the concept of the *Essais* had a sparkling career,[54] and Voltaire reintroduced it into France, probably stimulated by that experience.

As subjectivism, skepticism constitutes an essential aspect of all modern philosophy. Science was held to be objective as long as religious and worldly knowledge had not been separated and the earthly order appeared as posited by God. The structure of the universe which human beings strove to comprehend was its true structure; the central concepts mirrored objective relations, genuine ideas according to which nature, human beings, and society were ordered. Nominalism shook this conception. The Aristotelian doctrine that things have their essence within them, and that we know them according to that essence, lost its authority. Its dissonance with the reality of the new society became apparent with the advancing disintegration of the medieval *Ordo*. Reality is not characterized by the harmony of form and matter, but rather by their opposition: the opposition between a refractory external world that must be conquered and the individuals confronting it with their own purposes and ideas. Skepticism is the quintessence of nominalism. It lies hidden in all those tendencies at the advent of the modern era that ran counter to Aristotelian scholasticism. For the subjectivization of knowledge, about which the most antagonistic systems concur, is a skeptical function. The Platonist Ficino also opposes the view that objective reality makes its way into the mind in any sense. In truth, thought comprehends only itself and that which it brings forth. Knowledge is by no means the reflection of an object. "Judgment follows the form and nature of those judging, not of the object judged."[55] In this respect, Descartes, Hume, and Kant belong to the same school. At the same time that progressive science experienced the triumph of extending the validity of natural laws infinitely in spatial and temporal terms and of no longer giving any quarter to heavenly bliss, it itself sank to the level of a subjective medium of information. Its concepts amount to signposts. As long as this philosophical tendency went together with an exalted conception of the human being, as with Pico, its skeptical content remained obscure. But such beliefs founder in the Renaissance.[56] The reduction of philosophy to a logic and an epistemology whose object is the general, eternal forms of thought was completed in the next few centuries. Accordingly, the sciences are the manner in which individuals find their way by means of these forms in the chaos of given facts. The isolated ego, a point of power [*Kraftpunkt*], is the only comprehensible reality; there is no meaningful connection with the rest; the world becomes an incomprehensible "out-there," the existence of which is not even certain but must rather be demonstrated by way of complicated inferences. The ego is alone in an uncertain, ephemeral, deceptive world. Montaigne's style of thought thus fits in with modern philosophy's concept of knowledge.

The individual is the positive content of skepticism. Despite all the talk of its inconstancy and triviality, its incapacity for true knowledge, the ego with its powers remains the only principle we can rely on in theory and practice. Our happiness depends upon us ourselves. Hegel clearly recognizes this in the analysis to which he subjected skepticism. "The sceptical self-consciousness thus experiences in the flux of all that would stand secure before it its own freedom as given and preserved by itself. It is aware of this stoical indifference of a thinking which thinks itself, the unchanging and genuine certainty of itself."[57] The genuine skeptics' irony toward the weak, ephemeral, empirical ego in which we must trust is quite different from the pathos with which rationalism speaks of the subject as the principle of knowledge. Nonetheless, both see in the knowledge and action of the isolated individual the substance of an adequate philosophy. "We need little learning to live happily," says Montaigne. "And Socrates tells us that we have it in us, and instructs us how to find it and make use of it. All these acquisitions of ours that exceed the natural are well-nigh vain and superfluous. It is enough if they do not burden and cumber us more than they do us good."[58] Human beings must rely on their own powers.

Montaigne's opinion of what we can expect from them is tempered. The position of the human being in the universe is not impressive, and each individual is irrelevant in the overall course of things. The highest wisdom consists in developing our talents with common sense, pursuing calmly the happiness afforded us by nature, and adapting to nature as it is given to each of us—as the passage of life's stages, as physical and psychic temperament, as fate in the world. The maxim is to act naturally. Violence against oneself and others, against people and animals, is foolhardiness. There is no logical proof against tyranny and cruelty. Montaigne simply turns away from them. Free development, education without compulsion, the unfolding of naturally given individual powers is his humanistic program, which to be sure he lays out not as a doctrine but as his preference and private opinion. He makes no great distinction between Stoicism and skepticism. The essence of philosophy is *amor fati et naturae:* in the end, overcoming the fear of death. That is the quintessence of the wisdom of life that he sought to practice, at first through unceasing methodological preparation and later through observation of the common man, the "natural" human being.[59] Proper death as well as proper life are in the hands of individuals; they can make themselves independent of external vicissitudes. "The profit of life is not in its length but in the use we put it to: many a man has lived long, who has lived little; see to it as long as you are here. It lies in your will, not in the number of years, to make the best of life."[60] With respect to the possibility of suicide, he writes falsely: "No one suffers long but by his own fault."[61] Yet not only nature but the prison wardens have always taken precautions against this path of escape. The easy death within the reach of everyone reduces one's anxiety in the face of the terror that ultimately holds society together.

The natural, unconstrained manner of presenting oneself implied by Montaigne's view was the very paragon of the cultivated man throughout the bourgeois epoch. This is the goal of a good upbringing, and more recently of psychoanalysis. Those who demonstrate shortcomings in this respect draw suspicion upon themselves. They have not adapted; their relation to reality is out of order. They add something to reality, but are secretly aggressive. At the pinnacle of society and business, a refined instinct has developed for the unnatural quality of a personality. Those who do not move freely and without rancor in their dealings with the world can be quickly recognized through invisible signs, and have little success. At best they are neurotic; at worst, oppositional. The demand to give nature its due that went along with the emancipation of the bourgeoisie comes to mean that one should address oneself directly and without bias to a world in which nothing is in order. At the beginning of modernity, humanistic figures such as Montaigne emerge and assert the natural behavior of the cultivated personality as the norm of action. In the nascent bourgeoisie they can see that human beings can dispense with physical as well as religious compulsions. Despite all the differences between their theories and temperaments, these broad-minded spirits are united by the enjoyment of the intellectual and material fruits of culture, great political insight, sharp psychological judgment, and religious toleration. Relaxed satisfaction of individual needs in the status quo is their mode of life; they themselves belong to the cultivated bourgeoisie. There are among them examples of great personal courage and of solidarity with the oppressed—particularly Agrippa of Nettesheim, the deepest of these skeptics, but also Montaigne himself.[62] Any obligation is denied, however. Montaigne quotes an old philosopher "who said that the wise man should do nothing but for himself, seeing that he alone was worth doing anything for."[63] It is simply a matter of taste if at times he behaves differently.

In the face of such good sense, the Reformers seem inhuman. Mediated by their fanaticism, there emerges the bourgeois mass individual, who grows out of the childish condition of the medieval individual by way of the inversion of material desires, the subjugation of sensual impulses to a relentlessly driving ego, and the psychic incorporation of economic and political pressure as duty. Such individuals adapt themselves to the nascent bourgeois order—but with rancor and a strong faith, with jealousy and guilty feelings, with sexual envy and misanthropy. The idea of the maternal Church lost its historical basis to the extent that the church surrendered its protective function due to economic upheaval and took on parasitic traits. The Pope's unifying leadership of Christianity yields to the politics of national states, while ministering to spiritual needs gives way to the economic self-reliance of the individual. The devout assume a detached character, like the god in whom they believe, and God takes on the characteristics of the world he rules. They need the ruse of an inscrutable god in order to adapt, for their existence contravenes natural needs and any idea of justice. The size of their income, which is irrationally distributed according to the capitalist law of value, becomes the sign of grace which the hard-working can hope for, but not build upon. In this barbaric doctrine with which the spiritual leaders habituated the people to the new order, however, a concession is made to them: while God may abide in a distant inscrutability, while the heavenly order— with its dark predestination or its irrational justification through grace— may reveal itself as the image of earthly fate, a principle nonetheless exists that is not strictly identical with the world. Human destiny is not exhausted by humans' role in this order. To be sure, Luther conceived of inner freedom as the affirmation of external servitude, and reconciled Christian love and equality with oppression, exploitation, and massacre so long as this was directed at the rebellious masses and not the ruling authorities. Yet the very necessity of taking up Christian concepts and speaking of the Gospel in accessible language played a critical function, even if this ran counter to the will of the Reformers. To be sure, Calvin's concept of freedom was reduced almost to nothing; those who are not blessed choose evil of necessity, but without being forced. Despite such intricate doctrines, despite the careful limitation of the right of resistance incorporated into Calvin's teachings, even he is incapable of fully dissolving the tension between the ultimate sovereignty of God and the earthly powers.[64]

The Reformers were unable to fulfill their mission of creating individuals who freely subordinate themselves without incorporating into their doctrine, however distortedly, the contradiction between human beings and the order into which they had to deliver themselves. God and world, freedom and servitude, natural instinct and conscience, divine and earthly commandment remain in those teachings unresolved contradictions obscuring the real contradiction of the individual that seeks to develop itself with the relations of an emergent capitalism. The historical resolution of the contradiction can only take place at the end of the era, when the material conditions have developed for the abolition of classes. At the outset, no way out can be glimpsed; social inequality reveals itself as the means of progress and individuals are sacrificed to World Spirit, so to speak. However, the new religiosity was the form in which humanity came to know such injustice and in which it measured the existing against an ideal. The notion of a holy commandment or a duty which at that time constrained the Protestants to the repression or sublimation—or at least the postponement—of their material impulses has no direct connection with a rational society. Indeed, the function of the Reformers consisted in the introversion of the desires of the masses, the diversion of the demands of the dominated away from the rulers and toward their own inner nature.[65] Economic compulsion was mystified as divine. But humanity had come too far to consider the princes, officials, rich bourgeois, etc. as gods, and to view obedience to them as the absolute good. It had transcended the condition of a primitive fetishism. Renewed Christianity was no naked idolization of power and success, even if some tendencies promoted this attitude; rather, its concept of God contains the idea of human indifference toward social distinctions and points beyond the relations of class society. The insight that "they say Christ and mean cotton" illuminates the age, but it is valid in different measure for different classes. The oppressed said "Christ" and have always meant an existence worthy of human beings. Whether peasant rebellion—whose immediate intention was the realization of a more just manorial order—is considered simply a reactionary or, due to its ideas of equality, fraternity, and fairness, a progressive movement, the suffering peasants and proletarians who identified the reawakened Gospel with their demands did not simply fall prey to an illusion. That Luther knew no bounds in his instigation of a bloodbath among them is reminiscent of the rage of the renegade. He dimly recognized that his doctrine contained elements to which they could with some justice subscribe.[66] The more a superior, rational form of human organization becomes visible with the evolution of bourgeois society and emerges as a conscious objective of social groups, the more inappropriate the religious form of expression becomes for these progressive historical tendencies. In the entire period of early capitalism, from the emergence of the mendicant orders into the early nineteenth century, however, the Gospel had not simply a mystifying but a revolutionary significance as well. The Reformers, at least, did not identify it directly with the earthly order, and oppositional religious thinkers from Münzer to Tolstoy have held it up to the status quo as "a law as it is written in the heart."[67]

The Gospel is thus the negation of skepticism, according to which action is a matter of taste or a question of individual cleverness. To the skeptics, humaneness appears as a sort of adornment of their persons, as a temperamental idiosyncrasy like a fondness for travel. Their concept of the human being is exhausted in the notion of the isolated, empirical individual put together out of life's many moments. However mild they may be toward human beings and animals, their thought remains logically centered around the internal tranquillity and security of the empirical ego. They refuse to accept—even in thought, and contrary to their own existence and capacity for experience—anything against which the ego would decline in importance, or where the ego would extend beyond itself in solidarity. Thus, for the skeptics, the psychological condition of an extremely impoverished and abstracted soul becomes the highest structuring principle and the highest—indeed, the sole—philosophically relevant value (despite the rejection of all objective values). A more transcendent interest plays no conscious role for them, and is in their opinion not necessarily immanent in human beings. Montaigne hates oppression, whether social or private. But to assume the effort to abolish that injustice is, according to his own testimony, beyond his ken. According to a modern study of him, "Montaigne wishes neither to rule, nor to rule himself, nor to be ruled; he is moved and blinded by moral phenomena;

he surrenders himself to contemplation of the many-sided play of the inner life; he grows, ages, and dies in the condition of a pleasant and lax passivity; he rejects exertion; he does not practice it."[68]

More recently, the relationship between skepticism and religiosity has changed. In the seventeenth century the emphasis was primarily on the contrast between the two. Pascal recognizes Montaigne's quietism, saying that the latter made a "soft pillow" of the correct principle that human reason understands itself to be inadequate and that everything outside of faith is uncertain. Fearing that he would probe too deeply into problems by remaining with them for a long time, according to Pascal, he skimmed over them too lightly.[69] Vauvenargues later repeated the judgment. He despises Montaigne's indecisiveness and neutrality.[70] Rationalist philosophy also distanced itself from Montaigne. The same historical tendencies which, in religious terms, saw human beings as divided between conscience and instinct, lead in epistemology to the doctrine of the rational ego that must master the emotions. Religion corresponds to the masses whose historically necessary subordination is not grounded in rational motives, but must rather be taken on as a burden; philosophy refers to the behavior of the bourgeoisie, which postpones immediate gratification out of self-interest. The straightforward description of the empirical conditions of one's own ego, of customs, of worries and predilections, of physiological and anatomical idiosyncrasies, as they can be found in the *Essais*, has, according to Malebranche, nothing to do with the study of mind [*Geist*]. To him, Montaigne's fabled psychological insight is superficial.[71] Descartes, too, seems to have turned away in later years from the conformist worldly wisdom deriving from it.[72] Even Locke, who strongly followed Montaigne in epistemological and pedagogical teachings, calls him (in good Puritan fashion) "full of pride and vanity."[73]

But the contrast lost its clarity; with the transition from the abolutist to the liberal period, the progressive aspects of religion were obscured. Under the particular conditions of Germany's historical underdevelopment, they found a new form in German idealism, whose development as the official philosophy was arrested in the face of a triumphant liberalism, and continued only in the proletarian opposition. Among the dominant classes, however, religion became the uninterrupted affirmation of social forms. Its moral teaching coincides

with the praxis of the decent businessman, and its pedagogy with socialization into frugality and profit making. The distinction is eradicated between the ways of God and the capitalist mechanism for
distributing wealth. Troeltsch has described the difference between
old and new Protestantism in detail:

> Faith becomes simply trust and devotion to the blessed and holy will of God,
> as it is expressed in the contemporary decision of a conscience shaped by the
> community. . . . Dogma moves well behind ethics. At the same time, the ten-
> sion is moderated between Christian and non-Christian ethics, between mun-
> dane and Christian life; the idea of conversion is transformed into that of
> purification. However much sin may constrain and hinder the human being,
> . . . the world of creation has not in essence been changed by original sin. The
> greater part of Protestant ethics makes its infinitely multifarious compromise
> with the new ethical theories . . . , and no longer concerns itself with the old
> Protestant contradiction between this world and the next, or with the old
> Protestant unity of a Christian cultural life.[74]

Liberal theology abandons the significant distinction between action
based on custom and tradition tempered by inner reserve, which
skepticism teaches, and the absolute religious demand. There remains only the matter of prospering in business, of which "culture"
only constitutes another branch.

The liberal's relation to religion corresponds to the skeptical mode
of thought. This is nothing less than a militant atheism. The belief in
a hidden meaning cannot disappear in an order in which the results
of human beings' social labor, the vicissitudes of the market, economic
laws and crises appear to them in the form of autonomous powers, as
fate or natural law. Religion plays diverse roles in the lives of members of different classes. It may be a consolation to those who must
carry the burdens of society—a consolation which is supposed to keep
them from despair as well as from revolution. For the individual of
the dominant class, however, it sanctions his personal relations and
those of the bourgeois organization of society as a whole. In the liberal
period, it is also indispensable as a tool of education, even in the upper classes. The bourgeois virtues rest on the postponement of material impulses behind the more enduring interests of the abstract ego.
Economic gain is pursued not for the enjoyment it yields but rather
for the sake of further gain, and with each new success this striving
asserts itself anew as its own true aim. The individual becomes the

agent of capital. This attitude cannot be developed through reason, or through physical force alone. In religious belief, therefore, the pedagogy gives disciples the means for developing the socially required qualities in themselves. Where in education the notion of reason (or indeed that of "cooperation") [75] takes the place of God, as is common in the contemporary American system, it is also irrational—an imperious, quasi-religious power that instructs human beings to rely on themselves, to subordinate the present to the future, to recognize economic utility as the law of their action, and to persist in competition. Later, in the consciousness of adults, the irrational, religious grounding of their rationalist mode of thought recedes into the background, and they come to view their conduct in their calling and in other aspects of life as the product of their own character, or even of some human essence. Montaigne helped to usher in the relation to religion in this period. No negative judgment is made of it, even if it is only "esoteric," only held in secret. [76] But its role in thought and action changes. The specifically religious contents and the particular affairs, concerns, and aims of the individual go separate ways; the spheres of bourgeois life, the private and the public as well as the social, the religious, and the political come to oppose each other. The adult's freedom from religion, the peculiarly bourgeois unbelief consists in the fact that anyone can think anything without this coming into conflict with their faith—indeed, without drawing from it any other consequence than that which is socially required in any case. The mediation between thought and existence, which have diverged since the emancipation of the individual, grows infinitely differentiated. The most highly esteemed ideas are secretly considered a sham. Repressed into the unconscious, the most despised attitude, misanthropy, dominates this world of classes and competition. The interruption of mediation no longer disturbs anyone. Everyone knows what prisons and madhouses are all about; everyone is familiar with the condition of freedom, equality, and justice, those divine ideas; everyone tolerates the condition and reproduces it. In this period, the whole is kept going only by individuals, and all individuals wipe their hands in innocence; they appeal to the superior power, which in turn appeals to them. Society is dissolved into innumerable spheres and subjects, and has not yet put itself together as a subject.

Hume, whose skepticism is representative for liberal philosophy and science, distances religion still further from cognition and action than does Montaigne. He, too, has a sharp eye for misery and injustice; he anticipates Schopenhauer. "Were a stranger to drop, on a sudden, into this world, I would show him, as a specimen of its ills, an hospital full of diseases, a prison crowded with malefactors and debtors, a field of battle strewed with carcasses, a fleet floundering in the ocean, a nation languishing under tyranny, famine, or pestilence. To turn the gay side of life to him, and give him a notion of its pleasures; whither should I conduct him? to a ball, to an opera, to court?"[77] However, according to Hume—and in this he is only a consistent disciple of Montaigne—these insights are not in the least prejudicial to the state religion. Religious ideas assume such an exalted position in consciousness that they can neither influence the understanding [*Einsicht*] linked to praxis nor be undermined or confirmed by it. Where the contradiction between religion and the conditions of reality is taken seriously, and has advanced to the negation either of religion or of reality—as is the case with genuine religious thinkers as well as with militant atheists—the skeptic is appalled. Philosophy accords religion its due respect.

'Tis certainly a kind of indignity to philosophy [Hume begins in a genuinely antique frame of mind], whose sovereign authority ought every where to be acknowledg'd, to oblige her on every occasion to make apologies for her conclusions, and justify herself to every particular art and science, which may be offended at her. This puts one in mind of a king arraign'd for high-treason against his subjects. There is only one occasion, when philosophy will think it necessary and even honourable to justify herself, and that is, when religion may seem to be in the least offended; whose rights are as dear to her as her own, and are indeed the same.... If my philosophy ... makes no addition to the arguments for religion, I have at least the satisfaction to think it takes nothing from them, but that every thing remains precisely as before.[78]

The philosophical thought of the liberal bourgeois does not go to the root of social matters. To the extent that it does not exercise occupational functions in one of the branches of this order, it grows increasingly idle, even to itself. In the nineteenth century, philosophy and literature are still rooted in the whole. On the one hand, however, they serve the continuation of the economic process in its given form through transfiguration, diversion, and reassurance. On the other, the works of radical writers who call into question the whole of reality in either religious, artistic, or philosophical terms are absorbed as mere topics of discussion in academic environments. Labor and economic gain as the content and aim of existence have become flesh and blood among the members of the bourgeoisie and large parts of the dominated strata. They sit so deeply that they no longer come to the level of reflection. That which, according to Balzac, "skepticism recognizes—namely, the omnipotence, the omniscience, the all-congruity of gold,"[79] has become the true god. Those who own the means of production of social wealth dispose over labor. The freedom of the others consists in their ability to buy. The type and extent of the goods that serve the maintenance and enrichment of life are determined by the process of capital accumulation. In itself, human life has no value in this system. It acquires value only to the degree that it is inserted in the economic dynamic, and even here not for its own sake—because the individual should live—but rather as a cost element in the profit-oriented economy. In the dominant scholarship, this fact is not indicated, except as one view opposed to others. Critical literature, which represents it in the form of the novel, is received as a mere work of art. Just as bourgeois individuals reserve philosophy for their leisure hours and thus turn it into idle thought, knowledge and critique are isolated in the society as particular aspects of business. They are supposed to procure culture, which under these conditions of production is reduced to entertainment. The distinction between truth and mere fun is socially eradicated. After the victory over feudalism, the critical spirit of the bourgeoisie is transformed from a general to a private affair, from a practical to a contemplative reaction. Thus spreads the skeptical mode of thought.

With the disappearance of liberalism in the monopoly capitalist period, skepticism once again changes its meaning. As at its inception, it sees itself confronted by an absolutism that it leaves untouched. This absolutism, however, is different from that of the sixteenth and seventeenth centuries. At that time, the role of the state consisted in the (admittedly antagonistic) protection of a burgeoning trade and commerce. In the present, the state tends to act as the organ of the strongest capitalist groups, even where reformist governments seek to make of it a guardian of the economically weaker groups. Its apotheosis is the Führer state, in which the consolidation of the industrial and political bureaucracies is realized. The Führer state advances by political means the economic expropriation of the smaller capitalists by the larger, and regulates trade and commerce in the interest of the industrial and political groups arising from the concentration and centralization of capital. The unprincipled character of skepticism reveals itself under these circumstances. Skeptical negation was quite conscious about not sparing the ego. Hume denied his own existence, and Montaigne, in his dedication to the reader, refers to himself as "a matter . . . frivolous and empty."[80] And yet they make the ego into almost the exclusive theme of philosophy. Indeed, the independence of the ego from external events—the attempt not to lose oneself—constitutes the very meaning and aim of the skeptical mode of thought. But the retreat to the ego is itself a process in the empirical world. It presupposes inner strength and personality. But personality doesn't fall from the sky; it is socially produced and dissolves with the conditions that created it. In bourgeois democracies it is in any case arbitrary which individuals have the potential for such development; the stratum involved is small enough. Under the domination of the totalitarian state, it completely disappears as a possibility. The ego not only no longer has the opportunity to develop itself into a personality; even the stability of the existing character types is accidental. If the individual falls into the clutches of power, it might be not just destroyed but twisted and turned upside-down, depending on the degree to which chemical and psychological technique is advanced. The illusion of skepticism is that in spite of everything it holds the ego to be a safe harbor. Yet its every sinew is bound up with material reality. The capacities that make it up—the senses, memory, and understanding—depend not only on a well-functioning body but on the steady unfolding of the social process. The social environment—its language, rules, and beliefs—determines the existence and forms of reaction of every single ego. The ego consists of reciprocal influence, even down to the nuances. The opinion that there is something permanent in it, something inherent, is mere superficiality. However active the individual ego may be, in itself it is merely abstract; those who reify it in its isolation into a principle or an inner anchor only make of it a fetish. The tension with the environment—the resistance an independent ego is capable of offering it—is heightened independence vis-à-vis the contemporary situation, not vis-à-vis history as a whole. In confrontation with reality, it has developed a relatively firm shape. Its elasticity and the ideas that it opposes to reality grew out of that reality itself. The skeptical ego creates not so much definite ideas as doubt about its essence, which it takes to be its element. It has yet to discover that it is equally capable of being anxiety and pain, affirmation or indignation. The self-consciousness and independence in which the ego seeks to maintain itself in the face of doubt can be traced back, as psychological factors, to the decline of liberal society. The freedom of judgment which constitutes the lifeblood of skepticism can only be realized through the freedom of the social whole which, contrary to skepticism's aloofness, requires personal intervention. If skepticism fails to sustain itself as a rational mode of thought—namely, by sublating itself and consciously becoming its other, a belief in the concrete possibilities of the human being; if, instead of opposing the dominant conditions, it leaves the present untouched as a result of its characteristic inner reservations, it thus seems to persist unchanged but in fact has already lost the quality of being an expression of mind [*Geist*]. The ego can sustain itself only by seeking to sustain humanity as a whole.

According to Montaigne, *Epoché*, the reservation of judgment, and inner tranquillity are not "frivolous." Indeed, they were not so at that time in the same degree as they are today. To keep oneself free from the historical upheaval: in the sixteenth century, skeptical moderation constituted a progressive attitude. "We may both love virtue too much, and carry a just action to excess. . . . I like temperate and middle natures. Want of moderation, even in the direction of the good, if it does not offend me, astonishes me, and I am at pains how to baptize it."[81] Therein lay historical reason; such moderation was identical with the preservation of one's own person, with going the objectively correct way of tolerance in the national state. It amounted to independence from the illusions of the religious parties. Attentiveness to one's own development, keeping an appropriate distance from popular movements with their veiled aims, was a progressive position conducive to the solution of the problems on the historical agenda. Like religion, it contains a dynamic element despite the conscious quietism. Montaigne's *Epoché* is not without solidarity with humanity. To practice it entails promoting the happiness with which he was preoccupied for the individual ego not just in particular, but in general. At present, however, only the futility of the principle is evident. The peace that the liberal skeptic today concludes with the authoritarian order expresses not humane praxis but its renunciation. Unlike the absolute state power of those times, fascism does not take under its aegis the most important social forces. The obedience preached by Montaigne, as a good skeptic, was owed to a monarchy locked in battle with reactionary forces. Obedience toward contemporary dictatorships, to which today's skeptics accommodate themselves, is a lockstep into barbarism. Montaigne's relative neutrality in the wars of the Huguenots and Guisards was his retreat into the library and into hostile foreign territory. Neutrality in the struggle against the Führer and the bureaucracies, accommodation to the relations of the authoritarian state in the twentieth century, is tantamount to participation in total mobilization. The alliance between absolutism and the bourgeoisie, to which Montaigne's attitude belongs, arises from the emancipation of the bourgeoisie from a bankrupt feudalism. The alliance between bourgeoisie and fascist organizations arises from anxiety about the proletariat. Out of the skeptical tolerance concerning freedom of conscience comes conformism with the regime of the secret police.

After all, Montaigne wrote: "I am so hungry for freedom that if any one were to forbid me access to some corner of the Indies I should feel my life to be a little more constrained. And as long as I can find earth and air free and open elsewhere, I will never lurk in a place where I must hide. Good heavens, how I should chafe if I were reduced to the condition of so many people I know of, riveted to a district of this kingdom, deprived of the right to enter the chief towns and courts and to make use of the public roads, for having quarrelled with our laws! If those laws I observe were to threaten only the tip of my little finger I should immediately go in search of others, wherever they may be."[82] These words express not only reactionary indifference, but a revolutionary humanism as well. Today's skeptics don't leave the country as long as the bureaucracy lets them be. In any case, it makes no sense to leave, for "earth and air" are no longer open anywhere, and that stretch of land in the Indies is ruled by the same laws that one seeks to flee. The authoritarian order imposed by capital upon some countries in its current phase is already beginning to span the world, and the skeptical statesmen of the other countries—the disciples of Montaigne and Montesquieu—fall collectively before it. Negotiation has different faces at different times. Today it consolidates the domination of the biggest capital throughout all of Europe. The national contradictions between the European industrial powers are at present subordinated to the necessity of political reorganization. In both domestic and foreign policy, the world creeps softly or strides boldly toward dictatorship, the most appropriate form of government for monopoly. Just as before the war the bourgeoisie came to know better technical methods and the so-called spirit of innovation of the expanding industrial countries, it must now become familiar with something that did not come easily to the conservative industrialists of Western Europe.

Due to the economic laws intrinsic to it, the reigning social order has reached a level in which individuals have completely lost that arbitrary and abstract freedom that they had under liberalism. If they are not congenial to power by nature and attitude, they can no longer find any way out, for the earth is rapidly becoming more uniform. The affirmation of personal freedom—not to speak of its modest use—belongs to that excess of virtue from which Montaigne was so estranged. Humanity, despite its infinitely advanced capacities, is hindered in the rational organization of its affairs by the terror of national cliques. When things have reached this point, skepticism's evasiveness, relativism, and liberal tolerance become the rationalization of misanthropy—an attitude that negates every value, not just theoretically but practically as well. This attitude fails to reveal solidarity with human beings, even unconsciously or in contradiction to itself. Humanity, which expressed itself among such figures as Montaigne and even Hume as diplomacy and a world citizenry, has long since cast off its peaceful form; at present, that attitude reveals only the desire to participate a bit in a decadent power. The idiocy of the notion that an individual or collectivity can save itself or the world by conciliation with the spreading rule of violence has now become so patently obvious that it can only be understood as a thinly veiled sympathy with that rule, or as an anxiety about sunk capital. The skeptical diplomats of the nonauthoritarian countries of Europe, who make concessions to barbarism out of a "love of culture," have behind them dogmatic bankers nervous about their assets. Indeed, even these assets will be difficult to rescue. Machiavelli writes "that a general who wishes to keep the field cannot avoid a battle when the enemy is determined upon fighting."[83] He scoffs at the "indolent princes or effeminate republics"[84] that instruct their generals only to be cautious. This accusation does not touch the skeptical individuals and polities that pursue this ineffectual tactic at the end of the bourgeois epoch; they don't even want to triumph. Neither the bourgeoisie as a whole nor its members see in the authoritarian order their true enemy: that perspective is illusorily attributed to them only in the wishful thinking of a few of its scattered members who have met misfortune for one reason or another. The style according to which those emigrants who have fled authoritarian states seek to "influence" the democratic environment by denouncing those states—how naive is this clever style, whereby the host countries are supposedly warned in their greatest interest! Despite all the internal and external contradictions that promote war, the representatives of the old order have a common and greater enemy: the rational community of humankind, the possibility of which takes on firmer outlines in popular consciousness, and which can be extinguished in the longer term only by naked terror. Today, skepticism stands opposed to nothing other than the interest in a better future.

The transformation of skepticism from a humanistic cast of mind into pure conformism is anticipated in the economic principle of the epoch. The independence of the ego to which the skeptic retreats is rooted in the freedom of the individual that each subject enjoys in a commodity economy. In contrast to the slave states of antiquity, this freedom is universal in the modern period. Individuals exist by receiving in exchange for the labor they contribute to the life of society a quantity of goods equivalent to the effort expended. All are free; "every man carries within him the entire form of the human constitution."[85] Humanity is not undermined by the fact that the individual stands in the center of philosophy, or that the author of the *Essais* thematizes himself. In a society that rests on such a principle of exchange, all persons may retreat to themselves, they are their own masters, and their relations with others proceed in an orderly fashion. Given an existence regulated in this manner, the skeptical rejection of revolutionary activity and the hostility toward critique of the totality has nothing cynical about it. Individuals are recognized as equals. But the principle of bourgeois society has another side whose unfolding in capitalism governs history and drives it toward its own dissolution. Where labor and disposition over the means of production are not unitary but socially divided—that is, distributed among different classes—free exchange takes place as a labor contract. One party offers its productive capacity, while the other furnishes the money to replenish that capacity via food. This act corresponds to the principle. Normally, the labor power expended by workers can be replenished with the products they can buy with their wage; they can get by. The social result, however, is that equality disappears. Infinitely more labor time than is necessary for the reproduction of the workers' lives is congealed in the products that laboring humanity brings forth on the basis of these contracts. Capital disposes over the difference. The equality of free individuals, which renews itself through the exchange, the labor of each as the basis of their possessions and power, in short, the principle of the bourgeoisie—upon which rest its ideology, its justice, and its morality—thus reveals itself as a mere facade that masks the true relations. The further society develops, the more obviously this principle, and with it that of bourgeois freedom, reveal their internal contradictions. The continued dominance of this principle, the skeptical rejection of revolutionary activity, and the hostility toward critique of the totality thus have something cynical about them. They reveal subordination to irrational relations, not integration into rational ones. Skepticism is prepared to respect the freedom of each individual—to the extent that individuals do not forfeit it through the effects of the economic laws and their political consequences. With this contradiction, the modern skeptical attitude together with its tolerance, subjectivism, and liberalism bears a harsh, misanthropic quality; it is not as just and open as it sometimes appears. The essential harmony with forms of life that rest on social inequality—and that are mediated through the life-and-death struggle of competition—makes the reigning version of skepticism deeply unjust and destructive, even if it is occasionally cooperative and open within the framework of the possible (that is, without touching upon its basis). The notions of equality and fair chances for the virtuous, so successfully promulgated by the upper classes, should be evaluated according to the feelings with which one of them loses their fortune. Because they have enjoyed the goods which all could enjoy with the current development of social powers, they would become aware that a life is hell in which one has nothing to sell but one's labor power.

Montaigne's successors since Hume have only slightly changed their rhetoric. In essence, the same thing is repeated over and over: that all conceptual knowledge is subjective, a mere ordering, while theory is relative and separate from praxis. The skeptics remain liberal now as before; they demand that an intellectual substance be accorded even to those who are not necessarily congenial to the dominant party. Such professions do not have far-reaching consequence. On the one hand, the skeptics believe that, in the universities, critical tendencies should be voiced only toward fantasies—so-called ideologies—and not at all toward things as they are. This is harmless if for no other reason than that the foundation of authoritarian domination lies not in the delusions with which it rationalizes itself, but in the social structure of production that rules the age and shapes the character of human beings according to their place within it. Ideologies are not primary. Precisely because the conditions of existence make the bourgeois type so sober, and because skepticism toward mind [*Geist*] reveals itself as an essential characteristic in the monopoly capital period as in liberalism, fascism can change its slogans almost as often as it does its generals. What human beings consider important today remains individual advancement; any other kind is superficial. With the establishment of mind in its own sphere—that is, precisely through its emancipation as mind—it also became ideology, mere appearance. In liberalism, ideology proves itself relatively constant and substantial; the abstract consciousness of freedom is its essential content. Under the domination of monopoly, in the period of bourgeois decline, one slogan after the other takes hold of manifest thought. The skeptics, who stand up against racial and other misguided doctrines without theory and purely in the name of doubt, are Sancho Panzas who dress themselves up as Don Quixotes. They know that they are, in essence, tilting against windmills.[86] On the other hand, their campaign has the merit that, in the eyes of the public, the truth may easily slip through under the guise of another misguided doctrine. The skeptics no longer traffic in ideas, but only in illusions: the distinction no longer exists.[87] Those who attack ideology without analysis of the base criticize badly, or indeed not at all—regardless of the incisiveness of the criticism. The so-called penetration and dissolving of ideology undertaken without a definite theory, which Montaigne adopted from the ancients as the confrontation of temporally and spatially distinct moral and religious views, carries the day now. But the proper object of a theoretical and practical critique is the social totality, not ideology.

Not only the intellectuals who seek to make their peace with the domination of monopoly capital, but the common man, too, remains fundamentally the same. It is mistaken to think that the mass individuals of the modern period, particularly as they appear in the authoritarian states, are free of skepticism. The economic conditions from which they arise have not changed their essence since the era of liberalism; instead, they have created a social form in which the individual counts even less. The period has a crippling effect on thought; it replaces the idea of the universal [*Allgemeinheit*] with the fetish of the *Volk*. But "free, philosophic thought has this direct connection with practical freedom, that as the former supplies thought about the absolute, universal and real object, the latter, because it thinks itself, gives itself the character of universality. Thinking means the bringing of something into the form of universality."[88] The emancipation of civil society[89] from the Middle Ages was a reaction, so to speak, "of the element of Universality against the Real World as split up into particularity."[90] The principle that governs civil society has a higher universality than that of the feudal order. According to it, all should find their justice and their happiness. The ambiguity of the economic principle discussed above, however, necessarily reproduces and widens inequality, and in such a way that its foundation disappears from human consciousness. Thought loses its character in that fascism, under the rubric of the nation and the "people's community" [*Volksgemeinschaft*], abolishes certain formal residues of feudalism—external signs of status privileges, religious upbringing, and the other remnants of childishness and idleness—and indeed corrupts some groups with material advantages, in order the more brutally to sharpen the economic inequalities. This result emerges, too, from the fact that fascism organizes the whole militarily in the service of the dominant groups, and thus forces the life of the community "totally" under the profit motive of the few. The concepts *Volk*, nation, and fatherland have real validity, but they are not concrete, goal-oriented ideas. Separated from the interest in a rational society, removed from the reach of all critical thought and puffed up in its given form into the Most

High, the concept of the *Volk* sinks to the level of a false idol. In revolutionary France, death had a different meaning than did military service under Napoleon or MacMahon. In the mouth of the Führer, however, the fatherland of freedom tends to remain the same fatherland, even if freedom has already been eradicated and the last opponent banished or slain. The compulsion imposed upon thought to remain unconditionally in tune with such reified concepts—this prescribed aim that is contrary to its essence—becomes a fetter upon it under which it decays. Because people today are too advanced to take very seriously such a prescribed attitude, and at the same time are too dependent to overcome it consciously, they absorb the *völkisch* content superficially (in the same way that the liberal bourgeois always appropriated mind), but internally they become disappointed skeptics who, like the liberal bourgeios, believe in nothing beyond advancement and success. As at the demise of antiquity and in the Renaissance, skepticism and mysticism today reveal their affinity; today, however, skepticism is no longer religious but *völkisch*.

The insubstantiality of all the motifs upon which each person draws in order to explain the relations—from the belief in the Führer's God-given talents to the notion of the Jewish world threat—is experienced in varying degrees of vagueness. This feeling leads to cynicism, and this has progressive implications. Underneath uniform action and speech, the needs of modern life give rise to the development of correct knowledge—the loosening of the relation of ideology and faith, the hidden development of rationality even among retrograde strata— if only as instinct, as vague intuition, precisely as deep skepticism toward all that exists. These processes take place independent of the will of the dominant powers. They accelerate the pace of older tendencies. After liberalism, society has by no means consolidated itself into a subject. It still has no consciousness with which it could develop in freedom and justice. In the Führer, however, it has a voice acknowledging society's injustice and oppression. Together with more rigid economic organization (which anticipates a historical necessity, even if in a distorted way), the thoroughgoing lack of illusions of a fascist mentality misunderstood as idealistic and frenzied lends it superiority over the liberal environment. Individual freedom in domestic policy and even the idealistic embellishment of an imperialist foreign policy was an ideology whose contradiction with reality became increasingly apparent. To the extent that the religion of power and a brutal realism serve the maintenance of the social hierarchy of monopoly better than does Christianity, as Machiavelli had already intuited, fascism's cynical and enthusiastic skepticism is well beyond the idealistic skepticism of the previous century.

Fascism is not opposed to bourgeois society, but is rather its appropriate form under definite historical conditions. Given the lawlike quality intrinsic to the system, capital in the contemporary period is capable of occupying a growing majority of the population with tasks unrelated to the satisfaction of general needs. It takes on the character of the oligarchical cliques that prepare to divide the world anew in order to exploit it with modern means. That is the direction of European development. In this period, the mediating categories cast off their humanistic appearance. Money, the universal equivalent, which seemed to equate human beings to each other in a fundamental way, sheds the ephemeral character of independence. It has always mediated and expressed social relations. This becomes openly manifest today. The national group that has good apparatuses of production and repression, and which develops on this basis a rigid military and social organization, becomes increasingly independent of money—or, rather, presses it into its service. Domestic finance is formally taken in hand by capital and its state. The latter determines how the dominated groups shall live. State expenditures with the purpose of binding the masses to the regime, dividing them from themselves, and organizing them instrumentally; public works; official charities, etc.— so-called socialism—encounter serious resistance only in the transition to fascism, so long as the government is not unambiguously sworn to big industry. The complaints of smaller employers are harnessed until the proper authoritarian power is formed, in the face of which rebelliousness is reduced to harmless grumbling. Obstruction goes only this far, and demonstrates the powerlessness of all but the fascist approach. The apparent independence of financial power disappears along with that of parliament. The stratum that controls the means of material production, the industrial and political bureaucracy, emerges formally as authoritative. Competition has always functioned merely as a mediating factor; now it recedes in domestic affairs. In Germany, heavy industry—which came to open domination with the authoritarian state—was at that moment insolvent, remaining far behind other industries. Measured on liberal principles of competition, it was quite unsound despite its power. In fascism, however, power competes in essence only internationally; domestically, it carries on the struggle against competing industries as well as against the labor force with state resources. Furthermore, it becomes clear that the work relationship was only formally based on the contract; decree and command now openly take its place. It wins new significance as agreement between equally strong cliques within the state, not unlike many relationships in the Middle Ages. In the new system of justice, the universality of law and the independence of judges are openly abandoned.[91] Under liberalism, inequality was masked by equal rights—which guaranteed a minimum of freedom because the mask itself was not without substance. Now, a clean sweep is made of human rights as just another ideology. Specific groups, indeed individuals are affected by the law; laws are enforced retroactively. The judges are freed from the pedestrian obligation of merely interpreting and promulgating the law; they are promoted to the immediate executors of higher orders, and thus become equals of the executioner. This unmasking takes place along with other decisive social factors.

In the face of the horror emerging from the current destruction of a historical form of human life, it looks as if—next to the *völkisch* mysticism that carries within it a skeptical nihilism—there returns the age of a more noble skepticism, which in antiquity was the despondent individual's final word. But history has advanced in the meanwhile, and humanity has conquered the means to create happiness on earth. Thus the skepticism of the educated, who quietly make their peace with things as they are, is today no more noble than the everyday skepticism of the fellow-travelers. Montaigne would find himself at odds with contemporary skeptics. It is Montaigne's desire, "and perhaps a little more than it should be, . . . [that I] would embrace a Pole as I would a Frenchman, subordinating this national tie to the common and universal one."[92] The basis for such professions can be sought only in part in the fact that Montaigne was bound to the Middle Ages and could not follow the national principle, which later proved so revolutionary. Brotherly love is never simply reactionary. It has nothing to do with neutrality toward fascism, with today's decadent skepticism. The fascist type of "human being" and its ideal, the abasement of the human being under others, are the opposite of humanism, whether religious or skeptical.

The majority of free people [says Montaigne, putting animals above human beings], for a very slight consideration, surrender their life and being into the power of others. . . . Have tyrants ever failed to find enough men pledged to devote themselves to their service, some of whom were besides obliged to accompany them in death as in life? Whole armies have so bound themselves to their captains. The form of oath in that rude school of men who fought to the bitter end contained this promise: "We swear to suffer ourselves to be fettered, burned, beaten, killed with the sword, and to endure everything that real gladiators suffer at the hands of their masters; most religiously lending both body and soul to his service": "Burn, if thou wilt, my head with fire,/ With sword my body strike, and cut/My back with twisted thong" (Tibullus). That was a covenant indeed;[93] and yet there were, in some years, ten thousand who entered into it and rushed to perdition.[94]

Despite all the admonitions to obedience that move Montaigne close to the Reformers, he nonetheless saw through a sadomasochism masked as personal loyalty to the bitter end. Conformism with a bad reality, the excision from thought of the idea of the universal, the limitation of thought to business and specialized knowledge leads in the present to the falsification of all essential concepts, even among the educated. Even the wise man cannot in the long run remain immune theoretically, if in practice he accommodates himself to the enemies of humanity.

The emergence of a new spirit can be traced in the nineteenth century's judgment of Montaigne. Increasing emphasis is laid on his personality, on his distance from actual events, and above all on his hatred of the masses. Montaigne is considered a great man. Some of the best bourgeois thinkers have recognized the impoverished condition of human beings and the mendacity of the public spirit in the liberal period, without seeing any way out other than the romantic illusion of a new aristocracy—the "noblemen," as Ibsen puts it. The harmonious, isolated personality, independent of the social environment and raised above the man-in-the-mass, was for them the historical goal. They could find support for this position in Montaigne. Mass culture was not his cup of tea. There are differences between human beings. Knowledge is to be valued very highly; what matters is only who possesses it. "A very useful accessory in a naturally gifted mind, pernicious and harmful to another. Or rather it is a thing of very precious use, which is not to be purchased at a low price; in some hands it is a sceptre, in others a fool's bauble."[95] His attitude toward the civil wars seems similar to that of Goethe, if one ignores the differences between the religious wars in France and the great French Revolution. "All the little caution I possess, in these Civil wars in which we are engaged," says Montaigne, "is exercised to prevent their curtailing my freedom of coming and going."[96] More directly, he writes: "I dislike innovation in any disguise whatever, and have reason to do so, for I have witnessed its very injurious effects."[97] Even in the nineteenth century, mistrust of popular movements contains not just a reactionary element, but—as in the social pessimism to which it belongs—insight as well. Pessimism's bitterness conceals the suspicion that things do not look good for the general happiness in the reigning social order, despite the assurances of its apologists. Conservative thinkers take seriously the contradiction between the achievements of technology and the growing pressure on the masses, between the successes of natural science and the increasing uncertainty, which the liberals seek to paper over with the notions of social harmony and of the possibility of unlimited progress. In the political movements that run through the age, the masses are furthermore not yet capable of achieving their own aims. They appear as the material of bourgeois politics, and are used for the development and renewal of the system whose burdens they themselves must bear. They set out to liberate themselves, and in the process liberate the bourgeois form of property. Their action is as contradictory as the order which, in the end, that action consolidates. The social-psychological experience articulated not only in the gruesome doctrines of de Maistre and Bonald, but by Goethe and Nietzsche as well, is better grounded than the myth of the strength of the people [Kraft des Volkes], the unswerving belief in the healthy instincts of the masses. For the theoretician of the proletarian groups which today push beyond the bourgeois order, naive respect is simply harmful. In the struggle for a society without classes, which has been on the historical agenda since the middle of the nineteenth century, the masses must first organize themselves from a mere material into a subject; they must cast off the character of a mass. The attitude of adulation toward theoreticians is inappropriate. The deprivation of the masses or the Volk as they are manipulated in bourgeois politics is included and sublated in the solidarity of the theoreticians with the plight of the oppressed. Solidarity refers not just to human beings as they are, but as they might be as well. The negative moment—knowledge of the darker traits of human beings—is not absent from dialectical thought; critique is its element.

Penetrating though the hostile analysis of the condition of certain bourgeois masses may be, the damning verdict of the conservatives is rooted in an untenable aristocratic ideal. The isolated conception of personality, whose essence that condemnation leaves untouched whether the personality exists in a cruel society or a rational one, had a more progressive function in the Renaissance than in the current period of decay. Nietzsche first distanced himself gradually from history.

The individual cannot live more fairly than in being prepared to die in the struggle for love and justice and in sacrificing himself to it. . . . We cannot be happy so long as everything around us suffers and creates suffering; we cannot be moral so long as the course of human affairs is determined by force, deception and injustice; we cannot even be wise so long as the whole of mankind has not struggled in competition for wisdom and conducted the individual into life and knowledge in the way dictated by wisdom.[98]

Such judgments—which to be sure were already weakened by that which is ultimately demanded, namely the tragic attitude—still have little to do with the aristocratic attitude of hostility toward the masses. Nietzsche put Montaigne in the proper relation to the present.

What the individual Montaigne signifies within the agitation of the spirit of the Reformation, a coming to rest within oneself, a peaceful being for oneself and relaxation—and that was certainly how his best reader, Shakespeare, experienced him—is what history is for the modern spirit. If the Germans have for a century been especially devoted to the study of history, this shows that within the agitation of the contemporary world they represent the retarding, delaying, pacifying power: which some might perhaps turn into a commendation of them. On the whole, however, it is a dangerous sign.[99]

Nietzsche's praise is ambiguous. "If I were set the task, I could endure to make myself at home in the world with him."[100] Later on, his admiration for the skeptical Frenchman grows along with repulsion for the Germans, as well as with his error concerning the meaning of the revolution. He glorifies the personality. Montaigne declares that he was ill-treated by all sides, that he was a Guelph to the Ghibellines and a Ghibelline to the Guelphs, but the accusations remained mute because he stayed meticulously within the law.[101] Nietzsche thus sees him already during his lifetime as "on the *Index librorum prohibitorum* of the Vatican, under suspicion from all parties," and speaks of "his dangerous tolerance, his reviled nonpartisanship."[102] He makes of him a hero, which he certainly was not.[103]

Nonetheless, Nietzsche expresses more the critique of a bourgeoisie in decline than veneration of capital's consolidation of its power. His admiration for Montaigne points to the human meaning of the utopia of the Superman, and permits us to see how the "leaders" of the present constitute its distortion. They represent the historical answer, so to speak, to Nietzsche's error that personalities can still exist in the future while the bourgeois mass continues, that the enslavement rather than the emancipation of the mass is the condition for a humane future. Nietzsche is contradictory, like Montaigne himself. The persistent tendency to reconcile Montaigne with imperial Germany by emphasizing his harsher characteristics emerges, by contrast, in a slip on the part of Dilthey. He claims that Montaigne concurs "with the Stoics in preferring strong, masculine, and joyful feelings to the compassion that he ascribes to women, children, and the conceited crowd."[104] But in the passage cited by Dilthey,[105] Montaigne does not so much agree with the Stoics as simply indicate that they had asserted this position. And according to Montaigne, not just women, children, and the common man[106] were subject to compassion, but he himself as well. As he puts it in the *Essais*, "Among other vices, I cruelly hate cruelty, both by nature and reason, as the worst of all the vices. But then I am so soft in this that I cannot see a chicken's neck wrung without distress, and cannot bear to hear the squealing of a hare between the teeth of my hounds, although the chase is a vehement pleasure."[107] He is more concerned here with dissipation than with killing and booty. Dilthey's minor error is only a symptom. The professorial disdain for the masses in the Wilhelmine era consisted not in enmity toward the system that produces the masses, but in hatred for the forces that could overcome it. Herein was registered the enthusiasm for the world war, which—inseparable from the economic conditions—found renewed ascendancy in the defeat and brings recovery to the entire world as a *völkisch* awakening, as was promised at the time. The nonpartisan skepticism of modern science thus adds the German scholars to this triumphal march, whether they intended this or not.

Liberal theology pointed the way to the new mentality even earlier than scholarship. D. F. Strauss had already shown how the transition could be made from theology into a naked, authoritarian attitude, hostile to workers.[108] This vulgar materialist theologian virtually anticipated fascism. The Ritschl school, which "owed much" to him, reached the apotheosis of the reconciliation of capitalism and Protestantism with its skeptical agnosticism. "It is in principle an unphilosophical and antiphilosophical theology. It only employs as much philosophy or epistemology as it needs to avoid competing with philosophy and metaphysics."[109] Reverend Traub was one representative of this school; his rebellious liberalism drove him into conflict with the Church before the war. The essence of the rebellion revealed itself during the war as the tireless affirmation of imperialist policy. For his iron propaganda he received a place in the High Consistory. Agnosticism, skeptical hostility toward any theory transcending specialized disciplines, and reconciliation with the reigning order characterize his theological viewpoint.

As well as in isolated Catholic circles, retrieval of the progressive elements of religion—of the Gospel as a tribunal that can also come into opposition to the status quo—can be found in various orthodox tendencies in Protestantism. Like many political conservatives and above all the small sects, Jehovah's Witnesses, and others who today count their martyrs, they at least have a faith which—like any faith in a divided society—consistently affirms the idea of justice. Within the limits of positive religion, however, faith can only continue to exist in a distorted way. In contrast to the total nihilism of the liberals, to be sure, the courage of the orthodox reveals a higher truth. The totalitarians drive them to the right side against their will, so to speak. But the latter cannot count on them, for their restriction to the biblical word and to cult status is already an obdurate faith, bearing conformism within it despite everything. Christian freedom is promulgated in the Gospel; each individual should possess and act upon it. This cannot be an exclusively inner condition, if only because even freedom of conscience is not compatible with every kind of political and social order. Luther and Calvin knew this; it was not for no reason that they themselves and their immediate supporters were drawn into political conflict. As capitalism developed out of its liberal phase and into the authoritarian, the illusion was more concretely refuted that inner freedom can be guaranteed by a clause in the constitution or the benevolent nod of the Führer. Christianity is not identical with the middle or late Academy of Athens. The notion that the Gospel espouses, like Arcesilaus and Carneades, a retreat into oneself and obedience toward existing authority—with the difference that the Christian can hope for salvation—would not merely sublate [*aufheben*] Christianity: it would destroy it entirely. The principle of conscience does not demand unmitigated subordination in all social questions, except for occasional outbursts when the state intervenes in the constitution of the Church leadership.

Conscience emerged from the introversion of social demands. In contrast to skeptical *Ataraxie*, it pushes toward the self-actuation of the individual, toward activity, toward labor. Even in the bourgeois economy, however, labor is not as formal a concept as it appears. Its significance lies rather in that it makes a contribution to the life of the society with all its individuals. The moment of freedom as well as of universality are both inconceivable without it. Conscience, too, thus has a direction in history; like the concept of god, it points beyond the relations of class society. "Christianity," writes Hegel, "in its adherents has realised an ever-present sense that they are not and cannot be slaves; if they are made slaves, if the decision as regards their property rests with an arbitrary will, not with laws or courts of justice, they would find the very substance of their life outraged."[110] This is true not only for the particular individual as an exclusively egoistic being, but for society as a whole. It does not mean that conscience can be at ease as long as Christians themselves are not slaves in the given sense while others are.

Law, property, ethical life, government, constitutions, etc. must be conformed to general principles, in order that they may accord with the idea of Free Will and be Rational. Thus only can the Spirit of Truth manifest itself in Subjective Will—in the particular shapes which the activity of the Will assumes. In virtue of that degree of intensity which Subjective Free Spirit has attained, elevating it to the form of Universality, Objective Spirit attains manifestation. This is the sense in which we must understand the State to be based on Religion.[111]

Religious freedom bears within it a dialectic that drives it beyond interiority.

What set the Reformation and skepticism against each other in the sixteenth century—fanatical spontaneity, on the one hand, and humanism on the other—has been released from these forms and transformed into a theory and praxis which, as active humanism, overcomes and retains the contradiction. It is critical theory, and the historical effort to which this belongs. It is to be met concretely among those in the authoritarian states (and in those that would like to become such) who build the cells of a new world. To them, even after the defeat, thought has not become an internal matter that remains internal and adapts itself to a contradictory reality. They do not wash their hands in innocence. It is possible that everything will go to rack and ruin, but even the most sober analysis demonstrates that a rational society is possible. Humanism consists in committing oneself to its creation. Knowledge without connection to a definite historical praxis that concerns the whole of humanity, the mass of apparently atheoretical facts with which one obstructs the thought of children and especially of students, the philosophical and political doctrines distributed cheaply in the used bookstores of relativistic intellectual history—all of this creates chaos. Its function is more to make one unaccustomed to the truth than to represent it. To say that religion and skepticism are rooted in past cultural achievements is misleading. They have been transformed at their core: not because their wording has changed, but rather because the world has changed. Far from them, splintered into theoretical and political groups and apparently already conquered, the spirit once immanent in them carries on a desperate struggle whose duration and outcome cannot be foreseen. There is spontaneity in this new attitude, because it does not languish by itself, but rather expresses itself in the will to bring reason and freedom into the world; there is humanity, because it maintains the cultural resources and the capacity for enjoyment within just this spontaneity.

Skepticism is a pathological form of intellectual independence; it is immune to truth as well as to untruth. If, according to Pyrrhus, Diogenes Laertius showed his traveling companion a pig that calmly continued to eat and declared that such *Ataraxie* must be that of a wise being,[112] the naturally carefree human attitude toward death—to be attained through reason—may also be appropriate. With respect to the interests of humanity, toward which the skeptical bourgeois practices it, the behavior of the pig is neither natural nor rational, however widespread it may be. Like dead religiosity, the churches, and hierarchy, a moribund skepticism—the closing off of human beings toward one another, their retreat into their own empty individuality—belongs to an intellectual disposition in contradiction with the current level of development of human powers. Despite all the horror, the superficial appearance of a depraved humanity, overwhelming and discouraging enough, is deceptive. As in those previous transitional periods—at the end of civic freedom in antiquity and in the Renaissance—conditions are likely to make the individual skeptical or religious or both. It is not this repetition, however, but active humanism as it arises from historical developments themselves that now plays the role that once fell to the skeptical philosophers and Reformers. Not just any old ideas but the true ones, in their historically adequate form, distinguish cultural development [*Bildung*] from mere knowledge. The pedagogical effort to make the pragmatic bourgeois immune from barbarism by means of tradition, Greece, and occasional doses of Thomism is quite naive. There is no humanism without a clear position toward the historical problems of the epoch; it cannot exist as a mere profession of faith to itself. The humanism of the past consisted in the critique of the hierarchical feudal order, which had become a fetter on the development of humanity. The humanism of the present consists in the critique of the forms of life under which humanity now perishes, and in the effort to transform them in a rational manner.

Hegel pronounced the ultimate judgment concerning the relation of critical and dialectical theory toward the specific content of skepticism. Dialectics bears a skeptical element within it, in that it reveals the one-sided, limited, and transient in isolated ideas and opinions. Unlike skepticism, however, dialectical thought does not therefore consider these views destroyed, and then retreat to the ego that created them until the ego itself appears as a deception or fiction absurdly triumphing over itself. Like the ancients, Montaigne concluded from the uncertainty of knowledge based on the senses or the understanding, as well as from the multiplicity of moral, metaphysical, and religious perspectives, that one simply cannot know anything. In contrast, the dialectic, in its negative application to ideas that consider themselves firm and absolute, sees the essence of the power of thought as that of the "negative." Theory consists not in mere repudiation but precisely in the analysis of the forms and contents that have consolidated themselves in thought and life, in the concrete knowledge of the reasons why they are one-sided and contradictory. The result is thus not that one can forget everything as worthless—the emptiness of consciousness as the ideal, so to speak. The result, rather, is the entire process of thought with all its assertions, analyses, limitations, etc. That process comprehends both the manifest opinions and the real relations in which they appear, in all their relativity and transitoriness—not as simply true or false, but rather as they are known according to the level of knowledge attained at the given historical moment.[113] Hegel called truth in this critical and historical form the speculative Idea; it has the power in itself to apply the negative to every determinate structure, to each of its own moments. According to him, truth coincides not merely with philosophical consciousness but with concrete history, which thus shows itself as the negative— that is, history in which all transitory things fall apart due to their limitedness and internal contradictions, and are transformed into a more differentiated, better-adapted form. "The Idea, as abstract Idea," writes Hegel, "is the quiescent and inert; it only is in truth in as far as it grasps itself as living. This occurs because it is implicitly dialectical, in order to abrogate that inert quiescence, and to change itself. But if the philosophic Idea is thus implicitly dialectical, it is not so in a contingent manner. Skepticism, on the contrary, exercises its dialectic contingently, for just as the material comes up before it, it shows in the same that implicitly it is negative."[114]

Unlike Hegel, the materialist dialectic in critical theory rejects the unity of thought and history. At present, real historical forms of life exist whose irrationality has already revealed itself to thought. The dialectic is not closed. There is no harmony between thought and being; rather, contradiction still proves to be the driving force—and not just that between human beings and nature, but between human beings with their needs and capacities and the society that they bring forth. Its overcoming thus takes place in the real historical struggle between the individuals who represent those needs and capacities, i.e., the universality, and those others who represent their ossified forms, i.e., particular interests. Thus the skeptical and critical moment in thought goes over into concrete historical activity rather than back into the ephemeral ego. And, as a consequence of this relation between thought and history, critical theory in its totality cannot claim for itself the purely logical criterion of uncontestable certainty, the search for which as an always-already-existing transforms skepticism into nihilism. Although many features distinguish true theories from false, theoretical certainty can no more be presupposed than practical, for it is subject to a historical process which includes both the rigor of understanding and, if necessary, the commitment of one's life.

In the concluding pages of the *Essais* can be found the sentence: "A man who can rightly and truly enjoy his existence is absolutely and almost divinely perfect."[115] Classical German idealism has already indicated that such a demand cannot be fulfilled in direct affirmation of the individual ego. According to it, the fulfillment of one's essence consists in the realization of the transcendental, not the empirical ego. In the course of development of this philosophy it became clear that the transcendental tribunal works itself out not just in the processes of the isolated consciousness but in the shaping of human relations as well. Hegel's concept of Spirit and the idea of a rational society as the meaning of the transcendental subject are rooted in Kant's notion of original apperception.[116] In a divided and repugnant society, the ego, too, is divided and repugnant. That it is at peace does not necessarily mean that it is happy, for happiness is not merely a feeling but a real condition of human beings.[117] One cannot deceive oneself about happiness. A social condition in which the dependence of human beings upon the universality, as well as their contribution to it, are masked and withdrawn from their will necessarily constrains the unfolding of their powers and thus their happiness, even if such shortcomings can hardly be conceived of. They cannot come to the enjoyment of their reason because reason exists in particular terms, as the calculation of individual advantage, and thus in inadequate form. In addition to the universal limitation connected with the organizational principle of all hitherto existing society, the capacities of most individuals are constrained physically and psychically by the pressure of labor, by indignities and deprivations. The degradation of the individual; the taboo on the display, not to mention the practice, of decisive instinctual impulses; the prohibition on enjoyment; the continuous anxiety about defeat in the competitive struggle and the false ambition that goes along with it: these "psychological" influences deform the individual every bit as much as the direct material damage to the senses due to hunger, sickness, and hard work. Montaigne's words can only be fulfilled in a more free organization of humanity. Skepticism transcends itself in this respect. Where happiness is made into a principle, revolutionary action is required.

Though this is manifest, skepticism in its liberal and authoritarian forms constitutes an aspect of the dominant bourgeois type of individual. The reason is that characterological structures are consolidated and transformed not by knowledge and enlightenment but by material conditions. The advances in weapons technology, by means of which entire peoples are held in check by a well-stocked army, are much more decisive for the persistence of skepticism as an anthropological characteristic than the arguments with which the skeptical attitude seeks to rationalize itself. One could counter that insights such as these constitute the very essence of skepticism. To be sure, it is typical of skepticism, as well as of the dominant character as such, to ascribe the vulgar motives—according to which alone the rulers of the world act—not to them and their principle, but to the idea of humanity itself. The difference here is that the critical theory which we espouse, in contrast to skepticism, does not make an antitheoretical absolutism of the insight into the inadequacy of things as they are and the transitoriness of cognition. Instead, even in the face of pessimistic assessments, critical theory is guided by the unswerving interest in a better future.

Beginnings of the Bourgeois Philosophy of History

Preface

The work before you is comprised of several studies that were undertaken toward the goal of self-clarification. Its purpose is not to provide any new solutions to questions of philological research. The author is of the opinion that current reflections upon history are themselves part of a more comprehensive set of historical relations whose roots go deeper than the present. This has given him cause to explore several traditional approaches to this topic (particularly their important earlier formulations) that seem essential for comprehending the set of issues currently facing the philosophy of history, for the quite practical purpose of learning something in the process.

Nevertheless, there may be some value in publishing this work. The author's basic convictions regarding the philosophy of history are not set forth here in any great detail; nevertheless, as a consequence of the original aim of this work, the problems dealt with are presented in their essentials, and are considered with an eye to the present.

Accordingly, the discussions of the Machiavellian *psychological conception of history* may be relevant not only to modern theories of history which are influenced by psychology, but to questions of philosophical anthropology as well.

The objections to Machiavelli's views essentially revolve around the concept of society one finds in his work, and this concept is taken up by Hobbes's *doctrine of natural law*. The fundamental ideas of the latter are still to be found in many current theories of the state and of the law. Even the problem of *ideology*, which has a specific function in social struggle, turns up in Hobbes's system. This problem is at the center of current philosophical and sociological discussions.

If ideology effects appearances, then *utopia* is the dream of the "true" and just ordering of life. It manages somehow to play a role in every philosophical consideration of human society. Ideology and utopia are to be understood as orientations of social groups that are derivative of the whole of social reality.

The lawlike dependence of cultural spheres upon the course of development of humanity as a whole was the main theme of Vico's *New Science*. His treatment of *mythology* as a mirror of political relations is nothing short of brilliant. At present mythology has attracted the attention of philosophers not only as an ideological form of consciousness, but equally as a means of getting at the essence of primitive thinking.

The problems in the philosophy of history to be treated here are united by more than their significance for current issues; in their early form, which is our focus here, they all arose out of the same situation: namely, the bourgeois society that was in the process of consolidating itself and freeing itself from the fetters of the feudal system. They are necessarily related to the determinate needs, desires, exigencies, and contradictions of this society. This is the reason why they have been identified here as questions of the "*bourgeois philosophy of history*."

Finally, a note on the notes: In light of the purpose of this work, the employment of notes has been kept to a bare minimum. Bibliographic documentation of our authors' works on the philosophy of history is therefore not to be found; such can be gleaned from various texts on the history of philosophy and of theories of the state. Similarly, reference to original editions has been avoided; as much as possible, citations are from the most readily available German [here, English] translations.

1. Machiavelli and the Psychological Conception of History

The foundation of modern natural science was established during the Renaissance. The aim of this science is to identify, with the support of systematically employed empirical knowledge, regularities in nature's course, by means of which one can then either effect or hinder certain effects as are required—in other words, to dominate nature to the greatest extent possible. The intellectual approach during the Middle Ages had concentrated on discerning the meaning and purpose of the world and of life, and was for the most part consumed by biblical exegesis and the interpretation of ecclesiastical and classical authorities. With the Renaissance, however, focus shifted away from the otherworldly purpose taken from tradition and toward inquiry into the secular causes of this world, which were to be established by means of empirical observation.

Accordingly, the conviction that there was a certain uniformity to nature's course lies at the heart of the new science. Observations such as the fact that a free-falling body falls at a particular velocity, or that the combining of two substances yields a new substance that exhibits properties different from its constituents, or that certain medicines act as antidotes to certain types of poisoning—such observations are of value to society only insofar as these results regularly recur in the same manner, i.e., only if the formula used to calculate the velocity of free fall remains constant, the combination of the two substances always yields the same results, and the efficacy of the antidote extends to future cases of poisoning as well. No matter how loosely one may wish to conceive of the similarity between future and past events, no matter how much one may wish to focus on the variation exhibited by each particular case, the possibility of contaminating factors, or the variability of conditions, one point remains: the value of laws of nature, everywhere so central to the new science established during the Renaissance, is dependent upon the future recurrence of those cases in which the laws are supposed to be valid, and hence upon the practicability of such laws.[1] In the new science of the Renaissance, the possibility of laws of nature—and therefore also of the domination of nature—appears to be logically dependent upon the premise of an orderliness to the workings of nature.

This belief in uniformity lies at the root of the development of physics and chemistry, the introduction of mathematical knowledge to these disciplines, and the emergence of a scientific anthropology and medicine. This uniformity is something that is not subject to scientific proof itself, but is instead a hypothetical model. The positivists of the nineteenth century tried to make an empirical fact out of this uniformity. They argued that we observe instances of such regularities everywhere, and that we can readily observe that an event in nature that has occurred in a certain way at any given place or time will occur in exactly the same way at any point in time thereafter, and that this is to be taken as an inductive proof of the claim of uniformity.[2] Ignored here is the fact that this very chain of reasoning is cogent only when the proposition to be proven is already presumed. The uniformity of nature in the past gives grounds for the proposition of uniformity in the future only insofar as we assume that the future will correspond to the past; this just begs the question. No ontological law in the usual sense, much less any insight of the kind typified by mathematical laws, gives grounds for this assumption. This is due to the fact that mathematics deals with pure possibilities, and the postulation of uniformity makes an assertion about something in the real world. To be sure, the distinctively modern concept of nature formed essentially by the mathematical-mechanical natural sciences certainly would have been impossible without this assumption. In its origins, bourgeois science is inextricably linked to the development of technology and industry, and cannot be understood apart from bourgeois society's domination of nature.

But society is not just based on the domination of nature in the narrower sense, nor merely on the invention of new methods of production or the construction of machines, nor on the maintenance of a certain standard of health—it is equally based on the domination of human beings by other human beings. The aggregate of the paths that lead to this condition, and of the measures which serve to maintain this domination, goes under the name of politics. The greatness of Machiavelli was to have recognized, on the threshold of this new society, the possibility of a new science of politics whose principles corresponded to those of modern physics and psychology, and to have expressed its fundamentals with such simplicity and certainty. This is not the place to examine the extent to which Machiavelli was conscious of this analogy himself, or to determine for which of his ideas he was indebted to the writings of ancient authors or contemporary researchers: his objective is quite obvious. In real society, human beings are dominated by other human beings; what was needed was to impart knowledge, on the basis of observations and of a systematic study of facts, as to how one achieves domination and how one maintains it. This is the exclusive purport of all of his writings (save his artistic endeavors): above all of his major work, *Discourses on the First Ten Books of Titus Livius*—not to mention the famous text *The Prince*, which can be seen as a self-contained portion of the latter—but also of his excellent *History of Florence*.[3]

Natural scientists, in the course of pursuing their objective of discovering regularities, generally have the objects of their investigations directly at hand. Apart from certain problems in astronomy, geology, and several other branches of the natural sciences, the material to be observed may be directly viewed in as much depth as the scientist desires. As a rule, scientists can generate their own experimental procedures. Their concepts and theorems for the most part are founded on some kind of empirical knowledge, which at least in principle can be replicated by other scientists. Physics and chemistry, as well as psychology and medicine, encounter their objects of observation as given and in the present; furthermore, there is a certain amount of latitude regarding whatever experiments one may wish to carry out. The material for Machiavelli's science, however, is furnished primarily by the past. To be sure, as a high official of Florence, one of the most advanced political systems of the time, he witnessed important political events both within and outside of Italy. During his downfall and his attempts to win influence again, social movements of no small significance took place before his eyes. His works prove that he followed the events of his own time to the utmost degree of detail. However, he essentially saw himself as relying mostly upon history: side by side with the present, it is the past which must furnish the political scientist with examples from which he can detect regularities. Thus when Machiavelli, with the aid of Livius, makes his thorough inquiry into Roman history, he is seeking the timeless rules by which people allow themselves to be dominated.

Accordingly, the proposition of the uniformity of events cannot be separated from this objective of Machiavelli. If groups of subjects in certain states in the present and the future do not react in the same manner as in the past, and if the passions connected with the reactions of such individuals do not remain the same, then all the writings of Machiavelli would have failed to achieve their author's goal, and he would have to view his own science as just a dream. This pragmatic conception even determines the outward form of Machiavelli's writings. Whoever looks at his main work, the *Discourses*, will find that, as often as not, the chapters begin with excerpts taken from Livius's description of an event, from which (usually on the basis of further examples cited from ancient or more recent history) a general proposition is then derived. In *The Prince,* political questions that would be important mainly for a prince are taken up one at a time in each of the small chapters, and as a rule are also treated in terms of examples. The whole of the *History of Florence* amounts to one single, extended historical example: it is a collection of recollections to serve the politics of the future.

In the *Discourses,* the claim that human beings are of the same essence takes the form that "all men . . . are born and live and die in the same way, and therefore resemble each other."[4] The theory of a uniform human nature determines Machiavelli's work at every turn. "Whoever considers the past and the present," he says in his major work, "will readily observe that all cities and all peoples are and ever have been animated by the same desires and the same passions; so that it is easy, by diligent study of the past, to foresee what is likely to happen in the future in any republic, and to apply those remedies that were used by the ancients, or, not finding any that were employed by them, to devise new ones from the similarity of the events."[5] In another place Machiavelli states, "Wise men say, and not without reason, that whoever wishes to foresee the future must consult the past; for human events ever resemble those of preceding times. This arises from the fact that they are produced by men who have been, and ever will be, animated by the same passions, and thus they must necessarily have the same results."[6] Those who consider his method impracticable and who do not want to believe that one can imitate the past and apply what occurred in it to the future are considered by Machiavelli to be uneducated and narrow, "as though heaven, the sun, the elements, and men had changed the order of their motions and power, and were different from what they were in ancient times."[7]

This raises a question that has always occupied the research on Machiavelli: whom does the science of politics serve? Who, according to Machiavelli, is supposed to rule over human beings? To phrase the question more in terms of the philosophy of history, which form of rule—or for Machiavelli, which form of state—has proven historically to be the best, or which ought yet to be created in the course of things? The most varied interpretations exist regarding Machiavelli's position here, all of which appear to rest on solid evidence. In *The Prince,* which he presented at the feet of a Medici, he praised monarchy in its most brutal form as the only way to unify Italy. Yet in the *Discourses* he just as unambiguously considers a republic the best form of state, and reveals thoroughly republican, indeed even democratic, sympathies.

In any case, Machiavelli holds the view that no form of state can exist indefinitely. Just as in the past one form of government broke up another, so it will occur in all eternity. There exists a determined cycle that runs its course with the regularity of a natural law. The original governmental form, which emerges out of the convergence of scattered individuals, is monarchy, which arose through the selection of the bravest, and later of the most intelligent and just. As soon as the princes are determined by descent, monarchy degenerates into tyranny, which leads to revolution, mutiny, and conspiracy against the princes. The instigators of unrest are not primarily the masses; rather, those of the greatest rank and power put an end to tyranny and form an aristocratic regime. The sons of these nobles are similarly incapable of sustaining their power in the long run since, according to Machiavelli, they always gave themselves over to "ambition, libertinage, and violence, and soon caused the aristocratic government to degenerate into an oligarchic tyranny, regardless of all civil rights."[8] This leads to their downfall and to the establishment of democracy. However, this form of government has the tendency to disintegrate in corruption and hence into anarchy, from which a people can again only be saved by a dynamic individual, a dictator or a monarch. Then the cycle begins anew. According to Machiavelli, one should of course not imagine that this entire sequence, much less its repetition, need occur in one and the same state, "which results from the fact that their duration is not sufficiently long to be able to undergo these repeated changes and preserve their existence."[9] Powerful states decline or end up under the power of neighboring states; but even in variations of those sorts the cycle of governmental forms—which Machiavelli, relying on Polybius, outlined—still continues.

Provinces often in the changes they make, pass from order to disorder, and after the disorder pass over to order again; for mundane affairs not being by nature conducive to stopping, as they arrive at their ultimate perfection, not being able to rise further, they must descend; and similarly, when they have descended and, through disorders, come to the ultimate baseness, of necessity not being able to descend further, they must rise; and thus from the good they always descend to the bad, and from the bad they rise to the good; for virtu brings forth tranquillity; tranquillity, idleness; idlenesss, disorder; disorder, ruin; and similarly from ruin arises order; from order virtu; and from this, glory and good fortune.[10]

Thus even if a particular governmental form may be the best possible, it will not have eternal duration, for each form contains the seeds of its own destruction within itself. Machiavelli discusses the advantages and disadvantages of individual governmental forms. He ultimately does not show an unconditional preference for any one of them. Of course, he vacillates basically only between monarchy and republic, and he rejects the rule of an aristocracy, for reasons that will be discussed later. As for the rest, he explains, "Let republics, then, be established where equality [of wealth] exists, and, on the contrary, principalities where great inequality [of wealth] prevails; otherwise the governments will lack proper proportions and have but little durability."[11]

We now know that, in Machiavelli's view, his suggestions could be of advantage to princes and republicans: he discusses the interests of the former with the same exhaustiveness with which he analyzes the measures that their opponents must take to overthrow them—and this often occurs even in the same chapter. He gives just as much advice to the respective government as he does to those who are conspiring against it. Was all that mattered for him thus only the play of powers in social life? Did the struggle for power as the most profound expression of life captivate him when, enthralled by the political battles of his age, he undertook to examine their laws out of passionate interest, unconcerned with the possible results? Under the influence of modern *Lebensphilosophie*, this is indeed how Machiavelli has come to be understood. The ardent propaganda for the independence of Italy in the final chapter of *The Prince* might suggest that his ostensible delight in the great and vital unfolding of power, and not its actual foundation, stands in the forefront. However, such an interpretation—even if it is not fully incorrect psychologically—fails to appreciate the objective meaning of Machiavelli's thought.

Amongst all the apparent contradictions, however, there exists a single evaluative standard, one which Machiavelli held to be self-evident. His reliance on this standard is invariable and unambiguous.

He does not lend counsel to monarchs and republican governments for their own sakes; rather, he wanted to promote the power, greatness, and the unshakable security of the civil state as such. While all of the commentaries devote a considerable amount of discussion to the political events in the Italy of Machiavelli's time and his personal participation in politics, there is little focus on the theoretically most important result of his experiences. Expressed precisely, this consists in the insight that the welfare of the whole depends upon the unfolding of trade, upon the unchecked spread of bourgeois efficiency in business and industry, and upon the free play of economic powers, and that such social development can only be secured by means of a powerful state authority. He reached this conclusion not only as a consequence of his participation in diplomatic projects and in the Florentine civil war, but also because he thought it confirmed by the entirety of world history, above all the period when ancient Rome was at the height of its power. For Machiavelli, politics becomes the most noble task of the thinker only insofar as the state is the condition for the development of the civic powers of the individual and of the whole.

A decisive concept in his science is *virtù*. Much has been written about the meaning of this term, and with good reason, for in fact one touches here upon a very important point in Machiavelli's historical thinking. The notion of *virtus* has played a decisive role in the history of philosophy. Its nuances in meaning are difficult to demonstrate because the respective meaning of the term can always be grasped only within the context of the entire life relationships of a certain age. In general, its content is best described when one adheres to the following: *virtus* (*virtù, vertu*) designates the sum of essential qualities deemed to be desirable and respectable in the social circle in which the notion is used. A man who possesses *virtus* is a "just man," a man as he should be. The devotion to the state and the martial enthusiasm embodying the Roman ideal, which left common labor to the slave, was considered to be *virtus,* just as much as Christian humility later was. For Machiavelli, this notion encompasses the classical qualities of nobility and bravery, but it further contains the modern moment of industriousness and efficiency. Machiavelli detests the noble not only because the latter regards reforms with spite, and generally stands in the way of civic development by thwarting the formation of central governmental authority and of large states, but also because he performs no civic labor. "And to explain more clearly what is meant by the term 'gentlemen,' " he thus states in his *Discourses*, "I say that those are called gentleman who live idly upon the proceeds of their extensive possessions, without devoting themselves to agriculture or any other useful pursuit to gain a living. Such men are pernicious to any country or republic; but more pernicious even than these are such as have, besides their other possessions, castles which they command, and subjects who obey them." [12] Whoever wishes to found a republic, according to Machiavelli's words, "will not succeed until he has destroyed" all of the nobles. [13] A state is good, it possesses *virtù*, if the conditions prevail in it whereby its citizens may develop *virtù*. They should be confident, strong, uninhibited individuals—which happen to be the very qualities that, under the conditions of that age, were required of a great entrepreneur, merchant, shipmaster, or banker. According to Machiavelli, the common weal depended upon the flourishing of these occupations. The fact that the rise of the bourgeois class in the Renaissance was indeed the condition for great social progress demonstrates his political vision. The full import of what is generally referred to as "Machiavellianism," in the sense of radical political unscrupulousness, of completely "amoral" action, can only be understood within this context. Machiavelli demands the subordination of all considerations to the goal that appeared to him to be the highest: the creation and maintenance of a strong, centralized state as a condition for civic welfare. If one wished to summarize the content of *The Prince* and of the *Discourses* with the phrase "the end justifies the means," one would at least have to append to this what end is at issue here, namely the creation of the best possible commonwealth. According to Machiavelli, religion and morality should be subordinated to this highest goal of human action. In the service of this goal one may, according to him, employ lies, deception, duplicity, cruelty, and murder.

The means of controlling people that Machiavelli derived from history have in fact always found application in politics, but as a rule they were employed without any intention whatsoever of advancing this highest end. When the famous eighth chapter of *The Prince* explains that the prince may break contracts, that he does not need to keep his word; when Machiavelli shows how religion has been useful in every age to keep the dominated social classes in line during times of peace; when he coolly calculates whether pagan or Christian religion is better suited for this purpose; when he discusses the extermination of entire groups of human beings under certain conditions as one such means; in short, when he demonstrates that the holiest expressions of loving kindness as well as the darkest of crimes have one and all been means in the hands of rulers throughout history, in so doing he has formulated a significant historical-philosophical doctrine. His mistake, which the ensuing period committed even more egregiously in the doctrine of *raison d'état*, was that his justification of means of domination that were essential for the rise of the bourgeoisie in the Italy of his time was extended by him to cover the past and the future as well. Such eternalizing of the temporally bound is a characteristic deficiency of modern philosophy of history.

Machiavelli wants the rulers from now on consciously to make use of the means that up to now had frequently been applied only instinctively. But the Renaissance man's naive joy in discovery comes to light in the fact that he completely neglected the most important maxim of such an application, namely concealment, secrecy, illusion. Religion is unusable as an instrument of politics when it is explicitly designated as such; crimes which become transparent to the public as necessary tools of government are of little use to the latter. For all of the structural similarities between Machiavelli's science and the disciplines of the natural sciences, whose foundations also were established in the Renaissance, a major difference exists between them in their application. When the natural scientist openly expresses the laws that he has discovered, he has nothing to fear regarding the possibility of their application. But the possibility of effectively exploiting the relationships identified by Machiavelli depends upon their being viewed as a calamity of the past whose continued existence into the present is denied. The very thing that so inspired the philosopher and statesman Bacon, as well as Hegel a few centuries later—namely that Machiavelli expressed what is, and not what should be according to some private opinion or some prevailing prejudice—fundamentally contradicts Machiavelli's own intention. When Frederick II wrote his *Anti-Machiavelli*, Diderot reports[14] that a great philosopher supposedly said to him, "Sire, I think that the first lesson Machiavelli would have given to his pupil would have been to reject his work."

Machiavelli's passionate proclamation of the strong state is based on his belief in the possibility of spiritual and moral progress. Culture's advance, and indeed its very emergence, both have material causes in his view. In the *Discourses* he teaches, "men act right only upon compulsion; but from the moment that they have the option and liberty to commit wrong with impunity, then they never fail to carry confusion and disorder everywhere. It is this that has caused it to be said that poverty and hunger make men industrious, and that the law makes them good."[15] Thus all life conditions relating to work in the end are not based upon an ideal origin, but rather are driven by material need. Even morality does not emerge from some set of cultural intentions worked out in the beginning, and it is certainly not based on any sort of moral instinct; rather, it is derived from social conditions that are themselves determined by need. Consequently, an action is "moral" when it corresponds to the laws and mores governing the civilized society. Neither humanity as a whole nor the particular individual possesses predilections toward nobility, grace, charity, or justice in complete form upon entering the world; rather, causal connections exist: education and the particular contents of a moral code are determined by the changing needs of social development. The status of human culture in general is indicated by the amount of *virtù,* which in the present means the amount of bourgeois freedom.

According to Machiavelli, an important vehicle of cultural progress up to now has been the history of conflicts between social classes. Accordingly, for Machiavelli such conflicts, which he was familiar with mainly in the form of civil wars, were certainly not to be taken as simply pernicious, but rather as an essential condition for advancement. The form in which he experienced them most directly stemmed from the bloody confrontations between the nobles and the bourgeoisie. "I maintain," he says in his major work, "that those who blame the quarrels of the Senate and the people of Rome condemn that which was the very origin of liberty, and that they were probably more impressed by the cries and noise which these disturbances occasioned in the public places, than by the good effect which they produced; and that they do not consider that in every republic there are two parties, that of the nobles and that of the people; and all the laws that are favorable to liberty result from the opposition of these parties to each other."[16] In the preface to his *History of Florence* Machiavelli explains, "And certainly, according to my judgment, it seems to me that no other example so much shows the power of our City as that which depends on these divisions, which have had the strength to destroy every great and most powerful City. None the less, ours seemed that it had always become great."[17] Discussing the means that the Roman plebs used in such battles—"to hear constantly the cries of the people furious against the Senate, and of a Senate declaiming against the people, to see the populace rush tumultuously through the streets, close their houses, and even leave the city of Rome"[18]—he makes the point that though these are matters that may horrify those who read of them, they are necessary in the life of the state. "The demands of a free people are rarely pernicious to their liberty; they are generally inspired by oppressions, experienced or apprehended."[19] Machiavelli argued that better and freer institutions are the usual result of such movements.

Furthermore, Machiavelli was well aware of the struggles between the nobles and the princes, but especially those between *popolo*, i.e., the bourgeoisie, and *plebe*, i.e., laborers employed in manufacturing, shipping, and navigation as well as the unemployed who scraped by in the countries or in the cities of the Renaissance. We see here the first beginnings of the modern proletariat: "But in Florence, at first the Nobles became divided among themselves; then the Nobles and the People [*popolo*]; and finally the People and the Plebs; and many times it happened that one of these parties remained superior although divided in two. From which divisions there resulted so many deaths, so many exilings, so much scattering of families, as never before had resulted in any other City of which there is a record."[20] In the *History of Florence* Machiavelli exhaustively outlines a wage and reform movement among workers who were active in the wool and other guilds. Machiavelli presents us with part of a speech given by one of "the most passionate and, at the same time, most experienced revolutionaries":

And it appears to me that we are going to a certain gain, because those who could impede us are disunited and rich: their disunion, therefore, will give us the victory, and their riches (when they become ours) will maintain us. Nor should you be deceived about that antiquity of blood with which they reproach us. For all men having had the same origin, are equally ancient, and by nature have been made in one way. Undress us naked, and you will see us all the same. Dress us in their clothes, and them in ours, and we, without doubt, will appear noble, and they ignoble; for only poverty and riches makes us different. It grieves me much to think how many of you repent of those things that have been done, and want to abstain from new ones. And certainly, if this is true, you are not the men I believed you to be. For neither conscience nor infamy should dismay you, since those who conquer, in whatever manner they win, never bring back shame. And we should not take conscience into account; for where there is (as there is in us) fear of hunger and prisons, the fear of hell cannot, and should not, hold sway. But if you note the manner in which men proceed, you will see that all who attain great riches and power, have attained it either by fraud or force; and those things which they have usurped either by deceit or violence, to disguise the brutishness of the attainment, they excuse (themselves) under the false title of honest gains. And those who, either from little prudence or too much foolishness, avoid those methods, always suffocate in servitude and poverty. For the faithful servants are always servants, and the good men are always poor.[21]

Hence we can see that Machiavelli knew and clearly described the various forms of class conflict in his age. Despite the sacrifices that they demand, this observer of world history thought them to be a necessary condition for human development. Humans are driven to these violent encounters by their external living conditions, and thus here too need reveals itself as the cause of progress. But is not the meaning of Machiavelli's undertaking thus thrown into question? Is this materialist theory compatible with his conviction that knowledge of historical laws can make things better? Are human beings at all able to participate in the course of history with conscious awareness?

Machiavelli addresses this question at one point in *The Prince,* and as always he has a practical purpose in mind: "How much fortune can do in human affairs and how it may be opposed."[22] By "fortune" he understands everything that is not dependent on human will:

It is not unknown to me how many have been and are of opinion that worldly events are so governed by fortune and by God, that men cannot by their prudence change them, and that on the contrary there is no remedy whatever, and for this they may judge it to be useless to toil much about them, but let things be ruled by chance. . . . When I think about them, at times I am partly inclined to share this opinion. Nevertheless, that our freewill may not be altogether extinguished, I think it may be true that fortune is the ruler of half our actions, but that she allows the other half or thereabouts to be governed by us. I would compare her to an impetuous river that, when turbulent, inundates the plains, casts down trees and buildings, removes earth from this side and places it on the other; every one flees before it, and everything yields to its fury without being able to oppose it; and yet though it is of such a kind, still when it is quiet, men can make provision against it by dykes and banks, so that when it rises it will either go into a canal or its rush will not be so wild and dangerous. So it is with fortune, which shows her power where no measures have been taken to resist her, and directs her fury where she knows that no dykes or barriers have been made to hold her. [23]

We will always have to reckon with natural elements; even the history of technology, in which man grapples with nature, is governed by certain inner laws that we cannot get around. But even if the forces of nature cannot be completely effaced, they are at least to a great extent controllable. This holds not merely for the processes of nature in the narrow sense, for the objects of natural science, but rather just as much for the processes in the nature of society. Even Machiavelli's cycle of governmental forms is fundamentally an unshakable law of nature. One can attempt to shorten the bad phases and lengthen the good ones; one can undertake by means of a combination of forms of rule such as existed in republican Rome (consuls, senate, tribune of the people), according to Machiavelli and his ancient source Polybius, to maintain a particular state of affairs for as long as possible. But to reverse the cycle, to act contrary to the course of time, leads to ruin. Machiavelli believes "that he is happy whose mode of procedure accords with the needs of the times, and similarly he is unfortunate whose mode of procedure is opposed to the times." [24] We thus find here already *in nuce* Hegel's doctrine of great men, who differ from the fantast in that they express and do what is timely, while the fantast dreamily disregards reality.

Machiavelli allowed room for human activity, within which the course of nature and of society could be influenced on the basis of resolutions of the will. But are these resolutions themselves free? Is there anything in human beings that is not attributable to natural factors, but rather to something that transcends nature, to an absolute, to mercy or to a free will? In contrast to Protestant currents, the thinker of the Italian Renaissance answered this question in the negative. When Machiavelli speaks of free resolution, he in no way means a faculty independent of the course of nature. Rather, the will is no less conditioned by natural elements, namely instincts and natural tendencies against which no one can act, than is the fall of a stone because of gravity. Though never fully established or developed by Machiavelli, his work paves the way for the philosophical view that human instincts are part of the great causal mechanism. Human beings are parts of nature and can in no way elude its laws. They possess freedom inasmuch as they can act on the basis of their own decisions; they do not possess it insofar as the term is understood to mean freedom from the conditions of nature. We shall discuss this more in the next section.

Great statesmen and princes of the epoch of absolutism that arose in his age subscribed to Machiavelli's view that all historical movement was political. They agreed with him as well when, to assure the strongest possible development of *virtù*, he proclaimed the powerful state as the wisest political course for historically acting individuals. But the more the economic and cultural leadership was transferred from the Italian republics to the great national monarchies, the more the republican *Discourses*, his major work, lost significance, leaving all attention to focus solely on *The Prince*. By the century of the Enlightenment one read almost exclusively the latter work, yet by then it was rejected both as a defense of tyranny and as an attack on justice and humanity. Machiavelli appears to defend the prince who despises people, who subjects himself to no moral law, who rules with poison and dagger, who breaks his word, and who protects the religion that he actually considers false. The deficiency that Machiavelli's critics have charged him with, up to the present day, is his moral indifference. He is blamed not only for having given immoral advice to governments, but also for failing to recognize moral strength as a factor in political power. In fact, Machiavelli did not overlook morality as a factor in power; for him, however, issues of authenticity or disingenuousness of character, or of whether there was a concurrence or a distinction between a moral phenomenon and the personal disposition of its medium, were meaningless. Disposition, as long as it remains socially ineffectual, was also brushed aside both by Hegel as the impotence of particular individuality and by Nietzsche as the insignificance of pure inwardness. Machiavelli, whose main concern is the founding of a good social order as the highest goal of historical action, had to judge characters not by their subjective morality but rather by their political importance.

The common feature of Machiavelli and the critics of his "morals" lies rather in the overestimation of the historical role of character. Both his opponents and his disciples, Richelieu and Frederick the Great, Diderot and Fichte, are in agreement with Machiavelli that whether those who make up a governmental body rule others justly or un-justly, cruelly or gently, fanatically or tolerantly is purely dependent on their psychological constitution. For the subjects, all that matters is an ultimate, personal aspect, which is, of course, dependent on a man-ifold of natural conditions: the character of the rulers. Frederick ex-plains that the kings have power to do good or evil "after they have decided it," and to prove his point, as it were, he balances out the likes of a Nero, Caligula, Tiberius by listing the names of the good Roman Caesars, "the sacred names of a Titus, a Trajan, an Antoninus."[25] Therefore, when in the Enlightenment not only philosophers but even princes condemn Machiavelli's principles, then according to the above psychological view of history, this must be because the princes in that later time coincidentally were better human beings than were the rul-ers of the Renaissance and Baroque, who entered the world as holy terrors. According to this view, human passions and instincts deter-mine the course of things and explain even the modulation between order and disorder and the cycle of governmental forms. The basic powers of the mind should remain essentially the same in any age; they are conceived as the other natural powers are, as ahistorical. The various combinations of these same basic elements, which constitute the character differences of the rulers, are not explained in this view of history but are just taken to be incidental. Even the real battles in history, as well as the ideas that people have, are to be explained pri-marily by an examination of various characters. The characters react to external influences, and to human and suprahuman environments. Thus a benevolent prince responds to the poverty of his subjects with social-political measures, a cruel one with despotic violence.

Physics and psychology explain the whole of human events. "I be-lieve," Machiavelli says in a letter, "that as Nature has given men dif-ferent faces, so she has given them different temperaments and imaginations; and each acts according to his own temperament and imagination."[26] The deficiency of Machiavelli's view of history lies in the fact that he allowed this particular manner of "thinking and feel-ing" to be dependent only upon historically unchangeable elements of nature and in no way upon social transformations that occur in the course of history. Within the context of the new science, the only thing amenable to his explanatory model is whatever remains constant rel-ative to what is changeable. As long as one considered atoms to be unchangeable units, they constituted the ultimate explanatory material of physics. Similarly, for Machiavelli the characters of human beings constitute the ultimate explanatory material of the course of history, because they are composed of undeviating psychic elements, of eternally fixed instincts and passions.

But this conception is dogmatic. It disregards the fact that both psychical and physical elements, which determine the structure of human nature, are incorporated into historical reality. These may therefore not be taken as fixed and invariable units which one may always depend upon as if they were ultimate explanatory factors. Certainly the enlightened princes of the eighteenth century ruled more humanely than did Alexander Borgia or Louis XIV. But if it is correct to say that the King of England had respect for his subjects because of his humanity, then it is just as true that he is humane out of respect for his subjects. Respect too is dependent upon historical conditions. Not only the manifest behavior of a government but also its character is determined by the real relations of power in the state, and these in turn are formed by social life as a whole. In the Renaissance, the bourgeoisie needed a brutal ruler armed with all means of power so that all hindrances to trade could be eliminated; the first philosopher of history of the modern age outlined a corresponding ideal. By the time of the Enlightenment, the bourgeoisie had already become so powerful, and had already achieved such a position of actual power by way of the functions it served that were necessary for the life of society, that it no longer needed to tolerate the arbitrariness of an authoritarian ruler or even just an overly extravagant court. Absolutism had already fulfilled its historical task, the suppression of feudalism, and had produced the necessary governmental centralism. A successful prince who considers himself the first servant of the state is a product, and not the cause, of the social transformation that has been effected. In the Renaissance his rule would likely have met a quick end.

Machiavelli, along with the proponents of the psychological conception of history, could perhaps submit to this view—of course with a decisive qualification. Certainly, they might concede, the prospects for particular character types change along with the times. Nevertheless, the very same types of people that existed, for example, in the Renaissance also existed in the eighteenth century, but historical

conditions excluded them from prominence and ruled out the possibility of their having any impact. As Machiavelli writes, "because times
vary and condition of things change, one man's efforts result as he
desired them; and he succeeds who does things according to the times;
but conversely, he is not fortunate who does things in opposition to
the times."[27] But even this cannot save the doctrine of the unchangeable nature of human beings. In the Renaissance, no Fredericks or
Voltaires blossomed behind the scenes; rather, they never existed.
Among the guild masters of the medieval city, there were no modern
entrepreneurial types or trust managers who simply lacked appropriate outlets for their activity nor, among guild journeymen, was there
the unnoticed and silent consciousness, as it were, that is characteristic
of the industrial worker today. Only the vaguest of analogies can be
made. Characters abstracted from their age are entirely unreal; if one
separates these persons from the contents of the Enlightenment itself,
then all that remains is a phantom. Similarly, there existed no Cesare
Borgia in Frederick's Prussia; it is just so much idle talk to designate
some fallen noble adventurer who ends up on the gallows as a "Borgia
character" who simply was born at the wrong time. Practical institutions, forms of government, and laws are not the only things changed
by a radical transformation of actual conditions; human nature is
changed as well. The basis of all human relations, i.e., the way in which
people sustain their lives, is subject to a process of change, which provides the impetus to transformations in the spiritual and intellectual
realms, hence in science, art, metaphysics, and religion.

The doctrine is false that even though the times change, the psychological makeup of human beings remains the same. Whether rulers want to govern human beings justly or unjustly, cruelly or gently,
fanatically or tolerantly, does not depend on the character of the rulers. The doctrine of an eternally fixed human nature—an idea that
turns up again and again in the historical-philosophical thinking of
the modern age—this doctrine of the same instincts and passions is a
mistake. Of course, neither can we maintain the opposite, that people
of different times and cultures differ radically from one another
and that we therefore have no access whatsoever to an adequate understanding of individuals of past epochs. Such historical agnosticism
would leave no option but to renounce any understanding of history.
A corresponding psychological doctrine would be one of mutually

inaccessible milieu-worlds of particular human beings and animals. In the domain of history this skeptical radicalism is opposed primarily by the following consideration: only exceptionally can a human being at a primitive stage of civilization conceive of or predict a more developed life; but our more highly organized faculty of reason, together with the fact that we ourselves remain rather primitive on important psychic levels and often react like the human beings from earlier stages of development, makes it possible for us to perform successful research on those human beings whose psychological makeup is structured differently from our own. Furthermore, we understand people from other cultures because our own life in society is formed in such a way that we have thoughts, feelings, and goals that in substance are in agreement with theirs. Thus the social forms that are known to us were founded essentially on the basis of an organization that allowed only a relatively small portion of the population full enjoyment of the respective culture, while the great masses were forced to continuously renounce their instincts. The form of society dictated by material conditions up to this point was separation of management and labor, of ruler and ruled. This is why, for example, the will to justice in the sense of social equality, i.e., the will to the overcoming of these oppositions, must form a subject matter for consciousness that will surpass that of former times. The demand for justice as the elimination of privileges and the institution of equality stems from the lower, dominated classes. To this are opposed the notions of the rulers—efficiency, nobility, worth of the personality—which serve to maintain the social inequality. Such notions could disappear only with the social foundations that determine them. However, because of the social conditions that have prevailed up to now, they easily appear as eternal characteristics of human nature.

Machiavelli's error does not simply consist in his assertion of uniformities of character shared by all who have emerged in the course of history, but rather in his neglect of the social conditions underlying the preservation or transformation of psychological traits. With the exception of Hegel, scarcely a philosopher of the modern age has avoided Machiavelli's mistake. In contemporary analytic psychology, the mental life of the individual is understood in terms of a development conditioned by environmental situations. We have learned to regard the family as the most important environmental factor; but the family itself varies according to the historical epoch and the position of its members in society. Though certain patterns of human reaction have doubtless up to now remained relatively constant, it is now possible to go a long way toward a scientific explanation of the dependence of character upon the social conditions in which a particular individual develops. A philosophical anthropology, i.e., a doctrine of a particular human nature that consists of definitive pronouncements about some immutable concept of human essence that is untouched by history, is thus impossible. Insofar as such current attempts strictly adhere to the state of current empirical research and, at the same time, recognize their provisional nature, they have the value of broadening the range of questions and inquiries emerging out of the specialized spheres of science and of fruitfully applying them to a framework for examining the interconnections of reality. Further, they are able to sharpen our ability to sense which conception of humanity is implied by our historical and sociological theories. We can, of course, only speak of the essence of humanity insofar as it manifests itself. All finality in statements about the essence of what is real contradicts the fact that all predictions regarding actual events include an element of probability. Today we can avoid Machiavelli's ontological assumption of an unalterable human psyche without thereby having to renounce psychological explanations in history.

Criticism of Machiavelli does not at all tend to be directed against his static notion of man, but against what is called his naturalism. He is accused of looking at historical events as natural processes, of wanting to derive all occurrences in a strictly causal manner on the basis of material need and of the natural inclinations of human beings engaged in political struggle. But this cannot hold as a sound objection. Just as for every event in the world as a whole the task of science consists in explaining this event from known conditions within the context of an established law, so also is the attempt to research historical events within the context of their causal complexity similarly justified. The accusation of naturalism dogmatically assumes a fundamental, methodological difference between the investigation of nature and of history. To criticize the notion of naturalism on these terms means to reject enlightening research into historical relationships. Human action is here hastily hypostatized as unconditioned, not unlike in the abovementioned error in Machiavelli's psychology.

The accusation of naturalism can justifiably be raised against Machiavelli only if one understands this term to mean that the dialectical relations between nonhuman and human nature are simplified inasmuch as they are examined in a manner essentially suited only to nonhuman nature. Machiavelli in fact treats human beings as genera within nature just like any other animal genus. Each individual, irrespective of the group or time to which it belongs, is regarded as an exemplar of a single and well-defined genus, just as one can always take a particular bee or ant or even an atom as an example of all individuals of the genus. When one speaks of differences between individuals, these are natural differences only in a rather narrow sense, meaning only that one cannot take a worker bee for a drone or an especially weak, sick, or abnormal exemplar for a normal one of the genus. Human beings appear here as interchangeable exemplars of a biological genus: the influences of inorganic and organic nature are brought to bear upon individuals, to which each reacts according to the characteristics of the genus, and the sum of individual reactions is then history. What is naturalistic in this is that human beings' modes of reaction are derived from the notion of individuals belonging to a biological genus, without taking into consideration those moments through which the individual is determined not by nonhuman nature, but by the developing society and by the encroaching social patterns. Society has its own laws. Absent an investigation of these laws, one can no more understand human beings than one can understand society without individuals or individuals without nonhuman nature.

The exclusively biological conception of human beings, no less in the case of Machiavelli than of anyone else, corresponds to a naturalistic conception of nature, in which nature is essentially viewed as something that "surrounds" and determines human beings, and not as something determined, shaped, and changed by the latter. What we call nature is dependent upon human beings in a twofold sense: first, humanity's process of development continuously transforms nature through the course of civilization; second, the very conceptual elements through which we give content to the word "nature" depend upon the epoch in which humanity finds itself. In other words, the object of the knowledge of nature, like this knowledge itself, is conditioned. Hence the naive acceptance of natural laws and of the concept of nature determined by those laws as an absolute starting point for all explanations is similarly naturalistic. What nature is depends just as much on the life process of human beings as, conversely, this life process depends on nature. The same holds for the relationship between individual and society; we cannot recognize the content of either side of this relationship apart from the determinations of the other, and all of these determinations are themselves not fixed but have their own history. Initial steps toward the overcoming of naturalism, i.e., toward the recognition of specifically social laws, are found in Machiavelli partly in his doctrine of the necessary succession of governmental forms, and partly in his chapters where conflicts between classes are presented as decisive for cultural advances. But the fact remains that he did not fruitfully apply these insights into the driving forces of society to his principal ideas, for he thought he could explain even the activity of classes, along with political life in general, entirely in terms of isolated individuals.

2. Natural Law and Ideology

Machiavelli, the first modern philosopher of history, championed the ascent of civil society. The principles of his examination of history oriented themselves toward the advancement and development of this rising sector. During his time, a unified Italian nation was required in order to make the Italian bourgeoisie competitive. Yet Machiavellianism is characteristic of all countries that required a strong, centralized government in order to eliminate the barriers posed by the constraints of a fettered medieval economy and the associated vestiges of feudalism. Such governments had to overcome recalcitrant and disruptive elements. On top of all the human horror and misery that always accompanies periods of transition, relentless force was further required to make unhampered, secure, and uniformly regulated commerce possible—in short, to clear the way for a bourgeois order whose territorial domain was to be as extensive and autonomous as possible. It was with Machiavellian principles that Richelieu created the centralized nation-state in France. Napoleon, whose historical mission was to introduce civil security and order after the turmoil of the French Revolution (and who was left in the lurch by the French bourgeoisie immediately after fulfilling this function), wrote an essay on Machiavelli. Fichte, who advocated bourgeois freedom and values, wrote a defense of Machiavelli. The philosophy in which the German bourgeoisie (whose economic and political development was being impeded throughout the prerevolutionary period) found the clearest expression of its ideas was that of Hegel, who not only found himself to be in agreement with Machiavelli on many practical and factual matters, but who personally held him in the utmost esteem. Hobbes was the son of a country that, during his lifetime, was in the process of laying the foundations for the unimpeded development of civil society. In contrast to Machiavelli, whose ideas initially had no actual influence in his own country, Hobbes's philosophy of history may be taken to be just as much a cause as an effect of praxis.

Hobbes was born in 1588, the year of the destruction of the Armada. Son of a modestly educated preacher, he was to become one of the most important philosophers in modern history. Though a devotee of Machiavelli in the domain of the philosophy of history, in all other disciplines he was a student of the great Francis Bacon, who—in contrast to views widely held today—must be given due regard as a thinker who first brought many of the seminal ideas of modern philosophy to the fore. The life of Hobbes, spanning some 91 years, largely coincides with the period of the final struggle between the English bourgeoisie and feudalism. He had occasion to see how the crown required unconditional authority in order to save itself from falling; yet he also saw how, for the sake of preserving its continued existence, it had to devote this authority to "national" interests, i.e., to those bourgeois interests in England that at the time essentially coincided with those of the Protestant plutocracy.

Hobbes witnessed the last part of Elizabeth's reign, the weak rule of James I, and, ultimately, the fall of the English crown, this last the result of the royal family's single-minded political goal of augmenting dynastic power. He always personally considered monarchy the best form of government, and consequently had to flee London and seek refuge in France for eleven years when the "Long Parliament" convened in 1640. This personal conviction notwithstanding, he never strayed from the view—quite in the spirit of Machiavelli—that the *form* of the state was relatively inconsequential when weighed against the factual existence of a strong sovereign authority of whatever sort. These factors explain how Hobbes as an emigrant could tutor and eventually even befriend the exiled Prince of Wales (the future King Charles II, who at the time was holding court at St. Germain), yet subsequently have a falling out with him over Hobbes's recognition of Cromwell's republican government. Indeed, he returned to London under the amnesty of Parliament as a loyal citizen of the new regime toward the end of 1651. When Charles II upon his own return made reconciliatory gestures toward Hobbes, the king doubtless knew that Hobbes had remained a monarchist. Yet this he was only as a private individual, so to speak—as a philosopher he was the servant of whatever strong government happened to be at the helm and considered it his highest duty and mission to strengthen the government's power. He devoted his political science neither to a monarch nor to a republic; rather, like Machiavelli, he devoted it to the strongest political power.[28]

The Florentine statesman, in whose work abstract considerations or foundational questions are only rarely to be found, never moved beyond a naive understanding of the analogy between politics and physics, between the modes of explanation of natural science and of history. In contrast, Hobbes's philosophical system, one of the most brilliant and subtle intellectual documents of its time, is essentially based on a theoretical analysis of this analogy in the structure of natural and social formations, i.e., of physical systems and the union of human beings in a state. His doctrines concerning the state and history cannot be understood without some knowledge of his conception of nature, itself founded on the mechanistic understanding of nature with which the rising new society confronted the medieval cosmos.

Galileo had traced back all events to mechanical events, indeed to movements of the smallest particles of matter. Even the most complicated processes, such as the transformation of great masses, he attributed to the motion of atoms. Against the medieval idea—still encountered today in the "natural" conception of the world—that the state of rest is the original and, as it were, appropriate state of all things, Galileo's doctrine that uniform and linear motion was to be taken as the most elementary physical concept—or, more generally, that rest and motion had to be regarded as relative—was a world-historical achievement. According to Galileo, it is not motion as such that is to be explained, but rather acceleration, deceleration, and change of direction. As a consequence, the God of Aristotle, the unmoved mover of the world, the prime mover and at the same time the preserver of motion, became superfluous, at least in natural philosophy.

In a radical fashion, Hobbes gave full systematic expression to this new view that was established during the Renaissance. According to him, all science is knowledge of causes, and therefore must never rest content with the mere determination or description of facts. The causes of all changes of bodies are movements of their parts. However, Hobbes was not, strictly speaking, an atomist. For this school, whose adherents included Hobbes's friend Gassendi, everything that exists consists of final, immutable, indivisible, independent particles—the atoms. These atoms have specific properties such as weight and impermeability, if no actual sensible qualities. Hobbes did not acknowledge any such smallest particles of matter: for him, small and large are relative concepts that only have meaning in relation to the apprehending subject. Even what appears to the physicist to be the smallest particle is not necessarily such in any absolute sense. Yet Hobbes was convinced that nothing that has its place in space is real as such. Such real entities he referred to not as matter (which was for him just an abstract and general idea that was too reminiscent of Aristotle) but as bodies. Everything that can rightly be referred to as substance or reality is a body; all changes were movements of the components of bodies, which must in turn be traced to ever smaller submotions. Extension and shape are fixed properties of bodies; color, odor, sound are merely subjective modes of apprehending them. The supreme laws of motion are the supreme laws of the natural world—and no other world exists.

What distinguishes the human being—which for Hobbes is also a mechanism consisting of bodily parts—from all other bodies in nature is not that there are any human processes that obey other than mechanical laws; rather, it is distinguished solely by the greater complexity of its organization and functions. Hobbes compared the heart to a spring, nerves to strings, and joints to wheels, which all set the body in motion. Although Hobbes may have been occasionally bothered by the problem that the human being must at minimum be distinguished from some of the other bodies by virtue of its consciousness, and even though he approached this problem from various angles at several points in his life, he nonetheless never really addressed the issue in a clear or consistent manner. He vacillated between the doctrine that even sensations and processes of consciousness are as much completely material processes as everything else, and the view that certain processes could alternatively be considered as either physical or psychological (in which case it is not really a matter of any real differences, but only of different possibilities of classification). In any case, he was of the opinion that the fact of consciousness warrants no other explanation of human activity than a mechanical one; in any case, human movements are to be understood in precisely the same manner as, for instance, movements of particles are understood as the causes of movements of the atmosphere.

The relation of the state to the individual is the same as the relation of the latter to the material components of its body, i.e., the same as the relation of any physical system to its material components.

For as in a watch, or some such small engine, the matter, figure, and motion of the wheels, cannot well be known, except it be taken in sunder, and viewed in parts; so to make a more curious search into the rights of States, and duties of Subjects, it is necessary, (I say not to take them in sunder, but yet that) they be so considered, as if they were dissolved, (i.e.) that wee rightly understand what the quality of humane nature is, in what matters it is, in what not fit to make up a civill government, and how men must be agreed among themselves, that intend to grow up into a well-grounded State.[29]

For Hobbes, just as one must examine the properties of the smallest particles of matter in order to understand large objects, and just as in physics one must probe ever further into the infinitely small, so too must the formation and maintenance of the state, the larger entity, be explained in terms of the properties of its smallest constitutive parts, namely human beings.

This move in Hobbes's systematically grounded theory illuminates even more sharply the fundamental error of Machiavelli's explanation of history. All social changes in the various spheres of the state, politics, religion, ethics, and law are to be explained on the basis of the notion of the isolated individual, whose properties Hobbes, by means of a deliberate analogy to the properties of inorganic bodies, takes to be eternal and immutable. Each of these individuals reacts to external movements out of unconditional necessity. Viewed internally, human reactions manifest themselves as specific experiences, feelings, and instinctual impulses. Hobbes's anthropology is based on the fundamental idea that all affects, the basis of our action, are strictly necessary consequences of mechanical processes within our body and within the external world as well. The functions of the human body are set into motion and sustained by the heart, whose action in turn is sustained by the continuous impulses produced by certain materials during respiration. The heart pumps blood through the body and in this manner sustains the activity of the organs. Whatever stimulates circulation causes pleasure, and whatever impedes it causes aversion. Aesthetic delight, for instance, is determined by ethereal vibrations emanating from luminous bodies, which are transmitted through the retina, the optic nerve, the brain, and finally to the heart, at which point pleasure is produced. Movements which originate in the natural environment, or in the interior of the body itself, are in every respect the causes which regularly lead to pleasure and aversion. With lawlike necessity, furthermore, the individual's acts of will arise from pleasure and aversion, or considered physically, from the stimulation and impediment of the circulation. In an exact analogy to mechanics, the "movements" of the soul are divided up between those which attract and those which repel. Under the former are classified love, desire, and the wish to acquire and to keep; under the latter, pain, antipathy, and fear. To the extent that common sense makes the distinction between mental and corporeal pain, this is only due to an unawareness of the fact that, in both instances, what is at issue is qualitatively the same: the only difference is that in corporeal pain only a circumscribed part of the body is affected, whereas in mental pain the whole body is affected in its function. It is along these lines that Hobbes divides up all passions between those directed at attraction and acquisition and those that resist or repel.

Hence there can be no room for so-called freedom of the will in this philosophy; and indeed, textbooks on the history of philosophy usually portray Hobbes as having this view. Yet more important than this is the distinction Hobbes makes between freedom of the will and freedom of action; this was his fundamental contribution to the problem of freedom. The doctrine of freedom of the will—which in the heyday of Scholasticism had not yet acquired the significance that it would later attain during the Reformation and Counter-Reformation in express opposition to the growth of the new natural sciences—is based upon the proposition that human action cannot be explained in terms of natural causes. On the contrary, according to Hobbes, there exists within us a faculty [*Instanz*] that possesses the *liberum arbitrium indifferentiae,* which realizes a particular possibility of action out of the many that are available; it does this not in conformity to natural law, but of its own accord—which is to say, arbitrarily. At stake in this doctrine is not just a religious interest but a social interest as well. Without freedom of choice it becomes difficult to defend the notion of one's accountability to God, or of damnation either in this world or the hereafter. Scholars of jurisprudence have only recently taken it upon themselves to decry the standard practice of justifying the legal system in terms of the doctrine of freedom of the will; yet this only gives us occasion to observe that Hobbes (and afterward the Enlightenment) had long since refuted this theory with powerful arguments.

Should a particular case come to our attention in which the instinctual causes of a behavior are unknown to us, this need not lead us to conclude that the reaction in question cannot be causally related in any way. For Hobbes and the Enlightenment, the theoretical assumption of positive freedom in lieu of an explanation amounts rather to an artificial restriction of the sciences, whose very nature precludes ever stopping short at any point in research. In those cases where the mechanisms of human action are unknown to us, it is true that we have no right dogmatically to construct causal chains of events—yet neither may we block off further inquiry on account of some notion of freedom which has the effect of prematurely setting limits to science. For, writes Hobbes,

LIBERTY, that we may define it, is nothing else but an *absence of the lets, and hindrances of motion,* as water shut up in a vessell is therefore not at liberty, because the vessell hinders it from running out, which the vessell being broken, is *made free.* And every man hath more or lesse *liberty,* as he hath more or lesse space in which he employes himself: as he hath more *liberty,* who is in a large, then he that is kept in a close prison. And a man may be *free* toward one part, and yet not toward another, as the traveller is bounded on this, and that side with hedges, or stone walls, lest he spoyle the vines, or corne, neighbouring on the high way. And these kinde of lets are externall, and absolute; in which sense all *Servants,* and *Subjects* are *free,* who are not fetter'd and imprisoned. There are others which are arbitrary, which doe not absolutely hinder motion, but by accident; to wit, by our own choyce, as he that is in a ship is not so hindered, but he may caste himselfe into the Sea, if he will: and here also the more wayes a man may move himselfe, the more *liberty* he hath, and herein consists civill *liberty*. . . . But this priviledge *free subjects* and *sonnes* of a family, have above *servants*, (in every government, and family, where servants are) that they may both undergoe the more honourable offices of the City or family, and also enjoy a larger possession of things superfluous. And herein layes the difference between a *free subject,* and a *servant,* that he is FREE indeed, who serves his City onely; but a SERVANT is he who also serves his fellow subject: all other liberty is an exemption from the Lawes of the City, and proper only to those that bear Rule.[30]

These remarks of Hobbes clearly show that he is not speaking of the freedom to will, but of the freedom to act. Freedom of the will in the idealistic sense does not exist for him, but only freedom from hindrances which restrict our possibilities of action. Such freedom varies according to the individual, situation, and class position. Our actions are restricted not only by external obstacles but by internal ones as well, e.g., by the consequences anticipated from action. No ocean traveler will jump into the sea if he is "normal," even though this path is open to him. To the uninterested passerby, it is irrelevant whether entry into a house is physically blocked off or punishable by death. In both cases, which Hobbes divides into indirect and direct hindrances, the will itself is not free but determined by a series of causes.

The metaphysical freedom of the will rejected by Hobbes would be an element [*Moment*] which would unite people from all stations in life without exception: rich and poor, infirm and robust, young and old. It would be a joint property [*ein gemeinsames Vermögen*] in the sense of theology, which views all people equally as children of God, and would have a similar meaning for the Enlightenment, which emphasizes the equality of all people for political reasons. On the other hand, freedom of action, which Hobbes does acknowledge, differs from case to case; in his treatment of it, greatest prominence is accorded to disparities in the social situation. In the last quotation, mention was made, with respect to the servant and his lord, of "things superfluous," i.e., luxury. Should both servant and lord possess the will to take pleasure in such things, or to derive enjoyment with their aid, then they are completely indistinguishable according to the concept of idealistic freedom: the purely philosophical debate, as to whether their desire is in this sense free, pertains equally to both. The theoretical result of such a debate indiscriminately unites the two under a common concept and attributes to both either a common dignity or a common tragedy, and hence to that extent diverges from reality, "goes beyond it." By comparison, the Hobbesian concept of freedom leads to reality. For the physical mechanist and the follower of Machiavelli, it is a matter of a priori certainty that the servant and his lord must desire and will by their very nature. But when the lord takes his pleasure, he can enjoy it to the fullest; were the servant to satisfy the same yearning, he would pay for it with his life. It is this difference in freedom that matters in social reality; in any case, the other concept of freedom contributes nothing to an examination of this difference.

In order to understand Hobbes's inquiry into how human beings (whose actions, as we have seen, are to be explained in terms of causes) unite themselves in a state, create culture—in short, make their history—it needs to be emphasized that Hobbes did not primarily want to depict the actual emergence of the state. His reasoning, rather, which is characteristic of many philosophers of history from Rousseau to Kant and beyond along the lines of the doctrine of the social contract, leads him to the following: in order to discover the actual causes which in all times and places occasion the existence of the state, we need not study history any more than the scientist, according to Hobbes, needs to map out how something in nature actually comes into being in order to be able to identify the causes that gave rise to it. For the physicist knows the properties of the material particles of which nature is composed, apart from their relationship within a particular body. This is the reason why, based on their knowledge of the properties of the constituent parts (in this case, the laws of motion of matter), physicists can construct conceptual models of how things physically come into being. In like manner, we need only reflect upon individuals in abstraction from their relations within the state—which is to say, how they would have to act in the absence of a state, or in a "natural" state—in order to identify the causes that lead to the formation of the state. The physics of the time regarded the properties of particles, corpuscles, or atoms as the key to understanding the objects formed by them, as well as to understanding how they caused the world to emerge out of chaos, i.e., out of matter thought to be intrinsically relationless. The idea, then, was similarly to abstract from the social relations of individuals, such that the state could be seen to have emerged out of a set of relations within which the isolated individual was the basic unit. In order to understand the historically given state, it was thought that one need only look at how relationless individuals in the "state of nature" [*im "Naturstaat"*] were impelled by virtue of their innate qualities to forge relationships and consolidate them in the state.

For Hobbes, therefore, neither world history nor natural history, properly understood, should be confused with the actual science of politics; on the contrary, the latter is taken to be constructed out of pure thought. Its principles can be defined as follows: since human beings are only motivated either by pleasure or aversion, then life must be the highest good, and death the greatest evil. In the state of nature [*Naturzustande*], the life of the individual is highly precarious. Although each person has a natural right to everything in such a state of lawlessness, one must also continually expect to be robbed of everything by someone stronger, or occasionally even by someone who is weaker. Indeed, it is even possible for the weaker person to rob the stronger of the highest good, i.e., of life. The vitalistic romantic claim that, in nature, the biologically superior will always triumph over the inferior, is wrong. The state of nature [*natürliche Zustand*] is characterized by the boundless appetite of the individual—as well as by the individual's fear of everyone else. The "bellum omnium in omnes" reigns supreme. From such fear arises the need for security, and from the latter arises the willingness to forego unlimited (and continually threatened) freedom in order to be able to peacefully enjoy a measure of limited freedom. And so the social contract arises out of horror and hope, a compromise between our boundless aggression and our boundless anxiety.

The original contract could not have been between some government and the people it governed, since no government exists in the state of nature; rather, it was agreed to amongst the future citizens of the state. On the strength of their concurrent will, individuals transfer their sovereignty to *one* person or to *one* assembly, which is henceforth empowered by this contract to exercise authority. All the power and might of those who entered into the contract is placed at the disposal of the sovereign, whose will represents the will of all. Authority hence has its origin in the people, and its basis in the will of all individuals, or at least in that of the majority of the originally assembled group. Beyond this origin, however, individuals have no freedom whatsoever vis-à-vis the state (i.e., the sovereign), to whose laws they must wholly submit: the will of the state is identical with the will of the ruler, whether it has its origin in a single person (in a monarchy) or in a presidency (in a republic). As an unqualified absolutist, Hobbes regards any limitation placed upon the highest authority as contrary to the intent of the original contract. Of course, the contract also ascribes responsibilities and duties to whomever holds the power of state; but citizens cannot bring such obligations to bear against the ruler, who is accountable only to God and Reason.

Once such authority has been relinquished and handed over to the sovereign, no individual can revoke this transfer of power, even if he can manage to get many others to join forces with him. Hobbes develops here the analogy from natural philosophy between the state, whose source is convention, and mathematical concepts, which are established by convention. One has the freedom of determination, to define one's concepts as one wishes, only once. As soon as general agreement has been achieved, however, it is no longer subject to alteration. To contravene definitions in geometry is to commit an error; to contravene the laws of the state is to be a criminal or a rebel. Geometrical conventions were ultimately established in order to build machines; likewise, the convention of the original contract was arrived at in order to erect the greatest machine of all: the state. The function of this gigantic machine is to hold at bay the horror and anarchy of the original condition, to keep down all the monsters capable of endangering civil peace and security, above all the "behemoth": the monster of rebellion. Yet in truth, the state itself is none other than the most powerful monster, the "leviathan": the "mortal god" that governs as it pleases, and before whom the will of all other mortals keeps dumb.

Thus for Hobbes, the state arises of necessity from the intrinsic character of individuals. This derivation also provides natural law's basis for fundamental political obligations. While positive law is identical with the actual laws of the state, for Hobbes natural law refers to everything that necessarily ensues from human nature for individuals' action, insofar as it involves rational reflection. Moreover, it applies to everything which, in his own words, we must do or omit "for the constant preservation of Life, and Members, as much as in us lyes."[31] The task set by natural law [*die naturrechtliche Aufgabe*] for the state (which itself is supposed to arise from natural law [*natürlichen Gesetz*]) is to be the guarantor of civil peace.

When the professors and students at Oxford condemned Hobbes's writings and burned his books, they were well aware of the threat posed by theories of the social contract and of natural law. The medieval belief that those who governed (and by extension, the whole system of guilds and estates) were all ordained by God was irreconcilable with the view that both state and society derived their existence and justification from the will of the people, whose welfare was supposed to be their whole purpose. The feudal authorities had to justify the backward social hierarchy and its institutions—as well as their own special rights, privileges, and high-handed ways—in terms of their sanctification by God and tradition. The "venerable" and the "divine" (later romanticism called it *"das organisch gewachsene"*) was defended in opposition to the emerging bourgeois rational determination of ends in terms of the greatest possible happiness for the greatest possible number. Along with the classical contractarians and theorists of modern natural law such as Grotius and Pufendorf, Christian Wolff and Rousseau—not to mention Fichte as well as most of the great bourgeois philosophers until the beginning of the nineteenth century—Hobbes uses the original contract and natural law [*natürlichen Recht*] to undergird the demands of those classes wishing to free themselves from feudal forms that had become fetters. For according to these doctrines, even rulers have certain obligations. Although they need not submit to any bourgeois authority—for Hobbes, this would be logically excluded by the definition of the sovereign—rulers must indeed satisfy the spirit of the contract. According to Hobbes, the ruler has to provide for more than mere domestic tranquillity, even for more than just the bare preservation of life; the ruler must also proclaim, promulgate, and uphold laws whose aim is the most pleasurable existence possible for all citizens.[32]

Hobbes closely examines the way in which governmental measures appertaining to bourgeois welfare fit the situation at the time. In order to promote business and trade, which at that time were still just beginning to be developed, state measures in support of such activities had to be accorded far greater latitude than would be granted a few centuries later. Mercantilistic politics is essentially based on the

necessity of the state's active engagement in and nurturing of bourgeois business operations. Hobbes derives such claims from the natural rights of the original contract [*urvertraglichem Naturrecht*]. For
instance, he writes: "Since there are three things only, the *fruits of the
earth and water, Labour,* and *Thrift,* which are expedient for the enrich-
ing of subjects, the duty of Commanders in chief, shall be conversant
onely about those three. For the first, those lawes will be usefull which
countenance the arts that improve the increase of the earth, and water,
such as are *husbandry,* and *fishing.* For the second, all Lawes against
idlenesse, and such as quicken industry, are profitable"[33] (in this context we may also make mention of the laws against begging and va-
grancy, by means of which the unemployed were pressed into the
terrible conditions in the manufactories, as well as of subsidies, for
shipping in particular). Apart from navigation, Hobbes mentions as
especially important "the *Mechanicks,* (under which I comprehend all
the arts of the most excellent workmen) and the *Mathematicall sciences,*
the fountains of navigatory and mechanick employments."[34] It is expressly stated that "because such lawes are beneficiall to the ends above
specified, it belongs also to the Office of the supreme Magistrates, to
establish them."[35]

Hobbes's understanding of the bourgeois doctrine that the welfare
of the state must be the highest law, and in general the sense in which
the doctrine was understood by many of its earlier advocates, has since
been greatly modified by modern developments. While formerly the
emphasis had been placed primarily on the need to promote the welfare of the state, since this was taken to be the only way in which the
welfare of the individual could be secured, today this ethical position
in many respects signifies quite the opposite: the individual means
nothing as compared with the whole, on the contrary, the individual
is supposed to sacrifice himself and his life for the whole. The reason
for this transformation in the function of the concept of the state's
welfare, for this reifying and absolutizing of the concept of the state,
is to be sought primarily in the following circumstance: in the time
of Hobbes, the challenges to the state and the legislative demands
made by the bourgeoisie were made entirely in the spirit of raising
the material condition of what was far and away the largest sector of
society. In the course of history since that time, state interest and general interest have, by and large, hardly been equivalent concepts.

Consequently, it has often been difficult to muster support for complying with the edicts of the state on the basis of the latter's identification with the real interests of the individual. If, in the concept of the common weal, ends and means were originally linked in a naive relational unity, in the realm of theory it has gradually come to pass that the state has become an end in itself, reified into an independent entity.

To be sure, lack of clarity was characteristic of the earlier doctrines. The state as an undifferentiated national unit on the one hand, and the state as an amalgam of disparate social classes with disparate interests on the other—or in other words, state and society—still remain to be conceptually unraveled. However, in reality these differences are continuing to develop; from the mercantilist period to the present day they have been making themselves felt ever more sharply as contradictions of actual life, even if the conceptual matrices of numerous theories remain tied to Hobbes. The philosophical depreciation of evidence taken from reality, which in contemporary philosophy is being carried out principally amongst the various offshoots of phenomenology, may be viewed in the context of these problems. Even if the unity of state and society is no longer salvable factually, one nonetheless claims to see such a social form as a pristine essence. In thought [*in der Idee*], there is a tendency to embrace as "truth" that which is not susceptible to verification in reality, a tendency to look down upon mere "crude facts" that may indeed deviate from the idea, but which supposedly offer no evidence against it. It can nonetheless be demonstrated that state and society are distinct from one another. Society is not homogeneous but internally rent; and the role of the state depends upon which social groups it objectively represents in a given situation.

Hobbes expressly declares the absolutist regime to be a prerequisite for the well-being of all. Yet his naïveté is most tellingly revealed by his reluctance to make this the primary basis for a straightforward argument in favor of such a regime. Rather, he deems it equally necessary to deduce his position on the basis of natural law, particularly the obligations of the social contract. In essence, Hobbes substitutes natural law for the medieval divine commandment. There was an element within modern philosophy, right up to the eighteenth century, that sought to sanctify the new order by appeal to nature and reason, much as the old order had been consecrated by a steadfast religiosity. Such a consecration was crucial for the philosophers not only in relation to their reading audience but in relation to themselves as well; this is not a consequence of purposeful deliberation, but of a socially operative psychological mechanism. In a philosophical debate that spanned from Hobbes to the Enlightenment, the central question was whether state institutions were to be taken as having been established by God or by natural reason. Even if the latter supposition was indeed the more progressive at the time, the fact remains that both postulations are illusory, and that both conceal the real reasons for the rise of the state. The founding of the state in terms of natural law and social contract contains the veiled notion that the state was a product of the natural and vital interests of human beings. The fact that such interests are not uniform, that they can become divergent and transformed, and that consequently the state can change from an expression of objective universal interests into an expression of particular interests—such an insight is obscured by the myth of the contract. Machiavelli's doctrine of the change and deterioration of the forms of the state, in which revolution was not just a crime but a historical necessity as well, is more comprehensive and balanced than the rigid doctrine of natural rights of Hobbes and his successors. For this latter doctrine is blind to the transformations in the depths of social life; moreover, it just bolsters the belief (which has since grown even stronger) in the eternal persistence of the state of affairs proclaimed by the philosophical theorists of the state.

In this respect, then, Hobbes proves to be inferior to the instincts of the great Renaissance politician. Yet he set forth Machiavelli's fragmentary observations on the relationship between politics and nature in a systematic form. At least part of the reason why accusations of immorality, as well as the hostility that arises from unveiling the actual connections between thought and reality, have not been directed at Hobbes with even greater intensity than at Machiavelli is that, as a function of their unsystematic manner of organization, Machiavelli's books have been of greater accessibility than the more abstract accounts of Hobbes. Hobbes certainly has just as sharp a tongue as that of the Italian; indeed, Hobbes's causticity is thrown into even greater relief as a consequence of his theoretical comprehensiveness. Perhaps hostile attention was also diverted away from Hobbes by the fact that

Spinoza, whose *Tractatus theologico-politicus* shortly afterward shook the world, focused on the same key questions and resolved them in a manner similar to that of Hobbes. Already advanced in his years, Hobbes read Spinoza's book shortly after it appeared and—most probably out of fear of the still smoldering ash heaps in England—indicated in only the vaguest of terms that Spinoza's treatise echoed the thoughts of his own works, only in bolder language.

Drawing upon his general philosophical principles, Hobbes arrives at conclusions about politics and culture as a whole that converge with a number of other thinkers' views of the philosophy of history. One might call this the materialistic tendency in the philosophy of history of the rising bourgeoisie. It is characterized by Machiavelli, Spinoza, Pierre Bayle, and Mandeville, as well as by certain radical thinkers of the French Enlightenment, such as Holbach, Helvétius, and Condorcet.

The chain of thought runs as follows: apart from natural objects which extend in space, there is no reality. Human beings themselves are of a piece with nature, and are thus just as subject to its general laws as all other beings. History is nothing more than the account of a series of events in human nature, just as the rest of natural history describes events within other realms of nature. True knowledge always refers to natural reality, which is to be found as much in inorganic, vegetative, animal, and human nature as in individuals and the society they constitute. As organizational forms of individuals, state and society (which have yet to be conceptually distinguished from each other) belong to reality as well. Like any other functioning machine, they must be considered real since they are themselves a relationship of real elements. Even the problem of the connection between body and soul does not conceptually take us beyond the natural world; for there exist no self-contained souls, disconnected from or independent of the body. Nor are there ghosts or spirits, nor angels nor devils, which are to be taken as anything more than nature: all human actions—unconscious or conscious, voluntary or involuntary—are subject to the necessity of natural law.

But if such is the case, then the question arises as to how ethical, metaphysical, and religious notions arose in the first place, how belief in the existence of unnatural and otherworldly things held sway over people for millennia. What gave rise to these peculiar and erroneous ideas, and to what end are they sustained? These questions fundamentally bring to bear the problem of ideology, a problem that was first addressed with adequate methods in the post-Hegelian period. To be sure, the solution of Hobbes and his successors (and adumbrated by Machiavelli as well) was rather simple: all ideas which deviate from the exact theory of human and nonhuman nature are invented by human beings in order to dominate other human beings. Cunning and deception stand by the cradle of all these ideas. Their cause is the will to dominate on the one hand and ignorance on the other; their purpose is the maintenance of the power of those who propagate them. Consistent with the antagonism toward the form of society these modern theories oppose, it is the church and priesthood that end up appearing as the authors of these errors in the history of ideas. This doctrine enters the scene with a universal historical claim. Its scope was intended to extend even beyond all the social strata of past history that ever exerted a determining influence on government—for Machiavelli, Hobbes, and Spinoza are united in the view that these methods were indispensable to any conceivable form of social domination, which would therefore include even the new state. In fact, so they would argue, the state must seize the ideological instruments of power from the old authorities and turn them to its own use, albeit within prudent limitations. The fact that these thinkers made their shared view on the necessity of ideology into a general principle of the philosophy of history is surely a reason for their rejection in the later literature. Consider the following passage in *Leviathan:*

For I doubt not, but if it had been a thing contrary to any mans right of dominion, or to the interest of men that have dominion, *That the three Angles of a Triangle should be equall to two Angles of a Square;* that doctrine should have been, if not disputed, yet by the burning of all books of Geometry, suppressed, as farre as he whom it concerned was able.[36]

Hobbes produces closely detailed analyses of the advantages accruing to the clergy by religion; he relates even the most obscure philosophical doctrines of the Scholastics to real interests. An example of this is to be found in the first dialogue of *Behemoth,*[37] a book which treats this problem in a particularly characteristic manner. The interlocutors are called A and B. After a lengthy consideration of Scholasticism, A expounds on the question of what significance the adoption of Aristotelian philosophy is supposed to have had. This philosophy was also

made an ingredient in religion, as serving for a salve to a great many absurd articles, concerning the nature of Christ's body, and the estate of angels and saints in heaven; which articles they thought fit to have believed, because they brought some of them profit, and others reverence to the clergy, even to the meanest of them. For when they shall have made the people believe that the meanest of them can make the body of Christ; who is there that will not both show them reverence, and be liberal to them or to the Church, especially in the time of their sickness, when they think they make and bring unto them their Saviour?

B: But, what advantage to them, in these impostures, was the doctrine of Aristotle?

A: They have made more use of his obscurity than of his doctrine. For none of the ancient philosophers' writings are comparable to those of Aristotle, for their aptness to puzzle and entangle men with words, and to breed disputation, which must at last be ended in the determination of the Church of Rome. And yet in the doctrine of Aristotle, they made use of many points; as, first, the doctrine of *Separated Essences*.

B: What are *Separated Essences*?

A: Separated beings.

B: Separated from what?

A: From everything that is.

B: I cannot understand the being of any thing, which I understand not to be. But what can they make of that?

A: Very much, in questions concerning the nature of God, and concerning the estate of man's soul after death, in heaven, hell, and purgatory; by which you and every man know, how great obedience, and how much money they gain from the common people.—Whereas Aristotle holdeth the soul of man to be the *first giver of motion* to the body, and consequently to itself; they make use of that in the doctrine of *free will*. What, and how they gain by that, I will not say—

The discussion touches further on several other doctrines of Aristotle, including the differences between him and the Scholastics, and then suddenly takes the following turn:

B: I see what use they make of Aristotle's logic, physics, and metaphysics; but I see not yet how his politics can serve their turn.

A: Nor I. It has, I think, done them no good, though it has done us here much hurt by accident. For men, grown weary at last of the insolence of the priests, and examining the truth of those doctrines that were put upon them, began to search the sense of the Scriptures, as they are in the learned languages; and consequently (studying Greek and Latin) became acquainted with the democratical principles of Aristotle and Cicero, and from the love of their eloquence fell in love with their politics, and that more and more, till it grew into the rebellion we now talk of.

That which the radical Frenchmen of the eighteenth century wanted propagandistically to transform into a motor of historical events for the awakening bourgeoisie of their country was the very thing that had earlier struck Hobbes (in whose country the bourgeoisie had already secured for themselves a wide share of public power) as a direct, if pernicious, cause of previous historic events: enlightenment arising from material motives, which paves the way for revolution.

But unlike the French philosophers, who for the most part enter the historical scene storming the last bastions of feudalism, Hobbes heralds the dawn of the new order. Hence his immediate interest in this insight is to spell out its consequences for the new state. Since as a consequence of their instinctual predisposition, human beings are easily directed by means of moral and religious ideas, and since the past certainly shows such ideational influences to be an important instrument of rulers, it is essential that the state wrest this instrument from the powers of old and deliberately use it for its own ends.

According to Hobbes, in the Middle Ages this kind of influence on ideas was brought to bear primarily through the universities. Great numbers of scholars were trained at these universities; they had to master no small amount of intellectual skills in order to maintain their status as the only group qualified to render judgments on the most critical human issues. At the universities they learned

the trick of imposing what they list upon their readers, and declining the force of true reason by verbal forks; I mean, distinctions that signify nothing, but serve only to astonish the multitude of ignorant men. As for the understanding readers, they were so few, that these new sublime doctors cared not what they thought. These schoolmen were to make all the articles of faith, which the Popes from time to time should command to be believed. . . . From the universities also it was, that all preachers proceeded, and were poured out into city and country, to terrify the people into an absolute obedience to the Pope's canons.[38]

This tool, whose obvious importance has been demonstrated throughout the course of history, must now be placed in the service

Beginnings of the Bourgeois Philosophy of History

of a new and noble cause: the bourgeois state. According to Hobbes, internal peace for the most part depends on the ideas instilled in people. Thus for Hobbes it follows that scholarly activity at universities, the most important sites where dominant ideas are inculcated, must be organized in a manner consistent with the aims of the state. What the universities achieved for the church in the Middle Ages, they should now achieve for the powerful new nation-state, which is of course the best form of government from the perspective of natural rights. Hobbes is unequivocal on this point:

Those errors which [are] inconsistent with the quiet of the Commonweal, have crept into the mindes of ignorant men, partly from the Pulpit, partly from the daily discourses of men, who by reason of little employment, otherwise, doe finde leasure enough to study; and they got into these mens mindes by the teachers of their youth in publique schooles. Wherefore also, on the other side, if any man would introduce sound Doctrine, he must begin from the *Academies:* There, the true, and truly demonstrated foundations of civill Doctrine are to be laid, wherewith young men being once endued, they may afterward both in private and publique instruct the vulgar. And this they will doe so much the more cheerfully, and powerfully, by how much them selves shall be more certainly convinced of the truth of those things they profess, and teach.[39]

The marvelous simplicity with which these views are expressed is even more in evidence in his discussion of what public institutions of learning should be teaching in the areas of ethics and the exposition of religion. Since it was just at that time that the interests of the state he was promoting corresponded to those of the social strata in England that enjoyed the best economic prospects, he was in a position to strongly advance his proposal that the security of the state be openly presented to students as the one and only legal basis for all individuals' obligations. Since the distinction between state and society had yet to be recognized, there was a good deal of credibility to the proposition that all morality—to the extent that it had not already been deduced from natural law as a bourgeois virtue of sociability—was to be seen as identical with the laws enacted by the state. Otherwise it wouldn't have been possible for Hobbes to continue to overlook that which had eluded Machiavelli: the effective use of ideational instruments of power, whose usage is inherited from the past, cannot dispense with the mysterious obscurity that in the past had cloaked their purpose. For Hobbes,

the state is identical with the guarantee of the greatest possible prosperity for the greatest possible number of its citizens. It should be no
surprise, then, that in those instances where the state fails to meet this
condition, which consequently puts it in greatest need of its instruments of power, Hobbes's method of laying bare the connections between the state's power and intellectual commodities [*ideelen Gütern*]
yields the most dire of consequences. He had himself claimed that a
condition of the success of public instructors was a firm conviction in
the truth of what they taught and promulgated. Yet this idea takes on
a peculiar twist in regard to the historical use of truth as an instrument of power. In fact, there seems to be something of an alliance
between truth and ascending classes. Truth, however, is labile as well
as unfaithful. It gradually extracts itself from the ideas that attained
currency through the consolidation of these strata. Although the actual words, originally proclaimed with great conviction, may remain
the same, they come to be as much abandoned by truth as the "liberté,
égalité, fraternité" posted over the prisons of the French Republic.

Furthermore, there was never any doubt in Hobbes's mind that the
truth by itself was not enough to ensure the ruler's political survival.
When he says that the state must enlist the services of the church and
religion, he is talking about the state's exploitation of illusions—indeed he identifies knowledge with natural and political science. "I like
not the design of drawing religion into an art, whereas it ought to be
a law; and though not the same in all countries, yet in every country
indisputable."[40]

Hobbes believes it necessary that the state declare as a religion those
illusions most useful for its own purposes, make its form of worship a
matter of law, and (following the example of the English High Church)
sustain and extend it by means of state-sponsored ecclesiastics. Just as
priests had deliberately invented and maintained religion to serve their
own ends, reasoned Hobbes, it has now fallen to the state to do the
same thing: "The fear of invisible powers, whether it be invented or
handed down from tradition, is religion when established for the sake
of the state, and superstition when not established for the sake of the
state."[41] Hence fear, the most basic element of human nature, is to be
delivered by religion into the service of the state, principally to foster
obedience to the law, or more broadly, to induce the proper conduct
of the citizenry.

All that is required, both in faith and manners, for man's salvation is (I con-
fess) set down in Scripture as plainly as can be. *Children obey your parents in all
things: Servants obey your masters: Let all men be subject to the higher powers, whether
it be the King or those that are sent by him: Love God with all your soul, and your
neighbour as yourself:* are words of the Scripture, which are well enough understood; but neither children, nor the greatest part of men, do understand why
it is their duty to do so. They see not that the safety of the commonwealth,
and consequently their own, depends upon their doing it.[42]

Acceptance as an article of faith that Christ was the savior promised
in the Old Testament was for Hobbes a sufficient condition for salvation; for this makes one inclined to accept that obeying the commandments is the key to everlasting bliss. As we find at the conclusion
of the important first dialogue of *Behemoth,* "I am therefore of your
opinion, both that men may be brought to a love of obedience by
preachers and gentlemen that imbibe good principles in their youth
at the Universities, and also that we never shall have a lasting peace,
till the Universities themselves be in such manner . . . reformed; and
the ministers know they have no authority but what the supreme civil
power gives them."[43] This amounts to a conscious use of religion, the
"fear of invisible powers," to facilitate the control of society.

Quite in accord with the historical position of this early bourgeois
philosopher, Hobbes's style of thinking is marked not only by a marked
propensity toward stability but by an equal propensity to critically
penetrate social ideas and theories. As he himself wrote, "A private
man has alwaies the liberty, (because thought is free,) to beleeve, or
not beleeve in his heart, those acts that have been given out for Miracles, according as he shall see, what benefit can accrew by mens belief, to those that pretend, or countenance by them, and thereby
conjecture, whether they be Miracles, or Lies."[44] This view contains
an explosive historical dialectic at precisely the point when merely
"private" thoughts and those restricted to the belief in miracles acquire public efficacy as a sweeping critique of prevailing ideas.

The fundamental problem which Hobbes's philosophy of history
raises at this point is—as just mentioned above—that of ideology. This
concept (which in reality is a much richer one) is to be found in Hobbes's
texts in spirit if not by name. Yet he ends up reducing the concept to
the sum of those beliefs holding sway during a specific period in a
specific society that are particularly suited to maintain the form of

that society. Hobbes's view, not to mention that of Spinoza as well as the thinkers of the Enlightenment, may be roughly formulated as follows: the course of all previous history can be fully understood only if we take into account the direction of individuals by ideological means as one of the most important factors. During the late Middle Ages, it was primarily the nobility and the priesthood that were to be seen as having preserved a social formation by means of ideology; their predominance fundamentally depended on the long-term continuity of this formation. Ideology becomes contrasted with reason. The latter, which Hobbes frequently calls "right reason," is identical with science and natural law; it is the sum of all propositions based upon genuine insight.[45]

Hence for Hobbes and the Enlightenment, reason consisted of a series of cognitions that at any time can be extended on the basis of experience or as a consequence of logical thought. But the items in such a series are to be taken as established facts that, once discovered, should be unassailable and unalterable from that point forward. Such a view entails not only a concept of nature (whose validity is taken to be self-evident), but also a concept of morality and of the true interests of all people—a concept of universal validity through time and space. All categories associated with an idea of society and the state that were once recognized to be correct are deemed to be eternal categories. Hence history essentially appears as the process whereby humanity acquires full possession of reason, among the immediate consequences of which would be the best arrangement of society, which is aspired to as an ultimate state of affairs. Since the latter is determined by the principles of natural law—preservation of the general welfare by means of the ensured activity of individual egos—and since these principles formulate the basis of civil society, the objective significance of this theory is its conception of history as progress toward the ideal of bourgeois society, with its property arrangements and free competition. This process is measured against these thinkers' own historically conditioned ideas (which they nonetheless regard as timeless).

There is a distinction to be made here between Hobbes and the Enlightenment thinkers. The former naively assumes that reason was a completed whole that had been given from the very beginning, so to speak, and which has been concealed as a consequence of certain machinations, particularly tactics of confusion on the part of the church. Yet for the thinkers of the Enlightenment (with the exception of Rousseau), reason can only be acquired on the basis of socially organized experience—which on their view, of course, would include overcoming the difficulties posed by the ruling class. For Hobbes, knowledge is present from the beginning, much as the Bible would have it, obscured by human wrongdoing and consequently impeded in its efficacy. But for the Enlightenment, it is a natural law that ideology is present from the beginning, and can only be thrust aside in the course of the historical process.

Yet what unites all of these conceptions is the idea that reason remains forever the same, and that we are able, here and now, to grasp truth in all its manifold varieties for all time. Whether truth is an object toward which individuals draw closer or from which they distance themselves, it remains something untouched by history or human fortunes. Hence this theory, whose dubiousness first becomes clear in the philosophy of Hegel, exhibits a similarity with that which it rejects as ideological, namely religion: both promise to deliver absolute and final truth. It is simply taken for granted that the moment at which the theory itself appears has come into possession of the truth as such.

And so, naturally, modern philosophy considers its theory of nature and society to be definitive and final; just as naturally, it depicts history exclusively in black and white terms. All previously held convictions that stand in opposition to modern philosophy are attributed to deception, or error at best; past intellectual achievements are a product either of an impoverished conscience or of an impoverished understanding. To be sure, one can point to quite a number of medieval thinkers, and to even more thinkers of antiquity, whose ideas have certain things in common with current thinking. In contrast to their received status in the Middle Ages, for instance, one tends to heap encomia upon the likes of a Democritus or an Epicurus as a pioneer or a herald, or perhaps as chance occurrences of genius. But it is precisely this kind of assessment that reveals even more sharply the confidence of the belief in itself and in a transtemporal truth which, in contrast to the temporal and spatial world around us, one firmly possesses. What this has in common with the religious thinking criticized here is that ideas perceived at some remove are torn out of their original context, compared to one's own views, and then either cast aside or approved of—and through all this one never reaches the point of being able to grasp the historical role of such views. Just as the true believer sorted out heretics from saints on the basis of revelation taken to be eternal truth, bourgeois materialist philosophy distinguishes deceivers and fools from martyrs and sages based on its own "reason."

Evaluating cultural phenomena of the past with a curt thumbs-up or thumbs-down, simply comparing them instead of understanding them—such an attitude was portrayed by Hegel as follows:

The whole of the history of Philosophy becomes a battlefield covered with the bones of the dead; it is a kingdom not merely formed of dead and lifeless individuals, but of refuted and spiritually dead systems, since each has killed and buried the other. Instead of "Follow thou Me," here then it must indeed be said, "Follow thine own self"—that is, hold by thine own convictions, remain steadfast to thine own opinion, why adopt another? . . . But following upon what has gone before, it would rather seem that other words of Scripture are just as applicable to such a philosophy—the words which the Apostle Peter spoke to Ananias: "Behold the feet of them that shall carry thee out are at the door." Behold the philosophy by which thine own will be refuted and displaced shall not tarry long as it has not tarried before. . . . The facts within [the history of philosophy] are not adventures and contain no more romance than does the history of the world. They are not a mere collection of chance events, of expeditions of wandering knights, each going about fighting, struggling purposelessly, leaving no results to show for all his efforts. Nor is it so that one thing has been thought out here, another there.[46]

Whatever happens, every individual is a child of his time; so philosophy too is its own time apprehended in thoughts. It is just as absurd to fancy that a philosophy can transcend its contemporary world as it is to fancy that an individual can overleap his own age, jump over Rhodes.[47]

According to Hegel, we can grasp the meaning of the ideas that emerge in the course of history only after we understand their specific historical contexts, i.e., once we see their relation to all spheres of social life.

A nation's religion, its laws, its ethical life, the state of its knowledge, its arts, its judiciary, its other particular aptitudes and the industry by which it satisfies its needs, its entire destiny, and its relations with its neighbours in war and peace—all these are extremely closely connected. . . . What matters most is that the real nature of the relationship in question should be defined.[48]

It is true that such a connection was repeatedly asserted from Hobbes to the Enlightenment (Hegel himself reminds one of Montesquieu), but it was grasped only at the surface level. The point is made that all the life expressions of a society [*Volk*] interrelate, and that they are to be attributed to a *Volksgeist*; but no attempt is made to base a systematic explanation of the actual content of religious, metaphysical, or moral conceptions on the structure of the given society. Yet this is precisely the problem of ideology. It is correct to say that false consciousness exposes itself as such against the standard of real science [*Wissenschaft*]. But for purposes of historical knowledge, it is wholly inadequate to treat as mere errors those religious or metaphysical ideas that can no longer be brought into accord with the current state of knowledge, just as one discards a false hypothesis in the natural sciences as the error of some researcher. It doesn't even begin to make sense to attribute religion to the subjective contrivances of priests; the personal qualities assumed by Hobbes, among others, to be the motivating factors behind the priests and noblemen (especially the acquisitive drive) are psychical motives first developed in the context of bourgeois society. Although Hobbes clearly saw such motives operating all around him and was able to draw thoughtful conclusions from what he observed, the fact remains that such impulses are in no way characteristic of, for instance, the early Middle Ages.

The predominant ideas of an epoch have roots that go deeper than the ill intentions of certain individuals. Such ideas are endemic to a given social structure, whose outlines are given by the way in which individuals sustain themselves at the time. The basic process whereby primitive hunters or fishermen secure their existence dictates not only their material mode of life, but in a certain sense their intellectual horizon as well. Similarly, the form of life based upon this primitive level of development not only conditions the actual life of the individuals, but also has a significant influence on their knowledge of the external world, as well as on the content and structure of their general understanding of life. The same point applies to more differentiated forms of society: the intellectual life of individuals is bound up with the life process of the social body of which they are a part and which determines their activity. Reality is not a solid object, nor is consciousness a blank mirror which, as the Enlightenment would have it, could either be fogged up by the hot air of the ignorant or the malicious or polished by those who possess knowledge. On the contrary, the whole of reality is identical with the life process of humanity, in which neither nature, nor society, nor the relation between the two remain unaltered. This is why it is impossible to understand the content or nature of people's intellectual makeup without knowledge of the epoch in which they live, or indeed (leaving the primitive peoples aside) without knowing the specific position they occupy in the social production process. The vital functions necessary to sustain and further human existence have not been combined within every single individual since the time of the primitive hunters and fisherman; rather, such functions are distributed amongst the various groups within society. But this also entails the differentiation of the whole of thought [*geistige Leben*], which develops internal contradictions. Hence it is chimerical [*Konstruktion*] to speak of art, philosophy, and science in terms of a unified history of ideas that encompasses long stretches of time and that restricts itself to developmental trends that are purely intellectual.

Hobbes and the Enlightenment produced the first modern philosophies of history that broached the problem of ideology, i.e., how the social situation relates to prevailing ideas that come to be recognized as false. But rather than understanding ideology in terms of its contingency upon society, they stopped short at the psychology of the individual, with the end result that psychological determinants of the bourgeois world—such as private interest, shrewdness, the acquisitive drive, cheating, and profit—were made to appear as the content and purpose of medieval religiosity. But knowledge and ideology remain fairly undifferentiated within this religiosity, which in point of fact is the form of medieval reason—though this is revealed only by an examination of the whole social dynamic. Yet the static philosophy under consideration here essentially stops at the simple juxtaposition of "Reason" and ideology, without ever understanding either in terms of their historical roles. Had there been critical self-consciousness regarding the permanency of one's own set of conceptions, headway might have been made toward such a realization. One would have had to recognize the material and intellectual development of the preceding periods as a necessary prerequisite for the Enlightenment; the Enlightenment would have been, as Hegel put it, "enlightened about itself."[49] Moreover, the fundamental mutability of categories and their overall historical conditionedness would have become clear, and the rigid concept of reason of this period, an age that believed in itself as staunchly as did the Middle Ages, would have crumbled.

The theory that the building blocks of the intellect are historically conditioned does not lead to historical relativism. The relativity of a proposition and ideology are two rather different sorts of things. The limits to what may be rightly be called ideology are constantly set by our current state of knowledge.[50] The error of Hobbes and his successors was not that they took seriously the science of their time, or that they began to depict doctrines which were incompatible with their own as socially operative illusions. On the contrary, their error lay in hypostatizing their own stock of knowledge *in summa* as eternal reason, rather than recognizing their intellectual advances as yet another moment in the overall social process—which with the advance of history is subject not only to analysis but also to verification and, in certain cases, to change.

Having confidence in rigorous, conscientious thinking on the one hand, and being aware of the conditionedness of the content and structure of cognitions on the other—far from being mutually exclusive, both attitudes are necessarily of a piece. The fact that reason can never be certain of its perpetuity; or that knowledge is secure within a given time frame, yet is never so for all time; or even the fact that the stipulation of temporal contingency applies to the very body of knowledge from which it is derived—this paradox does not annul the truth of the claim itself. Rather, it is of the very essence of authentic knowledge never to be settled once and for all. This is perhaps the most profound insight of all dialectical philosophy. As Hegel puts it in the *Encyclopaedia*, "*modesty* of thought, as treats the finite as something altogether fixed and *absolute,* is the worst of virtues; and to stick to a post which has no sound ground in itself is the most unsound sort of theory. . . . [Such modesty] is a retention of this vanity—the finite—in opposition to the true: it is itself therefore vanity."[51] In another passage Hegel claims that it is the dialectic "which again makes this mass of understanding and diversity understand its finite nature and the pseudo-independence in its productions, and which brings the diversity back to unity."[52] For Hegel, this is not just a fragment in the unfinished history of human beings, but already achieved in Absolute

Spirit. Hegel himself falls prey to the same delusion as the Enlightenment that he so bitterly attacks: he applies the dialectic only to the past, fancying it something against which his own position is somehow inured. Hegel is also guilty of taking a historical moment in his thinking and making it into something eternal. But since he took reality to be a representation of the Idea, he also had to use his philosophy quite literally to deify and worship the political basis upon which it arose, i.e., the prerevolutionary Prussian state. This stance of humility before the existing was the false "modesty" of his own thought.

3. Utopia

Faith in the organizational form of civil society is expressed clearly in Hobbes, Spinoza, and the Enlightenment. The form itself, as well as its realization, is the goal of history. Its fundamental laws are the eternal laws of nature, whose fulfillment represents not only the highest moral imperative but also the guarantee of worldly happiness. The great utopias of the Renaissance, on the other hand, are the expression of the desperate classes who had to bear the costs of the transition from one economic form to another. The history of England in the fifteenth and sixteenth centuries provides stories of ordinary peasants driven from house and home by their manorial lords and of entire village communities transformed into sheep pastures in order to supply wool profitably to Brabant cloth manufacturers. The fate of the migrating, plundering hordes of hungry farmers was horrendous. Tens of thousands were killed by the government, many others forced to work in manufacturing plants under the appalling working conditions developed in that age. It is precisely among such classes that the first incarnation of the modern proletariat emerges. While they were liberated from serfdom, they were at the same time emancipated from all means of stretching out their meager existence. Their situation furnishes the basis for the first great utopia of the modern age, the *Utopia* of Thomas More (1516), from which all subsequent utopias derive their name. The author was executed in prison after a conflict with the king.[53]

The utopians realized that profit was becoming the driving force of history in the burgeoning trade economy. Enormous factories and financial ventures emerged before their eyes from the riches that had been accumulated in the cities. These new enterprises decimated the old system of guilds and introduced a new system of production. The possession of all labor potential came to be consolidated among one group: the educated and skilled entrepreneurs controlled not only the knowledge and organizational capabilities necessary for the new modes of production, but also the working space, raw materials, tools, ships, and other components. Without these elements profitable labor was no longer possible. Hunger, misery, and complete privation of all resources were concentrated among the rest. The survivors of serfdom, the starving masses of the large cities, and all other human refuse of the foundering system became wage laborers who had no choice but to sell their labor power.

The utopians reacted to these new conditions with the cry: private property is at fault! In the Middle Ages wealth had a significance different from that in the modern age. Then, it appeared essentially as goods amassed for immediate enjoyment, and did not necessarily entail power over other human beings. Given the situation since the Renaissance, it is understandable how the utopians could suddenly come to regard private property as the devil. For power was becoming decreasingly a matter of titles and inherited rights; it depended less and less on who ascended to the throne or who would be allowed to become a master of a trade. Rather, control over humans and their labor powers became increasingly indistinguishable from wealth now understood as the possession of the means of production. The new economic form allowed this control to be exploited without limit. Both domestic circumstances as well as emerging national competition among Italian cities were having bloody consequences. The utopians grasped the fact that these wars and the expulsion of the tenant farmers by their English landowners shared the same origin: profit.

It is no coincidence that the two great utopians, Thomas More and Tommaso Campanella, were Catholics. Henry VIII had his former chancellor executed because he held firmly to Catholicism and refused to acknowledge the ecclesiastical authority of the king. While in prison Campanella inveighed against heretics and composed impassioned treatises calling for an expansive Spanish papal world empire. At the conclusion of his trial—the death sentence had just been announced—Thomas More exclaimed to his judges, "I am, you say, a traitor and a rebel against the king. No, my lords. It is you who are. By separating yourselves from the true church you destroy its unity and peace. You are paving the way for a horrible future."[54]

The emancipation of individual powers and of the new, competitive economy led to the destruction of unity and peace in Europe. This annihilation threatened the future of Europe and was inextricably linked to the emergence of bourgeois nation-states. Under these circumstances, the medieval notion of a unified Christianity must have come as the embodiment of paradise to these two men, who were schooled in history and took their religion at its word. Although at the Councils of Trent the Church made allowances for the new historical conditions, the world could still represent for the Catholic church, as it would for a traditional folk religion, an order that was founded according to religious principles, one in which fatherly attention was extended toward everything and everybody. In the thinking of the masses, the church of the Middle Ages was still viable and was responsible for important social functions, above all generous care for the poor. But now that the church had intentionally begun to amass power in the form of material possessions and money, it stopped performing these functions. Together with a broad array of social strata, More and Campanella remained true to their faith out of honest belief in the greatness and beneficence of Catholic doctrine. The fundamental notion of a unified humanity, in Campanella's language a "universal monarchy," must have inspired them, especially during a period of bloody conflicts within Europe, which were the direct result of the new, anarchic economy.

These thinkers must have hated Machiavelli. What the Florentine considered an eternally valid law, namely, the use of religion as a means of conquering morality in the service of *raison d'état*, was for them a sign, indeed the root, of all evil in the present age. "Almost all princes are Machiavellian politicians," Campanella complained, "and they use religion only as an art of domination."[55] Both utopians despised what they saw infecting not only the great rulers, but especially the petty Italian and German princes: religious enthusiasm as phraseology, as the shabby veil for the courts' most ignoble financial transactions.

For More and Campanella, religion was the vessel that preserved the demand for justice in the face of actual misery. They wanted to achieve a holy community on earth that would replace the laws of free competition with the commandments of Christ. Their vision could not be sustained by Hobbes's conception of human beings' wolflike nature, which was in essence an interpretation of their age. According to their way of thinking, humans were not by nature evil, but rather became so through their involvement in worldly institutions, above all that of private property. Campanella reproached Machiavelli on the grounds that he seemed to know only the evil motives of human beings, for egoism could not be taken as the sole motive behind human action; the divine impulses of charity also had to be taken into account.

The utopians therefore anticipated Rousseau's theory that human beings, who are by nature good, become ruined by private property. "When I consider, I repeat, all these facts," Thomas More says in his *Utopia*, "I become more partial to Plato and less surprised at his refusal to make laws for those who rejected that legislation which gave to all an equal share in all goods. This wise old sage, to be sure, easily foresaw that the one and only road to the general welfare lies in the maintenance of equality in all respects. I have my doubts that the latter could ever be preserved where the individual's possessions are his private property. When every man aims at absolute ownership of all the property he can get, be there never so great an abundance of goods, it is all shared by a handful who leave the rest in poverty."[56]

For the utopians of the Enlightenment as well, private property was the historical origin of the evil attributes of the human soul. Thus even Morelly, in contrast to Hobbes and Machiavelli, writes,

Consider just once the vanity, the foppishness, the arrogance, the ambition, the deceit, the hypocrisy, the infamy; examine also the majority of our ostensible virtues. Everything gets resolved into that subtle and dangerous element: the desire to possess. You will even find this desire founded on disinterestedness. But could this universal pestilence, that is, private interest, this slithering fever, this tuberculosis of every kind of society, could it have gained ground where it could find not only no nourishment, but also not even the slightest number of fermenting agents? I believe that one cannot vie against the strength of the contention that where there is no private property of any kind, then none of its dangerous consequences can surface.[57]

And we read in Rousseau, "The first man who, having enclosed a piece of land, thought of saying, 'This is mine,' and found people simple enough to believe him, was the true founder of civil society."[58]

However, an important difference exists between Rousseau and the utopians: the former did not consider defending a notion of reverse historical development or, more precisely, of equal distribution of wealth. The utopians, however, speculatively outlined a communist society without private property whose realization they imagined to be possible with means available at the time. This is the reason why, in contrast to contemporary socialist models of future societies, or even to Bacon's *Nova Atlantis,* their dreamlands do not lie in the future, but only in spatial distance from the authors' own country. More's Utopia is situated on an ocean island; Campanella's City of the Sun is in Ceylon. For these philosophers, the perfect society can be established at any time and in any place if only human beings can be induced to accept a corresponding state constitution by means of persuasion, subterfuge, or even violence.[59]

The utopians share with Hobbes a detachment from actual historical circumstances. Just as social contract theory locates the foundation of society in the citizens' expression of free will, the utopians, without consideration of the historical circumstances, believe they can establish a new society simply on the grounds of free, rational human resolution. More argues that one need only propose the correct course of action to the rulers; for that which is better is the enemy of that which is good, and all things can become good only when human beings themselves have become so. This, he adds circumspectly, will take "a few" years.[60] It is even possible that he accepted Henry VIII's chancellorship with such utopian thoughts in mind.

A utopia leaps over time. It wants to generate a perfect society with means currently available: it is the dreamland of a historically bound fantasy. It creates this society out of desires that are shaped by the specific social situation, and that will be transformed concomitantly with a change in the society in question. The utopian fails to recognize that the historical stage of development, out of which the utopia arises as a prototype for a never-never land, has material conditions for its development, existence, and decline. These conditions must be precisely understood, and one must examine them in detail, in order to bring anything to fruition. Utopianism wants to eliminate the suffering of the present and retain only what is good in it. However, it forgets that these moments of good and evil instances are in reality two sides of the same coin, for the same conditions equally give rise to each. In a utopia, the transformation of existing conditions is not made dependent on the arduous and devastating transformation of the foundations of society. Rather, it is displaced to the minds of the subjects.

In this respect utopian doctrine contains a logical dilemma. Material property is presented as the factual basis of the actual spiritual state of human beings. Conversely, however, this same state is also supposed to be able to effect the elimination of private property. Expressed more generally, this logical inconsistency arises from the fact that human imagination, which is supposed to be influenced by the malign institutions currently in existence, is here not just asked to do the slow, meticulous work on existing reality that one might rightly expect of it. Rather, it is also burdened with mapping out an ideal society in substantive and meticulous detail. Here lurks the same presumptuous concept of absolute universal reason that we encountered in the theory of the original bourgeois philosophers. This theory, in contrast to that of the utopians, had the function of exalting the existing society and of passing off its categories as eternal.

More and Campanella are convinced that the goods necessary for society will be available in abundance and will be produced by means of a rationally ordered labor plan, not for the profit of particular individuals but for the needs of the general public. Except for criminals, everyone is obliged to work. For More, six hours per day suffices; for Campanella, just four. More's Utopia has the character of a universal alliance of free citizens, and allows for the election of public servants. Campanella's City of the Sun is closer to the model of a medieval cloister. The Utopians' social system is more humane, more liberal, more enlightened, more British than that of the City of the Sun, but Campanella ingeniously recognizes the possibility of exploiting scientific progress to control nature. He foresees a series of modern machines in his country of the future; in this respect, Bacon had already anticipated him. Furthermore, Campanella not only thinks that nature could be effectively controlled and utilized but that future generations within society could be governed with the aid of scientific eugenics.

The insistence on the creation of an ideal state and the failure to understand concrete developmental tendencies have taken their toll on the character of utopian systems. The economic preconditions for a rational organization of social affairs based on common property did not yet exist. On the contrary, the realization of their fantasy world would have required an artificial stifling of precisely the development that is contingent on the unfolding of creative individual initiative in free competition. This was an age in which the personality of a captain was not only crucial for navigational success, but in which the term "captain" was also the appropriate designation for the leaders of the other branches of trade that were showing great promise. Hence this was a time in which, owing to inefficiency in human production, an entire world divided the consciousness of the economic manager from that of the person executing the task, and in which a world of difference must have necessarily existed between the material living conditions of the manager and those of the executor. The common property and equal living conditions the utopians demanded would have been the death of civilization. Therefore, in comparison to More and Campanella, Machiavelli and Hobbes seem like visionaries. In *The Prince* Machiavelli is right when he says, with reference to utopian experiments, "my intention being to write something of use to those who understand, it appears to me more proper to go to the real truth of the matter than to its imagination; and many have imagined republics and principalities which have never been seen or known to exist in reality; for how we live is so far removed from how we ought to live, that he who abandons what is done for what ought to be done, will rather learn to bring about his own ruin than his preservation."[61]

Utopias actually have two aspects: the critique of what is and the representation of what should be. The significance of utopias lies essentially in the former moment. Desires bespeak a great deal about a person's actual circumstances. The condition of the English masses shows through More's happy Utopia; the humane chancellor lends form to their longing. Of course, he himself does not recognize that their longing is a reaction to the social situation in which both he and the masses live and suffer. Rather, More naively projects the content of this longing into a spatial or temporal beyond. The utopia of the Renaissance is the secularized heaven of the Middle Ages. The creation of a distant world that one could reach while alive certainly represents a radical change when compared to periods in which the poor could enter utopias only after death. But the pious believer of the

Middle Ages seldom saw the reflection of his own destitution in heaven, and just as seldom did the utopians see a reaction to the suffering of their age in their distant islands.

The utopians differ from philosophers who serve as apologists for what already exists or for what has just emerged. The utopian recognizes that within the bourgeois order, however completely thought through, true misery is not and cannot be eradicated, despite the emancipation of the individual from serfdom. When Hobbes and Spinoza announce that the new state is the expression of universal interests, they are correct insofar as the satisfaction of the demands of certain wealthy social groups and the development of their enterprises within a measurable period of time advance the society as a whole. One could say that these philosophers were the more practical physicians; they prescribed what was necessary immediately, even if it hurt in certain places. The utopians, in contrast, recognized that the causes of social misery lay in the economic realm, above all in the existence of private property. They made the ultimate cure dependent on a change not in the laws but in property relations.

Of course, comparing society to a sick or healthy organism is dangerous. It clouds over the fact that, to a very large degree, the connection between the happiness and life of broad social strata to the thriving of "the whole" is anything but "organic." Perhaps during the high Middle Ages such an organic relationship could be said to have existed between the individual and society in particular places in Europe (analogous to certain primitive tribes with collective economies), such that the society's welfare and privation were identical with those of each particular member; however, this no longer holds for the modern period. This state of affairs could be formulated in Hegel's language as the externality of the moments against one another and the diremption of the whole. The comparison with the sick body of society which must be saved even if it hurts in certain places overlooks the minor detail that these particular places consist of living human beings, each with a personal fate and a unique existence. The utopians, however, understood that this neglected detail actually represented suffering human beings forced by society into an inhuman existence. In their works we see the resolute conviction that no amount of merely juridical reforms but rather only the revolutionary upheaval of foundations could create unity in place of a fragmented, inhuman existence and justice in place of injustice.

Wherever one looks in these utopias, one sees that merit is duly honored—instead of the usual scenario, in which everything good yields to what is bad. Whenever—as in the present—economic laws are allowed to operate freely, the given entrenched disparity of wealth has the effect of distributing happiness and unhappiness not according to merit and worth but merely according to chance. Contained within utopias is the conviction that society can fulfill the goal prescribed to it by bourgeois natural law, that of satisfying the interests of everyone, only if it regulates its life process in the interest of everyone and abandons the blind mechanism of many competing individual wills as its economic foundation. This theory relates more than external prosperity to economic relations—it also relates these human relations to the development of morality and of science. In so doing, it links the dreams of the modern utopians to Plato's *Republic,* while also being at least as close to reality as are the apologetics of the existing order.

The more the interests of those individuals who have to bear the brunt of the suffering in the prevailing social order gain strength in that society, the more the utopians' doctrine concerning property becomes actuality. It was certainly a mistake to leap over the present and to overlook the possibilities that lie slumbering in the current state of things with the proclamation of having achieved an absolutely perfect order. But it is just as great a failure not to devise a better order or to recognize its preconditions. In his *Critique of Pure Reason* Kant remarks, in reference to the utopia of Plato, that "We should, however, be better advised to follow up this thought, and, where the great philosopher leaves us without help, to place it, through fresh efforts, in a proper light, rather than to set it aside as useless on the very sorry and harmful pretext of impracticability."[62] Kant joins the utopians in their error regarding what is required for perfect social conditions when he attributes their absence primarily to "the neglect of pure ideas in legislation." He contends that it is merely a matter of presenting these pure ideas to the "legislators." He too remains tied to the chimera of a harmonious society whose establishment depends simply on the correct insight and the good will of all members. However, those who understand the roots of the evil that utopias reveal, as well as the goal to which their emancipation is connected, are not the legislators but precisely those groups of individuals who suffer privation as a consequence of their position in the social life process.

Compared to the utopians' sidestepping of what actually existed, those who argued for principles of natural law at this time were wholly progressive and correct. They held that the new bourgeois state was in its essence an assurance of universal welfare and the best possible security for the life of its citizens. The fact that this account was directed invariably into the future, and did not continuously challenge social reality with its demands, ultimately resulted in its becoming purely ideological. Compared to the ideological apologetics of an order that was essentially characterized by the negation of medieval restraint, that is, by free competition, utopias were purely literary exercises that were at bottom expressions of impotent longing. But it goes without saying that this longing is able to cast off its impotence to precisely the same extent that society becomes riper for a transformation of its foundation and as it develops the powers to do so. As already noted, a collective economy was out of the question in the sixteenth and seventeenth centuries, and competition was still necessary as a condition for society's continuing development toward higher levels.[63] Although this is overlooked in the utopias, at least they formulate the ultimate goal in such a way that every political undertaking can be measured according to its standards.

Neither the impossibility of realizing this goal imminently nor the functionality of the property system under attack amounts to a justification for the contradictions that are operative in this system. The individual who is suffering under the new order can take refuge only in dreams and in subjectivity, which explains the vitality of religion in precisely this age among the lower classes. These individuals are the sacrifices that the "World Spirit" offers to its sublime goal, for they suffer during a period of historical development that is necessary for progress. To return to our organicist metaphor, whose ambiguity becomes especially clear in this case, they are the blood that is shed in order to heal. This very cure brings forth its own affliction, and it is an affliction that provides the utopia with its form. A social condition in which each individual is free to develop his own powers is the cause of world-historical burdens.

Here the difficulty of all idealism, even Hegel's, becomes evident. According to his idealistic conception, all reality is identical to the Absolute Spirit, "the necessity of nature and the necessity of history are only ministrant to its revelation and the vessels of its honour."[64] We see "Spirit manifesting, developing, and perfecting its powers in every direction which its manifold nature can follow. . . . In this pleasurable activity, it has to do only with itself."[65] This thought is not only problematic, it is frightening. The unique and factual death of individual human beings appears in this system as a mere illusion, or at least is justified as such, when viewed against the surviving spiritual essence, Absolute Spirit, or even transcendental consciousness. But there is no way to make death theoretically "meaningful." Rather, death reveals the impotence of any metaphysics that would impart meaning, as well as of all theodicies. Such actual suffering, of which utopias are the reflex, is doubtless conditioned by the same process that would permit deliverance from it. However, nothing contradicts the task of true philosophy more than the wisdom that rests content with ascertaining this necessity. History has realized a better society out of an inferior one, and in its course it can bring about one that is even better—this is a fact. But it is also a fact that the course of history passes over the suffering and misery of individuals. Between these two facts there exists a series of demonstrative associations, but no justifying meaning.

These philosophical considerations rule out any condescending dismissal of attempts that aim to achieve a utopia instantly and to introduce absolute justice on earth. In Germany at the time of Thomas More, one man, himself spurned by the English chancellor, began such a project. It was hopeless from the start, and his means were totally insufficient. This man was Thomas Münzer. He did not want to wait for an interminable sequence of suffering to pass before Christianity became fully realized. He proclaimed that even Christ had not been patient with injustice on earth, appealing to Christ's words themselves rather than to theological interpretations of them.

The patience of idealism was foreign to Thomas Münzer. The insight and knowledge of scholars and of experienced politicians concerning the complicated and protracted conditions required for even the most minuscule amelioration of social ailments could never satisfy this contemplative man of wisdom. Whoever demands forbearance with respect to suffering and death, inasmuch as they are contingent on human institutions, must consider that the prevailing forbearance toward the historical process is one of the main reasons why such waiting is necessary in the first place. At any rate, the historical-philosophical point is the following: the explanation of the prior course of history, an explanation that in great part must still be completed, is a matter different from the absurd justification of this course.

Nietzsche judged too critically and therefore ineffectively when, in his "On the Use and Disadvantage of History for Life," he cast grave doubt upon the scholarly investigation of history. However, one may invoke Nietzsche when reflecting on utopias within the context of history. Concerning the admiration for the so-called "power of history," he writes,

in practice [it] transforms every moment into a naked admiration for success and leads to an idolatry of the factual: which idolatry is now generally described by the very mythological yet quite German expression "to accommodate oneself to the facts." But he who has once learned to bend his back and bow his head before the "power of history" at last nods "Yes" like a Chinese mechanical doll to every power, whether it be a government or public opinion or a numerical majority, and moves his limbs to the precise rhythm at which any "power" whatever pulls the strings. If every success is a rational necessity, if every event is a victim of the logic or of the "idea"—then down on your knees quickly and do reverence to the whole stepladder of success! . . . And what a school of decorum is such a way of contemplating history! To take everything objectively, to grow angry at nothing, to love nothing, to understand everything, how soft and pliable that makes one; . . . I would say therefore: history always inculcates: "there was once," morality: "you ought not to" or "you ought not to have." Thus history amounts to a compendium of factual morality.[66]

Although Nietzsche's later philosophical development led him to idolize not human history but rather natural history and biology—he actually destroyed his health and vitality "in naked admiration of the success" of these sciences—he has formulated an idea from the Enlightenment here. A fully developed explanation, the sustained recognition of the necessity of an historical event can, for those of us who take action, become a means of introducing reason into history. However, regarded "in itself," history *has* no reason, nor is it an "essence" in the usual sense; it is neither "Spirit" before which we must genuflect nor "power," but rather a comprehensible collection of events resulting from the social life processes of human beings. No one is called into existence or is killed by "history." It neither confers tasks nor executes them. Only real human beings act, overcome obstacles, and are able to succeed in reducing individual or general suffering, which either they themselves or the powers of nature have created. The pantheistic promotion of history to the status of an autonomous, unitary, substantial being is nothing other than dogmatic metaphysics.

4. Vico and Mythology

For all events, as long as they are not the results of conscious human action, science acknowledges only the question of the cause and not of the end. However, the question "what for," especially when it arises from the fact of individual suffering and death, stems from an all-too-deep psychological source. It is thus incapable of being stifled. When attempts at satisfying everyone in the present age fail, when a utopia cannot be brought to fruition, and so the promise of eliminating random occurrences is denied, then a new philosophy of history must emerge. This philosophy must strive to recognize a hidden, beneficent intention behind the actual chaos of life and death, and within its designs every single, seemingly incomprehensible, meaningless fact must have determinate, situated value without itself knowing why. If it is true that the discovery of such a hidden intention comprises the essence of all true philosophies of history, then the Italian Giambattista Vico is the first real philosopher of history in the modern age. His intention in his major work is to show that providence is the guiding force in human history and that it realizes its goals through the actions of human beings, without their being or needing to be aware that this is the case. His greatness lies not, of course, in this framework but rather in the empirical investigations that he initiated on this count.

Vico was born in Naples in 1688 and died there in 1744. He was completely unknown in his lifetime. He began his career as a house tutor, then worked as an impoverished professor of rhetoric at the University of Naples. However, this man, a pious Catholic and a common citizen, is in fact not only one of the greatest philosophers of history ever but also a sociologist and psychologist of the first order. In addition to this, he revitalized the enterprise of philology, established the philosophy of art, and possessed an eye for important cultural processes unlike almost anyone in his own age or afterward. Vico provides proof that the study of history can have universal value if it does not aim just for a superficial recounting of events, but rather aspires to discover purposive laws and relationships.

Vico himself came to this realization through his polemic against Cartesian philosophy. Descartes died in 1650. In many ways, his philosophy pointed toward the future. Not only did it open the way for theoretically unbiased research on nature; but also, by establishing a critical epistemology, it provided the point of departure for advanced research in philosophy. The great intellectual dynamos that forged ahead in the unfolding and development of a mathematical natural science based their work upon this French thinker, the inventor of analytic geometry, and they employed his methods and terminology. But not just natural science: even Catholicism, which at this time was being revived, adopted Descartes's epistemology in order to adapt itself to progressive cultural development. Descartes was philosophically quite in vogue in Vico's age. It was impossible to avoid a philosophical engagement with his works.

Descartes's philosophy constitutes the philosophical analogue to the fact that modern society was, to a great extent, turning to mathematical natural sciences. The needs of the trade economy that was then in the process of unfolding, the necessity of technical mastery over inanimate nature, led to the idealization of mathematics as the only reliable form of knowledge. Descartes's *cogito ergo sum* and the profound observations of his *Meditations* function in his work as a whole to validate mathematics as the only certain form of knowledge. In his doctrine of the *cogito* he secures the criteria of clarity and lucidity. These criteria he finds fulfilled essentially only in mathematics, out of which, in all probability, he had derived them even before he discovered his *cogito*. Criticism of Descartes consists in disputing the question whether mathematics is the only true science and, at the same time, whether mathematical thinking constitutes the true manifestation of human essence.

Vico's major work, the *Scienza Nuova,* the *New Science Concerning the Common Nature of the Nations,* first published in 1725, has an allegorical illustration on its title page. Among other objects depicted is a large sphere that is resting on an altar. This sphere, upon which a woman with a winged head is standing, lies on the edge of the altar, and is supported by it only on one side. This implies that reality has up to now been observed from one side only, "only through the natural order."[67] Vico holds that philosophers "have not yet contemplated His providence in respect of that part of it which is most proper to men, whose nature has this principal property: that of being social."[68] Descartes defended mathematics as the only sure and true science on the grounds that we can know thoroughly only what we ourselves have made, a principle that can be traced historically from Bacon, Hobbes, and Descartes to Leibniz, Kant, and Fichte. By the word "we" Descartes means the abstract reflection of the faculty of understanding, the quintessence of the isolated thought apparatus according to the model of traditional logic. Vico adopts the principle that only that which one has created oneself can be truly knowable, and indeed makes it the guiding principle of his philosophy. However, he gives it an entirely new and unprecedented turn. What humans have created themselves—and what, for that reason, must necessarily be the most noble object of knowledge—and hence those creations in which the essence of mankind and of "Spirit" find fullest expression, are not the fictional constructions of mathematical understanding, but rather historical reality. In regard to his own enterprise Vico says, "Now, as geometry, when it constructs the world of quantity out of its elements, or contemplates that world, is creating it for itself, just so does our Science [create for itself the world of nations], but with a reality greater by just so much as the institutions having to do with human affairs are more real than points, lines, surfaces, and figures are."[69]

Machiavelli leafed through history merely for its use as an instruction manual in political activity, while Hobbes, in the construction of his social contract theory, repeatedly shut his eyes to actual historical events. For both of them, any true science, not only mathematics and natural science but also the science of mankind, remained distinctly separate and independent from history. Apart from Hegel and his school, modern philosophy views history mainly as a description of events, something that may be pursued toward some practical or edifying end but which is insignificant for important theoretical concerns. This metaphysics fancied that it could make the real world—and with it the essence of mankind—accessible without any fundamental historical research to support it. This theory was not effectively put to rest until the nineteenth century. In contrast to Descartes, whom he hated, Vico recognized that a meditation that issued only from one—supposedly autonomous—individual must necessarily be narrow and empty, but above all it must of necessity be false. Human self-knowledge is only possible when based on an analysis of the historical process in which humans act, and not on the basis of mere introspection, as subjective idealism has always held. Economy, state, law, religion, science, art—all of these particularly human creations originated in history: not from isolated individuals, but rather from the relationships among these individuals. In Vico's language: they are to be understood in terms of their social property.

When Vico calls providence "sovereign over the affairs of men"[70,] and when he says that his "new Science must therefore be a demonstration, so to speak, of what providence has wrought in history,"[71] it appears that in essence his philosophy amounts to faith in a divine meaning and in a sacred end to history. However, when he applies the notion of providence concretely, he understands it essentially as nothing other than the guiding agency or the law through which humans are led to social and cultural refinement despite their individualistic, barbaric, and egoistical drives. The surface phenomena of history, among which Vico includes above all the motives and actions of individual human beings, are not what is essential in history. Rather, a succession of forms of society asserts itself without individuals being conscious that this is occurring; in a manner of speaking, it asserts itself behind these individuals. This process makes the civilizing achievements of human beings possible.

The inquiry into these hidden laws is the actual theme of the "new science." Vico points out[72] that the true meaning of the word "providence," in its latinate form *divinitas,* stems from *divinari,* that is, to apprehend what is hidden. He considers the role of his main work to be "to understand what is hidden *from* men . . . a demonstration, so to speak, of what providence has wrought in history . . . without human discernment or counsel, and often against the designs of men."[73] What Hegel later called "the cunning of reason," Vico attributes to *divinitas:* through chaotic human action in relentless conflict among individuals, social groups, and peoples; in all the pain and misery of personal fates; in spite of narrow-mindedness, greed, cruelty, fanaticism, indeed even *by means of* these moments, providence realizes a humane order and ultimately a rationally determined social existence.

Of course, it is impossible to discuss either a utopia and its ideal system of justice or the benign intention of providence while human beings are trampled under the foot of history, which is supposed to lead them into the light. Vico finds comfort for this in his Catholicism: regardless of whether a human being lived in a dark or a bright historical period, the highest judge will pass the appropriate sentence on him after his death. Thus for Vico, judgment upon the individual transcends history. For Hegel, the world court coincides directly with world history. His religion consisted essentially in a belief in an immanent teleology, that is, in the fulfillment of absolute justice in history. Because of his idealistic denial of the essential being of individuality, the question of individual suffering is irrelevant to Hegel. The examples of Hegel and Vico illustrate that, in the modern age at least, sincere belief in a revealed, transcendent religion allows for an inquiry into this world that is less prejudiced than one that stems from a pantheistic conflation of God and world, reason and reality. Because he preserves a notion of transcendental jurisdiction for the individual, Vico is able to examine the course of history relatively impartially and can undertake to uncover history's inner laws of motion and its hidden tendencies. If his work is less monumental and all-encompassing than that of Hegel (whose work strikes similar chords), it is much more empirical and significantly less structural than the speculations of the great idealist, who was primarily concerned with revealing the divine in this world.

An examination of some of Vico's work will give us an impression of the vast array of productive ideas he developed, ideas that for the most part have yet to be surpassed in scholarship. From Bacon, whom he admired greatly, Vico adopted an antipathy toward the view that the thinkers of classical antiquity, or other philosophers of some past age, possessed the highest knowledge of eternal things, and that the human race had made no progress but had only degenerated and declined. It is true that as a Catholic Vico had to put Paradise and divine creation at the beginning of history, as Catholic dogma holds. However, he used the biblical account of the Deluge to displace wholly the existence of that golden age from scientific inquiry, and allowed actual history to begin in darkness and barbarism, as was really the case. In *The New Science* Vico holds, "To this conceit of nations,"[74] which consists in "every nation . . . whether Greek or barbarian, [having] the same conceit that it before all other nations invented the comforts of human life and that its remembered history goes back to the very beginning of the world,"[75] "is added that of scholars, who will have it that what they know is as old as the world."[76] Vico, to his credit, wants "to sweep away all belief in the matchless wisdom of the ancients."[77] "This was the order of human institutions: first the forests, after that the huts, then the villages, next the cities, and finally the academies."[78] The human race begins its course in a dark and frightening prehistory.

The question arises, according to what laws is this advancement toward culture carried out? Vico explains his methodological principle in the following way: "In search of these natures of human institutions our Science proceeds by a severe analysis of human thoughts about the human necessities or utilities of social life."[79] Like Machiavelli, only much more logically and deliberately, Vico begins with the premise that human creations are to be explained by the notion of necessity, or, more precisely, by their origin in material conditions. According to Vico, the key to the explanation of human history lies in examining the outward manifestations of living conditions together with the primitive psychological makeup of earlier human beings. Traditions that have been handed down from these earlier periods, above all mythology, constitute the material by which this matter must be explored.

Vico outlines the beginnings of civilization in a grand design. The first inventions and customs of man emerged out of fear of the natural elements. Primitive races personified these elements by projecting their own nature into the cosmos. Thunder, lightning, and inclement weather in general forced people to seek shelter and, at the same time, inspired them with fear of superpowerful giants. This primitive reaction to natural phenomena by a projection of human nature into physical nature, that is, by animating the powers of nature, constitutes the origin of poetry, which emerges simultaneously with the beginning of civilization. These early people, whom Vico termed "The Giants," by their efforts to create shelter from the hardships of nature, gave the first impetus necessary for further cultural development. They now renounced "the bestial custom of wandering through the great forest of the earth and habituated themselves to the quite contrary custom of remaining settled and hidden for a long period in their caves."[80] This gradually increasing superiority of the will over the impulses of the body "was followed by the authority of natural law; for, having occupied and remained settled for a long time in the places where they chanced to find themselves at the time of the first thunderbolts, they became lords of them by occupation and long possession, the source of all dominion in the world. These are those 'few whom just Jupiter loved' (*pauci quos aequus amavit/Iupiter*) whom the philosophers later metamorphosed into men favored by God with natural aptitudes for science and virtue. But the historical significance of this phrase is that in the recesses and depths [of the caves] they became the princes of the so-called greater gentes, who counted Jove the first god. These were the ancient noble houses, branching out into many families."[81] After the giants were forced by nature to settle, their homes did not remain caves for long. They began to build huts and, since they had already initiated agricultural production, they inhabited the most fertile areas, as long as they could also find adequate protection there.

Especially interesting is how Vico explains the origin of the foundations of civilization from the interaction between external material conditions and human instincts. Although he invokes the notion of providence each time such interaction occurs without the conscious will of human beings, he nonetheless gives completely unprejudiced explanations that frequently accord in principle with the most modern views. Vico holds that there are four moments primarily involved in this interaction that function as civilizing conditions. He calls them, "four elements, as it were, of the civil universe; namely, religion, marriage, asylum, and the first agrarian law."[82]

We shall treat Vico's theory of mythology as an example here. According to him, myth emerged as a reaction of fear to overpowering natural forces. Humans project their own essence into nature, that is, natural forces appear to them from the beginning as living beings wholly similar to themselves, except that they are stronger, more powerful, and frighteningly real. Vico's account, which anticipates

Ludwig Feuerbach's anthropological interpretation of religion, is extraordinarily lucid and advanced. After he discusses the constitution of primitive human beings, he continues,

Of such natures must have been the first founders of gentile humanity when . . . at last the sky fearfully rolled with thunder and flashed with lightning, as could not but follow from the bursting upon the air for the first time of an impression so violent. Thereupon a few giants, who must have been the most robust, and who were dispersed through the forests on the mountain heights where the strongest beasts have their dens, were frightened and astonished by the great effect whose cause they did not know, and raised their eyes and became aware of the sky. And because in such a case the nature of the human mind leads it to attribute its own nature to the effect, and because in that state their nature was that of men all robust bodily strength, who expressed their very violent passions by shouting and grumbling, they pictured the sky to themselves as a great animated body, which in that aspect they called Jove, the first god of the so-called greater gentes, who meant to tell them something by the hiss of his bolts and the clap of his thunder.[83]

Vico thus explains "that divine providence initiated the process by which the fierce and violent were brought from their outlaw state to humanity and by which nations were instituted among them. It did so by awaking in them a confused idea of divinity, which they in their ignorance attributed to that to which it did not belong. Thus through the terror of this imagined divinity, they began to put themselves in some order."[84] In another passage Vico expresses the same thought in the following way: "All the things here discussed agree with that golden passage on the origins of idolatry: that the first people, simple and rough, invented the gods 'from terror of present power.' Thus it was fear which created gods in the world; not fear awakened in men by other men, but fear awakened in men by themselves."[85] Humans "thus . . . began to exercise that natural curiosity which is the daughter of ignorance and the mother of knowledge, and which, opening the mind of man, gives birth to wonder."[86]

If one advances Vico's doctrine regarding the historical origin of mythology against naive accounts concerning the duplicity of priests, which is how the Enlightenment at this time or a few decades later dealt with religion, only then does his accomplishment appear in its proper light. He examined the civilizing influence of religion down to its details. Thus he taught that religions have among other functions that of recompensing the great masses for their renunciation of instinctual drives, which life in society demands from them. Further, for Vico mythology served as a necessary and primitive form of knowledge, one that provides modern science with its roots, and he assigned to it a rank in society not unlike that of spiritual pursuits in modern civilization. "Wherever a people has grown savage in arms so that human laws have no longer any place among it, the only powerful means of reducing it is religion."[87] In contrast to the Enlightenment, Vico teaches us that false religions originated not through individual deceit but rather as a result of a necessary development.

Vico was perhaps the first to recognize consciously and explicitly the analogy between historically early peoples and primitive tribes still in existence. He also recognized the similarity between the mentality of primitive peoples and that of children, and thus the correspondence between human ontogenesis and phylogenesis. He made important discoveries in this area, above all that children and primitives are unable "to form intelligible class concepts of things," and in place of this, they "had a natural need to create poetic characters; that is, imaginative class concepts or universals, to which, as to certain models or ideal portraits, to reduce all the particular species which resembled them."[88] This doctrine holds that the early stages of intellectual development to a great extent lack any categorical framework and are characterized by prelogical thought, a view which accords with the findings of modern research, above all the work of Lévy-Bruhl.

Another of Vico's great achievements in the realm of mythological religiosity is the theory whose principle is contained in the phrase "that the first fables must have contained civil truths, and must therefore have been the histories of the first peoples."[89] He thus expresses the conviction that mythological conceptions are not free creations of the spirit, but rather social reality, albeit reflected in a distorted manner. If one applies this notion not just to metaphysics and art, as Vico has already done, but to all ideological forms of consciousness, then one arrives at a doctrine of the philosophy of history that is of immense consequence. The intellectual notions characteristic of a certain period arise out of social life processes in which nature and human beings stand in a reciprocal relationship. Their content, from the most nebulous idea to the clearest act of cognition, is reality, existence. It is simply a matter of recognizing the reality that lies at their foundation, which is reflected even in the darkest cult.

Vico's interpretation of the Cadmus saga provides an example of his method. The rulers of the first community descended from the giants, who had settled on the best and most fertile plots of land. They started families and opened sanctuaries for those who, because of their material circumstances, were less fortunate. Hence the first agricultural law stabilized property relationships, that is, it confirmed the lords in their supremacy. Thus according to Vico, "the cities were to be born, based on the two communities of men that composed them, one of the nobles to command, the other of plebeians to obey. . . . Hence emerges the *matter* of political science, which is nothing other than the science of commanding and obeying in states."[90] The giants as rulers—Vico means the archaic Greeks and Romans, who came to exalt themselves as gods—Vico terms heroes: Cadmus

first . . . slays the great serpent (clears the earth of the great ancient forest). Then he sows the teeth (a fine metaphor for his plowing the first fields of the world with curved pieces of hard wood, which, before the use of iron was discovered, must have served as the teeth of the first plows, and teeth they continued to be called). He throws a heavy stone (the hard earth which the clients or *famuli* wished to plow for themselves). From the furrows armed men spring forth (in the heroic contest over the first agrarian law the heroes come forth from their estates to assert their lordship of them, and unite in arms against the plebs, and they fight not among themselves but with the clients that have revolted against them; the furrows signifying the orders in which they unite and thereby give form and stability to the first cities on the basis of arms, as is all set forth above). And Cadmus is changed into a serpent (signifying the origin of the authority of the aristocratic senates, for which the ancient Latins would have used the phrase *Cadmus fundus factus est,* and the Greeks said Cadmus was changed into Draco, the dragon that wrote the laws in blood). All of which is what we promised to make clear: that the fable of Cadmus contained several centuries of poetic history, and is a grand example of the inarticulateness with which the still infant world labored to express itself, which is one of the seven great sources of the difficulty of the fables.[91]

Over and over again Vico finds this theme of the emancipation of plebeians from the patricians, of the *famuli* from the lords, reflected in the myths, and he compares and identifies it with medieval systems of fealty and indenture. Sons were suddenly emancipated from familial subservience under monarchic authority and could themselves become fathers. However, the servants lived in hopeless slavery. Dissatisfaction and ultimately revolutions arose because of the pressure burdening the slaves. Thus, for Vico, the opposition between classes is the fundamental social fact and the key to understanding Greek mythology. The various forms of misery brought on by slavery find symbolic expression in the sufferings of Tantalus, Ixion, and Sisyphus,[92] and these myths contain just as many motifs of rebellion.

It is not just mythology that Vico understood as a reflex reaction to social conditions; he also relates metaphysics to historical reality. Socrates's notion of intelligible genera and Plato's doctrine of ideas stem, according to Vico, "from observing that the enactment of laws by Athenian citizens involved their coming to agreement in an idea of an equal utility common to all of them severally."[93] Furthermore, concerning Aristotle's new concept of justice, Vico says explicitly "that these principles of metaphysics, logic, and morals issued from the market place of Athens."[94]

This understanding of mythology and metaphysics, which in fact concerns how such things are connected and how they are "hidden," signifies a tremendous advance over the simple assessment of Hobbes that such doctrines are invented only to deceive others. For Vico, these essentially distorted forms of reality appear at an early stage of historical development. Just as the state did not emerge from a voluntary and conscious act of human reason—as natural law doctrines hold—language, art, religion, and metaphysics similarly lack any rational origin. The task of scientific inquiry is to understand these cultural products as surface manifestations of history, to grasp the natural, instinctual social processes from which these manifestations issued and which are, in turn, reflected in them.

Vico's interpretations of mythology are exemplary cases of how to understand the "spiritual" elements that arise from determinant social processes. Vico is far from wanting to understand the process of artistic and religious creation as the conscious or even intentional recasting of a given reality that was previously unideological. From the vantage point of their creator, the aesthetic creations, in which the sociologist later sees the reflections of a particular society and its epoch, appear as innovative, thoroughly "originary" products. There exists no prestabilized harmony between the potential of creative works to express something of society and the individual intentions that give rise to such works. Works of art attain their transparency only in the course of history.

"The human mind is naturally impelled to take delight in uniformity."[95] Of course there is a wide gap between Vico's attempts at a unitary explanation of history and those constructive syntheses which putatively contain the principle by which one can not only understand the past but predict the future as well. Within such systematic approaches to the philosophy of history, history is, as it were, the body of a unitary framework of meaning that one can logically and clearly contemplate and envision in its final form. Hegel's monumental system as well as Spengler's simple framework both contain this structure, according to which one culture becomes domineering, experiences its youth, heyday, and decline, only to be superseded by the next one. Vico also offers us the satisfaction of a universal vision of history; in his works as well we find delight in "uniformity." Indeed, what in Spengler's schema may not be interpreted merely as historical-philosophical daydreams may not be thus interpreted in Vico's works either. However, in contrast to Spengler, Vico harbors the philosophical conviction that, in spite of the recurrence of old forms and of the fact that, at the end of each cycle, humanity sinks into barbarism, the eternal task is to establish the finite dominion of a just order. This thought is specifically grounded in the identity between the laws of history and divine providence.

Toward the beginning of *The Decline and Fall of the West,* Oswald Spengler says, "Let the words 'youth,' 'growth,' 'maturity,' 'decay' . . . be taken at last as objective descriptions of organic states . . . determine for each of these higher individuals [that is, cultures][96] what is typical in their surgings and what is necessary in the riot of incident. And then at last will unfold itself the picture of world-history that is natural to us, men of the West, and to us alone."[97] Vico, probably following Machiavelli, had long ago put this image, according to which the view of world history should unfold itself to us in the present time, to a use that offered itself to him without compulsion and which, in any case, is metaphysically unencumbered. Our science, he points out, comes to "describe at the same time an ideal eternal history traversed in time by the history of every nation in its rise, development, maturity, decline and fall."[98] For Vico, history does not develop from the free expression of Spirit, but rather, in its beginning and its development, it is necessarily determined by the forces of material conditions and their reciprocal relationship with primitive human beings; hence Vico is convinced that regardless of where a society is found, it must in every case follow the same course as others. One can thus in fact determine the main outlines of an "ideal history" according to which the destinies of all civilizations are fulfilled. As Vico formulates it: "Wherever, emerging from savage, fierce, and bestial times, men begin to domesticate themselves by religion, they begin, proceed, and end by those stages which are investigated here."[99]

Thus in the first epoch, the giants ruled: fantasy constitutes the form of knowledge, whose expression is fantastical poetry. The second epoch, which Vico calls the "heroic," witnesses the emergence of classes and states. The heroes, that is, the patricians, consolidate themselves as armed forces against the plebeians, the *clienteles,* in order to protect the property system and to defend themselves against those who own no property. Kings emerge from among the patrician leaders in such social conflicts. They are thus the ones who "lead the fathers in quelling the revolts of the *famuli.*"[100] "For the nature of the strong is to surrender as little as possible of what they have acquired by valor."[101] Vico examines the other stage of his "ideal" history, the "age of man," less thoroughly. He dedicates by far the greatest part of *The New Science* to the analysis of the poetic and heroic ages. The early monarchies are first followed by aristocracy, then democracy, then empire, and finally decline. "The nature of peoples is first crude, then severe, then benign, then delicate, finally dissolute."[102]

Thus Vico, like Machiavelli, is convinced that a regression to barbarism and a new beginning must follow each cycle. For Vico, the immediate reason for this conviction lies in the fact of the Middle Ages, which represents a new age of heroes, the second barbarism. There is hardly a more profound chapter in *The New Science* than the one in which Vico compares the Middle Ages in their dark cruelty and narrowness with earlier epochs to which classical mythology bears witness. This Catholic did not shrink from asserting that the title "Holy Royal Majesty" and the arrogation of spiritual worth among the medieval princes represented a recurrence of the self-deification of the heroes in Greek myths and was founded upon similar social conditions. Vico provides paradigms for a comparative sociology that—with the possible exception of Voltaire—far surpass anything else that was achieved in this area in the seventeenth and eighteenth centuries. It is also significant that Vico does not apply the framework of an ideal history speculatively in the sense of an *a priori,* that is to say, as a fate that is imposed from outside. Rather, he argues from empirical grounds, as when he explains the new barbarism as arising from historical mass migrations. Wherever humanity is cast back upon its origins through such events—be it a matter of natural occurrences, the invasion of uncivilized hoards, or the anarchic self-destruction of civilized peoples—then the entire developmental process must begin anew and run its course in the same way according to the social laws that Vico believes he has demonstrated in *The New Science.* Regarding his science he explains, "the course of the institutions of the nations had to be, must now be, and will have to be such as our Science demonstrates, even if infinite worlds were born from time to time through eternity, which is certainly not the case."[103]

Vico's doctrine of recurrence consists in a simple belief in the repetition of things human. We must follow him in his conviction that the possibility of a return to barbarism is always open. External catastrophes can play a role in its return, but so too can the events that humans themselves bring about. The migration of peoples is indeed an event of the past. However, beneath the deceptive veneer of the present age, tensions are at work within cultural states that very likely could bring about horrendous setbacks. Of course, fate is operative in human affairs only to the degree to which society is not able consciously to regulate its affairs in its own interest. When a philosophy of history contains a doctrine of a dark but self-governing, autonomous, and effectual meaning to history that one attempts to trace in schemata, logical constructions, and systems, one must counter by showing that there is precisely as much meaning and reason in the world as human beings realize within it. In as much as the discovery of lawlike regularities in history can serve as a means to such realization, then Vico, this early "interpretive" philosopher of history, was a path-breaking spirit.

Notes

The Present Situation of Social Philosophy and the Tasks of an Institute for Social Research

[This was Horkheimer's inaugural lecture on assuming the directorship of the Institute for Social Research at the University of Frankfurt in January 1931.—Trans.]

1. Immanuel Kant, *The Metaphysical Principles of Virtue*, trans. James Ellington (New York, 1964), p. 23 (translation modified).

2. *Hegel's Philosophy of Right*, trans. T. M. Knox (New York, 1942), §352, p. 219.

3. G. W. F. Hegel, *Lectures on the Philosophy of World History: Introduction*, trans. H. B. Nisbet (New York, 1975), p. 84 (translation modified).

4. Ibid.

5. Ibid., p. 73.

6. *Hegel's Philosophy of Right*, §189 Addition, p. 268.

7. Ibid., §182 Addition, p. 267 (translation modified).

8. Hegel, *Lectures on the Philosophy of World History: Introduction*, p. 69.

9. Ibid., p. 67.

10. Ibid., p. 89.

11. Ibid., pp. 94–95.

12. Hermann Cohen, *Ethik des reinen Willens*, 3d ed. (Berlin, 1921), p. 8.

13. Max Scheler, *Problems of a Sociology of Knowledge*, trans. Manfred Frings (Boston, 1980), pp. 40–41.

Materialism and Morality

1. *C. ep. Manich.* 6.

2. Cf. Dilthey's *Gesammelte Schriften,* vol. 2 (Leipzig and Berlin, 1921), pp. 110ff.

3. Nicolai Hartmann, *Ethics,* trans. Stanton Coit (London, 1932), vol. 1, p. 29.

4. Ibid., vol. 2, p. 285.

5. Ibid., vol. 1, p. 30.

6. Immanuel Kant, *Foundations of the Metaphysics of Morals,* trans. L. W. Beck (New York, 1959), p. 39.

7. Ibid., p. 50.

8. Ibid., pp. 67ff.

9. Arthur Schopenhauer, *The Basis of Morality,* trans. Arthur B. Bullock (London, 1915), p. 99.

10. ["Moralische Triebfeder": "Impulsion" follows Paton's rendering in his translation of the *Grundlegung*; Beck renders this as "incentive," but he also recommends "urge." —Trans.]

11. Immanuel Kant, *Critique of Practical Reason,* trans. L. W. Beck (Indianapolis, 1956), p. 89.

12. The psychological theory of conscience, as developed for example by Freud in his work *The Ego and the Id* [trans. James Strachey (New York, 1960), pp. 18ff., esp. p. 27], is thoroughly reconcilable with this explanation. Psychology provides knowledge about the mechanism by which the predisposition for morality reproduces itself and strikes firm roots in the individual. The ground of existence of this mechanism, however, lies deeper than in the individual soul.

13. E.g., *Foundations,* p. 51.

14. Ibid., p. 39.

15. David Hume, "On Suicide," in *Hume's Ethical Writings,* ed. Alasdair MacIntyre (London, 1965), pp. 304–305.

16. Cf. Immanuel Kant, *Gesammelte Schriften,* Akademieausgabe (Berlin, 1902–1942), vol. 8, pp. 425ff. ["Über ein vermeintliches Recht, aus Menschenliebe zu lügen"].

17. Claude Adrien Helvétius, "De L'Esprit," in *Oeuvres complètes,* Part 1 (London, 1780), p. 206.

18. Immanuel Kant, "Perpetual Peace," in *On History,* ed. L. W. Beck (New York, 1963), p. 117.

19. Ibid., p. 129.

20. Ibid., p. 134.

21. Ibid., p. 127.

22. Cf. Immanuel Kant, *Critique of Pure Reason*, trans. Norman Kemp Smith (New York, 1965), p. 312.

23. Ibid.

24. Kant, "Perpetual Peace," p. 121.

25. Ibid.

26. Schopenhauer, *The Basis of Morality*, p. 100.

27. [We have read the "Kategorie" of the original as "Kategorien."—Trans.]

28. I Corinthians 12:25.

29. Cf. Immanuel Kant, *The Critique of Judgement*, trans. James C. Meredith (London, 1952), sec. 10, p. 61 (First Part), and sec. 64, pp. 16ff. (Second Part).

30. Kant, *Foundations*, p. 52.

31. Cf., e.g., *Hegel's Philosophy of Right*, trans. T. M. Knox (New York, 1952), sec. 258, pp. 155ff.

32. "Explanatory Notes to *Thus Spake Zarathustra*," trans. Anthony M. Ludovici, in *The Complete Works of Friedrich Nietzsche*, vol. 16 (New York, 1964, reissue), p. 269.

33. Immanuel Kant, "Reflexionen zur Metaphysik," in *Handschriftlicher Nachlass*, Akademieausgabe, vol. 18, p. 454.

34. Henri Bergson, *Les deux sources de la morale et de la religion* (Paris, 1932), p. 66.

35. Ibid., p. 41.

36. Ibid., p. 54.

37. Ibid.

38. Ibid., p. 98.

39. Hartmann, *Ethics*, vol. 1, p. 86.

40. Ibid., vol. 2, p. 23.

41. Ibid., vol. 1, p. 247.

42. Ibid., p. 259.

43. Ibid., vol. 2, p. 387.

44. Spinoza, *Ethica*, Pars III, Propos. XIII, Schol.

45. Immauel Kant, *Metaphysische Anfangsgründe der Rechtslehre*, Sec. 24, Akademieausgabe, vol. 6, p. 277.

46. Ibid., sec. 26, p. 278.

47. Sigmund Freud, *Three Essays on the Theory of Sexuality*, trans. James Strachey (New York, 1962), p. 50.

48. Nietzsche, "Explanatory Notes to *Thus Spake Zarathustra*," p. 269, modified translation.

49. Kant, *Critique of Pure Reason*, p. 475 (note).

50. Friedrich Engels, Vorarbeiten zum "Anti-Dühring," Marx-Engels-Archiv, vol. 2 (Frankfurt am Main, 1927), p. 408.

51. Celestin Bouglé, *Les idées égalitaires* (Paris, 1925), p. 248.

52. "Die psychoanalytische Charakterologie und ihre Bedeutung für die Sozialpsychologie" [The psychoanalytic theory of the personality and its significance for social psychology], *Zeitschrift für Sozialforschung* (1932), pp. 268ff., esp. p. 274.

53. *De ludo globi* II, pp. 236ff., cited in Ernst Cassirer, *Individuum und Kosmos in der Philosophie der Renaissance* (Berlin, 1927), p. 46.

54. Max Weber, " 'Objectivity' in Social Science and Social Policy," in *The Methodology of the Social Sciences*, trans. E. A. Shils and H. A. Finch (New York, 1949), pp. 81, 83.

55. John Stuart Mill, *The Positive Philosophy of Auguste Comte* (Boston, 1866), p. 88.

56. Cf., e.g., the discussion led by Edward Claparède at the meeting of the Société française de Philosophie on March 12, 1932 (see the Bulletin of this society, July/September 1932, published by Armand Colin in Paris).

57. Lucien Lévy-Bruhl, *La morale et la science des moeurs*, ninth printing (Paris, 1927), p. 98.

Egoism and Freedom Movements: On the Anthropology of the Bourgeois Era

1. Niccolò Machiavelli, *The Prince and the Discourses* (New York, 1950), p. 64.

2. Heinrich von Treitschke, *Politik*, vol. 2 (Leipzig, 1922), pp. 546ff.

3. Cf. Machiavelli, *The Prince and the Discourses*, pp. 111–115, and *The History of Florence* in *Niccolo Machiavelli and the United States of America*, ed. Anthony J. Pansini (Greenvale, 1969), p. 811.

4. Jean Jacques Rousseau, "Discours sur l'origine et les fondements de l'égalité parmi les hommes," in *Œuvres complètes*, vol. 3 (Frankfurt am Main, 1853), p. 25.

5. Cf. Dilthey, *Weltanschauung und Analyse des Menschen seit Renaissance und Reformation*, in *Gesammelte Schriften*, vol. 2 (Leipzig and Berlin, 1914), pp. 433–435; and Bernhard

Groethuysen, "Philosophische Anthropologie," in *Handbuch der Philosophie,* part 3 (Munich and Berlin, 1931), pp. 38ff.

6. Cf. H. Oncken, Introduction to More's *Utopia,* in *Klassiker der Politik,* vol. 1 (Berlin, 1922), pp. 38ff.

7. Machiavelli, *The Prince and the Discourses,* p. 118.

8. Ibid., p. 103.

9. H. Lammers, *Luthers Anschauung vom Willen* (Berlin, 1935), p. 15.

10. Calvin, *Institutio Religionis Christianae* (German ed., Neukirchen, 1928), pp. 118–120; cf. H. Engelland, *Gott und Mensch bei Calvin* (Munich, 1934), p. 49.

11. Cf., e.g., the speech on "The Relations between the Religious and Moral Ideas and Republican Principles" in the *Rapport imprimé par ordre de la Convention nationale* of the 18 Floréal 1794 session of the National Convention, pp. 26f.

12. Ibid., p. 8.

13. Ibid., p. 7.

14. Cf. my remarks on "Materialism and Morality" [in this volume].

15. Cf. Jeremy Bentham. His basic moral principle is so indefinite that two German philosophers have interpreted it in exactly opposite words. According to W. Wundt, in "Über den wahrhaften Krieg" (Leipzig, 1914), pp. 21ff., there is no doubt that Bentham meant "Let each do what is useful to him." But O. Kraus [in J. Bentham's *Grundsätze für ein künftiges Völkerrecht und einen dauernden Frieden,* ed. O. Kraus (Halle an der Saale, 1915), p. 8] reads "Let each one make himself as useful as possible." The contradiction contained in this concept of egoism disappears if one refers back to the society whose classes it applies to in different ways. Depending on the individual's social situation it assumes one meaning or the other.

16. Cf. George Berkeley, *Alciphron,* 2nd Dialogue, §§ 4 and 5.

17. Bernard Mandeville, *The Fable of the Bees* (London, 1934), p. 121.

18. K. Burdach, *Briefwechsel des Cola di Rienzo,* part 1 (Berlin, 1913–1928), p. 448.

19. Cf. ibid., p. 445.

20. Cf. ibid., p. 163.

21. Ibid., vol. 2, part 3, p. 222: "nam sine parcialitate, dum vixero, perdurabo, pro pace et statu totius Tuscie et Italie laboro."

22. Gregorovius, *Geschichte der Stadt Rom im Mittelalter,* vol. 2 (Dresden, 1926), p. 312.

23. Ibid., p. 319.

24. Ibid., p. 314.

25. Ibid., p. 316.

26. Cf. ibid., p. 411.

27. Burdach, *Briefwechsel des Cola di Rienzo*, vol. 1, p. 161.

28. Gregorovius, *Geschichte der Stadt Rom*, vol. 2, p. 376.

29. Ibid., p. 380.

30. Burdach, *Briefwechsel des Cola di Rienzo*, vol. 1, p. 105.

31. Gregorovius, *Geschichte der Stadt Rom*, vol. 2, p. 381.

32. Cf. Burdach, *Briefwechsel des Cola di Rienzo*, vol. 1, p. 451.

33. Gregorovius, *Geschichte der Stadt Rom*, vol. 2, pp. 321–353.

34. Burdach, *Briefwechsel des Cola di Rienzo*, vol. 1, p. 449.

35. Ibid. vol. 2, part 4, pp. 112ff.: "non contentus officio Rectoris, varios titulos impudenter et temere usurpavit . . . christiane religionis mores abiciens ac priscos gentilium ritus amplectens, varias coronas laureasque suscepit ac fatuas et sine lege leges more Cesarum promulgare temptavit"; cf. ibid., vol. 1, p. 31.

36. Cf. Gregorovius, *Geschichte der Stadt Rom*, vol. 2, p. 320.

37. Ibid., p. 332.

38. Erich Fromm, *Studien über Authorität und Familie*, Schriften des Institutes für Sozialforschung, vol. 5 (Paris, 1936), pp. 120ff.

39. On the identity of the authoritarian and rebellious character, see ibid., p. 131.

40. A document on the beginnings of this social self-consciousness shortly after Cola's time is the famous speech by a worker in the Florentine uprising, reported by Machiavelli in his *History of Florence*, p. 811.

41. Karl Marx, *The Eighteenth Brumaire of Louis Bonaparte* (New York, 1963), p. 15.

42. Gregorovius, *Geschichte der Stadt Rom*, vol. 2, p. 308.

43. Cf. Burdach, *Briefwechsel des Cola di Rienzo*, vol. 1, p. 454; vol. 2, part 3, p. 164.

44. Cf. ibid., vol. 1, pp. 475, 479.

45. Ibid., p. 451.

46. Ibid., p. 450.

47. Gregorovius, *Geschichte der Stadt Rom*, vol. 2, p. 321.

48. Cf. J. Schnitzer, *Savonarola*, vol. 1 (Munich, 1924), p. 227.

49. Cf. K. Kretschmayr, *Geschichte von Venedig*, vol. 2 (Gotha, 1920), pp. 130ff.; also Schnitzer, *Savonarola*, vol. 1, p. 210.

395

Notes to Pages 69–76

50. *Trattato circa il reggimento e governo della città di Firenze.*

5l. Cf. R. Roeder, *Savonarola* (New York, 1930), p. 131.

52. Schnitzer, *Savonarola*, vol. 1, p. 199.

53. Ibid., pp. 204ff.

54. Ibid., p. 212.

55. Ibid., pp. 2l3ff.

56. Machiavelli's admiration for Cesare Borgia, who in some regards himself bears the traits of a dictator of the bourgeois epoch, referred mainly to his national political goals and not, for instance, to the state of the hierarchy.

57. Cf. Schnitzer, *Savonarola*, vol. 1, pp. 324ff.

58. Ibid., vol. 2, p. 630.

59. Ibid., vol. 1, p. 465.

60. Ibid., pp. 506ff.

61. H. Grimm, *Leben Michelangelos*, vol. 1 (Stuttgart, 1922), pp. 188ff.

62. H. Thode, *Franz von Assisi und die Anfänge der Kunst der Renaissance in Italien* (Berlin, 1926), p. xxiv.

63. Schnitzer, *Savonarola*, vol. 1, p. 204.

64. Luther, *Ausgewählte Werke*, ed. H. H. Borcherdt (Munich, 1923), p. 165.

65. Ibid., pp. 7ff.

66. Gregorovius, *Geschichte der Stadt Rom*, vol. 2, p. 321.

67. H. Grundmann, *Religiöse Bewegungen im Mittelalter* (Berlin, 1955), pp. 35ff.; cf. p. 37.

68. Ibid., pp. 164ff.

69. Thode, *Franz von Assisi*, p. xix.

70. Ibid., p. 25.

71. Since the turn of the century, the Reformation has been increasingly used as a background for idealist confessions; Dilthey still presented a national as well as a socio-logical vision. He attacks Ritschl for not recognizing that the "new religious valuation of life" set forth by Ritschl "sprang from the progress of German society. . . . Germanic activity, intensified by the state of society as a will to do something, to create realities, to deal adequately with the things of this world, makes itself felt in this whole period and in Luther" (W. Dilthey, "Weltanschauung und Analyse des Menschen seit Renais-sance und Reformation," in *Gesammelte Schriften*, vol. 2 [Leipzig, 1914], p. 216). Troeltsch, as usual, vacillates. The theologian defends himself against the suspicion of a materi-

alistic conception of the Reformation by stressing that "Luther's religious idea really has a high personal originality; it emanates purely from the inner movement of religious thinking itself. It did not originate as a reflex to social or even economic transformation, but has its essential independent cause in the initiative of the religious thought from which the social, economic, and political consequences themselves first come. . . . At most indirectly, certain influences of those elements are recognizable. . . . Precisely for that reason, the Reformation's world of ideas cannot be linked with any particular social class. If nonetheless one is inclined to accord it a bourgeois character, and in a certain sense rightly so, if it contrasted with the seigneurial early medieval Church and against the democratically-proletarianly infected sects, then that is due only to that indirect connection. But this in turn is based on the psychologically easily understandable fact that absolutely all individualization of spiritual life that seizes the broad masses is connected with urbanization" (E. Troeltsch, "Die Soziallehren der christlichen Kirchen und Gruppen," in *Gesammelte Schriften,* vol. 1 [Tübingen, 1923], pp. 432ff.). As if an "at most indirect" connection were not also a connection! Others spoke more clearly. With a loyalty of conviction, which can dissuade one from objective arguments, H. Delbrück, for example, announces that "economic factors cannot be accorded a place among the causes of the Reformation" (*Weltgeschichte,* part 2 [Berlin, 1931], p. 253). The confusion seems to stem from the need to set oneself off from a falsely understood historical materialism, such as that of Kautsky, for example. But this kind of didactic, *Weltanschauung* materialism, precisely because of its undialectical conception of the relation between historical facts and general principles, displays an affinity with the metaphysical prejudices of these historians; although this affinity is concealed by principles that are contradictory at the level of content, it is by no means superseded.

72. Schnitzer, *Savonarola,* vol. 2, p. 685.

73. Ibid., p. 682.

74. Cf. ibid.

75. F. W. Kampschulte, *Johann Calvin,* vol. 2 (Leipzig, 1899), pp. 33ff.

76. Cf. ibid.

77. Friedrich von Bezold, *Geschichte der deutschen Reformation* (Berlin, 1890), p. 570.

78. *Luthers Werke,* ed. Buchwald et al., third issue, vol. 2 (Berlin, 1905), p. 282.

79. *Die evangelische Kirchenordnung des 16. Jahrhunderts,* ed. A. L. Richter, vol. 2 (Leipzig, 1871), p. 181; cf. also the *Landesordnung* of the dukedom of Prussia of 1525, ibid., vol. 1, p. 34, the Esslingen Church regulation of 1534, vol. 1, p. 247, and many other regulations.

80. Kampschulte, *Johann Calvin.*

81. Karl Lamprecht, *Deutsche Geschichte,* vol. 5, part 2 (Berlin, 1922), p. 372.

82. Ibid., pp. 373ff.

83. Friedrich Engels, *The German Revolutions* (Chicago, 1967), pp. 39–40.

84. Luther, "Von Kaufhandlung und Wucher," in *Ausgewählte Werke,* vol. 6, pp. 123ff.

85. Luther, "Wider die mörderischen und räuberischen Rotten der Bauern," in ibid., vol. 4, p. 300.

86. Luther, "Ein Sendbrief von dem harten Büchlein wider die Bauern," in ibid., p. 310.

87. Luther, "Ob Kriegsleute auch in seligen Stande sein können," in ibid., vol. 6, pp. 157ff.

88. Cf. Luther, "Von Kaufhandlung und Wucher," p. 134.

89. Luther, "Ob Kriegsleute auch in seligen Stande sein können," p. 158.

90. Calvin, *Institutio religionis christianae*, p. 596.

91. Ibid.

92. Ibid.

93. Ibid., p. 587.

94. Kampschulte, *Johann Calvin*, vol. 1, pp. 42lff.

95. P. Joachimsen, "Das Zeitalter der Reformation," in *Propyläen-Geschichte*, vol. 5 (Berlin, 1930), p. 31.

96. Vilfredo Pareto, *Traité de sociologie générale*, French ed. P. Bovet, vol. 2 (Lausanne and Paris, 1919), §2034, p. 1298; cf. Herbert Marcuse, "Ideengeschichtlicher Teil," in Fromm, *Studien über Authorität und Familie*, pp. 223ff.

97. Giordano Bruno, "Die Vertreibung der triumphierden Bestie," German trans. L. Kuhlenbeck, in *Gesammelte Werke*, vol. 2 (Leipzig, 1904), pp. 113ff.

98. Calvin, *Institutio Religionis Christianae*, p. 135.

99. Ibid., pp. 161f.

100. *Luthers Werke*, ed. Buchwald et al., third issue, vol. 1 (Leipzig, 1924), pp. 96f.

101. Schnitzer, *Savonarola*, vol. 1, p. 392.

102. Kampschulte, *Johann Calvin*, vol. 1, p. 166.

103. Cf. Schnitzer, *Savonarola*, vol. 1, pp. 271ff.

104. Ibid., p. 282.

105. The fetishization of childlikeness goes so far that the diminutive, the childlike form, becomes the characteristic poetic means of expression in bourgeois mysticism.

106. Cf. M. Kowalewsky, *Die ökonomische Entwicklung Europas*, German trans. A. Stein, vol. 7 (Berlin, 1914), p. 386.

107. A. Mathiez, *La vie chère et le mouvement social sous la Terreur* (Paris, 1927), p. 586.

108. A. Mathiez, *La réaction thermidorienne* (Paris, 1929), p. 2. Compare the detailed discussion of the Ventôse decrees in G. Lefebvre, *Questions agraires au temps de la Terreur* (Strasbourg, 1932), pp. 46ff.

109. Cf. Mathiez, *La vie chère,* pp. 581ff.

110. Ibid., pp. 605ff.

111. Rousseau, *Œuvres complètes,* vol. 6, p. 98.

112. Ibid., vol. 3, p. 183.

113. Ibid., p. 179.

114. Buchez and Roux, *Histoire parlementaire de la Révolution française,* vol. 26 (Paris, 1836), p. 130.

115. Cf. the speech just quoted.

116. Cf. A. Aulard, *La Société des Jacobins,* Recueil de Documents, vol. 5 (Paris, 1895), p. 179.

117. J. Michelet, *Histoire de la Révolution française,* vol. 8 (Paris, 1879), p. 268.

118. Cf. E. Hamel, *Histoire de Robespierre,* vol. 2 (Paris, undated), p. 321.

119. Cf. ibid., vol. 3, pp. 160f.

120. Ibid., p. 380.

121. Among other things, Chénier's hymn "God of the people, kings, cities, lands, Luther, Calvin, and the Children of Israel" was intoned. Cf. A. Mathiez, *Autour de Robespierre* (Paris, 1926), p. 121.

122. Hamel, *Histoire de Robespierre,* vol. 3, p. 382.

123. Gregorovius, *Geschichte der Stadt Rom,* vol. 2, p. 332.

124. Burdach, *Briefwechsel des Cola di Rienzo,* part 1, pp. 116ff.

125. Michelet, *Histoire de la Révolution française,* p. 271.

126. Ibid.

127. Gregorovius, *Geschichte der Stadt Rom,* vol. 2, p. 311.

128. Rousseau, Lettre à M d'Alembert, in *Œuvres complètes,* vol. 8, p. 232.

129. C. A. Cornelius, *Historische Arbeiten* (Leipzig, 1899), p. 475.

130. Kampschulte, *Johann Calvin,* vol. 1, p. 444.

131. Ibid., p. 445.

132. R. S. Ward, *Maximilian Robespierre* (London, 1934), p. 229.

133. As quoted in ibid., p. 167.

134. *Rapport imprimé par ordre de la Convention nationale,* pp. 28f.

135. R. H. Tawney, *Religion and the Rise of Capitalism* (London, undated), p. 267.

136. Nietzsche's critique of "European nihilism" amounts ultimately to the denial of cultural development since the beginning of Christianity. The nihilism spoken of in this article is more narrowly defined. It concerns the secret self-contempt of the individual on the basis of the contradiction between bourgeois ideology and reality. This self-contempt is usually linked with an exaggerated consciousness of freedom and of one's own or another's greatness. Because Nietzsche understands the term too widely and therefore unhistorically, he cannot understand that nihilism is overcome either by society as a whole or not at all. "We have grown to dislike egoism," he complains in *The Will to Power* [*Complete Works* (New York, 1964), vol. 14, p. 11]. But what he intentionally promotes is, however, merely the abstract self-consciousness of ancient slaveholders, and unintentionally, the good conscience of modern tyrants who reproduce the general nihilism which they carry in themselves.

137. Cf. Hippolyte Taine, *Les origines de la France contemporaine,* vol. 3 (Paris, 1881), pp. 294ff.; also vol. 4, pp. 276ff.

138. A. Mathiez, *La Révolution française,* vol. 3 (Paris, 1928), p. 81.

139. "Bilanz der preussischen Revolution," in *Aus dem literarischen Nachlass von K. Marx und F. Engels,* ed. F. Mehring, vol. 3 (Stuttgart, 1920), p. 211.

140. Engels to Marx, letter dated 4.9.1870, in *Marx/Engels Briefwechsel,* vol. 4 (Berlin, 1951), p. 577.

141. Mathiez, *La vie chère,* p. 356.

142. J. Jaurès, *Histoire socialiste de la Révolution française,* vol. 8 (Paris, 1924), p. 259.

143. Saint-Just, *Oeuvres complètes,* vol. 2 (Paris, 1905), p. 248.

144. A theoretically important continuation within psychoanalysis comes from Wilhelm Reich. Cf. especially his *Mass Psychology of Fascism.* I agree on many points with his psychological interpretation of individual traits of the bourgeois character. Reich, however, remains a true disciple of Freud's by deriving them essentially from sexual repression; he ascribes an almost utopian significance to the changing of the present conditions toward the disinhibition of genital sexuality.

145. Sigmund Freud, "Instincts and Their Vicissitudes," in *Complete Psychological Works* (London, 1962), vol. 14, p. 139.

146. Sigmund Freud, *Civilization and Its Discontents,* in *Complete Psychological Works,* vol. 21, p. 170.

147. Ibid., pp. 118ff.

148. Ibid., p. 122.

149. Ibid., p. 112.

150. Sigmund Freud, "Why War?," in *Complete Psychological Works*, vol. 22, p. 210.

151. Ibid., p. 212.

152. Ibid.

153. Freud, "Thoughts on War and Death" in *Complete Psychological Works*, vol. 14, p. 282.

154. Ibid.

155. Sigmund Freud, "New Introductory Lectures on Psychoanalysis," in *Complete Psychological Works*, vol. 22, pp. 103–104.

156. *Hegel's Philosophy of Mind*, trans. Wm. Wallace and A. V. Miller (Oxford, 1971), p. 240.

157. *Hegel's Philosophy of Right*, trans. T. M. Knox (New York, 1971), p. 109, §153.

158. Sigmund Freud, "New Introductory Lectures," p. 104.

159. Quoted after H. Cunow, *Die Parteien der grossen französischen Revolution und ihre Presse* (Berlin, 1912), p. 334.

160. Cf. Kampschulte, *Johann Calvin*, vol. 2, p. 268.

161. Cf. ibid., p. 270.

162. Ibid.

163. Ibid., p. 271.

164. Nietzsche, *Complete Works*, vol. 11, p. 205.

165. Cf. chapter 6 of the *Poetics*.

History and Psychology

1. [In Heideggerian philosophy, *Dasein* (sometimes hyphenated as *Da sein*, "there being") refers to "existence," as opposed to *Sein* or "Being." *Dasein* is the mode of being that is open to an understanding of its Being, its essence. The term, which carries a host of technical meanings, is traditionally left in German. For further explication of the translation of *Dasein*, see David H. Krell, ed., *Heidegger: Basic Writings* (New York, 1977), p. 48n.—Trans.]

2. J. G. Fichte, "Sun-Clear Statement to the Public at Large Concerning the True Nature of the Newest Philosophy," *Journal of Speculative Philosophy* 2, no. 2 (1868), p. 69.

3. Heinrich Rickert, *Die Grenzen der naturwissenschaftlichen Begriffsbildung*, 2d ed. (Tübingen, 1913), p. 487. [This passage does not appear in the abridged translation, *The Limits of Concept Formation in Natural Sciences*, ed. Guy Oakes (New York, 1986).—Trans.]

4. G. W. F. Hegel, *Lectures on the Philosophy of History,* trans. J. Sibree (London, 1914), p. 31.

5. Ibid.

6. [In his translation of the *Philosophy of Right* (New York, 1942), p. 375, T. M. Knox notes that " 'World history is the world's court of judgment' is a phrase from Schiller's poem 'Resignation' (*Gedichte der zweiten Periode*). Hegel does not insert quotation marks, and it may be for this reason that the phrase is sometimes falsely attributed to him."— Trans.]

7. Ibid., §360, p. 222.

8. E. Bernheim, *Lehrbuch der historischen Methode und der Geschichtsphilosophie,* 5th and 6th ed. (Leipzig, 1908), p. 677.

9. G. Tarde, *L'opinion et la foule* (Paris, 1922), p. 172. [The translation here is from Horkheimer's German.—Trans.]

10. Freud has taken an important step beyond the prevailing theories of mass psychology (Le Bon, McDougall) in his book *Massenpsychologie und Ich-Analyse.* [First published in 1921; English translation, *Group Psychology and the Analysis of the Ego,* trans. James Strachey (New York, 1959).—Trans.]

11. Immanuel Kant, *Critique of Pure Reason,* trans. Norman Kemp Smith (New York, 1965), p. 183.

12. In general, the sociological literature—even when it wants sociology radically distinguished from psychology, as in the Durkheimian school—contains deeper psychological insights than traditional academic psychology. Leopold von Wiese, for instance, objects to the burdening of his science with specifically psychological tasks, though he is certainly incorrect to assert that processes of consciousness are the only object of psychology. Yet his work shows evidence of a more differentiated knowledge of psychological processes than does that of those who subordinate sociology to psychology.

13. Wilhelm Dilthey, "Ideas about a Descriptive and Analytical Psychology," in *Selected Writings,* ed. H. P. Rickman (New York, 1976), p. 90.

14. Ibid.

15. Dilthey, "Ideen zu einer beschreibende und zergliedernde Psychologie," in *Gesammelte Schriften,* vol. 5 (Leipzig and Berlin, 1924), p. 236. [This passage is not translated in Rickman, ed., *Selected Writings.*—Trans.]

A New Concept of Ideology?

1. Karl Mannheim, *Ideologie und Utopie* (Bonn, 1929). [Except in the translators' notes, page numbers in parentheses refer to the English translation, *Ideology and Utopia: An Introduction to the Sociology of Knowledge,* trans. Louis Wirth and Edward Shils (New York, 1936). We have quite frequently found it necessary to retranslate this text, however, in order to reveal the substance of Horkheimer's critique of Mannheim. Passages of the translation that we have modified are indicated by the symbol [M.]. Ironically, in order to lend Mannheim's study an idealistic and universalistic veneer more acceptable

to an Anglo-American audience, the translators often exaggerated precisely those characteristics of Mannheim's analysis to which Horkheimer objects, namely, his resurrection of an idealist metaphysics in the guise of a sociology of knowledge that lays claim to scientific status.—Trans.]

2. [The English version does not include any translation of the term "*Zurechnungssubjekt.*" On Mannheim's use of the term "*Zurechnung,*" see Mannheim, *Conservatism: A Contribution to the Sociology of Knowledge,* trans. David Kettler and Volker Meja from a first draft by Elizabeth R. King, edited by David Kettler, Volker Meja, and Nico Stehr (New York, 1986), p. 42n, where the translators write of his exposition there: "Mannheim [uses] . . . the term '*Zurechnung*' to cover . . . claims about correspondence of meanings between some analysed occurrence and another, presumably more comprehensive or systematic structure, and claims about empirical linkages between concrete intellectual phenomena and unit(s) of analysis constituted by sociological and/or historical study."—Trans.]

3. [This phrase is emphasized in the German but not in the English translation.—Trans.]

4. Wilhelm Dilthey, *Das Erlebnis und die Dichtung* (Leipzig and Berlin, 1919), p. 307. [This portion of *Das Erlebnis und die Dichtung* is not translated in Rudolf Makkreel and Frithjof Rodi, eds., *Poetry and Experience,* vol. 5 of Dilthey's *Selected Works* (Princeton, 1985).—Trans.]

5. Wilhelm Dilthey, *Meaning in History,* ed. H. P. Rickman (London, 1961), p. 138.

6. Wilhelm Dilthey, *Gesammelte Schriften,* vol. 1 (Leipzig and Berlin, 1927), p. 422.

7. Ibid.

8. Karl Mannheim, "The Problem of a Sociology of Knowledge," in *Essays on the Sociology of Knowledge,* trans. and ed. Paul Kecskemeti (London, 1952), p. 177.

9. Ibid., p. 172.

10. See Martin Heidegger, *Being and Time,* trans. John Macquarrie and Edward Robinson (New York, 1962), pp. 268ff.

11. Mannheim, "The Problem of a Sociology of Knowledge," p. 137, n. 1.

12. Machiavelli, *Florentine Histories,* trans. Laura F. Banfield and Harvey C. Mansfield, Jr. (Princeton, 1988), p. 123.

13. See Mannheim, "The Problem of a Sociology of Knowledge," pp. 184ff.

14. Karl Mannheim, "Das konservative Denken," *Archiv für Sozialwissenschaft und Sozialpolitik,* vol. 57, p. 76. [The English translation—"Conservative Thought," in *Essays in Sociology and Social Psychology,* ed. Paul Kecskemeti (New York, 1953)—does not include this passage. The passage given here is from Mannheim's recently translated dissertation, *Conservatism,* p. 76 (translation modified).—Trans.]

15. Mannheim, "The Problem of a Sociology of Knowledge," p. 185 (translation modified). Emphasis in the original.

16. Mannheim, "Conservative Thought," p. 101.

17. Mannheim, "Competition as a Cultural Phenomenon," in *Essays on the Sociology of Knowledge*, p. 210.

18. Ernst Troeltsch, "Die theologische und religiöse Lage der Gegenwart," *Gesammelte Schriften*, vol. 1 (Tübingen, 1919), p. 8.

19. Ibid., p. 9.

20. [This passage does not appear in the English translation. It is to be found in the original at p. 3.—Trans.]

21. Mannheim, "Conservative Thought."

Remarks on Philosophical Anthropology

1. Max Scheler, *Man's Place in Nature*, trans. Hans Meyerhoff (New York, 1971), p. 88.

2. Paul Ludwig Landsberg, *Einführung in die philosophische Anthropologie* (Frankfurt am Main, 1934), pp. 29–30.

3. Scheler, *Man's Place in Nature*, p. 92.

4. Ibid., p. 94.

5. Landsberg, *Einführung in die philosophische Anthropologie*, p. 41.

6. Max Scheler, *Formalism in Ethics and Non-Formal Ethics of Values*, trans. Manfred S. Frings and Roger L. Funk (Evanston, 1973), pp. 89–90.

7. Joseph de Maistre, *Ouevres Complètes*, vol. 2 (Lyons, 1892), p. 339.

8. Scheler, *Man's Place in Nature*, p. 6.

9. Leopold von Ranke, *Zwölf Bücher preussischer Geschichte*, Akadamie-Ausgabe, first series, 9, vol. 2 (Munich, 1930), p. 534.

10. Cf. R. Koser, *Geschichte Friedrichs des Grossen*, vol. 1 (Stuttgart and Berlin, 1912), pp. 402–403.

11. Thomas Hobbes, *Selections*, ed. F. J. E. Woodbridge (New York, 1958), p. 292.

12. Friedrich Nietzsche, *Werke*, vol. 12 (Leipzig, 1919), p. 360.

13. Ibid., vol. 13, pp. 212–213.

14. Friedrich Nietzsche, *Thus Spoke Zarathustra*, trans. Walter Kaufmann (New York, 1972), p. 321.

15. Cf. Wilhelm Dilthey, *Gesammelte Schriften*, vol. 2 (Leipzig, 1914), pp. 451ff.

16. Edmund Husserl, "Philosophy as a Rigorous Science," in *Phenomenology and the Crisis of Philosophy*, trans. Quentin Lauer (New York, 1965), p. 136.

17. Aristotle, *Politics,* 1254a 23.

18. Hermann Diels and Walther Kranz, *Fragmente der Vorsokratiker* (Berlin, 1956), fragment 242. Translation from Kathleen Freeman, *Ancilla to the Presocratic Philosophers* (Cambridge, Mass., 1978), p. 113.

19. Diels and Kranz, *Fragmente,* fragment 33; Freeman, *Ancilla,* p. 99.

20. Hegel, *Early Theological Writings,* trans. T. M. Knox (Philadelphia, 1981), p. 233.

21. Bernhard Groethuysen, "Philosophical Anthropology," in *Handbuch der Philosophie,* part 3 (Munich and Berlin, 1931), p. 205.

On the Problem Of Truth

1. C. Sigwart, *Logic* (Freiburg im Breisgau, 1889), vol. 1, p. 111.

2. Immanuel Kant, *Prolegomena* §13, Note III, in *Gesammelte Schriften,* Akademieausgabe (Berlin, 1902–1942), vol. 4, p. 293.

3. Edmund Husserl, "Formale und transzendentale Logik," *Jahrbuch für Philosophie und phänomenologische Forschung,* vol. 10 (Halle, 1929), p. 241.

4. "Materialism and Metaphysics," in Max Horkheimer, *Critical Theory: Selected Essays* (Herder and Herder, 1972), pp. 40f.

5. Cf. J. S. Bixler, *Religion in the Philosophy of William James* (Boston, 1926), pp. 126ff.

6. William James, *Human Immortality* (Boston and New York, 1898), p. 27.

7. F. C. S. Schiller, *Riddles on the Sphinx* (London, 1891), p. 295.

8. G. W. F. Hegel, *Phenomenology of Spirit,* trans. A. V. Miller (Oxford, 1977), p. 29.

9. Ibid., p. 51.

10. G. W. F. Hegel, *The Philosophy of Fine Art,* trans. F. P. R. Osmaston (London, 1920), pp. 130ff.

11. Ibid., p. 131.

12. Trendelenburg, *Logische Untersuchungen* (Leipzig, 1870), vol. 1, pp. 42ff.

13. Cf. G. W. F. Hegel, *The Philosophy of History,* trans. J. Sibree (London, 1900), p. 350.

14. Hegel, *Phenomenology of Spirit,* p. 234.

15. *Hegel's Logic* (Being Part One of the *Encyclopaedia of the Philosophical Sciences* [1830]), trans. Wm. Wallace, foreword by J. N. Findlay (Oxford, 1975), pp. 91f. (§60).

16. Cf. G. W. F. Hegel, *Science of Logic,* trans. W. H. Johnston and L. G. Struthers (New York, 1929), pp. 226f.

17. Husserl, "Formale und transzendentale Logik," p. 140.

18. [*Bewährung* is the noun form of the more easily rendered *sich bewähren:* to prove oneself/itself, to stand the test, to demonstrate one's/its effectiveness or worth, to prove to be true. It is the single most important word in the section on pragmatism, arguably in the entire essay, and it does not mean "corroboration." We have found it impossible, however, to render *Bewährung* into an English substantive that matches Horkheimer's usage. Though Horkheimer himself translates "corroboration" as *Bewährung* in the passage from Dewey cited in note 25, "corroboration" is too weak to capture what Horkheimer intends with the term. The pragmatist use of the term "corroboration" connotes a sense of constancy and reliability; when Horkheimer discusses the relation of *Bewährung* to truth, the implicit (and sometimes explicit) connection is always with *praxis.*—Trans.]

19. Edmund Husserl, *Logische Untersuchungen* (Halle an der Saale, 1913), vol. 1, p. 115.

20. Epicurus, translated by W. Nestle in *Die Nachsokratiker* (Jena, 1923), vol. 1, p. 202.

21. Goethe, Letter to Zelter, December 31, 1829.

22. Friedrich Nietzsche, *The Will to Power,* in *The Complete Works of Friedrich Nietzsche,* ed. Oscar Levy (New York, 1974), vol. 15, pp. 49f.

23. Friedrich Nietzsche, *Werke* (Leipzig, 1911), vol. 11, p. 186.

24. William James, "Pragmatism," in *Writings of William James* (New York, 1968), p. 436.

25. John Dewey, *Reconstruction in Philosophy* (Boston, 1957), p. 156.

26. James, "Pragmatism," p. 436.

27. Ibid., p. 435.

28. Max Adler, *Marx als Denker* (Berlin, 1908), p. 75.

29. Max Scheler, "Erkenntnis und Arbeit," in *Die Wissenschaften und die Gesellschaft* (Leipzig, 1926), pp. 250ff.

30. Ibid., p. 485.

31. Ibid., p. 44.

32. Ibid., p. 484.

33. Ibid., p. 486.

34. In the *Phenomenology* (p. 21), Hegel himself described the dialectic as the "science of experience, which creates consciousness." Nicolai Hartmann considers this definition the only authoritative one (see his essay "Hegel und das Problem der Realdialektik," published in French in the collection *Etudes sur Hegel* [Paris, 1931]; cf. esp. pp. 17ff.). In the materialistic interpretation it acquires a more fundamental meaning than in Hegelian logic itself, since Hegel's closed metaphysics rules out, in the future course of history, decisive experience which could change currently valid conceptual structures. Hartmann's contemplative point of view causes him to misunderstand the interaction between concept and object, so that he one-sidedly interprets the dynamic nature of

thought as a "subjective law of thought" arising from the effort of the subject to follow reality and adapt itself to it. The problem of the changes occurring in praxis in the relationship between the two principles in the course of the historical process is not posed; instead, both are preserved in their isolation.

35. *Kant's Introduction to Logic,* trans. T. K. Abbott (New York, 1963), p. 3.

36. Ibid., p. 53.

37. Ibid., p. 54.

38. Hegel, *Phenomenology of Spirit,* p. 32.

39. *Hegel's Logic,* p. 18 (§12).

40. See "The Rationalism Debate in Contemporary Philosophy" [included in this volume].

41. *Hegel's Logic,* p. 121 (§83, A.).

42. G. W. F. Hegel, *The Philosophical Propaedeutic,* trans. A. V. Miller (Oxford, 1986), p. 126.

43. Friedrich Nietzsche, *Werke,* second series (Leipzig, 1919), vol. 11, p. 171.

44. Ernst Troeltsch, "Zur religiösen Lage, Religionsphilosophie und Ethik," in *Gesammelte Schriften* (Tübingen, 1922), vol. 2, p. 535.

45. Ibid., pp. 190ff.

46. Ibid.

47. Ibid., pp. 191ff.

48. Ibid.

49. Ibid.

50. Ibid., p. 311.

51. Cf. ibid., p. 802.

52. Nietzsche, *Ecce Homo,* in *Werke,* second series (Leipzig, 1933), vol. 11, p. 115.

The Rationalism Debate in Contemporary Philosophy

1. David Hume, *A Treatise on Human Nature,* ed. L. A. Selby-Bigge, 2d ed., rev. P. H. Nidditch (New York, 1978), p. xvii.

2. David Hume, *An Enquiry Concerning Human Understanding,* in *The Empiricists* (Garden City, 1974), p. 312.

3. Hume, *Treatise,* p. xviii.

4. Hermann von Helmholtz, "On Academic Freedom in German Universities," in his *Popular Lectures on Scientific Subjects*, trans. E. Atkinson (London, 1908), p. 246.

5. Hegel, "Proceedings of the Estates Assembly in the Kingdom of Wurtemberg, 1815–1816," in *Hegel's Political Writings*, trans. T. M. Knox (Oxford, 1964), pp. 282–283.

6. Ernst Troeltsch, "Die Restaurationsepoche am Anfang des 19. Jahrhunderts," in his *Gesammelte Schriften*, vol. 4 (Tübingen, 1925), pp. 587–614.

7. Ernst Krieck, *Nationalpolitische Erziehung* (Leipzig, 1933), p. 111.

8. Ernst Jünger, *Der Arbeiter*, 2d ed. (Hamburg, 1932), p. 71.

9. Erich Rothacker, *Logik und Systematik der Geisteswissenschaften*, in *Handbuch der Philosophie*, part 2 (Munich and Berlin, 1927), p. C130.

10. Wilhelm Scherer, *Vorträge und Aufsätze zur Geschichte des geistigen Lebens in Deutschland und Österreich* (Berlin, 1874), pp. 340–341.

11. See, e.g., Max Scheler, *On the Eternal in Man*, trans. Bernard Noble (New York, 1961), pp. 95ff.

12. Heinrich Rickert, *Die Philosophie des Lebens* (Tübingen, 1922), p. 30.

13. Ibid., p. 102.

14. Ibid., p. 54.

15. Cf. Heinrich Rickert, *System der Philosophie*, part 1 (Tübingen, 1921), p. 368.

16. Rickert, *Die Philosophie des Lebens*, p. 148.

17. See the works of W. Köhler, M. Wertheimer, A. Gelb, K. Koffka, et al.

18. Oswald Spengler, *The Decline of the West*, trans. Charles Francis Atkinson, vol. 1 (New York, 1934), p. 353.

19. Ibid.

20. Ludwig Klages, *Der Geist als Widersacher der Seele*, vol. 3 (Leipzig, 1929–1932), pp. 451–452.

21. Ibid., pp. 766–777.

22. Ibid., p. 452.

23. Martin Heidegger, *Being and Time*, trans. John Macquarrie and Edward Robinson (New York, 1962), p. 175.

24. Dacque, *Natur und Erlösung* (Munich and Berlin, 1933), p. 53.

25. Jünger, *Der Arbeiter*, p. 161.

26. Claude Adrien Helvétius, "De l'Homme," in *Oeuvres complètes*, part 5 (London, 1780), p. 29.

27. Henri Bergson, *An Introduction to Metaphysics,* trans. T. E. Hulme (New York, 1912), pp. 24–29.

28. *Hegel's Logic,* trans. William Wallace (New York, 1975), §227 Addition, p. 285.

29. Ibid., §79, p. 113.

30. Hegel, *Lectures on the History of Philosophy,* vol. 3, trans. E. S. Haldane and F. H. Simson (London, 1896), p. 176.

31. Karl Marx, Afterword to the second German Edition of *Capital,* ed. Friedrich Engels, trans. Samuel Moore and Edward Aveling, vol. 1 (London, 1974), p. 28.

32. *Hegel's Logic,* §38 Addition, p. 63.

33. *Hegel's Science of Logic,* trans. A. V. Miller (London, 1969), p. 50.

34. Ludwig Feuerbach, "Principles of the Philosophy of the Future," in *The Fiery Brook: Selected Writings of Ludwig Feuerbach,* trans. Zawar Hanfi (Garden City, 1972), §50, p. 239.

35. Ibid. [Translation modified.]

36. For some of these conditions, see Martin Heidegger, "What Is Metaphysics?," in his *Basic Writings,* ed. D. F. Krell (New York, 1977): "Profound boredom, drifting here and there in the abysses of our existence like a muffling fog, removes all things and men and oneself along with it into a remarkable indifference. This boredom reveals beings as a whole. Another possibility of such revelation is concealed in our joy in the present existence . . . of a human being whom we love. . . . The founding mode of attunement [*Die Befindlichkeit der Stimmung*] . . . reveals beings as a whole in various ways. . . . In the clear night of the nothing of anxiety the original openness of beings as such arises: that they are beings and not nothing" (pp. 101–105).

37. [In English in the original.—Trans.]

38. *Hegel's Philosophy of Right,* trans. T. M. Knox (Oxford, 1953), §270, p. 164.

39. Friedrich Nietzsche, "The Genealogy of Morals," in *The Birth of Tragedy and the Genealogy of Morals,* trans. Francis Golffing (Garden City, 1956), p. 193.

40. *Hegel's Science of Logic,* p. 516.

41. Othmar Spann, *Gesellschaftslehre* (Leipzig, 1930), p. 562.

42. Ibid., pp. 562–563.

43. Othmar Spann, "Universalismus," in *Handwörterbuch der Staatswissenschaften,* vol. 8 (Jena, 1928), p. 456.

44. Spann, *Gesellschaftslehre,* p. 100.

45. See the excellent critique of this approach by M. Hartmann in *Die methodologischen Grundlagen der Biologie* (Leipzig, 1933).

46. Jünger, *Der Arbeiter,* p. 170.

47. See in particular Sigmund Freud, "Instincts and Their Vicissitudes," in his *Collected Papers*, vol. 4 (New York, 1959), pp. 69–76.

48. Nietzsche, "The Genealogy of Morals," p. 256.

49. Ibid., p. 271.

50. Ibid., pp. 271–272.

51. Max Scheler, "Tod und Fortleben," in *Schriften aus dem Nachlass*, vol. 1 (Berlin, 1933), p. 26.

52. See, e.g., Lucretius, *De rerum natura*, Book II, lines 58–60, and Book V, lines 1–55. [For an English translation, see Lucretius, *The Nature of Things*, trans. Frank O. Copley (New York, 1977), pp. 2, 113–114.—Trans.]

53. Heidegger, *Being and Time*, p. 175.

Montaigne and the Function of Skepticism

1. [The Diadochi were the generals and successors of Alexander the Great (from the Greek word *diadochos*, "successor").—Trans.]

2. Jacob Burckhardt, *Griechische Kulturgeschichte*, vol. 4, in his *Gesammelte Werke*, vol. 8 (Basel and Stuttgart, 1978), pp. 492–493.

3. H. See, *Französische Wirtschaftsgeschichte*, vol. 1 (Jena, 1930), p. 57.

4. See ibid., pp. 120–126.

5. Jules Michelet, *History of the French Revolution*, trans. Charles Cocks (Chicago, 1967), p. 34.

6. See Montaigne's own accounts, e.g., *Les essais*, ed. Pierre Villey (Paris, 1930–1931), Book II, chapter 32, pp. 781–782. [Unless otherwise indicated, further citations of Montaigne will be from the English translation, *The Essays of Montaigne*, 2 vols., trans. E. J. Trechmann (New York, n.d. [1935?]). The passage here is from vol. 2, p. 173.—Trans.]

7. Gustave Fagniez, *L'economie sociale de la France sous Henri IV* (Paris, 1897), pp. 78–79.

8. Ibid., p. 167.

9. Montaigne, *Essays*, vol. 2, Book III, chapter 9, p. 437.

10. Ibid., vol. 1, Book II, chapter 12, pp. 499–500.

11. Ibid., p. 501.

12. See Eduard Zeller, *The Stoics, Epicureans, and Sceptics*, trans. Oswald J. Reichel (New York, 1962 [reissued]), p. 518.

13. Ibid., p. 536 n. 1.

14. Montaigne, *Essays,* vol. 2, Book III, chapter 1, p. 244.

15. Henri Hauser, *La prépondérance espagnole* (Paris, 1933), p. 57. See in particular Albert Elkan, *Die Publizistik der Bartholomäusnacht* (Heidelberg, 1905), pp. 87ff.

16. See Goethe, "Besprechung des deutschen Gil Blas," *Sämtliche Werke,* Cotta'sche Jubiläumsausgabe (Stuttgart and Berlin), vol. 37, p. 206.

17. Goethe, "Besprechung der Principes de philosophie zoologique von G. de St.-Hilaire," *Sämtliche Werke,* vol. 39, p. 228.

18. See Zeller, *The Stoics, Epicureans, and Sceptics,* p. 534.

19. Ibid., p. 562.

20. Montaigne, *Essays,* vol. 2, Book II, chapter 12, p. 35.

21. See Eduard Zeller, *Die Philosophie der Griechen in ihrer geschichtlichen Entwicklung,* part 3, section 2 (Leipzig, 1923), pp. 71–73. See also Raoul Richter, *Der Skeptizismus in der Philosophie und seine Überwindung,* vol. 1 (Leipzig, 1904), pp. 102–103.

22. [In his translation of Hegel's *Phenomenology of Spirit* (Oxford, 1977), p. 124, Miller renders *Ataraxie* as "stoical indifference."—Trans.]

23. Montaigne, *Essays,* vol. 1, Book I, chapter 39, p. 240.

24. Ibid.

25. "Conversation of Pascal with de Saci, on Epictetus and Montaigne," in *The Works of Pascal,* trans. and ed. George Pearce (London, 1849), vol. 2, pp. 287–288.

26. Montaigne, *Essays,* vol. 1, Book I, chapter 39, pp. 237–238.

27. Ibid., vol. 2, Book III, chapter 9, p. 438.

28. Ibid., p. 454. [In French in the English translation.—Trans.]

29. The Neoplatonic theosophist Philo disputes the possibility of knowledge on the same grounds—indeed, with the same words—as the skeptics. See Zeller, *Die Philosophie der Griechen,* pp. 9–10, 390.

30. See the quotations in "Egoism and Freedom Movements" [reprinted in this volume, p. 86].

31. See Villey's introduction to Book II, chapter 12 of *Les essais,* pp. 208–209.

32. Montaigne, *Essays,* vol. 1, Book II, chapter 12, p. 441.

33. Ibid., vol. 2, Book II, chapter 17, p. 83.

34. John Calvin, *Institutes of the Christian Religion,* trans. John Allen, 6th American edition (Philadelphia, n.d. [1813?]), vol. 1, pp. 244–245.

35. Montaigne, *Essays,* vol. 1, Book II, chapter 12, p. 482.

36. Ibid., vol. 2, Book II, chapter 12, p. 8.

37. Ibid., vol. 1, Book II, chapter 12, p. 502.

38. Ibid. [We have generally translated Montaigne's singular *l'homme* in the plural: "they," "them," "their," "themselves."—Trans.]

39. Calvin, *Institutes,* p. 255.

40. See J. Bohatec, *Calvins Lehre von Staat und Kirche* (Breslau, 1937), p. 117. Bohatec also recognizes that Calvin concurs with Montaigne on this point.

41. Martin Luther, *Kritische Gesamtausgabe* (Weimar, 1883ff.), vol. 2, p. 240.

42. Luther, "Sermo Die Epiphaniae," in ibid., vol. 1, pp. 123–124.

43. Luther, "Quaestio de viribus et voluntate hominis sine gratia disputata 1516," ibid., p. 148.

44. Calvin, *Institutes,* p. 247.

45. See Montaigne, *Essays,* vol. 2, Book III, chapter 13, p. 545.

46. Ibid., vol. 1, Book II, chapter 12, p. 429.

47. Ibid., vol. 2, Book II, chapter 19, p. 119.

48. See E. Lavisse, *Histoire de France* (Paris, 1904), vol. 4, pp. 57–59, on the meeting of the Catholic dignitaries with the Duke of Württemberg two weeks before the massacre in Vassy, which Guise described to the Duke as an "accident."

49. Montaigne, *Essays,* vol. 1, Book II, chapter 12, p. 433.

50. See Lavisse, *Histoire de France,* p. 181.

51. Jean Bodin, *The Six Bookes of a Commonweale,* reprint of the English translation of 1606, ed. K. D. McRae (Cambridge, Mass., 1962), Book 4, chapter 7, p. 539.

52. Montaigne, *Essays,* vol. 2, Book II, chapter 12, p. 2.

53. See E. Cassirer, *The Platonic Renaissance in England,* trans. James P. Pettegrove (Austin, 1953), p. 158.

54. See G. Lanson, *Les Essais de Montaigne* (Paris, 1930), pp. 326–327.

55. Marsilio Ficino, *Theologia platonica de immortalitate animorum,* cited in E. Cassirer, *Das Erkenntnisproblem in der Philosophie und Wissenschaft der neueren Zeit,* vol. 1 (Berlin, 1911), p. 92. See the entire account of Ficino given there.

56. See the excellent account in H. Ritter, *Geschichte der Philosophie,* vol. 10 (Hamburg, 1851), pp. 288ff.

57. *Hegel's Phenomenology of Spirit,* trans. A. V. Miller (New York, 1977), p. 124.

58. Montaigne, *Essays,* vol. 2, Book III, chapter 12, p. 511.

59. See Villey's introductions to chapter 20 in Book I (p. 145), and to chapter 12 in Book III (pp. 504–505) of *Les essais*.

60. Montaigne, *Essays*, vol. 1, Book I, chapter 20, p. 89.

61. Ibid., vol. 1, Book I, chapter 14, p. 63.

62. Montaigne let stand the remark about the barbaric justice of the Christians in the chapter on cruelty (ibid., Book II, chapter 11, p. 423), even though the representative of the Inquisition politely and halfheartedly urged its modification during Montaigne's visit to Rome. The essay on the cannibals (Book I, chapter 31), from which Shakespeare and Goethe included passages *verbatim* in their own literary works, is among the most beautiful of his oeuvre. One finds there the remark directed against the terror of the powers that be: "I think there is more barbarity in eating a live than a dead man, in tearing on the rack and torturing the body of a man still full of feeling, in roasting him piecemeal and giving him to be bitten and mangled by dogs and swine . . . than in roasting and eating him after he is dead" (vol. 1, Book I, chapter 31, pp. 209–210). In other words, the powerful within Christianity rank lower than the cannibals.

63. Ibid., vol. 1, Book I, chapter 50, p. 296.

64. See the discussion of Luther's and Calvin's attitudes toward authority in Herbert Marcuse, "A Study on Authority," in *Studies in Critical Philosophy*, trans. Joris de Bres (Boston, 1973), pp. 56–78.

65. On this mechanism, see "Egoism and Freedom Movements" [included in this volume].

66. See Friedrich von Bezold, *Geschichte der deutschen Reformation* (Berlin, 1890), pp. 500–501.

67. See Günther Franz, *Der deutsche Bauernkrieg* (Munich and Berlin, 1933), p. 418.

68. François Tavera, *L'idée d'humanité dans Montaigne* (Paris, 1932), p. 239.

69. *The Works of Pascal*, vol. 2, p. 287.

70. See Vauvenargues, *Oeuvres*, ed. Gilbert, vol. 1 (Paris, 1857), pp. 22, 274–276.

71. See *Nicolas Malebranche: The Search after Truth*, trans. Thomas M. Lennon and Paul J. Olscamp (Columbus, 1980), Book II, part 3, chapter 5.

72. See Charles Adam, *Vie et oeuvres de Descartes* (Paris, 1910), p. 415.

73. Peter King, *The Life of John Locke, with extracts from his correspondence, journals and common-place books* (London, 1830), vol. 1, p. 296.

74. Ernst Troeltsch, "Geschichte der christlichen Religion," in *Die Kultur der Gegenwart*, part I, section IV, I, second half (Leipzig and Berlin, 1922), pp. 615–617.

75. [In English in the original.—Trans.]

76. The characterization of Montaigne as a pagan in F. Mauthner's otherwise exact description (*Geschichte des Atheismus*, vol. 2 [Stuttgart and Berlin, 1922], p. 188) is incorrect. In contrast, see M. Dreano, *La pensée religieuse de Montaigne* (Paris, 1937).

77. David Hume, "Dialogues Concerning Natural Religion," in *The Empiricists* (Garden City, 1974), p. 488.

78. David Hume, *A Treatise of Human Nature,* ed. L. A. Selby-Bigge, 2d ed., rev. P. H. Nidditch (Oxford, 1978), pp. 250–251.

79. Honoré de Balzac, *The House of Nucingen,* trans. William Walton (Philadelphia, 1896), p. 8. [Translation modified.]

80. Montaigne, *Essays,* p. 1.

81. Ibid., vol. 1, Book I, chapter 30, p. 197.

82. Ibid., vol. 2, Book III, chapter 13, p. 548.

83. Niccolo Machiavelli, *Discourses,* Book III, chapter 10, in *The Prince and the Discourses* (New York, 1950), p. 444.

84. Ibid.

85. Montaigne, *Essays,* vol. 2, Book III, chapter 2, p. 258.

86. Gide regrets that Cervantes's book appeared only after Montaigne's death. It seemed to Gide to have been written especially for Montaigne. "It was at the expense of Don Quixote that, little by little, Sancho Panza came to great stature in him." There can be no doubt of the affinity of the contemporary skeptics with Sancho. What is new is that they carefully pretend to be Don Quixotes. Their recipe consists in being philosophically radical and socially conformist. The fact that Montaigne is so understood is the secret of his continuing popularity. See André Gide, *Montaigne, An Essay in Two Parts,* trans. Stephen H. Guest and Trever E. Blewith (New York, 1929), p. 91.

87. See on this point R. Aron, "La sociologie de Pareto," *Zeitschrift für Sozialforschung,* vol. 6 (1937), pp. 489–521.

88. G. W. F. Hegel, *Lectures on the History of Philosophy,* trans. E. S. Haldane and F. H. Simson (London, 1892–1896), vol. 1, p. 95. [Haldane's and Simson's translation, based on the second, amended edition of Hegel's *Geschichte der Philosophie* (1840), reverses the order of these two sentences and includes some wording not found in the edition from which Horkheimer quotes. Horkheimer's quotation of Hegel reads as follows: "Denken heisst, etwas in die Form der Allgemeinheit zu bringen; sich denken, heisst, sich in sich als Allgemeines wissen, sich die Bestimmung des Allgemeinen geben, sich auf sich beziehen. Darin ist das Element der praktischen Freiheit enthalten."—Trans.]

89. [Hegel's term "bürgerliche Gesellschaft" is normally translated "civil society." Horkheimer, however, tends consistently to use a Marxist phraseology that implies the translation "*bourgeois* society." Except where it is clear that Horkheimer wants to discuss Hegel's conception, we revert to the latter formulation.—Trans.]

90. G. W. F. Hegel, *Lectures on the Philosophy of History,* trans. J. Sibree (London, 1914), p. 388.

91. See F. Neumann, "The Change in the Function of Law in Modern Society," in *The Democratic and the Authoritarian State: Essays in Political and Legal Theory,* ed. Herbert Marcuse (New York, 1957), pp. 22–68.

92. Montaigne, *Essays*, vol. 2, Book III, chapter 9, p. 439.

93. The oath comes not from reality but from belles-lettres. E. J. Trechmann argues (*Essays*, vol. 1, p. 453 n. 1) that it is taken seriously by neither real gladiators nor those of fiction. It thus expresses even more exactly the attitude of the present-day followers of authoritarianism.

94. Ibid., vol. 1, Book II, chapter 12, pp. 452–453.

95. Ibid., vol. 2, Book III, chapter 8, p. 390.

96. Ibid., vol. 2, Book III, chapter 13, p. 548.

97. Ibid., vol. 1, Book I, chapter 23, p. 115.

98. Nietzsche, "Richard Wagner in Bayreuth," in *Untimely Meditations*, trans. R. J. Hollingdale (New York, 1983), p. 212.

99. Ibid., p. 207.

100. Nietzsche, "Schopenhauer as Educator," in *Untimely Meditations*, p. 135.

101. See Montaigne, *Essays*, vol. 2, Book III, chapter 12, p. 517.

102. Nietzsche, *Werke*, Grossoktavausgabe, vol. 14 (Leipzig, 1917), pp. 176–177.

103. In reality, criticisms of Montaigne during his lifetime were not of a particularly threatening nature; see Pierre Villey, *Montaigne devant la posterité* (Paris, 1935), pp. 56ff. After reading the *Essais*, the Inquisitors of the Sacro Palazzo assured Montaigne that they respected his intentions and affection for the Church. He should, they said, remain in Rome and live with them in harmony; see *Montaigne's Travel Journal*, trans. Donald M. Frame (San Francisco, 1983), pp. 101ff. Indeed, Roman citizenship was bestowed upon him. The wording of the document, as he himself remarks, was as honorable as that of the Duke of Sore, the Pope's own son (ibid., p. 98). He was referred to as "Socrates de France" in the Vatican; see Montaigne, *Journal de Voyage*, 2d ed. (Paris, 1909), p. 268n. Nor was his life lacking in other honors. The *Essais* were first included in the *Index* in 1676, almost 100 years after their original appearance; see P. Bonnefon, *Montaigne et ses amis*, vol. 2 (Paris, 1898), p. 38. Nietzsche's conclusion corresponds to the version in Henry Thomas Buckle's *History of Civilization in England*, vol. 1 (New York, 1858), p. 374: "Under the guise of a mere man of the world, expressing natural thoughts in common language, Montaigne concealed a spirit of lofty and audacious inquiry. . . . He was bold, since he was undaunted by the reproaches with which the ignorant, who love to dogmatize, always cover those whose knowledge makes them ready to doubt."

104. Wilhelm Dilthey, "Weltanschauung und Analyse des Menschen seit Renaissance und Reformation," in *Gesammelte Schriften*, vol. 2 (Leipzig and Berlin, 1921), p. 37.

105. Montaigne, *Essays*, vol. 1, Book I, chapter 1, p. 4.

106. The "conceited crowd" [*der eingebildete Haufe*] is either a typographical error or a misunderstanding.

107. Montaigne, *Essays*, vol. 1, Book II, chapter 11, p. 421.

108. See in particular David F. Strauss, *The Old Faith and the New,* trans. Mathilde Blind (New York, 1873), vol. 2, pp. 90–123.

109. See Ernst Troeltsch, "Half a Century of Theology: A Review," in *Writings on Theology and Religion,* trans. and ed. Robert Morgan and Michael Pye (London, 1977), pp. 61–62.

110. *Hegel's Philosophy of Mind,* trans. William Wallace (Oxford, 1894), pp. 101–102.

111. Hegel, *Lectures on the Philosophy of History,* p. 434.

112. See Montaigne, *Essays,* vol. 1, Book II, chapter 12, p. 485. [The passage in Montaigne says nothing about Diogenes Laertius.—Trans.]

113. On the relation between skepticism and dialectics, see also my essay "On the Problem of Truth" [included in this volume].

114. Hegel, *Lectures on the History of Philosophy,* vol. 2, p. 331.

115. Montaigne, *Essays,* vol. 2, Book III, chapter 13, p. 600.

116. On this point, see "Traditional and Critical Theory," in Max Horkheimer, *Critical Theory: Selected Essays,* trans. Matthew J. O'Connell et al. (New York, 1972), esp. pp. 202–204.

117. On this point, see Herbert Marcuse, "On Hedonism," in *Negations: Essays in Critical Theory* (Boston, 1968), pp. 159–200.

Beginnings of the Bourgeois Philosophy of History

1. The formulation of laws of nature which have questionable future applicability indeed has a classificatory value for the new science; but such value is based on the possibility of finding other laws whose realization is not similarly limited.

2. John Stuart Mill characterizes this proposition as "an instance of induction." See *A System of Logic* (London, 1970), p. 201.

3. *I tre libri de' Discorsi sopra la prima deca di Tito Livio* (1531), hereafter cited as *Discourses;* *Il Principe* (1532), hereafter cited as *The Prince; Dell'istore Fiorentine* (1532), hereafter cited as *History of Florence.* Page references to the first two works are taken from the Modern Library volume *The Prince and the Discourses* (New York, 1950). References to the third work are from *Niccolo Machiavelli and the United States of America,* ed. Anthony J. Pansini (Greenvale, 1969).

4. *Discourses,* p. 149.

5. Ibid., p. 216.

6. Ibid., p. 530.

7. Ibid., p. 105.

8. Ibid., p. 113.

9. Ibid., p. 114.

10. *History of Florence*, p. 811.

11. *Discourses*, p. 257.

12. Ibid., p. 255.

13. Ibid., p. 256.

14. Denis Diderot, *Œuvres complètes* (Paris, 1876), vol. 16, p. 33.

15. *Discourses*, p. 118.

16. Ibid., p. 119.

17. *History of Florence*, p. 680.

18. *Discourses*, p. 120.

19. Ibid.

20. *History of Florence*, p. 680.

21. Ibid., pp. 764ff.

22. *The Prince*, p. 91.

23. Ibid.

24. Ibid., p. 92.

25. Frederick the Great, *Antimachiavell*, Preface.

26. Letter to Pier Soderini, in *Niccolo Machiavelli and the United States of America*, p. 1153.

27. Ibid.

28. The following works are especially relevant: *De Cive* (1642), *Leviathan, or the Matter, Forme, and Power of a Common-wealth, Ecclesiasticall and Civill* (1651), and *De homine* (1658). Of particular interest, however, is the book *Behemoth or the Long Parliament*, a treatment of the course of the Cromwellian revolution from 1640 to the Restoration, presented in the form of a dialogue. Hobbes was never able to obtain an imprimatur for this posthumously published work—despite his reconciliation with Charles II, and despite the attacks on Cromwell and the Independents that he interpolated into the book out of precaution—due to the ever-increasing influence of his intellectual opponents at the king's court. Hobbes lived to see his writings banned by Catholics and Protestants alike. Three years after his death, Oxford University issued a decree against the pernicious doctrine that all civil authority emanates from the people (see Ferdinand Tönnies, *Thomas Hobbes: Leben und Lehre* [Stuttgart, 1925], p. 65), and the books *De Cive* and *Leviathan* were publicly burned by the students there. The backward Stuart throne was at bottom simply opposed to all interests of the English bourgeoisie.

29. Thomas Hobbes, *De Cive (Philosophical Rudiments Concerning Government and Society), The English Version*, ed. Howard Warrender (Oxford, 1983), p. 32 (Preface).

30. *De Cive,* pp. 125f.

31. Ibid., p. 52.

32. Ibid., pp. 157ff.

33. Ibid., p. 164.

34. Ibid., pp. 164ff.

35. Ibid., p. 165.

36. Thomas Hobbes, *Leviathan,* ed. C. B. Macpherson, Penguin English Library, 1982 reprint (orig. 1651), p. 166.

37. The following passages are taken from *Behemoth or the Long Parliament,* ed. Ferdinand Tönnies (London, 1889), pp. 41–43.

38. Ibid., p. 41.

39. *De Cive,* p. 161.

40. *Behemoth,* p. 43.

41. [Horkheimer's reference is an "ibid.," but we have not been able to locate this passage anywhere in *Behemoth,* hence what appears in the above text is actually a rendering of the German. Horkheimer's note here most likely refers to a citation that had been excised at some point in the editing/revision process. We presume the original passage to be attributable to Hobbes.—Trans.]

42. *Behemoth,* p. 54. Even Hegel still saw piety "of the right sort" as creating reverence for truth and the state's system of law and order (cf. *Hegel's Philosophy of Right,* trans. T. M. Knox [New York, 1971], p. 6).

43. *Behemoth,* p. 59.

44. *Leviathan,* p. 478.

45. For the entire French and English Enlightenment, the concept of "Reason" denotes correct knowledge and the human condition of being in possession of it. German philosophers, following Christian Wolff, took the word *raison* to refer merely to a psychical property, which resulted in a hopeless confusion that even Kant failed to untangle completely.

46. *Hegel's Lectures on the History of Philosophy,* vol. 1, trans. E. S. Haldane and Frances H. Simson (New York, 1968), pp. 17ff.

47. *Hegel's Philosophy of Right,* p. 11.

48. Hegel, *Lectures on the Philosophy of World History, Introduction: Reason in History,* trans. H. B. Nisbet (Cambridge, 1975), pp. 101ff.

49. *Hegel's Phenomenology of Spirit,* trans. A. V. Miller (Oxford, 1979), p. 344.

50. Recognizing the historical conditionedness of a theory is in no case identical with proving that it is ideological. For such a claim, rather complicated evidence is required to demonstrate the theory's social function.

51. *Hegel's Philosophy of Mind, Being Part Three of the Encyclopaedia of the Philosophical Sciences (1830)*, trans. W. Wallace (Oxford, 1971), pp. 22ff.

52. *Hegel's Logic, Being Part One of the Encyclopaedia of the Philosophical Sciences (1830)*, trans. W. Wallace (Oxford, 1975), p. 278.

53. In this chapter a series of other utopias of similar content will be explored, above all *City of the Sun* (1623) by the southern Italian monk Tommaso Campanella, who was one of the greatest philosophers of his age; for an account of Campanella, see especially Friedrich Meinecke, *Die Idee der Staatsräson in der neueren Geschichte* (Munich and Berlin, 1925). There exists a great deal of utopian literature by the radical disciples of Cromwell, from the Levelers to the French Enlightenment. Abbé Morelly's *Code de la Nature* (1755) appears to have been their paradigmatic utopia. The utopias of the nineteenth and twentieth centuries, which have a different historical-philosophical significance, are excluded from our analysis here.

54. Quoted from the court files examined in Emile Dermenghem, *Thomas Morus et les Utopistes de la Renaissance* (Paris, 1927), p. 86.

55. Meinecke, *Die Idee der Staatsräson*, p. 123.

56. Thomas More, *Utopia*, trans. Edward Surtz (New Haven, 1973), p. 53.

57. Morelly, *Code de la Nature ou le véritable esprit de ses lois* (Paris, 1910), p. 16.

58. Jean-Jacques Rousseau, *A Discourse on Inequality*, trans. Maurice Cranston (New York, 1987), p. 109.

59. Campanella has proven in his own life that the utopian model in its essence allows for persuasion and violence as means toward the realization of a better order. After his revolt was extinguished, he pursued his ideal further and sought to persuade those in power by means of his writings.

60. More, *Utopia*, p. 53.

61. Machiavelli, *The Prince*, p. 56.

62. Immanuel Kant, *The Critique of Pure Reason*, trans. Norman Kemp Smith (Toronto, 1933), pp. 168–169.

63. Since the goal and the available means were grotesquely mismatched, the peculiar paths taken by utopians for the realization of their ideas are understandable. More wants to persuade the rulers, and Campanella prepares an insurrection among monks in Calabria.

64. Hegel, *Encyclopaedia of the Philosophical Sciences*, trans. W. Wallace, in *G. W. F. Hegel: Selections*, ed. Jacob Loewenberg (New York, 1957), pp. 218–280, here pp. 268–269.

65. Hegel, *The Philosophy of History*, trans. J. Sibree (New York, 1956), p. 73.

66. Friedrich Nietzsche, "On the Use and Disadvantage of History for Life," in *Untimely Meditations,* trans. R. J. Hollingdale (Cambridge, 1983), p. 105.

67. Giambattista Vico, *The New Science of Giambattista Vico,* trans. Thomas Goddard Bergin and Max Harold Fisch (Ithaca, 1975), p. 3.

68. Ibid., p. 3.

69. Ibid., pp. 104–105.

70. Ibid., p. 92.

71. Ibid., p. 102.

72. Ibid.

73. Ibid.

74. Ibid., p. 61.

75. Ibid.

76. Ibid.

77. Ibid., p. 76.

78. Ibid., p. 78.

79. Ibid., p. 103.

80. Ibid., p. 122.

81. Ibid., pp. 122–123.

82. Ibid., p. 235.

83. Ibid., pp. 117–118.

84. Ibid., p. 70.

85. Ibid., p. 120.

86. Ibid., p. 118.

87. Ibid., p. 70.

88. Ibid., p. 74.

89. Ibid., p. 73.

90. Ibid., p. 235.

91. Ibid., p. 257. Vico unknowingly interprets Greek myths in their ancient Roman variations. The reason for that may be left undiscussed here, since we are primarily concerned with the principle.

92. Ibid., p. 208, pp. 272ff.

93. Ibid., pp. 391.

94. Ibid., p. 392.

95. Ibid., p. 73.

96. [The brackets are Horkheimer's.—Trans.]

97. Oswald Spengler, *The Decline of the West,* vol. 1, trans. Charles F. Atkinson (New York, 1962), p. 21.

98. Vico, *The New Science,* p. 104.

99. Ibid., p. 124.

100. Ibid., p. 82.

101. Ibid., p. 212.

102. Ibid., p. 79.

103. Ibid., p. 104.

Index

Absolutism, monarchic, 27, 172, 182, 188, 220, 266, 271, 285, 292, 328, 330, 345, 348
Adler, Max, 200
Aggression, 173, 281
Agrippa of Nettesheim, 281
Altruism, 173
Anthropology, 50–51, 55, 120, 152–175, 263, 318, 331–335, 339–343
Anti-intellectualism, 85–87. *See also* Irrationalism, philosophical
Antiquity, 75, 127, 151, 168, 261, 265, 269, 271, 294, 298, 306, 308, 324–325, 327, 329
Antirationalism, 221
Anti-Semitism, 101, 298
Aquinas, Saint Thomas, 40
Arcesilaus, 306
Aristippus, 108
Aristotle, 40, 44, 110, 166, 168, 206–207, 279, 338, 352
Arnold of Brescia, 84
Asceticism, 93–94, 103, 109, 255–257, 271
Augustine, Saint, 15
Authoritarianism, 169, 289–290, 292–294, 296–298, 305–306, 311. *See also* Absolutism, monarchic; Fascism

Bacon, Francis, 323, 336, 367, 377, 379
Balzac, Honoré de, 215, 289
Bayle, Pierre, 350
Beethoven, Ludwig van, 35
Bentham, Jeremy, 25, 108, 393n15
Bergson, Henri, 31–32, 40, 196, 202, 221, 224, 229, 234, 249
Bible, 29, 180, 211
Bleuler, Eugen, 104
Bodin, Jean, 277
Bonald, Louis Gabriel Ambroise, vicomte de, 215, 302

Borgia, Alexander (Rodrigo Borgia, pope Alexander VI), 71, 330
Borgia, Cesare, 331, 395n56
Bourgeoisie. *See also* Petite bourgeoisie
economic and political order, 18–21, 70, 162–166, 170, 172, 188, 218, 221, 266–267, 302–303, 321, 322, 330, 335–336, 346–347, 353, 370
and fascism, 278, 290–300, 305–306
historical epoch, 22, 49, 181, 266, 285, 289, 322–323, 335–336 (*see also* Absolutism; Liberalism; Monopoly capitalism)
ideology and culture, 25, 34–38, 41–44, 49, 54–58, 60, 86, 101, 153–174, 178–183, 202–203, 211–215, 220, 238, 243, 271, 277–278, 281, 285–289, 291–295, 301, 335–336 (*see also* Liberalism)
psychology, 51, 101, 180, 281–282, 285, 287, 311 (*see also* Individual, concept of)
Bruno, Giordano, 85
Burckhardt, Jacob, 265–266

Calvin, John, 52–53, 77–82, 86, 107, 269, 274–276, 282–283, 305
Campanella, Tommaso, 364–369
Cardano, Geronimo, 50
Carneades, 269, 270, 306
Cartesianism, 218–222, 247, 262, 376. *See also* Descartes, René
Catholicism, 52–53, 84, 85, 178, 215, 269, 273–278, 305, 364–365, 376, 379
Ceremony. *See* Pageantry, political
Cervantes, Miguel de, 413n86
Charles II, king of England, 337
Christianity, 165, 211–215, 258, 299, 306. *See also* Catholicism; Protestantism
Class consciousness, 131
Class division and conflict, 39, 70, 79, 129, 146, 151–152, 240, 267, 283–284, 287, 295, 324–326, 363–364

1425

Index

23Progressive forces, Horkheimer's judgment of, 35, 36, 41, 69, 83, 136, 188,
230–231, 238, 291
Promises. *See* Contracts
Prophets, 71
Protestantism, 44, 52–53, 78, 212, 283,
286, 305, 327
Reformation, 60, 73–74, 76, 80–85,
98–99, 267, 269, 273–278, 282–284,
307, 308, 395–396n71
Proudhon, Pierre Joseph, 39
Psychoanalysis, 281, 399n144
Psychology, 11–13, 113, 115–116, 118–
128, 135, 142–143, 214, 234, 235–237,
247–248, 257, 263, 278, 313, 316,
390n12. *See also* Depth psychology;
Freud, Sigmund; Gestalt psychology;
Psychoanalysis
and economic order, 103–110, 125–
126, 250
of political movements, 51, 67–69,
100–101, 310–311, 329–335
Pufendorf, baron Samuel von, 346
Pyrrhus, 265, 268–269, 307

Rationalism, 120, 217–264, 280, 285,
278
Reason, 29, 30–31, 85, 154–155, 274,
278, 358
Reich, Wilhelm, 399n144
Reinach, Adolf, 6
Relativism, 177–178, 188, 193, 269, 362
Religion, 1, 15, 32, 57, 152, 156, 157,
180–183, 185–186, 211–215, 258,
281–288, 305–308, 322, 350–352,
354–356, 364–366, 379, 382–383. *See
also* Catholicism; Christianity; Protes-
tantism
Renaissance, 16, 50, 228, 261, 265, 279,
298, 303, 308, 314–331, 338, 363. *See
also* Humanism
Revolutions, characteristics of, 59–62,
72, 95–103, 123, 267
Ricardo, David, 3
Richelieu, Armand Jean du Plessis, cardi-
nal de, 328, 335
Rickert, Heinrich, 113, 225–226
Rienzo, Cola di, 60, 64–71, 76, 92, 93
Ritschl, Albrecht, 305, 395n71
Robespierre, Maximilien François Marie
Isidore de, 53, 66, 88–95, 103
Romanticism, 247
Rothacker, Erich, 223
Rousseau, Jean Jacques, 49, 53, 64, 90,
95, 109, 343, 346, 358, 366–367

Sade, Donatien Alphonse François, mar-
quis de, 109
Saint-Just, Louis de, 103
Savonarola, Girolamo, 60, 66, 69–74,
76–77, 86–87
Say, Jean Baptiste, 3
Scheler, Max, 6, 7, 10, 12, 32, 112, 153,
157, 159, 200–203, 222, 225
Scherer, Wilhelm, 223–224
Schiller, Johann Christoph Friedrich
von, 18, 64, 166, 180
Schlegel, August Wilhelm von, 226
Schleiermacher, Friedrich, 18, 213
Scholasticism, 340, 351–352
Schopenhauer, Arthur, 5, 18, 27, 36,
138, 288
Sciences, physical and natural, 8–9, 45,
171, 180, 181, 201–203, 214, 229–230,
232–233, 237, 254, 302, 317, 343, 345,
350, 374, 376
historical development of, 233, 278,
279, 314–316, 337–340, 362
Sebond, Raymond, 274
Sermons, 75–77
Shaftesbury, Anthony Ashley Cooper,
3rd Earl of, 53
Simmel, Georg, 229
Skepticism, 160, 179, 184, 223, 228,
265–311
Slavery, 114, 118, 168, 172, 207, 294
Smith, Adam, 3
Social contract, 343–347, 349
Socialism, 299, 367
Social philosophy, development of, 1–14
Sociology, 8, 13, 135–136, 138, 177,
401n12
Sociology of knowledge, 129–134, 136,
141, 146, 147–149
Socrates, 75, 280, 385
Sombart, Werner, 7
Spain, history of, 59
Spann, Othmar, 6, 252
Spengler, Oswald, 229, 231, 386
Spinoza, Baruch, 16, 34, 50, 169, 229,
278, 350, 351, 357, 363, 370
Spirit (Hegelian concept), 2–3, 5, 12, 30,
116–117, 187, 310, 373
Sports, 57
State, 1, 4–5
Stoicism, 271–272, 280, 304
Strauss, David Friedrich, 211, 305
Subject. *See* Individual, concept of, as
subject
Suicide, 22
Symbols, political, 63, 66–68, 91–92, 97

Studies in Contemporary German Social Thought

Thomas McCarthy, General Editor

Theodor W. Adorno, *Against Epistemology: A Metacritique*

Theodor W. Adorno, *Hegel: Three Studies*

Theodor W. Adorno, *Prisms*

Karl-Otto Apel, *Understanding and Explanation: A Transcendental-Pragmatic Perspective*

Seyla Benhabib and Fred Dallmayr, editors, *The Communicative Ethics Controversy*

Richard J. Bernstein, editor, *Habermas and Modernity*

Ernst Bloch, *Natural Law and Human Dignity*

Ernst Bloch, *The Principle of Hope*

Ernst Bloch, *The Utopian Function of Art and Literature: Selected Essays*

Hans Blumenberg, *The Genesis of the Copernican World*

Hans Blumenberg, *The Legitimacy of the Modern Age*

Hans Blumenberg, *Work on Myth*

Susan Buck-Morss, *The Dialectics of Seeing: Walter Benjamin and the* Arcades Project

Craig Calhoun, editor, *Habermas and the Public Sphere*

Jean Cohen and Andrew Arato, *Civil Society and Political Theory*

Helmut Dubiel, *Theory and Politics: Studies in the Development of Critical Theory*

John Forester, editor, *Critical Theory and Public Life*

David Frisby, *Fragments of Modernity: Theories of Modernity in the Work of Simmel, Kracauer and Benjamin*

Hans-Georg Gadamer, *Philosophical Apprenticeships*

Hans-Georg Gadamer, *Reason in the Age of Science*

Jürgen Habermas, *Justification and Application: Remarks on Discourse Ethics*

Jürgen Habermas, *On the Logic of the Social Sciences*

Jürgen Habermas, *Moral Consciousness and Communicative Action*

Jürgen Habermas, *The New Conservatism: Cultural Criticism and the Historians' Debate*

Jürgen Habermas, *The Philosophical Discourse of Modernity: Twelve Lectures*

Jürgen Habermas, *Philosophical-Political Profiles*

Jürgen Habermas, *Postmetaphysical Thinking: Philosophical Essays*

Jürgen Habermas, *The Structural Transformation of the Public Sphere: An Inquiry into a Category of Bourgeois Society*

Jürgen Habermas, editor, *Observations on "The Spiritual Situation of the Age"*

Axel Honneth, *The Critique of Power: Reflective Stages in a Critical Social Theory*

Axel Honneth and Hans Joas, editors, *Communicative Action: Essays on Jürgen Habermas's* The Theory of Communicative Action

Axel Honneth, Thomas McCarthy, Claus Offe, and Albrecht Wellmer, editors, *Cultural-Political Interventions in the Unfinished Project of Enlightenment*

Axel Honneth, Thomas McCarthy, Claus Offe, and Albrecht Wellmer, editors, *Philosophical Interventions in the Unfinished Project of Enlightenment*

Max Horkheimer, *Between Philosophy and Social Science: Selected Early Writings*

Hans Joas, *G. H. Mead: A Contemporary Re-examination of His Thought*

Reinhart Koselleck, *Critique and Crisis: Enlightenment and the Pathogenesis of Modern Society*

Reinhart Koselleck, *Futures Past: On the Semantics of Historical Time*

Harry Liebersohn, *Fate and Utopia in German Sociology, 1887–1923*

Herbert Marcuse, *Hegel's Ontology and the Theory of Historicity*

Gil G. Noam and Thomas Wren, editors, *The Moral Self: Building a Better Paradigm*

Guy Oakes, *Weber and Rickert: Concept Formation in the Cultural Sciences*

Claus Offe, *Contradictions of the Welfare State*

Claus Offe, *Disorganized Capitalism: Contemporary Transformations of Work and Politics*

Helmut Peukert, *Science, Action, and Fundamental Theology: Toward a Theology of Communicative Action*

Joachim Ritter, *Hegel and the French Revolution: Essays on the* Philosophy of Right

Alfred Schmidt, *History and Structure: An Essay on Hegelian-Marxist and Structuralist Theories of History*

Dennis Schmidt, *The Ubiquity of the Finite: Hegel, Heidegger, and the Entitlements of Philosophy*

Carl Schmitt, *The Crisis of Parliamentary Democracy*

Carl Schmitt, *Political Romanticism*

Carl Schmitt, *Political Theology: Four Chapters on the Concept of Sovereignty*

Gary Smith, editor, *On Walter Benjamin: Critical Essays and Recollections*

Michael Theunissen, *The Other: Studies in the Social Ontology of Husserl, Heidegger, Sartre, and Buber*

Ernst Tugendhat, *Self-Consciousness and Self-Determination*